The
Criminal
Event

The Criminal Event

An Introduction to Criminology

Vincent F. Sacco
Queen's University

Leslie W. Kennedy
University of Alberta

with contributions by
Peggy Plass
James Madison University

Wadsworth Publishing Company
I(T)P™ An International Thomson Publishing Company

Belmont • Albany • Bonn • Boston • Cincinnati • Detroit • London • Madrid • Melbourne
Mexico City • New York • Paris • San Francisco • Singapore • Tokyo • Toronto • Washington

Criminology Editor: Sabra Horne
Developmental Editor: Alan Venable
Assistant Editor: Claire Masson
Editorial Assistant: Louise Mendelson
Production Editor: Angela Mann
Managing Designer: Ann Butler
Print Buyer: Karen Hunt
Permissions Editor: Jeanne Bosschart
Art Editors: Emma Nash/Kevin Berry
Cover and Interior Design: Ellen Pettengell
Copy Editor: Tom Briggs
Technical Illustrator: Patricia Isaacs/Parrot Graphics
Photo Researcher: Laurel Anderson
Cover Photography: Lynn Sugarman
Compositor: G & S
Printer: Banta Company

 This book is printed on acid-free recycled paper.

Library of Congress Catalog Card Number 95-61504

ISBN 0-534-26448-4

For more information, contact Wadsworth Publishing
Company:

Wadsworth Publishing Company
10 Davis Drive
Belmont, California 94002, USA

International Thomson Publishing Europe
Berkshire House 168-173
High Holborn
London, WC1V 7AA, England

Thomas Nelson Australia
102 Dodds Street
South Melbourne 3205
Victoria, Australia

Nelson Canada
1120 Birchmount Road
Scarborough, Ontario
Canada M1K 5G4

International Thomson Editores
Campos Eliseos 385, Piso 7
Col. Polanco
11560 México D.F. México

International Thomson Publishing GmbH
Königswinterer Strasse 418
53227 Bonn, Germany

International Thomson Publishing Asia
221 Henderson Road
#05-10 Henderson Building
Singapore 0315

International Thomson Publishing Japan
Hirakawacho Kyowa Building, 3F
2-2-1 Hirakawacho
Chiyoda-ku, Tokyo 102, Japan

To Tiia, Daniel, Katherin, and Ema
Ilona, Alexis, Andrea, and Grandparents

CONTENTS

PREFACE

For a number of years we both taught introductory criminology using a fairly conventional approach. We discussed definitions of crime, reviewed the important theoretical debates, talked about measurement, the correlates of crime, and the nature of societal reaction. While this style of course organization provided all of the material that an introductory student needs, it left us both feeling a bit dissatisfied. We felt that students were learning the "basic facts of crime," but that the approach was disjointed. Like a story without a theme, it became a collection of seemingly unrelated anecdotes about what different researchers were saying about how we should study what we study. In talking to others who have taught introductory students, we found a similar frustration with the lack of an integrating theme in the books they were using.

We believe that introductory criminology has long paid too much attention to the different elements of crime and ignored the integrating nature of the criminal event in its entirety. In this book, we use the idea of the criminal event to provide the missing theme. This theme runs through our discussion of what motivates people to commit crime, of who suffers and how, and of what we should do about the problem of crime. This perspective allows us to examine the determinants of crime, as well as individual choice and opportunity, as part of a more complete explanation of criminal outcomes.

Further, we believe that we should look at crime in different contexts, since variations in situations and settings produce variations in the ways in which crime evolves. We have identified three domains of crime that guide our analysis of context: the family, leisure, and work. These domains include most daily behavior and have been the prime areas of study in research on crime and its consequences.

The text that appears here, then, reflects our effort to achieve the objectives laid out above. We have been careful to include the major theories in our discussion. We have also made a concerted effort to include as much contemporary research on crime as possible. As Richard A. Wright has said, introductory criminology books have failed to reflect the current state of the research.

We have tried not to fall into the trap of simply repeating old truths but have sought confirmation of our points in current empirical studies.

To recap:

- Our use of an integrating theme—that of the criminal event as a whole—enables the reader to understand crime as more than simply a collection of loosely connected elements.
- Because it is important to study crime in different contexts, we have identified three domains of crime—family, leisure, and work—and used these to guide our discussion of context.
- We give careful consideration to all of the major criminological theories.
- We use as much contemporary research as possible to inform our points of discussion.

This book was made possible largely through the efforts of Charlotte Forbes at Nelson Canada. Charlotte showed great patience and perseverance in initiating this project. It is her commitment to getting things done that makes her such a great editor. We owe her a great deal. We are also in the debt of Sabra Horne, our editor at Wadsworth, who saw the value of this manuscript and sold its merit to her colleagues. Her strong commitment to this project made it the success that it is. The staff at Wadsworth worked hard to get constructive feedback for us on our ideas. We are grateful to Alan Venable and Angela Mann for all their time and attention as our manuscript moved through its various development stages. We also appreciate the patience and dedication of Tom Briggs who undertook the job of copyediting the manuscript. The external reviewers Alex Alvarez, Northern Arizona University; Jim Anderson, John Abbott College; John Casey, Grant MacEwan Community College; Anthony Doob, University of Toronto; L. B. Gaiters, Tennessee State University; John Galleher, University of Missouri, Columbia; Karin Kaercher, Camosun College; Peter Kratcowski, Kent State University; Scott Nicholls, Humber College, Lakeshore Campus; Xin Ren, California State University, Sacramento; Douglas Skoog, The University of Winnipeg; Ruth Triplett, Sam Houston State University; and Ed Wells, Illinois State University provided us with countless suggestions and encouraged us to improve certain parts of the text that needed more work. We thank them for their efforts on our behalf. We have a special thanks for Peggy Plass who helped to assure that the content of the book, specifically the data and numerous examples, match the needs and interests of students in the United States as well as in Canada. We will miss the daily e-mail conferences that we had with her (particularly the updates on how wonderful the Virginia spring (and fall and winter) is. We promise her that we will continue to write.

Les Kennedy would like to thank his colleagues, support staff, and students at the University of Alberta for their support of this work. Specifically, he would like to thank Fran Russell, Kelly McGuirk, and Kerri Calvert for their help. Tina Papadopoulos did a fine job creating the index. Also, he is grateful for the financial aid provided through the Centre for Criminological Research, which was funded through a contributions grant from the Solicitor General of

Canada. In addition, he appreciates the ongoing support and friendship of David Forde and Steve Baron. Of course, special thanks go to Ilona, Alexis, and Andrea for providing perspective as well as the moral support that is needed to complete a long, intensive job of writing.

Vince Sacco would like to thank his friends and colleagues in the Department of Sociology at Queen's University. Roberta Hamilton, Reza Nakhaie, Frank Pearce, Terry Willett, and Elia Zureik, as always, provided support and encouragement. The help provided by Wilma Bauder and Joan Westenhaefer as the project was nearing completion is greatly appreciated. Finally, and as always, the biggest thank you is owed to Tiia, Katherin, and Daniel.

Both of us would like to make special mention of the support that our friend Bob Silverman has provided to us over the years. In his role as colleague and mentor, he has kept us honest to the profession and committed to the field of criminology.

The Authors

Vincent F. Sacco
Queen's University

Leslie W. Kennedy
University of Alberta

The
Criminal
Event

PART ONE

INTRODUCTION

CRIME ATTRACTS A GREAT DEAL OF PUBLIC ATTEN-
TION. CRIMINOLOGY HAS DEVELOPED AS A FIELD
OF STUDY TO EXAMINE HOW CRIME EVOLVES
FROM SOCIAL EVENTS. THROUGH DIFFERENT PER-
SPECTIVES, CRIMINOLOGISTS LOOK AT MOTIVA-
TIONS OF OFFENDERS, CRIMINOGENIC FORCES
IN SOCIETY, AND OPPORTUNITIES FOR CRIMINAL
ACTIVITIES. THE PUBLIC'S REACTIONS, THROUGH
DEFINITIONS OF CRIMINAL BEHAVIOR, THROUGH
CHANGES IN THE LAW, AND THROUGH THE ACTIONS
OF THE POLICE, ARE ALSO A FOCUS OF CRIMINO-
LOGICAL STUDY.

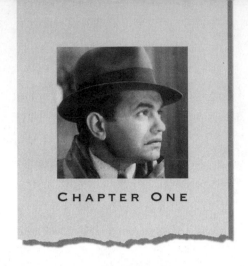

Crime, Criminology, and the Public View

KEY TERMS

criminology

classical school

positivist school

crime

offender

crime *mala in se*

crime *mala prohibita*

actus reus

mens rea

constructive intent

juvenile

duress

self-defense

morality

consensus theory

conflict theory

peacemaking

feminist

battered women's syndrome

proactive policing

reactive policing

National Crime Victimization Survey

index crimes

crime news

improvised news

urban legend

crime myths

WHAT'S IN CHAPTER ONE

In this chapter, we introduce criminology as a discipline and examine two major schools of thought: positivism and classicism. Classicists view the offender as rational, deterred only by the threat of sanction. Positivists argue that explanations of criminality—and hence the secret to crime cessation—are found in forces that cause criminal behavior. We also explain what constitutes crime, focusing on the ideas of *actus reus* (the guilty act) and *mens rea* (the guilty mind). We explore, as well, the different views presented by consensus versus conflict theorists. The former advocates a commonly accepted definition of crime while the latter argues that criminal definitions are open to debate as they are often imposed by self-serving interest groups. In addition, we examine the role of the police and the media in defining the extent and pervasiveness of crime. Finally, we discuss myths about crime.

The victim's wife wept. She called the decision unbelievable. Her husband was dead, and she thought she knew who was responsible. Twenty-six other men were dead as well, and their relatives, too, had hoped for a murder conviction for the people they held responsible. However, the court had ruled that there was insufficient evidence to support the allegations and therefore had dismissed the case. The families of the victims were not to find out why the men died or who was to blame, compounding their grief and frustration.

This case did not involve a mass murderer wielding an assault weapon and mowing down innocent bystanders in a shopping mall or targeted victims in a factory. The men died in a mine explosion at the Westray coal mine in Nova Scotia. Murder charges alleging failure to enforce proper safety standards in the workplace had been brought against Westray's mine manager and underground manager (*Globe and Mail*, 1993: A1).

In the Cicero area of Chicago, on the same day, one teenager was killed and four other people were wounded when gunfire, apparently triggered by gang rivalries, broke out at a crowded public swimming pool on Cicero's northeast side (*Chicago Tribune*, 1993: Section 2, 2). Meanwhile, in Los Angeles, a former Bank of America branch manager was sentenced to twenty-four years in prison for her role in a drug and money-laundering operation. According to the U.S. attorney, the woman worked for a major drug trafficking ring that distributed cocaine, marijuana, and methamphetamines. Prosecutors claimed that members of the operation hid large amounts of cocaine in the roofs of tour buses traveling from Mexico and unloaded the cocaine in Fontana, where it would be repackaged and sold (*Los Angeles Times*, 1993: B2).

These three events appear to be very different from one another. However, there are consistent ways in which we can approach these and other crimes, ways that allow us to make sense of what happened and to put it into a broader context. While we may not be able always to understand why people do certain things, we can search for the motivations behind crime by examining such factors as circumstances, characteristics of offenders and victims, and their relationship to one another. What events led up to the act? Who else was involved? Where did the event take place? What did the police do? We also want to know what was done after the event occurred to deal with its consequences. What punishment was handed down to ensure that similar events did not happen again? While the examples presented here may seem to be unique social events, they share many characteristics that allow us to make sense of them as a singular type of behavior—that is, acts that are criminal.

In presenting an overview of explanations of crime, we will introduce the major theories of criminology as well as the research methods and data that are used to test hypotheses and identify trends in crime. We will also present findings from the considerable research literature, with particular emphasis on crime that occurs at home, during leisure, and at work, the times when and places where most crimes occur. Because explanations of crime heavily

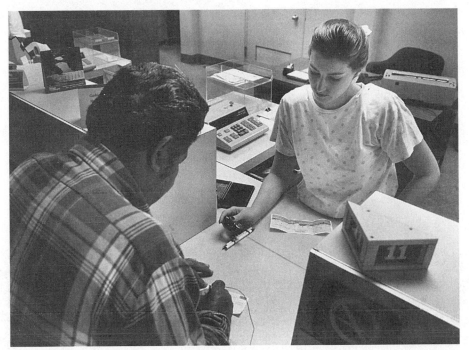

Crime occurs in a variety of settings but some environments are more threatening than others; as our examples of the mine, the street, and the bank discussed in the book attest.

influence views of how society should respond to it, it is important to understand what the current program responses are and how they can be brought into line to more effectively deal with crime.

Our approach to the study of crime is defined by the discipline of criminology, a school of inquiry that has gained in stature and credibility over the years. Strong traditions have developed within this school of thought, many of which are complementary, as we will see. Let us begin by looking at criminology as a discipline, as practiced in the United States and elsewhere, before we review the various factors that influence the study of crime.

WHAT IS CRIMINOLOGY?

Criminology is a subject area that draws on a number of different disciplines as it seeks to clarify the nature of the criminal event. Through this interdisciplinary perspective, criminologists attempt to understand not only the motivations of the offender but also the nature of the circumstances leading up to the act and its consequences for the victim(s), for others in the community, and for society at large. Criminologists are also called on to provide insights into how we should respond to crime (for example, through changes in policing strategies or through the development of crime prevention programs). Finally, criminologists monitor the ways in which changes in the laws and their interpretation can affect how people behave in society and, in turn, how agents of social control respond to this behavior.

The interdisciplinary nature of criminology means that people with quite different types of training contribute to the understanding of criminal events. Criminologists include historians, psychologists, political scientists, economists, legal scholars, and sociologists. For the most part, though, when criminology is taught outside of departments of criminology and criminal justice, it is treated as a subdiscipline of sociology. The fact that sociology has become the major focus of criminological training in North America can be explained by the tendency of sociologists to be more involved than researchers from other disciplines in the study of social problems. In addition, the major figures in the teaching of criminology have been sociologists by training, a fact reflected in the courses that are offered. The tendency in Europe, in contrast, is for criminologists to reside in law schools, which gives a more legal orientation to the research that is pursued there.

The interdisciplinary programs in criminology have been very successful in creating a focus for many people who are interested in the study of crime. For example, the strong emphasis in quantitative sociology on survey research has provided the impetus to accumulate important data through victimization surveys. Economic perspectives, too, have made important contributions in the understanding of offender motivations.

WHAT IS IT?

Criminology

Criminology uses an interdisciplinary perspective to understand not only the motivations of the offender but also the nature of the circumstances leading up to the act and its consequences for the victim(s), for others in the community, and for the society at large. Criminologists study ways in which we should respond to crime through changes in policing strategies or through the development of crime prevention programs. In addition, criminologists pay close attention to the ways in which changes in laws and their interpretation can affect how people behave in society and, in turn, how agents of social control respond to this behavior.

Many would argue that the growth of modern criminology has been strongest in the United States, particularly as a result of federal funding for research in the 1970s and 1980s in response to the problems of large-scale social disorder in American cities. More recently, the U.S. government has spent large sums on the study of drug-related crime but less liberally in other areas of research. Still, relatively little money is spent on criminological research when compared with the amounts committed to other areas, such as medical or biophysical research. This disparity exists despite the large costs that some criminological research entails, particularly large-scale victimization surveys and longitudinal studies of offenders.

There is a great deal of interest in the study of crime in countries outside of the United States. Many of these countries have become involved in large-scale victimization surveys. Some, like Canada, with the Canadian Centre for Justice Statistics, and Britain, through the Home Office Research Unit, have applied criminological research to the development of policing policy, community crime prevention programs, and offender programs. Again, we will draw on this work in this book.

Our presentation will be heavily influenced by recent thinking in criminology that places great significance on the routine nature of crime and maintains that individual lifestyles bring offenders and victims together in time and space to create crime opportunities. The crime that results creates consequences for all parties concerned, as a result of either police intervention or the actions of third parties.

CLASSICAL AND POSITIVIST VIEWS OF OFFENDERS

Studying the crime event as a consequence of routine does not mean that we ignore the importance of criminological thinking that has been developed over the centuries to explain offender motivations or the role of punishment in deterring crime. Criminological thought goes back to the ideas of Cesare Beccaria, who wrote in the late 1700s about the need to account for the psychological reality of the offender. The state, he argued, needs to use the fear of pain to control behavior. Beccaria's view emphasized reform of the repressive and barbaric laws of eighteenth-century Europe, a period in which the administration of justice was arbitrary and abusive. The standing of the person in the community had a direct impact on the treatment that he or she could expect from the courts; justice therefore was relative rather than absolute.

According to Beccaria, the degree of punishment should be sufficient to outweigh the pleasure one derives from a criminal act (Martin, Mutchnik, and Austin, 1990: 8). It was Beccaria's views, together with those of Jeremy Bentham after him, that so heavily influenced modern thinking about deterrence and punishment. According to this **classical school** of thought, the "rational man" would act to avoid punishment—hence the importance of laws that were clear about both how one should act and what the costs of deviating from this lawful behavior would be.

Beccaria is better described as a social reformer than as a criminologist in the modern sense of that term. He was more interested in changes that would make the criminal justice system effective and fair than he was in explaining the causes of crime. Still, implicit in Beccaria's view is a model of what offenders are like and why they offend. For Beccaria, the offender's behavior could be understood in terms of a principle of "hedonism." In short, the offender is seen as a kind of rational calculator who seeks to maximize pleasure and minimize pain. From this perspective, a person commits crime when the pleasure that the offending promises outweighs the pain that the law threatens.

The classical model of "rational man" led to a view that the law could be used as an instrument of control. This assumed, however, that men and women were not only free to judge but also equal in their ability to do so. In the late 1800s, Cesare Lombroso's positivist views began to question this assumption. His basic belief was that human behavior was *determined*, a view that stands in direct opposition to Beccaria's assumption that people have free will. For Lombroso, the individual's constitution predetermined responses to surroundings and was influential in creating deficiencies in human behavior that led to criminality; thus, heredity was a principal cause of criminal tendencies (Martin, Mutchnik, and Austin, 1990: 29). These assumptions led Lombroso to argue for a perspective that emphasized the development of crime types.

For Lombroso, one important category was the "atavistic criminal." His use of the term *atavism* was meant to imply that such offenders were throwbacks to an earlier period in human evolution. In other words, their behavior was less likely to conform to the demands of contemporary social life because they were related to a more primitive human condition. Lombroso believed that the physical signs of atavism could be described and measured in a scientific manner. Born criminals not only acted in a particular way but looked a particular way. The atavistic criminal might be expected to have ears of unusual size, fleshy lips, pouches in the cheeks, and a head of unusual size and shape (Vold and Bernard, 1986). Lombroso was not suggesting that such characteristics caused criminal behavior in any simple sense, but rather that they served as visible indicators of the type of person who was likely to behave in this way.

Lombroso's ideas were very influential and even found their way into the popular culture of the period. For instance, the title character in Bram Stoker's novel *Dracula* is based on Lombroso's description of the atavistic criminal (Wolf, 1975). However, despite their popularity, these ideas were largely discredited even during Lombroso's lifetime. Lombroso's lasting contribution is not the specific content of his theories but rather his more general approach to the problem of crime. Unlike the classical writers who preceded him, Lombroso did not see crime as a product of free will; instead, according to this **positivist school**, crime was something that could be understood in terms of causes and effects.

We should stress that the legacies of **classical and positivist thought** are alive and well in the context of contemporary criminology. However, they have

Are "criminal tendencies" reflected in personal appearance? Can you guess which of these individuals is a notorious bank robber?

taken researchers in somewhat different directions. The positivist tradition has come to be linked to theories of criminal motivation. As we will see in Chapter 3, these theories encourage us to ask questions about the kinds of factors that push or pull people into criminal conduct. In contrast, the classical legacy is linked to theories and research that emphasize the factors that constrain people from developing or acting on criminal motivations. In this view, as we will discuss in Chapter 4, when these constraints are weak, people have more freedom to do as they please—which sometimes means behaving criminally. As will become clear, these ideas are not necessarily contradictory in the

WHAT DOES IT MEAN?

Classical vs. Positivist

Classical criminology still views the offender as rational, deterred only by the threat of social sanctions. Positivists argue that explanations of criminality—and hence the key to crime cessation—are found in factors that influence criminal conduct.

modern criminological context. As Felson (1994: 22) observes, societies provide both temptations and controls, and "as any society generates more temptations and fewer controls, it invites a crime wave."

For all their differences, the various theories that fall roughly into these two schools of thought have in common a fixation on criminality rather than crime; that is, they focus little attention on the dynamics of the criminal event itself, except as it relates to offender actions (for example, trying to explain why an individual would act in a particular way at a particular time). Only in recent years has the criminal event in its totality served as a focus of criminology (Gottfredson and Hirchi, 1990).

Following from this orientation, there has been an intensive investigation into the relationship between situational factors and individual lifestyles that allows us to consider simultaneously motivation and structural conditions in the environment, including the deterrent effects of possible detection and punishment. We have begun to understand more clearly what happens in crime events and to apply this knowledge as a basis for predicting certain outcomes. Using this approach, modern criminology has emerged with a more holistic view of the crime problem (Miethe and Meier, 1994).

DEFINING CRIME

Criminologists study and teach about crime, but they are not the only sources of information about this phenomenon. Through its depiction in the media and through public debate, we develop particular views of what crime is, how extensive it is, and what we can do about it.

CRIME AS LAWBREAKING

CRIME AND LAW

In Western society, **crime** is defined strictly as behavior that breaks the law and is liable to public prosecution and punishment. In a fundamental way, terms like *crime, offender,* and *victim* are legal concepts. An **offender**, for instance, is someone who is recognized as having behaved in a way that contravenes the criminal law. Whether it is appropriate, however, to label an event participant as an offender, criminal, or lawbreaker may be debatable. Individuals who are judged to be offenders by the law may not see themselves in this way or be regarded as such by witnesses or even victims. To a considerable degree, criminal trials are organized, state-sponsored attempts to determine who should be considered an "offender."

Social events have meaning as criminal events, then, only in reference to law. As Nettler (1984: 32) states, "Crime is a word, not a deed," and to label something a crime is to invoke the moral evaluation of the behavior that is embodied in the law. Thus, the law may be understood as a form of social control that evaluates the moral nature of the behavior in question. When we describe an act as criminal, we imply that the act is disvalued. It is a form of wrongdoing that "good people" should avoid at the risk of punishment. One of the major functions of the law is to deter people from engaging in the behavior that the law prohibits. The law comprises a set of written rules that are supported by state authority and accompanied by a standardized schedule of penalties.

> ### WHAT IS IT?
>
> ### *Crime*
>
> In Western society, crime is defined strictly as behavior that breaks the criminal law and is liable to public prosecution and punishment. A criminal intention (*mens rea*) without the action (*actus reus*) is not a crime.

EVOLVING PERCEPTIONS OF CRIME

Even when there is a clear agreement that an offense has been committed, there may be disagreement about what type of offense and what to do about it. In a startling break from tradition, a judge decided in early 1992 to accept a charge of second-degree murder directed against a couple who had grievously assaulted their foster child. The judge ruled that, even though the child was not technically dead (parts of the child's brain stem were still functioning, and he continued to breathe spontaneously), sufficient evidence existed that the persistent vegetative state that resulted from the child's injuries should be incorporated into the legal definition of death. This judgment sparked a heated debate over what might be considered to be a fairly straightforward issue: the definition of life and death.

Subsequently, the charge was reduced to aggravated assault, and the couple was convicted. John Dosseter, a bioethics expert, commented on the reduced charge. "I don't think society is ready for such an important matter [changing the definition of life and death] to be decided in such a way in the courts. The matter needs more debate and I don't think a simple court decision is going to do it" (Moysa, 1992: A1). The public and lawmakers must debate changes in the law such that death would be recognized as something beyond the complete cessation of life.

In a similar way, the law is undergoing changes in how it considers actions such as murder. As illustrated in the Westray case, one does not have to wield a knife or fire a gun to be labeled a murderer. That same case also exemplifies the difficulty of establishing motives. Did the Westray managers intend to kill? Did they know that what they did might result in death? These are among the questions that arise in cases in which neglect or incompetence have deadly consequences.

THE FOCUS ON OFFENDERS

In general, the law is more concerned with crime or criminal behavior than with criminal events (Gould, 1989). In other words, the law focuses on what offenders do (rather than on other event elements) in deciding what a crime is or when a crime occurs. From a legal standpoint, crime is largely synonymous with the actions of the offender.

Criminologists often find it useful to distinguish between crime *mala in se* and crime *mala prohibita*. This distinction alerts us to the fact that not all crimes resonate to the same degree with popular morality. **Crimes *mala in se*** are crimes that are seen as wrong in and of themselves. They are acts that most people would see as wrong even if they were not against the law and that have been widely condemned both historically and cross-culturally. Murder, robbery, and other predatory crimes are examples of crimes *mala in se*. In contrast, some types of behaviors are not as widely or as consistently condemned. **Crimes *mala prohibita*** are acts that are wrong not in and of themselves but by prohibition. Alcohol consumption and certain sexual activities, for instance, are viewed as criminal only in some societies and only at some points in history.

FEDERAL AND STATE LAWS

The United States has two systems or levels of criminal law—federal and state. Federal crimes are those actions that violate the federal criminal code; for example, most white-collar crimes are covered by federal law. Federal law is uniform for all U.S. citizens. Many crimes, however, are specifically defined on the state level. While similarities exist from one state to another, different states may also define a given criminal act differently. Federal law (and the Constitution) provides guidelines, but within these guidelines, individual states have the power to interpret criminal law for themselves.

On both the state and federal level, the law also distinguishes between two different types of crime—felonies and misdemeanors. The difference between felonies and misdemeanors is found in the potential consequences of an action. Typically, a *felony* is defined as a violation of criminal law that could result in a prison sentence of a year or more (or the imposition of the death penalty). A *misdemeanor* is usually defined as a violation of a criminal law that carries a maximum penalty of less than one year in jail or prison.

CONTEXT

Regardless of whether an act violates a federal or a state law or whether it qualifies as a felony or a misdemeanor, context also is important in determining criminality. The fact that someone behaves in a way that *seems* to be inconsistent with the requirements of the law does not mean that he or she has committed a crime. To be criminal in a legal sense, an act must be intentional (Barnhorst, Barnhorst, and Clarke, 1992). The mere physical act—what is legally known as the *actus reus*—is not enough. There must also be a willful quality to the act—what the law refers to as *mens rea* (Nettler, 1984). Moreover, to be criminal, an act must be committed in the absence of a legally recognized defense or justification (Parker, 1991). For example, while the law defines assaultive behavior as a crime, a particular assaultive act may not be criminal if it was accidental (rather than intentional) or was committed in self-defense (and therefore legally justifiable).

INDIVIDUAL ACCOUNTABILITY

All criminal law derives from a model of behavior that accounts for individual psychology. Individuals must employ judgments in controlling their acts so that accidents do not occur. The law traditionally has sought to hold able but negligent people accountable for their actions. To do this, it has included the concept of **constructive intent**. The penalties for doing damage through negligence are usually lighter than those for being deliberately criminal, yet the term *crime* applies to both. A criminal intention (*mens rea*) without the action (*actus reus*) is not a crime. Since intent is part of the definition of crime, prosecutors must establish such purpose in the perpetrator. They sometimes try to do this by constructing the motive (Nettler, 1984), asking, "Why would the person act as he or she did?" Establishing a motive does not establish guilt, however; intent and action together are required to obtain a criminal conviction.

Courts can also define the criteria used in judging guilt. Felony murders are a case in point. Under the law, an accidental (and nonnegligent) death that occurs in the context of the commission of any other felony would nevertheless be defined as a murder. Thus, the law defines as "murder" an action that would otherwise not be considered as such, based solely on its connection with the commission of another felony (Rush, 1994).

In some cases, individuals may commit acts that are beyond their control to prevent. This situation is covered by a judgment of competence, which may be restricted because of age, duress, self-defense, or insanity. With respect to age, all criminal behaviors of youths are handled not in the criminal justice system, but rather in the juvenile system. The philosophy and organization of the juvenile court system is notably different from that of the adult or criminal system in many ways. For example, the juvenile system has as its primary mission the well-being of children, whereas the criminal courts are primarily designed to punish crimes. Although the legal definition of **juvenile** varies somewhat from state to state, most juvenile courts set the minimum age of jurisdiction somewhere between 6 and 10, while the maximum age of jurisdiction is most likely to be 18. (There are exceptions to this. Connecticut, New York, North Carolina, and Vermont, for example, set the maximum age of jurisdiction for the juvenile court at 16.)

Individuals operating under **duress** may also claim that they did not intend to commit a crime and therefore are not guilty of an offense. In these cases, it must be proven that some unlawful constraint of influence was used to force an individual to commit an act that he or she would otherwise not have committed (Rush, 1994). The idea that one is under duress when committing a crime is often difficult to prove. The degree of force used must be commensurate with the degree of harm the individual perceived was being directed his or her way. Duress, however, is never a defense against murder.

SELF-DEFENSE

Self-defense involves actions taken to protect oneself or one's property in the face of a threat involving reasonable force. These cases are not always straightforward, and our view of self-defense is evolving. Originally, the doctrine of self-defense held that the danger must be immediate and severe in order to justify criminal actions. More recently, in delineating situations in which self-defense claims may be made, the law has begun to recognize issues such as power differentials between victims and offenders and/or the presence of a long-term pattern of abuse and the fear that might be associated with it. An example of this can be found in the use of "battered women's syndrome," in which a battered woman who kills her abuser in a situation in which she had reasonable cause to think that her life might be in danger (regardless of whether she had actually been physically abused in the immediate incident) claims self-defense. The battered women's syndrome defense was first used in a U.S. court in 1979 (Gillespie, 1989).

INSANITY

When it comes to proving insanity, it is incumbent on the defense to prove a state of insanity; the prosecution is not required to prove sanity. Putting the onus on the defense has the effect of restricting the extent to which an individual can claim that a limited capacity to form intent resulted from mental breakdown.

BOX 1.1 THE INSANITY DEFENSE

Many reasons for the [insanity] defense have been offered, most turning on the strong and widespread sentiment that a person should not be punished for what he cannot help doing. If his criminal act is part of an illness, it seems unjust to punish him for what the illness causes him to do. Put another way, the criminal law exists to inhibit and to punish wrong choices by people; if there was no freedom of choice, there should be no punishment. . . .

The most frequently quoted statement of the reason for an insanity defense is Judge David Bazelon's in the *Durham* case: "Our collective conscience does not allow punishment where it cannot impose blame." In practice, it may be hard to go much further than to say that we do not wish to "blame," and therefore punish, the "sick."

Compared with a total prison population in 1984 of some 463,000, fewer than

4,000 persons were held in mental hospitals because they had been adjudged "not guilty by reason of insanity." The defense of insanity is, thus, a relatively rare plea, generally advanced only in serious cases and where there is no other reasonably valid defense.

While the defense of insanity is not confined to the charge of murder, it is most often used as a defense to this charge. One reason for this is that, under recent case law, a person found not guilty by reason of insanity may be held in a mental hospital longer than if he had been convicted and sentenced for the maximum possible lawful term. This provides a strong disincentive to use of the plea except in extreme cases, particularly cases where capital punishment may be a possibility.

The insanity defense is recognized in the federal system and in all states except Montana and Idaho.* The various insanity defense standards . . . are set out in Table 1.1.

The details of the law concerning the hospitalization and release of persons acquitted by reason of insanity (NGRI's) vary from state to state. In most states, the broad outlines are similar. A person found NGRI will be committed to a mental hospital for assessment as to his present psychological condition and, if found to be mentally ill, as routinely happens, he will be confined until the mental health authorities recommend to a court that he is no longer mentally ill or that he is no longer dangerous. The final release decision in all but a few states rests with the court.

Data have not been collected on whether, in practice, those found NGRI spend more time in mental hospitals than they would have spent in prisons had they been convicted—probably less is the best present guess. But since the decision of the United States Supreme Court in *Jones* in 1983, it is constitutional to hold them longer than if they had been convicted and sentenced.

One final insanity defense development warrants comment. In the wake of the Hinckley case [John Hinckley attempted to assassinate former President Reagan in 1981], eight states have provided the defense of "guilty but mentally ill." This is supplementary to the other defense of insanity and allows a jury to find the accused guilty but to require the prison authorities to provide for his psychiatric treatment, as necessary, during the course of his imprisonment. . . . Thus, "guilty but mentally ill" merely compels prison authorities to do what they were in any event empowered to do, and were doing. Prison systems deal with many more cases of mentally ill criminals than does the insanity defense. The quality of prison psychiatric services varies from very good, in the federal system and some states, to very bad in others.

For Discussion

What do these rules about the insanity defense mean for the ways in which people are held accountable for their actions? Are these rules, as people generally believe, open to abuse?

*Currently, Utah also has no insanity defense.

SOURCE: Norval Morris, "Insanity Defense," *Crime File Study Guide* (Washington, DC: National Institute of Justice, 1988).

Table 1.1
Insanity Defense Standards

Test	Legal Standard Because of Mental Illness	Final Burden of Proof	Who Bears Burden of Proof
M'Naghten	"didn't know what he was doing or didn't know it was wrong"	Varies from proof by a balance of probabilities on the defense to proof beyond a reasonable doubt on the prosecutor	
Irresistible impulse	"could not control his conduct"		
Durham	"the criminal act was caused by his mental illness"	Beyond reasonable doubt	Prosecutor
Brawner–A.L.I.	"lacks substantial capacity to appreciate the wrongfulness of his conduct or to control it"	Beyond reasonable doubt	Prosecutor
Present federal law	"lacks capacity to appreciate the wrongfulness of his conduct"	Clear and convincing evidence	Defense

LEGAL AND SOCIAL CONTROLS

The legal system plays an important role in managing criminal events. Legal definitions of crime may appear to be immutable, determined by clear-cut rules of evidence in establishing guilt or innocence, but in reality, this is not the case. Legal responses can be and are heavily influenced by circumstance, public tolerance, and judicial discretion. Police and courts apply the law not only to fight crime and punish criminals but also to reduce social conflict. Any study of crime needs to account for behavior that is disorderly or dangerous but not yet unlawful. Alternative or informal legal responses set the outside limits of criminality by redefining criminal justice system responses to misbehavior.

Law is only one form of social control (Black, 1976). Social life is also regulated by informal expectations about how people should and should not behave. Whether we call these expectations etiquette, professionalism, or simply good taste, people evaluate the morality of each other's behavior and respond accordingly through a variety of means. Gossip, ridicule, and ostracism are forms of social control that involve less formal social processes than do legal forms. When actions are classified as crimes, much more is implied than the mere condemnation of the behavior. Calling an act a crime implies that the problem will be processed in a particular way and that specific state agencies will assume responsibility for solving it. In other words, to label a particular deed a crime is to confer "ownership" of the problem in question to the police, the courts, and other criminal justice agencies (Gilsinan, 1990).

If a problem is defined as one that involves an uninformed public acting on the basis of incomplete or incorrect information, then educational experts might be expected to provide a solution. If a problem is defined as one that results from some medical condition, then mental or physical health professionals will dominate efforts at problem amelioration. However, when behavior is deemed criminal, the issue will likely be surrendered to law enforcement and crime prevention specialists. Evidently, these alternative views are associated with dramatically different consequences. As Gusfield (1989) notes, it makes a real difference whether we see social problems as involving people who are troubled or people who are troublesome.

CRIME AND MORALITY

The idea of crime starts with some conception of proper behavior that is based on an accepted form of **morality**. Society sets out general rules detailing what is permissible or normative behavior. Moral standards change whether we want them to or not, and accompanying the changes are variations in the content of crime. "The broad boundaries of offenses against property, person, and 'society' remain fairly steady, but the criminal content within these boundaries varies" (Nettler, 1984: 2). What we define as normative behavior is affected by our reactions to behavior as morality evolves over time.

A related issue involves the forces that bring about changes in public beliefs about morality. A question posed by Jack Gibbs—"With what frequency must a type of act occur before it is considered a norm?" (1981: 14)—can be asked with reference to delinquent or criminal behavior. Suppose that large parts of the society partake in what is considered to be criminal behavior. Does the fact that the behavior is widespread make it normative? Obviously, this depends on the degree of harm being done and on the willingness of the society to retaliate against this harm. For example, violence in the "Old West" was commonplace during the settlement years. The behavior of gunslingers appeared to be normative, but was it acceptable? Clearly, the strong demand by inhabitants of these settlements for law enforcement indicates that they wanted the violence to be curtailed. Criminologists must assess how legal and moral definitions of crime coincide with the circumstances that people face, circumstances that evolve into events that demand enforcement and result in labeling individuals as criminal.

Our approach to the study of crime takes into account the issues related to its normalcy, particularly in our review of the impact that changes in law have on definitions of criminality. But the definitions that victims and offenders themselves bring to criminal situations (definitions that we measure in victimization surveys, reports on crime, action by public interest groups, and reports in the media) heavily influence how we react to and what we do about crime.

The perspective that we offer in this book questions the recent tendency in positivist criminology to isolate one or two characteristics of individuals as a way of increasing our precision in predicting their criminal tendencies or identifying a "criminal type." We believe that this type of theory building is preclusive in that it sets up artificial borders around different aspects of crime and discourages criminologists from looking at the social bases of crime—that is, crime as it evolves out of social interaction and affects social structures.

The artificial boundaries placed around crime actually change through continuous negotiation of what constitutes criminal behavior, both in the ways individuals respond to criminal behavior and in the ways the criminal justice system tries to control it. While positivist approaches certainly simplify the number of elements we have to consider in our assessment of crime, they ignore the complexity of the criminal event—its precursors, the circumstances that prevail during the act, and its aftermath.

CRIME, POLITICS, AND THE LAW

Why are some kinds of criminal events aggressively prosecuted by the criminal justice system while others do not seem to arouse much indignation? How do some types of "crime problems" become the central concern of policymakers who talk about "the war on drugs" or the need for "zero tolerance" of family violence? Where do the laws that deem some types of events as criminal come from in the first place? Answering such questions requires a systematic study of the social processes that shape and constrain organized reaction to criminal events. Theoretical approaches to these issues help us to recognize that these reactions should be understood not only as the decisions of police officers, policymakers, or politicians but also as part of larger social processes that affect behavior at the individual level.

Two theoretical explanations have been advanced to account for reactions to crime. One argues that these reactions emerge out of and reflect a social consensus about morality and about the need to respond to particular types of events in particular ways. The other view suggests that reactions to crime have more to do with power, conflict, and inequality than with social consensus.

At a very broad level, these approaches may be distinguished with respect to the ways in which they conceptualize the role of social interests (Bockman, 1991). According to consensus theorists, the members of a society have many interests in common, and their reactions to crime may be said to serve these collective interests. Laws are written and enforced to meet the needs of the majority. Deviation from these laws is generally accepted as reason for punishment. Conflict theorists, on the other hand, argue that in a complex society, social groups may pursue different interests, and that the degree of success with which they do so depends on how powerful they are. In this framework, reactions to crime can be understood as reflecting particular class, cultural, or other social interests rather than more broadly defined collective interests.

In the study of reactions to crime, the concept of social consensus is meant to alert us to the apparently broad-based agreement in society about what kinds of acts are serious crimes warranting direct and immediate intervention and what types are not. **Consensus theory,** which relates to our discussion of crime as an attack on social morality, is associated with a number of important scholars (Durkheim, 1964; Parsons, 1951; Pound, 1943). It suggests that, even in a complex, highly differentiated society like our own, people who differ from one another in terms of gender, age, ethnicity, and social class are likely to agree about certain basic moral standards.

Punishment is directed toward a commonly agreed-upon set of behaviors that offend social mores. We punish murderers more severely than we punish other criminals because of the general social consensus that murder is among the most serious infractions that a person can commit. We "criminalize," through the passage of laws, behaviors that are widely understood as threatening to our shared values, and we attach the most severe penalties to those crimes that offend our sense of collective morality most deeply.

The consensus view has gone so far as to assert that crime is functional, an idea that originated in the work of Emile Durkheim. According to the functional approach, without the contrast to "normal" behavior that is provided by crime, we would have difficulty establishing acceptable and tolerable limits to human actions. Criminal definitions provide us with the boundaries of behavior beyond which we should, and dare, not go. As Kennedy (1990) notes, these boundaries create the illusion that crime is an isolated phenomenon, unrelated to other types of social activity. Theories of crime are based on classifications of the social forms and factors associated with criminal behavior (Cain and Kulscar, 1981–82: 386). The preclusive view of delinquent behavior that results from placing artificial borders around crime discourages criminologists from addressing conflict that occurs beyond these borders—and that may motivate crime in the first place. From a functionalist perspective, there is no need to address the idea that the boundaries around crime may change as a result of changes in both individual and criminal justice system responses to criminal behavior.

From the functionalist point of view, reactions to crime, as expressed in criminalization or punishment, comprise one of the most basic ways in which

WHAT DOES IT MEAN?

Consensus vs. Conflict

Social consensus is meant to alert us to the apparent broad-based agreement in society about what kinds of acts are serious crimes deserving of direct and immediate intervention and what types are not. Conflict approaches argue that responses to crime must be seen as part of a larger struggle among groups that attempt to use the law, or legal control, in the pursuit of their interests.

The majesty and symbolism of the court sometimes obscures our understanding of the political character of the legal process.

our sense of collective morality is communicated. The moral indignation reflected in the passage of a law, the policy decision to increase the penalties for a given type of crime, the punishment of an offender—are all reminders of what binds us together as members of a society. Consistent with this view, a large body of public opinion research indicates that, by and large, our legal responses to crime reflect widespread social sentiments (Cullen, Link, and Polanzi, 1982; Goff and Nason-Clark, 1989; Hansel, 1987; Miethe, 1982; Rossi et al., 1974; Sigler and Johnson, 1986; Warr, 1989).

The consensus position and the research it has spawned have attracted much criticism. Most generally, opponents have argued that the consensus view oversimplifies the complex relationships among groups that pursue different interests with varying levels of resources. To measure consensus in a public opinion survey begs the question as to where the consensus comes from in the first place. It is one thing to argue that consensus spontaneously emerges from the collective will of the population. It is quite another to suggest that consensus results from the fact that some individuals have a vested interest in reacting to criminal events in a particular way and are able to convince the rest of the population that their world view is the right one. In either case, we might find that public opinion data reveal widespread agreement about the relative seriousness of different crimes.

BOX 1.2 DON'T SOME LAWS REFLECT CONSENSUS?

The view that laws emerge out of and reflect special interests seems to be contradicted by the commonsense observation that some laws, at least, appear to reflect the interests of everyone in society. For example, laws against murder, robbery, or sexual assault would seem to be in everyone's interest, not just those who have the most power.

However, the late British sociologist Steven Box (1981) argued that it is not really correct to say that the law prohibits murder, sexual assault, or robbery. Rather, it prohibits certain types of such behaviors while at the same time not prohibiting other behaviors that, while very similar, are likely to be committed by more powerful people.

With respect to murder, for instance, Box wrote that

the criminal code defines only some types of killing as murder; it excludes, for example, deaths which result from negligence such as employers' failure to maintain safe working conditions in factories or mines . . . or deaths which result from government agencies' giving environmental health risks a low priority . . . or death resulting from drug manufacturers' failure to conduct adequate research on new chemical compounds before conducting aggressive marketing campaigns. [Therefore,] criminal laws against murder, rape, robbery and assault do protect us all, but they do not protect the less powerful from being killed, sexually exploited, deprived of their property, or physically or psychologically damaged through the greed, apathy, negligence and the accountability of the relatively more powerful. (48–49)

For Discussion
Are there behaviors that everyone believes should be outlawed? Does this apply in all countries in the same way?

Further, by assuming that crime is functional, we justify actions that are taken by the state to repress certain groups. The actions of the police and the judiciary become focused on the disadvantaged, on visible minorities, and on other groups that lack the resources to escape this kind of attention. Such criminalization is dysfunctional in that it exacts a human cost and at the same time devalues initiatives that attempt to deal with the problems faced by these groups in ways other than through law enforcement.

Sellin (1938) cautions that using an unqualified set of *legal* definitions as the basic units or elements of criminological inquiry violates a fundamental criterion of scientific inquiry. The scientist must be free to define his or her own terms in attempting to understand any phenomena, including the crime event. Accepting without qualification the definitions of crime and criminals as laid down in law renders criminological research theoretically invalid from the scientific point of view (Sellin, 1938: 24). What is necessary, claims Sellin, is an approach to crime in which the definitions of criminal behavior can change and evolve depending on the nature of the interactions among individuals and between them and the agencies that administer control over social behavior. The way in which we articulate the problem of crime can help us focus on its root causes. Adopting inflexible definitions of the criminal event will probably lead us to deal only with the symptoms of crime and not with the causes. However, we must know not just *what* these definitions entail but also *how* they are developed (Kennedy, 1990). Further, the negotiation of justice may be a reflection not only of what the agents of social control *can do* but also what they are *prepared to do* in attacking crime.

The definitions of crime through law, then, may be seen as unchangeable, determined by the rules of evidence in establishing guilt or innocence. Alternatively, law can be seen as defining the boundaries of unacceptable behaviors depending on circumstance, public tolerance, and judicial discretion. Agents of social control use the law not only to deter crime and punish criminals but also to reduce social conflict. Some behavior that is *not* dealt with through the formal application of law may nevertheless be disorderly, threatening, or dangerous. Any study of crime needs to account for behavior that has these characteristics but is not yet unlawful. Criminologists must also consider alternative responses, such as community-based mediation, that have developed as a means of dealing with this kind of behavior. Even though they do not elicit any specific legal sanction, alternative or informal responses establish the outer limits of criminality by redefining criminal justice responses to misbehavior.

CONFLICT, POWER, AND THE LAW

In contrast to the consensus view, **conflict theory** asserts that, even if a consensus exists about what constitutes a serious crime and what does not, the source of the consensus must be taken into consideration. Moreover, it is incorrect to maintain that this consensus is a spontaneous product of group life. As one critic of the consensus position has recently written, "Laws do not simply appear miraculously on our law books and do not reflect 'society's' values. Instead, the acts and people we call 'criminal' and our concern with crime at any given time reflect the activity of groups in this society seeking legal support for economic, ideological and status interest" (Sheley, 1991: 39). From this standpoint, definitions of crime must be seen as part of a larger struggle among groups attempting to use the law, or legal control, in the pursuit of their interests.

IDENTIFYING COMPETING SOCIAL GROUPS

There is little agreement among scholars as to what might constitute such competing groups in society. Marxian scholars, for instance, locate attempts to control the mechanisms for reacting to crime in the conflicts between social classes (Chambliss, 1986; Reiman, 1990). For these theorists, such conflicts are a central feature of capitalist societies. The powerful economic classes, which own property and industries, seek to expand and consolidate their control of the less powerful classes, which must sell their labor to the capitalist class in order to survive. The legal machinery provides one important means by which this may be accomplished (Schissel, 1992).

At the same time, Marxian scholars encourage us to recognize that industries that pollute the environment and victimize consumers are generally treated less harshly than the street criminal who robs a convenience store (Michalowski and Bohlander, 1976). This is because the criminalization or aggressive prosecution of these industry actions would not be consistent with capitalist interests. For the Marxian theorist, the fact that the average person might agree that the cold-blooded killer of a convenience store night clerk should be treated more harshly than the CEO of a corporation that sells defective—and potentially dangerous or even lethal—products does not demonstrate evidence of a spontaneous consensus about what types of crimes are more serious. It merely demonstrates the ability of powerful interests to manipulate the consciousness of the members of a capitalist society.

Other proponents of the conflict position favor a model of group relations that is more diffuse than the one embraced by the Marxians. Laws and other aspects of the legal machinery do not merely reflect class conflict but may involve a variety of other interests as well (Bernard, 1981; Gusfield, 1963; Jenkins, 1992; Turk, 1976). Conflicts arise between cultural, lifestyle, or ethnic groups, and the factors that propel groups to use the legal machinery in the service of their interests may be diverse. The conflicts in which social groups are involved are not necessarily fought on a level playing field. Groups differ in the degree to which they have access to resources that allow them to influence the outcome of the conflict. From this perspective, the machinery of legal control can be thought of as one such resource. Groups may wish to see laws passed in order to have their values officially recognized by society; or they may wish to see the law used to control a group they believe threatens their values or social position.

PEACEMAKING

In a recent interpretation of conflict theory, Quinney and Wildeman (1991) offer a perspective that emphasizes peace and social justice. They argue that many of the dilemmas and contradictions in mainstream ("bourgeois") criminology in the United States at the end of the twentieth century are the result of a theoretical chaos in the field. As Quinney and Wildeman see it, this chaos stems from the persistence of certain popular beliefs that dominate the thinking about crime. As originally outlined by Pepinsky and Jesilow (1984), these include the following:

- Crime is increasing.
- Most crime is committed by the poor.
- Some groups are more law-abiding than others.

Successful crime prevention depends on neighborhood involvement in problem solving.

- White collar crime is nonviolent.
- Regulatory agencies prevent white-collar crime.
- Rich and poor people are equal before the law.
- Drug addiction causes crime.
- Laws make people behave themselves.

In Quinney and Wildeman's (1991) view, these beliefs fail to address the fundamental inequality in a society in which the power to control punishment, which lies in the hands of the state, dictates that certain groups will be unfairly treated by the criminal justice system. In this respect, criminalization is a means of imposing violence on the underclass.

Quinney and Wildeman encourage us to consider both alternative ways of responding to social ills and the broader issues that generate criminality, including social and economic disadvantage. Their solution is to offer a criminology of **peacemaking**, which involves reducing punishment/imprisonment and promoting programs that encourage treatment, rehabilitation, alternatives to prisons, mediation, and enhanced social justice. Peacemaking's nonviolent approach to crime reduction includes strategies of problem-oriented policing in which the emphasis is on *preventing* crime rather than *reacting to* crime in a punitive way (Quinney and Wildeman, 1991: 107).

THE FEMINIST APPROACH

The idea of peacemaking has found its way into feminist approaches to criminology (Simpson, 1989). In the **feminist** view, felicity and harmony are regarded as the highest values, and much emphasis is placed on the themes of caring, sharing, nurturing, and loving. According to Harris (1991):

> *This contrasts sharply [with] the orientation that values power and control above all else. Where the central goal is power, power conceived as "power over" or control, people and things are not viewed as ends in themselves but as instruments for the furtherance of power. Hierarchical institutions and structures are established both to clarify power rankings and to maintain them. The resulting stratifications create levels of superiority and inferiority, which carry differential status, legitimacy, and access to resources and other benefits. Such divisions and exclusions engender resentment and revolt in various forms, which then are used to justify greater control. (88)*

A major part of the feminist effort, Harris suggests, involves attempts to identify and confront characteristics and values that are not conducive to the full realization of human potential. In addition, feminists reject negative values that are used to justify stereotyping and that work to support the groups in power. Consistent with the ideas offered in the criminology of peacemaking, the feminist view proposes that the emphasis on control (which is epitomized in incarceration) be replaced by an emphasis on strategies that address the serious disharmony in society. Undermining social inequalities and enhancing social interaction are ways in which the potential for violence and crime can be reduced.

FEMINIST EXPLANATIONS OF CRIME RATES

In addition to seeking to understand the overall causes of crime, feminists explore the basic issues related to female criminality, starting with why the female crime rate is so much lower than that for males. Naffine (1987) examines the different theoretical approaches that have dominated criminological thinking and finds them wanting in their explanation of female involvement (or noninvolvement) in crime.

Theories that Naffine characterizes as masculinity theories, as exemplified by the work of Silverman and Dinitz (1974), have argued that men and women differ in terms of the traits that create a propensity toward criminal behavior. According to Naffine, these perspectives give rise to a basic but serious empirical problem. "Those who theorize the significance of masculinity for criminality (and femininity for conformity) have never managed to specify exactly what it is about masculinity and femininity which triggers this behavior, let alone define these concepts in a consistent and convincing manner" (Naffine, 1987: 60).

Feminist criminologists argue that the reasons we have seen a limited growth in female crime over the past decades is not that women are more passive and conforming but rather that they are more interested than men are in seeking alternatives to confrontation and aggressive action. Female crime occurs not because women become more like men but rather because the structural supports that women require to maintain relationships or to achieve their goals either are not available or are being used against them. Feminists have called for a new view of social control, one that moves away from the notion of the "reasonable man," with its emphasis on decision making based on the male experience and toward a perspective that encompasses the experiences of all individuals (Naffine, 1987: 1).

BOX 1.3 REPORTING RAPE TO THE POLICE

Is rape a unique crime in terms of the factors that relate to victims' decisions to report the event to the police, or is it similar to other forms of assaultive violence? Criminologist Alan J. Lizotte (1985) attempted to answer this question using data from the National Crime Victimization Survey.

He found that those factors that make a strong case for prosecution are more closely related to the reporting of rape than to the reporting of other kinds of assault. In other words, those factors that make the incident "more serious" in a legal sense and that make prosecution easier are likely to have important effects on the decision to notify the police. Lizotte found that:

- The more property stolen by a rapist, the more likely the incident was to be reported. The theft might be perceived by the victim as making prosecution easier, even if the rape itself was questioned by the police.
- In the case of rape, unlike for other types of assaults, the more familiar the relationship between victim and offender, the less likely the event was to be reported. This probably reflects the view that rapists who have a prior relationship with their victims are more difficult to convict.
- Rapes were more likely to be reported when the offender was an intruder rather than someone who had a right to be in the place where the rape occurred.
- If serious injury resulted from the attack, victims were more likely to report it. However, the effects were stronger for rapes and assaults on women than for assaults involving male victims.
- Victims of rape were more likely to report the rape to police if they were married. If assaulted by a nonspouse, being married could imply to the police and the courts that the sexual assault was uninvited.

For Discussion
What do these findings say about women's views of the criminal justice system? Why do you suppose that these factors have more to do with the decisions made by female as opposed to male victims?

SOURCE: Based on A. J. Lizotte (1985), "The Uniqueness of Rape: Reporting Assaultive Violence to the Police," *Crime and Delinquency* 31(2): 169–190.

The feminist reinterpretation of social control is consistent with the fact that, in the legal landscape, an increasing number of claimants are not only representing certain groups as victims but also negotiating to have offenders considered in a different light. A similar trend can be seen with respect to the cases of women who kill their husbands after suffering long-term physical abuse. What has confounded the courts in dealing with these cases is that often there is no evidence of self-defense at the time of the murder, and, in many instances, the crime actually appears to have been premeditated. However, advocates argue that women charged with such crimes should not be judged solely based on the evidence gathered on the scene. Rather, adjudication of the act should include consideration of the pattern of abuse that preceded it.

As stated previously, courts have come to accept as an acceptable defense the claim that ongoing violence directed against women creates a **battered women's syndrome.** This syndrome is characterized by a sense of helplessness whereby women come to believe that they can neither leave the abusive relationship nor effectively act to reduce the physical abuse; hence, violence is their only recourse. Striking back when the abuser is asleep or otherwise vulnerable makes the act appear premeditated.

Until fairly recently, women who killed their abusive partners in such circumstances were routinely convicted of manslaughter or murder and often were sentenced to long prison terms. In the late 1970s and early 1980s, however, U.S. courts began to allow expert witness testimony regarding the battered women's syndrome, and how the experience of long-term abuse might impart a sense of imminent personal danger (generally required in a self-defense plea) in a woman who killed an abusive partner (Gillespie, 1989). The battered women's defense is still not recognized as a special category of justification for the commission of a homicide, but the use of expert witness testimony in such cases continues to be allowed and to influence decisions regarding guilt or innocence. In other countries—for example, Canada—the battered women's defense has been officially recognized as a special type of self-defense plea by the Supreme Court (Silverman and Kennedy, 1993).

WHAT DOES IT MEAN?

Battered Women's Syndrome

This syndrome is characterized by the sense of helplessness felt by women who come to believe that they can neither leave an abusive relationship nor effectively act to reduce the violence.

THE POLICE AND CRIME

The discretionary aspects of policing strongly affect which events will be targeted and acted on. No group is more influential than the police in designating crime events.

When an event comes to their attention, the police may invoke a wide array of discretionary powers (for example, collecting evidence, investigating the claims of the victim(s), and arresting the offender or offenders). In short, the police have the power to "certify" an event as a crime by assessing the match between the event as they understand it and their working knowledge of what the law disallows.

How do the police encounter situations that they might designate as crimes? Attempts to answer this question have tended to emphasize the distinction between proactive and reactive policing services. Black (1970) notes that, in the case of **proactive policing,** the police become involved in incidents when their own investigative or patrol activities bring to their attention events that may be designated as crimes. Only about 10 percent of the cases in which the police are involved are the result of proactive policing. By contrast, in the case of **reactive policing,** the police become involved in criminal events when asked to do so by a member of the general public. Thus, it is important to understand the circumstances under which citizens request police intervention.

> **WHAT DOES IT MEAN?**
>
> ### Proactive vs. Reactive Policing
>
> In proactive policing, the police become involved in incidents as a result of their own investigative or patrol activities, which bring events that may be designated as crimes to their attention. In reactive policing, the police become involved in criminal events when requested to do so by a member of the general public.

Surveys of crime victims have proven to be a valuable source of information in this regard. In 1992, data from the **National Crime Victimization Survey (NCVS)** showed that only about 39 percent of the criminal events described to survey interviewers by victims had been brought to the attention of law enforcement officers. The police were most likely to be informed about completed motor vehicle thefts (92.2 percent of these events were reported) and about completed or attempted aggravated assaults (62 percent reported). Victims were least likely to report crimes of personal theft—only about 30 percent of these events were reported to the police in 1992 (U.S. Dept. of Justice, 1994).

Most crimes that come to the attention of the police are reported by the crime victims themselves (U.S. Dept. of Justice, 1985). In 1992, the NCVS found that people who report crimes to the police were most likely to say they did so because they hoped to recover stolen property (19 percent), because "the offense was a crime" (15 percent), or because they wished to prevent being further victimized by the offender (12 percent). Most common reasons for *not* reporting criminal victimization were because the object was recovered or the offender was not successful in his/her attempt (25 percent), because the crime was reported to "another official" (15 percent), or because victims felt there was a "lack of proof" (11 percent) (U.S. Dept. of Justice, 1994).

Victims may also, of course, have other reasons for not reporting crimes. For example, they may prefer not to report because they feel that the police cannot be of assistance to them—about 11 percent of victims in the 1992

NCVS said they did not report either because they thought the police would not want to be bothered (8 percent) or because they felt the police were inefficient, ineffective, or biased (3 percent). Further, victims may choose not to report because they perceive the crime to have been of a personal or private nature. For example, rates of reporting for stranger-perpetrated crimes are generally slightly higher than for those crimes perpetrated by someone known to the victim (U.S. Dept. of Justice, 1994).

Victims choose not to call the police for other reasons as well. Victims may themselves be involved in some form of criminal activity at the time of the incident and may therefore be reluctant to invite a police investigation (Block, 1974). In some instances, victims do not report crimes because they have at their disposal other means of dealing with the situation (Kennedy, 1988). For example, a teenage boy who has been assaulted by a peer may be more likely to seek retaliation through personal action than through police intervention.

Members of some social groups are somewhat more likely than members of other groups to report crime to the police, although differences in this regard are not particularly strong (Gottfredson and Gottfredson, 1988). Crimes involving female or elderly victims, for instance, have higher levels of reportability. This is perhaps because many women and many elderly have at their disposal fewer alternative resources for dealing with victimization and its consequences (Fattah and Sacco, 1989; Skogan, 1976). While people who view the criminal justice system negatively might be expected to be less likely to contact the police, the influence of such attitudes actually appears to be slight (Block, 1974; Gottfredson and Gottfredson, 1988).

In contrast, available data indicate that reporting decisions are strongly influenced by the characteristics of the criminal events themselves. The more serious the event, the greater the probability that it will be reported to the police. Thus, incidents that involve physical injury, significant property loss, or the use of a weapon, or that occur in or near the victim's residence, are more likely than incidents without these characteristics to be brought to the attention of the police (Block, 1974; Gottfredson and Gottfredson, 1988; Skogan, 1977).

These findings are consistent with the view that people report crimes to the police when there is good reason to do so but decline to report crimes when the costs of reporting outweigh any potential benefits. For victims of sexual assault or wife

Reactive policing involves mobilization that results from citizens' requests for action.

abuse, fear of retaliation or concerns about stigmatization or mistreatment by police negate the advantages associated with reporting. In general, reporting crime is best viewed as part of a rational decision-making process that takes account of the crime, the offender, the victim's resources, and the perceived limitations of police responsiveness (Gottfredson and Gottfredson, 1988).

HOW MUCH CRIME?

Now that we have some sense of what constitutes crime and which factors may affect its reporting, what does this mean for the overall volume of crime that comes to the attention of the police? The Federal Bureau of Investigation (FBI) collects statistics annually on the occurrence of seven important criminal events called the **index crimes**—homicide, rape, aggravated assault, robbery, burglary, larceny, and motor vehicle theft—which provide good indicators of variations in rates of all criminal activity. As can be seen in Figure 1.1, the rate of index crime offenses increased dramatically in the United States between

Figure 1.1
Crime Victimization Rates per 100,000 Population, 1960–1993

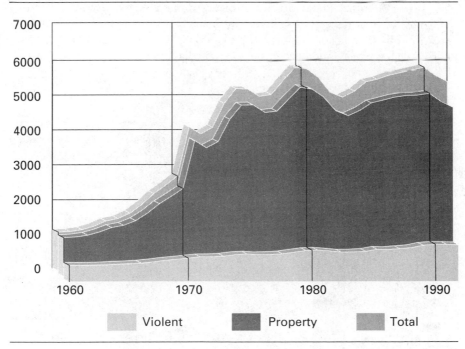

NOTE: Violent index crimes are homicide, forcible rape, robbery, and aggravated assault. Property index crimes are burglary, larceny-theft, and motor vehicle theft. Data for arson are *not* included in this table.

SOURCE: FBI Uniform Crime Reports, 1970, 1980, 1990, 1993.

1962 and 1993. Rates of increase were similar for violent and property crimes, with each rising almost 400 percent during this thirty-year period.

Table 1.2 gives a somewhat clearer picture of each of the index offenses for 1993. Here we can see that property crimes far outnumbered the violent crimes, which comprised only about 14 percent of all the index crimes reported. Larceny-theft was the crime most likely to occur in 1993, while homicide was least likely to occur.

Crime rates also vary somewhat by geographical region. Figure 1.2 shows rates of property and violent index crime victimization in various regions of the United States. Rates of both types of crime are highest in the West. Property crime rates are lowest in the Northeast, while rates of violent criminal victimization are lowest in the Midwest. Patterns of and trends in crime are heavily influenced by changes in the population and by the socioeconomic forces that impinge on daily life. We will examine these factors in greater detail in later chapters.

THE PUBLIC INTEREST IN CRIMINAL EVENTS

The fact that violent crime still constitutes a small proportion of all crime events is at odds with the public perception about the extent and pervasiveness of this type of crime. Public attitudes toward crime are strongly influenced by the extensive treatment of this subject in the media. Of course, there is a widespread public fascination with the topic of crime. Lawbreaking figures prominently in what we see and hear in the mass media and in the conversations that

Table 1.2
Index Crime in the United States, 1993

Offense Type	Number	Rate per 100,000	% of Total Index Crime
Homicide	24,526	9.5	0.2
Rape	104,806	40.6	0.7
Robbery	659,757	255.8	4.6
Aggravated assault	1,135,099	440.1	8.0
Total violent crime	**1,924,188**	**746.1**	**13.6**
Burglary	2,834,808	1,099.2	20.0
Larceny-theft	7,820,909	3,032.4	55.3
Motor vehicle theft	1,561,047	605.3	11.0
Total property crime	**12,216,764**	**4,736.9**	**86.4**
Total Violent and Property Crime	**14,140,952**	**5,482.9**	**100%**

SOURCE: FBI Uniform Crime Reports, 1993.

Figure 1.2
Regional Violent and Property Crime Rates per 100,000 Population, 1993

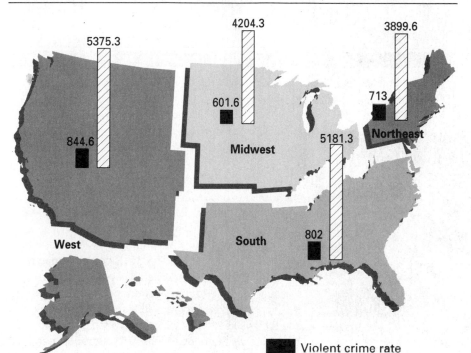

SOURCE: FBI Uniform Crime Reports, 1993.

we have with one another. What are these popular images of crime? Where do they come from? What implications do they have for the ways in which we think about and respond to crime?

CRIME NEWS

THE INTEREST IN CRIME NEWS

While there are differences across media types and across communities with respect to the amount of coverage that crime receives (Liska and Baccaglini, 1990), generally speaking crime is widely reported by all popular news media (Dominick, 1978; Ericson, Barnek, and Chan, 1991). Why is this? The simple answer may be that media audiences are interested in such stories, and journalists therefore rely on crime news because it "sells" (Gordon and Heath, 1981). Some audience members may view crime news as an important source of information about the "facts" of crime, while others may be caught up in the dramatic and sometimes lurid nature of crime news.

BOX 1.4 CRIME TOURS

The public ambivalence about crime manifests itself in various ways. Much of the popular culture that we find in television, books, and movies focuses on the sensational character of crime in society. Even while most members of the general public express concern about the crime problem, it remains an endless source of fascination.

Alcatraz, now a popular tourist attraction, was once the prison home of "public enemies" like Al Capone.

This fascination has extended in recent years to the tourist experience. In many large American cities, visitors may take guided tours of famous local crime scenes. In Chicago, Untouchable Tours provide customers with a scenic view of the city's most famous gangland locations, including the Biograph Theater (where the FBI shot and killed bank robber John Dillinger) and the former headquarters of gangster Al Capone. A tour company in New York City offers the Sidewalks of New York tour, which allows paying guests to visit famous Manhattan murder scenes.

Visitors to Hollywood can ride in a Cadillac hearse as they visit local sites, including the places where Janis Joplin and John Belushi overdosed on drugs and the homes where mobster Bugsy Siegal and Nicole Brown Simpson were murdered.

Vacation planning is made easy by travel guides such as *Unauthorized America* ("a travel guide to the places the Chamber of Commerce won't tell you about") by Vince Staten, *New York Notorious* ("a borough-by-borough tour of the city's most famous crime scenes") by Paul Schwartzman and Rob Polner, and *Murder USA* ("a true-crime travel guide to the most notorious killing grounds in America") by Tom Philben.

For Discussion

Why do you think that there is so much public fascination with crime, particularly when we fear its consequences? Do you think that notorious murder scenes of today will be the tourist attractions of tomorrow?

SOURCE: Based on "Crime Tours," *Crimebeat* (January 1992): 29–31.

Katz (1987) argues that audience fascination with crime news has little to do with a search for the truth about crime or with the dramatic qualities of crime reporting. Instead, he maintains, crime news allows audience members to work out their own positions on moral questions of a general yet also personal nature. For example, many crime stories deal with the competence or insensitivity of offenders. As Katz (1987) expresses it, we read accounts of "ingenious, vicious, and audacious crimes—of deceptions that trick the close scrutiny of diligent customs inspectors, of the most bloody murders, of big heists in broad daylight" (50). Such stories demonstrate to the audience the nature and the limits of human competence and human sensibility. They are of interest to the audience precisely because the dilemma of assessing personal competence and maintaining one's own moral sensibility is routinely encountered in day-to-day life. For Katz (1987), reading crime news is a "ritual moral exercise [and, as such,] appears to serve a purpose similar to the morning shower, routine physical exercise and shaving" (72).

THE CONTENT OF CRIME NEWS

Studies on the content of **crime news** have yielded informative findings. First, there appears to be little direct correspondence between the amount of *crime news* and the amount of *crime* (as measured, for instance, in official statistics). In other words, objectively measured trends in crime do not correspond closely with trends in the amount of crime news (Garofalo, 1981; Katz, 1987). Second, the degree of media attention to crime depends on the type of offense. Violent, relatively infrequent crimes like homicide are emphasized, while property crimes, white-collar offenses, and other nonviolent, frequently occurring crimes are underreported (Graber, 1980; Humphries, 1981; Randall, Lee-Sammons, and Hagner, 1988; Skogan and Maxfield, 1981). Third, crime news presents an exaggerated image of the proportion of offenses that result in arrest (Sacco and Fair, 1988; Skogan and Maxfield, 1981)—that is, the media portray police as far more effective than they really are. Fourth, media attention is focused on the early stages of criminal justice processing (detection and arrest); the later stages of legal processing are largely ignored (Hans, 1990).

Analyses of crime news also indicate that media coverage is notable not only for what it includes but also for what it excludes. Crime reporting is often criticized for ignoring the relationship between crime and broad social conditions. Jon Katz (1993) reports that gun murders have now become so common in the large U.S. cities that major newspapers and networks tend to ignore them. Katz states that the readers of large dailies primarily reside in suburbs outside of the areas in which the violence is the greatest. As a result, only the most sensational of the violent crimes are reported, leaving the inner-city residents with no mainstream media to report on their most urgent problems.

Humphries (1981) suggests that while news reports associate criminal violence with youth, maleness, and minority membership, they ignore the historical view of how labor markets and related institutions shape employment opportunities and the size and composition of the pool of people vulnerable to arrest. This tendency to portray crime as perpetrated mainly by pathological individuals precludes alternative explanations. For instance, a report about a single mother accused or convicted of child abuse may describe her as "disturbed" and ignore the following questions: "Was the mother receiving

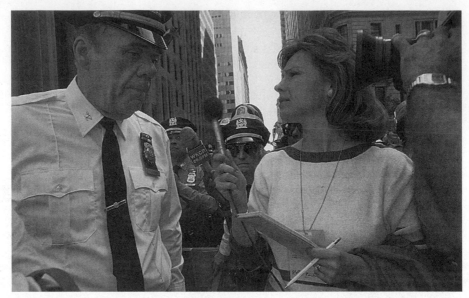

Most crime news finds its origins in the well-developed relationships that link police and members of the news media.

welfare or was she unemployed? Was the child attending a day-care program or receiving any other social services? Had the mother been a victim of child abuse?" (Gorelick, 1989: 423).

The biased nature of media crime reporting is clearly illustrated in Voumvakis and Ericson's (1984) study on newspaper accounts of attacks against women. While the accounts covered in this study offer explanations for the "crime wave," they do so by emphasizing (1) the ways in which the victims' actions placed them at risk; (2) the need for a more coercive, and presumably more effective, response from the criminal justice system; and (3) offender pathology. Voumvakis and Ericson maintain that these terms of reference, although not necessarily unreasonable, are restrictive in that they rule out alternative interpretations, particularly those that link crimes against women to more general patterns of gender inequality. Reporting that emphasizes the need for more police, more punishment, and more vigilance by women does not allow for discussion of broader programs of social reform that might correct these inequalities.

THE SOURCES OF CRIME NEWS

Studies of news production practices emphasize the ways in which judgments of **"newsworthiness"** come to be applied to categories of events (Chib-

WHAT DOES IT MEAN?

Newsworthy

To be newsworthy, incidents first must have spatial and temporal characteristics that lend themselves easily to news production routines. Second, reports of such events must be viewed by journalists as readily comprehensible to an audience and thus as requiring little in the way of background information. Finally, the crimes must lend themselves to a dramatic narrative.

nall, 1977; Fishman, 1978). Such judgments reflect the ways journalists view their society, the work in which they are engaged, and the audiences that they serve. Criminal events (especially violent ones) conform closely to the professional values of journalists for several reasons (Ericson, Baranek, and Chan, 1987).

First, such incidents have spatial and temporal characteristics that lend themselves easily to news production routines. Murders, thefts, and sexual assaults are discrete events that occur in the period between the publication of successive editions of a newspaper or between successive radio and television newscasts. Second, reports of criminal events are readily comprehensible to an audience and thus require little in the way of background information. In addition, because there is an almost limitless supply of crime news, the number of crime-related stories can be expanded or reduced depending on the needs of media decision makers and on the amount of space or time that must be filled on any given day (Warr, 1991). Finally, many crimes lend themselves to a dramatic narrative form that features the exploits of clearly defined "good guys" and "bad guys" (Ericson, 1991).

The reliance of news organizations on a continuous flow of crime news has led to the establishment of well-defined relationships between news organizations and those who are viewed as reliable and credible suppliers of such information (Gordon and Heath, 1981). The police are the principal source of crime news, and the "police wire," press release, news conference, or beat reporter provides the link between the world of crime and the news media (Ericson, Baranek, and Chan, 1989). Because the police are able to supply a steady stream of stories that are "entertaining, dramatic, amusing and titillating" (Ericson, 1991: 207), journalists implicitly adopt a police perspective on the problem of crime (Fishman, 1981).

The police–journalist relationship is mutually beneficial (Katz, 1987). It allows journalists regular access to a valued news commodity, and, through reference to the police as the official spokespersons on crime, it lends credibility, authority, and objectivity to media reporting. Correspondingly, the relationship allows police to present themselves as experts on crime and at the same time reaffirms police ownership of the problem of crime.

This exploration of the role that police sources play in the production of crime news helps to explain why interpersonal violent crimes such as homicide or robbery receive greater coverage than crimes by or against businesses (Ericson, 1991). First, the established source–journalist relationships that exist with respect to so-called common crimes generally do not exist in the case of business crime. Second, stories about business crime may be judged as less newsworthy because they are generally more complex, less dramatic, and often more difficult to personalize (Randall, Lee-Sammons, and Hagner, 1988).

CRIME DRAMA

Crime drama has been an important part of television since the medium's inception. From "Dragnet," "The Untouchables," and "Racket Squad" to "Homicide," "Law and Order," and "New York: Undercover," each decade has witnessed countless lawyers, police detectives, and private investigators engaged in the prime-time pursuit of law and order. As in the case of crime news, television crime drama conforms closely to the stylistic and commercial requirements of the medium. These programs rely heavily on dramatic conventions that emphasize suspense and violent action. The storytelling formula of crime shows typically provides a format in which these conventions can be conveniently maximized (Ericson, 1991). As crimes are investigated, and as wrongdoers are pursued and ultimately brought to justice, opportunities abound for car chases, fistfights, and gunplay. It is rumored that a television executive was once asked why so many of the programs on his network dealt with police officers and private detectives. He responded, "I suppose we could do a one-hour dramatic show about mail carriers. But just exactly what would we have them do every week?"

BOX 1.5 GUNS AND GLAMOR

Pocketfuls of Fear
Armed with special permits, America's elite are carrying concealed weapons

In New York City these days, there's a new list to beat all others. Comedian Bill Cosby is on it. Joan Rivers, too. And Donald Trump and William F. Buckley Jr. There's even a Rockefeller on it: Laurence.

All are members of a select group of New Yorkers who have been granted the privilege of firepower. Each possesses a permit from the New York Police Department to carry a concealed weapon when they step out onto the streets of the city.

Harry Connick Jr. is not on the list, and it cost him a night in jail. Mr. Connick, a Frank Sinatra–style crooner, got a pistol from his sister for Christmas. He was arrested when he tried to take the unlicenced weapon with him on a recent trip to New Orleans.

The militarization of New York's cultural elite comes at a time when the perception of violence is on the increase in America's cities, says Dr. Gary Kleck, an expert on American gun culture and author of the book *Point Blank.* Never mind that figures show violent crime has "experienced a mild decrease since the 1970s," except against young black males, says Dr. Kleck. The rise in gun lust appears to be the best-kept secret in New York's cultural constellation.

Indeed, gun culture has become almost a fashion statement. Sylvia Heisel, a designer for clothier Barneys New York, recently created a low-cut, full-length bullet-proof evening gown for the fearful set.

Meanwhile, well-heeled politicians, entertainers, doctors and businessmen pay up to $1,500 (U.S.) a year for the opportunity of letting off some high-calibre steam at the exclusive Downtown Rifle and Pistol Club, according to Bill Messick, the club's director.

Who are they? "We don't give out names," sniffs Mr. Messick.

Pornography mogul Al Goldstein, editor and publisher of *Screw Magazine* and producer of the late-night TV cable show *Midnight Blue* (which he hosts in the nude), has been trying to get on the "gun-carry" list since 1978, after his colleague, Hustler Magazine publisher Larry Flint, was crippled by an assailant's bullet. After a string of rejected applications, he has taken his case all the way to the New York State Appeals Court.

"If the crooks and crazies are packing Uzis or Mac-10s, at least let me carry a Beretta," says the card-carrying member of the American Civil Liberties Union and the National Rifle Association.

The application process concerning gun-carrying permits varies considerably throughout the U.S., according to Dr. Kleck. In the state of Iowa, law-enforcement officials must prove an applicant is unfit to possess a gun-carry permit. Los Angeles, which has one of the most restrictive gun-carry policies in the country, recently granted its first permit for a concealed weapon since 1974 to the city's new Commissioner of Police, Willy Williams. New York City's policy regarding gun-carry permits is one of the most arbitrary systems in the nation, says Mr. Kleck.

Mr. Goldstein insists that his case reflects the perks available to those at the top of the heap in New York. Indeed, the process has been kind to those with fame, power and influence.

The New York Times publisher Arthur Ochs Sulzberger said he needed to carry a gun to safeguard the wads of money he carries around town. He got one. The photographer Irving Elkin requested and received a permit on the grounds that he carries "money and expensive cameras." The entertainer Bill Cosby was issued a permit in 1988 after stating that he and other family members had been the object of unspecified death threats. Real-estate mogul Donald Trump and radio host Howard Stern also cited death threats. "Threats, as ever," wrote conservative journalist William F. Buckley, on his application for renewal of his gun carry permit.

Thomas Certoni, the officer who rejected Mr. Goldstein's application, testified that he could not think of another New Yorker who has received more death threats than the porn publisher. Nevertheless, Mr. Certoni concluded that Mr. Goldstein could not prove extraordinary need to obtain a gun-carry permit.

Mr. Goldstein says he has more reason to be fearful than any of the other notables who have been given police approval to carry a concealed weapon. The police granted him a permit to keep a .38-calibre revolver in his apartment, but he says it isn't enough. The 4th Street massage parlours and downtown S&M clubs he frequents in the wee hours to review the sex world for his magazine are not only unsavoury, he says, they are unsafe.

Furthermore, the incendiary tenor of his editorials—designed to offend and incite—attract a degree of crackpot hostility that is potentially lethal. Mr. Goldstein says he was pistol-whipped more than 10 years ago by thugs in his midtown office for writing an "unfavourable review" of what he believes is a Mafia-controlled massage parlour.

A lewd attack in the pages of *Screw Magazine* on the late Ayatollah Khomeini—after he placed his *fatwa* on writer Salman Rushdie—occasioned a battery of death threats.

The reaction was serious enough to prompt an investigation by the FBI and the New York Police Department. . . .

Because the essentially escapist nature of television crime drama is well recognized, no one really expects the world of crime portrayed in such programs to constitute a valid portrait of real-life crime and criminals. The images have more to do with the needs of the medium than with a desire to accurately map reality. Still, it is worth noting that crime in television drama, like crime in the news, tends to be disproportionately violent (Dominick, 1978). Additionally, television criminals are generally older than their real-life counterparts, with their age grouping more closely approximating that of the audience (Pandiani, 1978). Whereas crime data suggest that offenders are typically poor, television criminals are more likely to be affluent. Any suggestion of an association between crime and minority group membership is typically downplayed in crime dramas in order to avoid alienating a significant segment of the viewing audience, which would clearly not be in the best interests of a commercial medium. As a result of these influences, television criminals are typically "white materialists, motivated by greed and lasciviousness" (Newman, 1990: 263).

The distinction between television news and television drama is less clear than it once was (Hans, 1990; Newman, 1990). Programs such as "America's Most Wanted," "Unsolved Mysteries," "Top Cops," and "A Current Affair" combine traditional news documentary techniques with the familiar narrative style of dramatic television. These program formats (sometimes labeled "infotainment" or "reality television") have proliferated both because they have proven popular with audiences and because they are relatively inexpensive to produce. Crime, like other social problems, continues to be a source of both entertainment and income in the mass media (Gusfield, 1989).

The ongoing debate about violence in the media and its effects on audiences has recently intensified. Discussion of the issue in the United States Senate (in hearings chaired by Senator Paul Simon) has convinced many television officials that if they do not voluntarily do something about lessening the display of graphic violence in their shows, they are likely to face legislated standards. The effectiveness of the Simon hearings was reflected in the fact that all four American networks sent their presidents to testify as to the steps they had taken—including self-censorship—to address these problems.

TALKING ABOUT CRIME

People not only read crime news and watch crime shows on television but also talk about crime. A major study of reactions to crime in three major American cities found that people cited their friends and neighbors, rather than the mass media, as their principal sources of information about local crime conditions

(Skogan and Maxfield, 1981). Nonetheless, talk about crime is frequently focused on events that have achieved a high degree of media notoriety. Heavy media coverage of serial killings, child abductions, or crimes committed by or against celebrities is likely to generate considerable public discussion. Much talk also centers on crime in the local environment. Residents of high-crime neighborhoods tend to talk more about crime (Skogan and Maxfield, 1981); they are more likely to be personally acquainted with crime victims and thus to have more stories to tell about crime and its consequences.

In their study on fear of crime among the elderly, Kennedy and Silverman (1985) report the surprising finding that respondents who expressed high levels of fear also had higher levels of contact with family members than did other respondents. The continuous cautions that the elderly (particularly those who live on their own) receive from their families may have the paradoxical effect of exacerbating rather than calming their fears.

CRIME IN RUMOR AND LEGEND

Sometimes talk about crime seems to bear only a very tenuous relationship to social reality. In 1956, news spread throughout Taipei that a number of children had been victims of slashings with what appeared to be razor blades or similar weapons (Jacobs, 1965). In 1944, many residents of Mattoon, Illinois, were reportedly the victims of a "phantom anaesthetist" who entered their homes and sprayed them with a paralyzing gas (Johnson, 1945). In 1969, stories spread through the city of Orléans, France, that Jewish dress shop owners were kidnapping young women and selling them into the "white slave trade" (Morin, 1971). More recently, stories have spread in many communities in North America about the threats posed to children by Halloween sadists, who poison or otherwise contaminate the "treats" they dispense to unsuspecting children (Best, 1990).

There was no real evidence to corroborate any of these stories. Their fanciful quality suggests a close kinship with sociological definitions of "rumor" (Rosnow, 1988; Rosnow and Fine, 1976). Like all rumors, they represent forms of **improvised news** that express anxieties and uncertainties about some aspect of social life (Shibutani, 1966). For example, Best (1990) argues that the spread of stories about Halloween sadists during the 1970s was a response to three forms of social strain that characterized the period. The first was an increasing public awareness of, and concern over, the vulnerability of children to child abuse and a range of other victimizing experiences. The second was the general increase in the fear of crime and in the threats posed to personal safety by anonymous strangers. The third was an increasing mistrust of persons outside of one's group. Best (1990: 143) characterizes the Halloween sadist as a symbolic expression of these three anxieties: "The sadist, like other dangers, attacks children—society's most vulnerable members; the sadist, like the stereotypical criminal, is an anonymous, unprovoked assailant; and the sadist, like other strangers, should be met with suspicion rather than trust."

BOX 1.6 TERROR ON CAMPUS: AN URBAN LEGEND

Folklorist H. J. Brunvand (1993) describes an urban legend that circulated around university campuses in the American South and Midwest in 1988. According to rumors, a psychic had predicted on a television talk show that a mass murderer was going to terrorize campus residents on Halloween night.

From place to place, the specific details of the rumor changed. The talk show in question was variously named as "Oprah," "Donahue," and "Geraldo" among others. The universities in question were variously named as Florida State, Purdue, Ohio Northern, and Slippery Rock.

According to the version of the story that circulated in Florida, a psychic on the "Oprah Winfrey Show" had predicted that a knife-wielding maniac, dressed as Little Bo Peep, was going to slash his way through a dormitory or sorority house. The story persisted despite statements from the show's producers that no such guest had appeared and no such prediction had been made. An elaboration of the story described proposed action by university officials to evacuate residences on Halloween, although such action was never considered. At Purdue, it was said that the prediction involved the deaths of twelve students living in an "X-shaped" dormitory.

According to Brunvand, rumors of this type frequently circulate around university campuses in the fall. Usually, the stories describe killings that will occur at a school, the name of which begins with a particular letter or that is situated near a particular configuration of mountains or rivers. The target building is usually described as being of a particular shape and size or as having a particular type of name. Such stories have been circulating since at least 1968.

Brunvand states that, even though these stories lack a factual basis, some students are likely to react as though they are true. They may, for instance, move out of their residence on Halloween night or barricade their doors.

Real-life mass murders on campus (such as those at the University of Montreal) may lend to such stories an air of credibility.

For Discussion

Why do you think that there is so much concern about safety on college campuses?

SOURCE: Based on H. J. Brunvand; *The Baby Train* (New York: Norton, 1993).

WHAT ARE THEY?

Urban Legends

Urban legends are captivating and plausible but mainly fictional oral narratives that are widely regarded as true stories.

Folklorists use the term **urban legend** to characterize many of the crime stories that travel along interpersonal channels of communication (Brunvand, 1981, 1984, 1986, 1989). Brunvand (1984: ix) describes these legends as "highly captivating and plausible, but mainly fictional oral narratives that are widely told as true stories." Urban legends are widely circulated and typically deal with attempted abductions in shopping malls or amusement parks, psychopaths who terrorize babysitters, the contamination of children's "lick-and-stick" tattoos with hallucinogenic drugs, and criminally insane killers who stalk couples on "lovers lane." While these stories vary in their details from place to place and over time, their moral substance has remarkable durability.

Wachs (1988) argues that urban folklore regarding crime has considerable entertainment value in that both the telling and the hearing of the stories may provide opportunities for dramatic and frequently humorous release. She further characterizes these stories as "cautionary tales" that advise listeners of the dangers of urban life and the need for constant vigilance.

Some kinds of urban legends are more newsworthy than others. Stories about bicycle thieves generally have less currency than stories about killers on the loose. Skogan and Maxfield (1981) found that, in the cities that they studied, neighborhood talk about crime was largely dominated by stories about elderly or female victims.

While talk about corporate and white-collar criminals appears to be infrequent, it does exist (Kapferer, 1989). In recent years, for instance, stories have circulated that some major businesses are under the control of satanic cults (Brunvand, 1984) or are willfully contaminating food products (Kapferer, 1989).

Sometimes stories have very real consequences before it becomes evident that they are in fact hoaxes. In the summer of 1993, a media scare erupted over the "discovery" of hypodermic needles in Pepsi cans. All aspects of Pepsi's operations were scrutinized to determine how this could have happened. After much bad publicity, Pepsi was able to demonstrate that it is virtually impossible to insert a needle into a can during the high-speed canning processes employed in its plants. Subsequently, the story was exposed as a series of hoaxes, but not before serious damage had been done to Pepsi's image. Concerns have been raised not only about the serious consequences of such hoaxes but also about the media's role in sounding the alarm and perpetuating public doubts about a product.

CRIME MYTHS

Much of what we see on television or hear during late-night storytelling sessions can be described as **crime myths** (Kappeler et al., 1993): distorted and misleading information that nevertheless is accepted as fact. For instance, many people believe these crime myths:

- The elderly face the highest risks of victimization of any group in society.
- Most crime is violent.
- Serial killers account for a substantial number of murders each year.
- Rates of victimization have risen dramatically in recent years.
- The risk of wife assault increases substantially on Super Bowl Sunday.

However, according to the best social scientific evidence, none of these statements is true.

According to Kappeler and colleagues (1993), crime myths serve several important social functions. First, they help us to organize our views of crime and the criminal justice system within a ready-made framework that clearly identifies criminals, victims, and crimefighters. Second, these myths support and maintain established views about crime. Third, they help us to fill in the gaps in knowledge that social science has not or cannot fill. Finally, these myths provide an outlet for emotional responses to crime and help to establish the channels by which emotions can be transformed into action.

The problem of drunk driving demonstrates the power of myths. As Walker (1994) argues, drunk driving, like many problems in criminology, has been subject to active mythmaking. According to Walker, myths associated with drunk driving include the following:

- *Drunk drivers are responsible for half of all traffic fatalities.* According to Walker, this claim originated in a 1968 Department of Transportation report, and subsequent analyses have shown the figure to be greatly exaggerated.
- *The traffic safety problem is getting worse.* In fact, Walker claims, the rate of traffic accidents and traffic fatalities has been steadily declining since the 1920s.
- *Everyone drives drunk from time to time.* Instead, Walker maintains, studies have shown that the drinking habits of close to 80 percent of the population are unlikely to cause them to drive drunk.
- *Drunk drivers "get off" easily.* On the contrary, Walker states, even before the great crackdown of the 1980s, conviction rates for drunk drivers were fairly high.
- *Drunk drivers tend to kill other drivers or pedestrians.* Actually, Walker asserts, over 90 percent of the people killed by drunk drivers are the drivers themselves or their passengers.

Because crime myths are so pervasive and so durable, they sometimes interfere with our ability to approach the subject matter of criminology in an open manner. However, in the chapters that follow, the gap that separates cultural myth from empirical reality will become increasingly evident.

SUMMARY
■ ■ ■

The study of crime is an interdisciplinary endeavor that draws on a variety of techniques in highlighting different aspects of the criminal event. While crime is, strictly speaking, the breaking of the law, we need to understand more than simply offender motivation in explaining how and why crime occurs. A number of factors influence the definition of criminal behavior, including variations in legal interpretations, changing social morality, police actions, and (for various reasons) nonreporting of crime. Thus, we need to be sensitive to social as well as legal definitions of crime events.

In attempting to explain crime, criminologists generally adopt one of two perspectives. The first approach, classicism, views offenders as rational beings who weigh the benefits of criminal activity against the costs of apprehension. The second approach, positivism, looks instead at the offenders' behavior as something determined by their constitution and/or social and economic conditions. In addition, crime can be defined as based on consensus or conflict of special interests. The emphasis in these approaches is on the motivation of offenders.

Crime statistics compiled by the police indicate that the volume of reported crime has increased dramatically over the last thirty years. Property crimes represent most of all reported crime, while violent crime makes up about 14 percent of the total.

Crime events as presented in the media and in public discussions frequently do not accurately represent the true nature of crime. Media treatment of crime often creates the impression that certain types of crime (for example, homicide or armed robbery) are more prevalent than is actually the case. Both crime news and crime dramas emphasize the more exotic and "exciting" types of crime; their depictions of criminal events are often more entertaining than informative.

QUESTIONS FOR REVIEW AND DISCUSSION
■ ■ ■

1. What is the difference between an action in which there is no intent to harm and one in which an individual has this intent?
2. How much crime is there? Discuss both the incidence and extent of crime in the United States.
3. Do people who have psychological problems always get off based on an insanity defense? If not, why not?
4. In what ways do your family and friends talk about crime? How does this influence your sense of how much crime there is? How does their discussion of crime compare to what you read in or hear through the media?
5. Is news reporting of crime accurate? Discuss the factors that may create distortions in the extent and incidence of crime.

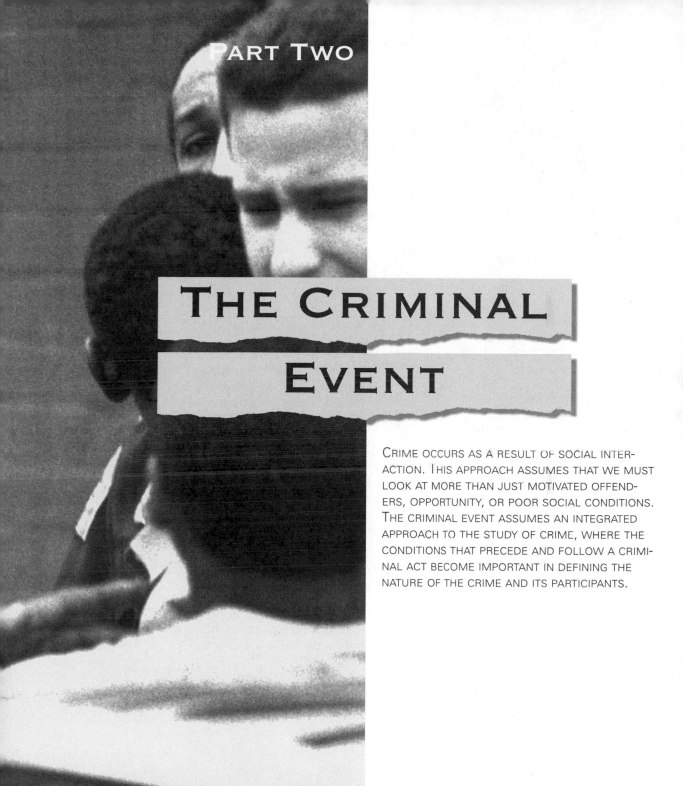

PART TWO

THE CRIMINAL EVENT

CRIME OCCURS AS A RESULT OF SOCIAL INTER-
ACTION. THIS APPROACH ASSUMES THAT WE MUST
LOOK AT MORE THAN JUST MOTIVATED OFFEND-
ERS, OPPORTUNITY, OR POOR SOCIAL CONDITIONS.
THE CRIMINAL EVENT ASSUMES AN INTEGRATED
APPROACH TO THE STUDY OF CRIME, WHERE THE
CONDITIONS THAT PRECEDE AND FOLLOW A CRIMI-
NAL ACT BECOME IMPORTANT IN DEFINING THE
NATURE OF THE CRIME AND ITS PARTICIPANTS.

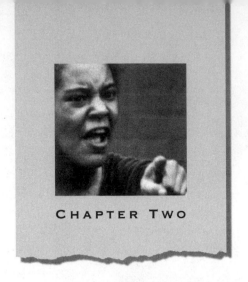

The Criminal Event

KEY TERMS

criminal events

excuse

justification

victim

victimless crimes

bystanders

mandatory charge
rule

modernization

defensible space

social domains

precursors

transactions

aftermath

WHAT'S IN CHAPTER TWO

In this chapter, we introduce the concept of the "criminal event," explaining how crime takes place through the convergence of motivated offenders, victims, and others who may increase the chance of harm or who may act to deter criminal behavior. We also detail the three stages of criminal events: precursors, transactions, and aftermath. Precursors relate to the way the law defines acceptable behavior in society and the way people in the community define morality. These factors affect how individuals treat one another. The transaction involves the criminal act itself. Key considerations here include the offender's behavior, the role of the victim in the transaction, and the part that third parties, including the police, play in affecting the nature of the event. The aftermath refers to the consequences of the crime, including harm to the victim, punishment of the offender, and public reactions to the crime.

In this chapter, we will outline a framework for organizing our integrated approach to the analysis of crime and crime control. This framework emphasizes the study of crime as **criminal events** (Gould, 1989). As we have already pointed out, throughout most of the history of criminology, researchers have attempted to understand crime largely in terms of the actions of criminal offenders (Cohen and Felson, 1979). The simple implication of this approach is that crimes represent little more than the enactment of the will of people who are motivated to behave criminally. If this view is valid, the task of the criminologist is to try to explain why some people behave criminally, while the task of the police and other criminal justice agencies is to prevent offenders from behaving criminally or to capture and reform them after they have done so.

Although we cannot hope to understand crime in society without reference to the lawbreaker, it is also true, as noted previously, that there is much more to crime than the offender. Crimes also involve, in many cases, victims who resist their victimization and in so doing affect the course of action (Kleck and Sayles, 1990; Webb and Marshall, 1989; Ziegenhagen and Brosnan, 1985). Further, crimes may involve bystanders and witnesses whose presence can deter an offender or whose apparent tacit approval of the offender's actions can facilitate the commission of the crime (Shotland and Goodstein, 1984). Bystanders or victims may also summon the police, whose appearance at the scene may affect the response of offenders.

The criminal event cannot be separated from the physical and social settings in which it occurs (Miethe and Meier, 1994). Many forms of crime are intricately linked to the routine activities in which both victims and offenders engage as well as to the places in which these activities occur (Sherman, Gartin, and Buerger, 1989). More generally, criminal events involve the members of the public whose response to perceived increases in crime levels results in pressure on police to pursue more aggressively some categories of offenders. On an even broader scale, crimes involve the actions of lawmakers and the social groups to whom they are responsive. The concept of the criminal event encourages us to conceptualize crime in terms that encompass but also extend beyond the study of offenders. In other words, rather than being *individual* events, crimes are *social* events (Gould, 1989).

CRIMES AS SOCIAL EVENTS

BOX 2.1 THE DIVERSE CHARACTER OF CRIMINAL EVENTS

Case One

I'm on the seventh floor of a seven-story building, and there are steps to go to the roof, and there's nothing on the roof except tarpaper. For some obscure reason, people manage to get into the building. There's no intercom system, and there's just a buzzer. One night, the door buzzed, and we buzzed back because we had expected company. We go to the door and look through the peephole. We see this body come up steps, come off the elevator, and start looking around. So Rob [Karen's husband] stuck his head out of the door and said, "Get the hell out of here!" And the guy said, "If you come after me, I'm gonna knife you to death!" Rob quickly beat a fast retreat and shut the door. So we went and called the cops. In the meantime, the guy comes up the steps to the roof, and we hear shuffling around on the roof [group laughter]. So we go to the door again, and we're looking around the door— shuffle— [laughter]—and the guy comes down again to the seventh floor, and a light goes on when you push the elevator button. He pushed the button at the *exact* second that the cops hit the button. So you couldn't tell if someone downstairs was coming up. But you never saw anybody get such a *surprise in their entire life* when he's standing there to open the elevator door and there's these cops: *"All right, get outta here!"* [group laughter] (cited in Wachs, 1988: 9–10).

Case Two

Buried in secret files of the Ford Motor Company lies evidence that big auto makers have put profits ahead of lives. Their lack of concern has caused thousands of people to die or be horribly disfigured in fiery car crashes. Undisclosed Ford tests have demonstrated that the big auto makers could have made safer automobiles by spending a few dollars more on each car (Anderson and Whitten, 1976: B7).

Case Three

One example of an independent auditor's complicity in the fraudulent schemes of its clients involved the now-defunct National Student Marketing Corporation. NSMC was launched with the aim of providing the burgeoning "youth market" with a network of campus representatives who would market products among students. The company was an immediate hit in the bull market of the times. Its stock originally went on sale at $6 a share, then soared to $80 a share in only six months, and peaked at $140 a share. NSMC quickly began acquiring other companies, including the cash-rich Interstate National Corporation. But it turned out that NSMC's success story was built upon fraud, misrepresentation, and deception. It was actually losing money when its financial reports claimed big profits. A partner and a former employee from Peat, Marwick, and Mitchell, one of the prestigious "big eight" accounting firms, were subsequently convicted of knowingly filing fraudulent statements with the Securities and Exchange Commission. Among other things, they filed reports showing profits for periods in which NSMC had none, and padded its accounts receivable and sales figures. One accountant was fined $10,000 and given sixty days in jail, and the other was fined $2,500 and given ten days in jail—the first time any employees of one of the big eight firms were ever sent to jail for professional misconduct (Coleman, 1989: 116).

Case Four

I remember one particularly violent time. When we were first married. He was out drinking and he came home stinking drunk. I suppose I must have said something. Well, he took a fit. He started putting his fist through the walls. Finally, he just picked up the Christmas tree and threw it at me (Gelles and Straus, 1988: 95).

Case Five

The accused had been attending a party on a cold winter night. During the evening he started the car to warm the engine so the car would start when he was ready to go home. He did not intend to drive home, however, and had arranged for someone else to drive since he knew he was impaired. The police found him behind the wheel with the motor running. The Supreme Court affirmed the decision of the Court of Appeal which held the intent to drive the vehicle is not necessary for the offense. The court stated: "Care or control may be exercised where the accused performs some acts or series of acts involving the use of the car, its fittings or equipment . . . whereby the car may be unintentionally set in motion creating the danger that the section is designed to prevent." (Barnhorst, Barnhorst, and Clarke, 1992: 236).

For Discussion

What is meant by a conceptualization of crimes as social events? How do the case studies represent crimes as social events?

To characterize crimes as "events" is to recognize them as incidents that occur at particular times and in particular places. Like any other type of social event—a dinner party, a corporate board meeting, or a car accident—criminal events are more likely to happen under specific circumstances and to involve specific types of people. This conceptualization of crime runs counter to our tendency to think about criminal events as merely the by-product of chance. We speak of the crime victim as having been "unlucky." We maintain that crimes occur because some people are "in the wrong place at the wrong time." If such events are accidents, however, they are *systematic* accidents (Felson, 1987). Like many other surprises in life, criminal events are made more or less likely by the choices people make about how and where they spend their time, energy, and money.

The term *event* also conveys an *episodic* quality. Criminal events, like all forms of social events, have a beginning and an end. This is not to deny that the participants in the event may have had a prior association or, in the case of a homicide, for instance, that some form of conflict may have predated the event (Luckenbill, 1977). It is to suggest, however, that the criminal event has its own dimensions, which are both related to and distinct from what went on before it. In a similar way, we can speak of the aftermath of criminal events, in which other social processes are set in motion. Much of the daily business of the criminal justice system is relevant in this respect. Offenders are accused and tried, court dispositions are carried out, and victims must learn to cope with the pains of victimization (Lurigio and Resick, 1990). In addition, members of the public who learn about criminal events through mass media reports or conversations with neighbors may become more concerned about their personal safety or about the crime problem and its effect on society.

The *social* character of criminal events derives from the fact that they involve interactions between people. If the event has several offenders, these offenders interact with one another as well as with victims or bystanders. The police interact with these and other event participants. Even an act of vandalism involving a lone youthful offender and an unoccupied school building has social dimensions. A sticker on the door advising that the property is patrolled by security guards may encourage the offender to weigh the risks associated with the offense. Conversely, a run-down building with broken windows may be read by the offender as announcing that no one cares about the appearance of the property (Wilson and Kelling, 1983). In either case, the offender reads and (using past experience as a guide) interprets the signs and then acts accordingly. The vandalism itself may be intended as a message to other youths or to unpopular teachers.

BOX 2.2 TWO CASES OF HOMICIDE

Andy and Bob's Story

Wrightstown had long been known as a tough blue-collar suburb. Residents rarely ventured downtown, with its open-air drug markets and drive-by shootings. Still, men were men—and their reputations depended on toughness, sexual and beer-drinking prowess, and family honor. Big Sunday afternoon beer-drinking parties were a local ritual, and everyone knew that some of the biggest and wildest happened at Andy's house.

In a tough town, Andy's friend Bob was one of the toughest. Like his father before him, Bob had begun drinking heavily as a teenager and had accumulated records of school fights and simple assaults. He nearly always won the fights, but had recently lost his job for missing work—he had been in jail after a bar brawl that got out of hand.

Late one Sunday afternoon, on a run to replenish the beer supply, Andy ran into his out-of-luck friend and invited him back to join the party. Once there, Bob quickly drank up a six-pack and began making passes at Andy's sister Charlene. Charlene had never liked Bob. The more she resisted his advances, the more aggressive he became, until she slapped him hard across the mouth. Bob stepped back and tripped over a coffee table. As he picked himself up, half the crowd was laughing at him.

The other half was yelling at Charlene to make it up to him like a good girl, but Andy saw his sister's honor at stake.

Andy came at Bob. The two fought in the living room until Andy's older brother told them to take it outside after they broke the coffee table. As the crowd moved out to the porch to watch and cheer, Bob yanked a tire iron out of his trunk and used it to knock Andy to the ground, unconscious. The crowd fell silent only after Bob jumped into his car, ran over Andy twice, and roared away. After what seemed like forever, an ambulance responded and took Andy to the hospital emergency room, where he died 4 hours later of massive internal injuries.

Jason and His Father's Story

Dave, Evelyn, and their 10-month-old son Jason were struggling. Jason was born just a few weeks after Evelyn's 20th birthday and 4 months before Dave was laid off from his job as a day laborer.

Things had clearly gone wrong since the layoff. Dave had become moody. They argued more frequently, mostly about money. During several of their arguments, Dave had slapped Evelyn, but begged forgiveness each time and promised never to hit her again. Worst of all, Dave seemed to have begun resenting Jason. He had never quite mastered feeding and changing and had stopped trying to learn. He had almost stopped playing with the baby, and what playing he did struck Evelyn as too rough.

Evelyn finally figured out a solution: she'd get back her old job as a waitress. Even though she would miss being away from Jason, they needed the money. Less financial pressure might relieve the psychological pressures that she believed were making Dave more abusive.

Dave didn't fight her idea, but Evelyn had mixed feelings about leaving Jason in his care. He was no model babysitter, but perhaps time alone together would build his bonds with Jason and take his attention off his joblessness. Anyway, there was no choice. She knew none of their neighbors, especially none whom she would trust with Jason, and the local day-care center had a 3-month waiting list.

As Evelyn left for her first day at work, Dave hit bottom. All the humiliations—over the layoff, the rejections, loans from Evelyn's parents, and his new status as a babysitter—descended at once. He heard Jason's bawling as yet another insult, not as a cry for mother. Whatever Jason's problem was, Dave couldn't fix it. The more he tried, the louder the bawling, and the deeper his own despair and frustration.

Dave's self-control finally broke when Jason wet him. He turned on the "hot" tap, filled the bathtub with scalding water, and held Jason in the tub by his arm and leg. Jason's crying eventually stopped, but not until third-degree burns covered 35 percent of his body, according to the medical examiner's report.

For Discussion

What structural, situational, and personality factors, in your view, led to the homicide in each case? What are the important similarities and differences that characterize these cases?

SOURCE: J. A. Roth, *Understanding and Preventing Violence* (Washington, DC: U.S. Department of Justice, 1994), pp. 5–6.

The behavior of any one participant in the criminal event, then, intersects with and influences the behavior of other participants. This interaction plays a key role in shaping the course of the event, determining the stages through which it proceeds and the extent to which it will be judged a serious one. In order to fully appreciate the complexity of criminal events, we must understand their behavioral and situational elements (Birkbeck and LaFree, 1993). A consideration of the principal participants in these events provides a useful starting point.

OFFENDERS

OFFENDER CHARACTERISTICS

The accumulated body of criminological research indicates that particular social characteristics are associated with a higher likelihood of offender involvement in criminal events. For most categories of offenses, offenders tend to be young, disadvantaged males. The relationship between age and offender status has been well documented through the use of a variety of data sources (Gottfredson and Hirschi, 1990; U.S. Dept. of Justice, 1988). Involvement in offending is highest among those in late adolescence and early adulthood. Property crime offending peaks at a somewhat earlier age than does violent offending (Flowers, 1989). Property crime arrests peak at age 16 and drop by one-half by age 20, while violent offending reaches a peak at age 18 (U.S. Dept. of Justice, 1988). Crimes such as embezzlement, fraud, and gambling do not conform to this general trend in that they are characterized by higher levels of involvement somewhat later in the life cycle (Steffensmeier and Allen, 1991).

Offender status is also strongly related to gender (Campbell, 1990). In 1993, 80.5 percent of all offenders who were arrested were males, while almost 90 percent of those arrested for an index violent offense (homicide, rape, robbery, or aggravated assault) were men. Table 2.1 shows that while the rate at which women are arrested has increased somewhat over the past thirty years, the offending rates of males continue to be higher than those for females in virtually every category of crime. Also noteworthy is the fact that most of the increase in women's offenses during this period came in the category of property crime—the violent crime offense rates for females has remained fairly steady. Although recent evidence indicates that the gender gap in offending has been closing, much of the rhetoric about the "new female criminal" has overstated the case. The narrowing of the gender gap has occurred primarily with respect to nonviolent property crime, for which the gender differential has always been less extreme than for violent crime (Flowers, 1989; Hartnagel, 1992). For most types of criminal events, offending is still very much a male activity.

For many so-called common varieties of crime, such as assault, burglary, robbery, and homicide, offending is associated with various measures of social and economic disadvantage (Silverman and Nielsen, 1992). These differences emerge most clearly when the most serious forms of crime are examined

Table 2.1

Females Arrested as a Percentage of Total Arrests for All Serious Crimes and for All Violent and Property Crimes, 1963–1987

Year	Crime Type			Year	Crime Type		
	Serious	*Violent*	*Property*		*Serious*	*Violent*	*Property*
1963	11.7%	10.3%	12.0%	1976	19.8%	10.5%	22.1%
1964	12.6	10.4	13.0	1977	20.1	10.4	22.4
1965	13.4	10.2	14.1	1978	19.9	10.2	22.4
1966	13.9	10.1	14.8	1979	19.5	10.2	21.8
1967	14.1	9.8	15.1	1980	18.8	10.0	21.0
1968	14.2	9.5	15.4	1981	19.1	10.1	21.4
1969	15.7	9.6	17.1	1982	19.7	10.4	22.1
1970	16.9	9.6	18.1	1983	20.1	10.8	22.5
1971	17.2	10.0	19.0	1984	20.8	10.7	23.4
1972	18.0	10.0	20.2	1985	21.4	10.9	24.0
1973	18.7	10.2	21.1	1986	21.1	10.9	23.9
1974	19.0	10.2	21.2	1987	21.6	11.1	24.4
1975	19.5	10.3	21.7				

NOTE: Violent crimes include criminal homicide, forcible rape, robbery, and aggravated assault. Property crimes include burglary, larceny-theft, and auto theft; as of 1977, arson is also included. Serious crimes include both violent and property crimes.

SOURCE: Caroline Harlow, *Comparing Federal and State Prison Inmates, 1991*, NCJ-145864 (Washington, DC: Bureau of Justice Statistics, 1994), p. 119.

(Harris, 1991). Arrest data reveal that offenders tend to be unemployed, temporarily employed, or employed in part-time, unskilled, or semiskilled jobs (Flowers, 1989). Offending is also associated with minority group membership. Such an association has been extensively documented with respect to African-Americans (Sampson, 1985). Corporate crimes suggest a departure from this pattern in that offenders involved in such crimes tend to be "predominantly well-educated people with good jobs" (Snider, 1992: 320). Table 2.2 shows data on a variety of convicted offender characteristics; Table 2.3 focuses on employment and income.

An emphasis on the social and demographic characteristics of individual offenders should not detract attention from the fact that, in the context of many criminal events, offending has collective dimensions. Most delinquent acts, for instance, are committed in groups rather than by individuals (Giordano, Cerakovich, and Pugh, 1986; Sampson and Lauritsen, 1990). Criminal events involving corporate offending or organized crime may involve several complex levels of organization (Snider, 1992). These differing levels of offender organization strongly affect the course of criminal events.

OFFENDER PERCEPTIONS

Those who are defined by others as offenders may not share this view of who they are or what their actions mean. Black (1983) argues that much of what is regarded as crime by the criminal justice system is seen as something quite the

Table 2.2
Characteristics of Sentenced Federal and State Prison
Inmates, 1991

Characteristics	Federal	State
Sex		
Male	92.2%	94.6%
Female	7.8	5.4
Race/Hispanic origin		
White non-Hispanic	38.4%	35.4%
Black non-Hispanic	29.9	45.6
Other*	3.8	2.4
Hispanic	28.0	16.6
Age		
17 or younger	0.0%	0.6%
18–24	9.3	21.3
25–34	36.0	45.7
35–44	32.9	22.7
45–54	15.0	6.5
55–64	5.7	2.4
65 or older	1.1	0.7
Median Age	36 yr	30 yr
Marital Status		
Married	37.9%	18.2%
Widowed	1.8	1.9
Separated	6.7	6.2
Divorced	21.0	18.5
Never married	32.6	55.3
Education		
8th grade or less	11.0%	14.2%
Some high school	12.3	26.9
High school graduate	48.5	46.5
Some college	18.8	10.0
College graduate or more	9.3	2.3
Median Education	12 yr	12 yr
Military Service		
Veteran	19.9%	16.3%
Vietnam era	4.2	2.7
Other	15.7	13.6
Nonveteran	80.1	83.7
Citizenship		
United States	81.6%	95.6%
Other countries	18.4	4.4
Mexico	4.1	2.1
Central/South America	6.3	0.6
Other	8.0	1.7
Number of Inmates	54,006	704,203

NOTE: Data were missing for marital status on 1.3% of cases, for education on 0.6%, and for military service on 0.3% for federal prison inmates. Data were missing for marital status on 1.1% of cases, for education on 0.7%, and for military service on 0.2% for state prison inmates.

*Includes Asians, Pacific Islanders, and Native Americans.

SOURCE: Rita Simon, *Women and Crime Revisited* (Washington, DC: Bureau of Justice Statistics, 1990).

Table 2.3
Pre-arrest Employment and Income for Sentenced Federal
and State Prison Inmates, 1991

	Federal	State
Pre-arrest Employment		
Employed	74.4%	67.4%
Full-time	65.4	55.5
Part-time	9.0	11.9
Not employed	25.6	32.6
Looking for work	10.0	16.3
Not looking	15.6	16.3
Pre-arrest Annual Income (Free at Least 1 Year)*		
No income	3.1%	2.9%
Less than $3,000	1.8	19.0
$3,000–$4,999	6.6	9.8
$5,000–$9,999	16.2	20.7
$10,000–$14,999	16.1	17.1
$15,000–$24,999	18.9	15.8
$25,000 or more	27.3	14.7
Number of Inmates	44,436	517,232
Pre-arrest Monthly Income (Free Less Than 1 Year)*		
No income	8.9%	6.7%
Less than $300	10.9	15.4
$300–$499	7.6	12.9
$500–$999	18.9	22.7
$1,000–$1,499	17.0	16.1
$1,500–$2,499	14.2	9.7
$2,500 or more	22.6	16.4
Number of Inmates	4,030	130,725

NOTE: Pre-arrest employment data were missing for 0.8% of federal inmates and 0.6% of state inmates. Income data were missing for 10.3% of federal inmates and for 8% of state inmates.

*Annual income figures based on inmates who reported being free at least one year prior to the offense for which they were sent to prison.

*Monthly income figures for inmates who were free less than one year prior to the offense for which they were sent to prison.

SOURCE: U.S. Department of Justice, *Violence Against Women* (Washington, DC: Bureau of Justice Statistics, 1990).

opposite by those whom the criminal justice system labels as offenders. From the offender's viewpoint, crimes frequently have a moralistic basis. According to Black, offending actually can serve as a form of social control when people use it to define and respond to behavior they regard as having violated expectations of appropriate conduct.

Seen in this way, those who commit assaults, acts of vandalism, or even murder may be understood as individuals engaged in a quest for justice (Agnew, 1990; Katz, 1988). This position recognizes that those who are judged to be offenders frequently feel victimized by those against whom they offend. Studies of homicide have shown that the eventual victim is often the first event participant to brandish a weapon or to threaten deadly force (Luckenbill, 1977; Wolfgang, 1958). Similarly, in many cases of assault, offenders may feel that they are merely responding to verbal or physical transgressions on the part of others (Felson, Baccaglini, and Ribner, 1985; Luckenbill, 1984). The wife who shoots her husband after years or decades of abuse may question a justice system that categorizes her as the offender and her husband as the victim.

If asked to explain their actions, offenders typically offer two types of accounts: excuses and justifications (Scott and Lyman, 1968). With an **excuse**, an individual admits that a given act is wrong but denies responsibility for the act. With a **justification**, on the other hand, an individual accepts responsibility for the act but denies the immorality of the act. Such accounts provide distinct interpretations of offenders, their victims, and their offenses.

A study of convicted rapists found that, while offenders admitted their offenses, they denied that they were to blame for what had happened (Scully and Marolla, 1984). By offering excuses relating to the use of drugs, alcohol, or the persistence of "emotional problems," they attempted to disown their blameworthiness. In a similar way, police use of force against suspects may be excused by defining it as a natural outcome of the strong emotions that arise in the course of police work (Hunt, 1985). White-collar offenders might argue that their crimes are committed out of ignorance or an inattention to detail and, further, that they must be considered in the context of an otherwise law-abiding life. Even contract killers may offer rationalizations that mitigate personal blame. Levi (1981) maintains that organized-crime hit men deny responsibility by emphasizing the need to avoid the potentially fatal penalties that could result from their failure to fulfil a contract.

> ## HOW DO THEY DIFFER?
>
> ### *Excuses vs. Justifications*
>
> Someone who offers an excuse admits that a given act is wrong but denies responsibility for the act. Someone who offers a justification accepts responsibility for but denies the immorality of the act.

Offenders may even claim that their crime has had positive effects. White-collar criminals, for example, might argue that their actions saved a failing business and thereby preserved much-needed jobs. They may also favorably compare their offenses with those of "real" criminals like robbers or rapists (Benson, 1985). People who are guilty of workplace theft or income tax evasion might defend their actions by arguing that "everyone does it" and "the only real crime is getting caught."

Offender accounts may also make reference to the culpability of victims. The rapist may contend that the victim seduced him or that she said no but really meant yes (Scully and Marolla, 1984). While these justifications do not deny the accusation, they do deny the moral and legal interpretations that others attach to the behavior. In the case of police violence, some types of people are defined by the police as legitimate targets of physical force because they are known "cop haters" or troublemakers (Hunt, 1985).

However, offender accounts may be driven by more than personal motivations. Frequently, they reflect pervasive cultural beliefs. The excuses and justifications articulated by the rapist, for instance, borrow from more general sexist beliefs in the blameworthiness of sexual assault victims. In addition, the cultural environment and the historical period partly determine the degree to which an offender account is viewed as plausible. In the late twentieth century, people tend to dismiss accounts that propose demonic possession as an excuse for crime, although such accounts would have been accepted in an earlier period. By contrast, the "culture" of large bureaucracies currently allows white-collar offenders to deny personal responsibility for their actions (Benson, 1984), but does so in a period in which public sentiment increasingly is that these individuals need to be held accountable for their actions (Snider, 1992).

Offender accounts also alert us to the fact that we apply the label of offender only with relative certainty. Most of us are unequivocal in our judgment of the man who hides in the bushes and sexually assaults a woman who happens by. Until recently, however, our feelings about labeling as rapists offenders who were intimately involved with their victims have been more ambivalent. Many people might argue that a husband who assaults a wife has somehow committed a less serious act than has a stranger who assaults another stranger (Bograd, 1988).

Our judgments about the suitability of an offender label may be further complicated by the social context in which the offending occurs. A homicide that results from a heated argument between drunken patrons of a bar may not seem as clear-cut as one that occurs in a more sedate environment. When we draw attention to the relationship between offender labels and offender characteristics, to the victim–offender relationship, or to the social setting, we are suggesting that the study of the offender is inseparable from the study of other dimensions of the criminal event.

When considering the offender, we must also take into account those factors that will restrict or curtail criminal behavior. The contemporary debate over deterrence strategies revolves around differing views about the effects of punishment. According to Williams and Hawkins (1986), individuals are less afraid of punishment per se than of being judged harshly by others for having received it. In contrast, Wilson and Herrnstein (1985), among others, argue that individuals are deterred only through a punishment scheme that takes into account their innate propensity to offend. This perspective focuses on specific efforts to incarcerate and immobilize, rather than on social stigma and the role of community forces, in reducing criminality.

VICTIMS

"VICTIMLESS" CRIMES

For many types of criminal events, it is useful to recognize a **victim** role. Victims include people whose purses are stolen and whose homes are broken into and who are murdered in the course of the event. For other event categories, such as drug use or gambling offenses, victims cannot be said to exist in any direct and immediate way, although many would argue that it is incorrect to consider such offenses **victimless crimes** (Schur, 1965).

The degree to which the law should be applied to victimless crimes revolves around the issue of harm. While there is widespread support for legalizing various forms of vice, great concern persists as to the potential negative effects of doing so. The prevailing view is that victimless crimes are not victimless and need to be regulated through criminal law.

Proponents for removing the legal sanctions associated with victimless crimes argue that policing these acts represents an overreach of the law and that consenting adults should have the freedom to partake in certain activities. Further, criminalization tends to affect only the disadvantaged and others who cannot pursue these activities in private. Advocates of legalization argue as well that many of the problems associated with victimless crimes would be eliminated were these behaviors permitted in regulated (but legal) environments. From their perspective, it is not the behavior itself but rather the fact that it has been driven underground that gives rise to the surrounding criminal subcultures.

VICTIM CHARACTERISTICS

Surveys of direct victims of crime demonstrate that involvement in criminal events as a victim, like involvement as an offender, is not a random matter. In fact, many of the social characteristics associated with offending are also associated with victimization. For one thing, like offenders, the victims of crime tend to be young. According to the National Crime Victimization Survey (NCVS), the highest rates of both violent and property (theft) crimes were experienced by people between the ages of 12 and 24. The violent crime victimization rates for young people, for example, was more than seven times greater than the rates of violent victimization reported by people in their fifties or sixties (U.S. Dept. of Justice, 1994a). This finding is consistent with that of similar surveys done in Canada and elsewhere (Fattah, 1991). Despite much talk about a crime wave against the elderly, people over the age of 65 are least likely to be victims of crime (Bachman, 1992).

Surveys of crime victims also indicate that, for most types of crime, males have higher rates of victimization than females (Smith, 1987). For example, the NCVS found that the male rate of violent victimization in 1992 was 39 per 1,000 while the rate for females was 26 per 1,000 (U.S. Dept. of Justice, 1994a). A notable exception to this pattern is found with rape, a crime in which the vast majority of victims are women. Note, too, that several researchers question the extent to which surveys like the NCVS accurately portray the levels of women's victimization, an issue we will return to in Chapter 7.

The link between social disadvantage and victimization is less clear-cut than in the case of offending (Cohen, Kluegel, and Land, 1981; Fattah, 1991). To some extent, the nature of the relationship depends on the type of event. For violent crimes, data from the NCVS suggest a steady decrease in the rate of victimization as income rises, although the relationship is less apparent for property crimes.

Finally, race and/or ethnicity also seem to be identifiable risk factors for victimization, especially for violent crime. For example, rates of homicide victimization for African-Americans are markedly higher than for white/European Americans. In 1992, the homicide victimization rate for whites was 5.0 per 100,000; for African-Americans, it was 35.4 per 100,000 (U.S. Dept. of Justice, 1994b). Table 2.4 presents data on victimization rates according to a variety of demographic characteristics.

VICTIM PERCEPTIONS

Like offenders, victims may be reluctant to define events in which they are involved as crimes. In some cases, even while the event is underway, it may feature ambiguous or unfamiliar elements that are not readily understood as criminal victimization. A study of mugging victims reported that many of those victimized did not immediately define the event as a predatory crime; some even thought the mugger was a neighbor in search of assistance or someone playing a joke (Lejeune and Alex, 1973).

Willingness to label an event a crime generally depends on the degree of coherence between the victim's definition of a "typical crime" and the characteristics of the event in question (Ruback, Greenberg, and Wescott, 1984). However, some types of crimes are inherently more ambiguous than others. The meaning of many forms of sexual victimization may be highly problematic with respect to the labels that victims assign to them. For instance, a study of ninety-four women who were sexually assaulted in a number of ways did not define the act as rape unless sexual intercourse was involved (Scheppele and Bart, 1983). Crime definitions are generally less ambiguous when the events contain elements that imply a high degree of legal seriousness (Agnew, 1985a).

The issue of family violence provides a particularly vivid illustration of the importance of victim definition processes. The reluctance of women to label as criminal or abusive violence occurring in the context of intimate relationships has been well documented (Ferraro and Johnson, 1983; Sedlak, 1988). As in the case of sexual assault, there has been (until recently) a firmly entrenched cultural tendency to blame women for their victimization in domestic relationships. If women remain in abusive relationships, they may be labeled "sick" or "masochistic" or they may be accused of "bringing it on themselves." If they attempt to flee the abuse or confront the abuser, they may find relatively few supports available. Moreover, such actions may increase rather than decrease the risk of future victimization. As parents, in-laws, and neighbors choose sides, many may blame the victim for breaking up the family and suggest that if she really loved her children she would have "made the best of it." These factors may discourage a woman from viewing herself as a victim, since acknowledging that one's mate is an abuser is the first—and hardest— step in re-evaluating and changing one's life circumstances, a process that might entail violent retaliation by the abusive partner. A denial of the violent character of the victimization and the victimizer may allow the abused partner to tolerate conditions an outsider would think intolerable (Ferraro and Johnson, 1983).

Table 2.4
Average Annual Rate (per 1,000 Persons) of Personal Victimization for Males and
Females, by Demographic Characteristics, 1987–1991

	Rate			
	Male		**Female**	
Characteristics	*Crimes of Violence*	*Crimes of Theft*	*Crimes of Violence*	*Crimes of Theft*
Race				
White	38.6	71.0	23.8	65.2
African-American	55.9	76.7	32.3	58.8
Other*	38.7	71.8	23.2	57.8
Ethnicity				
Hispanic	49.5	67.8	29.3	60.3
Non-Hispanic	39.7	71.9	24.4	64.4
Age				
12–19	97.1	114.0	31.1	64.1
20–24	87.3	126.2	52.1	108.6
25–34	43.8	85.8	28.5	63.9
35–49	24.9	61.2	18.5	63.1
50–64	10.8	40.1	7.8	37.0
65 or older	5.0	20.1	3.5	19.5
Education				
Some high school or less	54.2	66.2	31.8	58.8
High school graduate	33.4	58.7	20.0	47.9
Some college	48.5	92.7	28.1	82.9
College graduate or more	22.9	78.4	18.2	86.8
Family Income				
Less than $9,999	69.0	79.5	42.9	59.5
$10,000–$19,999	45.3	65.2	27.3	59.5
$20,000–$29,999	37.9	69.3	23.6	63.8
$30,000–$49,999	32.5	70.5	17.3	65.2
$50,000 or more	28.8	76.6	15.1	77.7
Marital Status				
Never married	78.8	110.6	46.6	101.1
Married	18.5	47.9	11.1	49.4
Widowed	12.7	33.5	6.8	24.8
Divorced/separated	51.1	95.3	55.2	62.1
Location of Residence				
Central city	55.9	90.2	34.4	79.1
Suburban	36.1	71.1	20.6	65.1
Rural	29.1	47.9	20.1	41.1
Total Personal Victimizations	40.5	71.6	24.8	64.2

NOTE: These data based on victimizations reported to the National Crime Victimization Survey (NCVS) from 1987–91. The NCVS is conducted by the U.S. Bureau of the Census for the U.S. Department of Justice, Bureau of Justice Statistics. Data for the NCVS are drawn from a continuous, nationally representative sample of households in the United States. Household members age 12 and older are interviewed. The victimization rates reported are average annual rates for 1987–91. The numerator of a given rate is the sum of the crimes that occurred each year from 1987 through 1991 for each demographic group. The denominator is the sum of the annual population totals for these same years and demographic groups.

*Includes groups such as Asians and Native Americans.

SOURCE: U.S. Department of Justice, Bureau of Justice Statistics, *Violence Against Women*, NCJ-145325 (Washington, DC: U.S. Department of Justice, 1994), p. 2.

In many cases, criminal events involve individuals other than those who can be described as offenders or victims. **Bystanders** in many events are more than passive spectators. They may by their very presence deter an offender from committing a crime or they may prevent an event from escalating. Conversely, they may facilitate the offender's actions. For example, a young male who is insulted by someone in the presence of his peers may be naturally inclined to respond in an aggressive fashion or else be encouraged to do so by his peers.

Bystanders may also call the police or offer to act as witnesses (Shotland and Goodstein, 1984). What bystanders do, if anything, depends on several factors. Their actions may be influenced, for example, by their view of or relationship to the victim and/or offender (Steffensmeier and Steffensmeier, 1977), by their assessment of the personal costs associated with intervention, and by their confidence in their ability to intervene (Shotland and Goodstein, 1984).

Bystanders are also affected by what they perceive to be transpiring between victim and offender. According to Shotland and Straw (1976), bystanders are less likely to intervene in a violent assault perpetrated by a man against a woman if they perceive them to be married rather than strangers (Shotland and Straw, 1976). In a highly publicized case that took place in New York City a number of years ago, a woman named Kitty Genovese was attacked by a man in the courtyard of a large apartment complex (Conklin, 1975). The attack continued for a long period of time, during which Genovese's screams for help went unanswered. She finally succumbed to the attack and died on the street. Although many people in the apartment block witnessed the attack, no one called the police, much less intervened. According to those who researched the event, the apartment dwellers had interpreted the attack as a quarrel between a married couple and, therefore, as a private affair. Similarly, Davis (1991) suggests that when people witness adults physically abusing children in public, their reluctance to intervene in a "private matter" outweighs their concern for the child's welfare.

Criminal events are frequently ambiguous from the standpoint of bystanders. We do not expect to witness a crime and may be so engrossed in our own activities that an event may be well underway before it comes to our attention (Hartman et al., 1972). By the time we make sense of the event and think of a response, it may be too late. The presence of several bystanders tends to reduce the likelihood that any one bystander will assist a victim, particularly if the bystanders are strangers to one another and do not share a common cultural frame of reference (Shotland, 1976). One bystander among many is required to accept only part of the responsibility for not acting; he or she may rationalize that somebody else would take action were something seriously wrong.

Bystanders may be asked to perform as witnesses. How valuable are eyewitness accounts in providing accurate depictions of the activities in a criminal event? The research suggests that these eyewitness accounts are quite inaccurate, with bystanders failing to remember even key characteristics of the offender or the event (Loftus, 1979).

POLICE

POLICE PRACTICE

Police involvement in criminal events may result from either proactive or reactive mobilization. As the police engage in routine patrol work, they may encounter individuals or situations they define as criminal. Proactive policing is not in any sense a random or arbitrary process. Rather, it is heavily influenced by police priorities, prevailing community concerns, available police resources, and the styles and traditions that characterize police work in given areas (Desroches, 1991). Ericson (1982) reports that police officers who are engaged in patrol activities use cues that structure their proactive work. For example, their attention may be attracted by individuals who appear in particular places at particular times of the day. Conversely, events that could be defined as

A wide variety of factors affect the circumstances that bring police and citizens together.

crimes are not labeled as such because the police choose not to stop and question a suspect.

In his study of the policing of a heroin-using community, Stoddart (1991) reports that heroin users who act as police informants are less likely to be pursued by the police than are heroin users who are perceived as interfering with police work. This finding suggests that proactive police activity is influenced not only by what the police do but also by the visibility of the offender's behavior. Stoddart argues that changes in the nature of the heroin-using community over time have increased the probability of arrest. Members of this community today are more apathetic than their predecessors about the fate of their colleagues and less attentive to the risks associated with illegal drug use. Such factors increase the visibility of the behavior, thereby facilitating police intervention.

It is worth noting that the line between reactive and proactive police mobilization is frequently unclear (Ericson, 1982). Citizens may decide to mobilize the police reactively as a result of police-sponsored crime prevention campaigns that encourage them to do so. Conversely, widespread public concern about specific crime problems may influence police to adopt a proactive mobilization strategy. Desroches (1991) reports on a police investigation of impersonal homosexual behavior in public washrooms, known as "tearooms." While the fact that evidence was gathered through police surveillance techniques would appear to suggest a proactive police stance on the problem, Desroches indicates this police involvement was largely a response to requests from citizens or businesses for more aggressive enforcement.

POLICE INVOLVEMENT IN DEFINING CRIMINAL EVENTS

The type of mobilization, whether proactive or reactive, does not indicate how the police will intervene in a particular event. The actions taken by officers may depend on a variety of contingencies, including the characteristics of the incident, the behavior of the participants, and the nature of the requests being made of the police (Bayley, 1986; Gottfredson and Gottfredson, 1988; Smith, 1987).

Police tend to respond most emphatically to (that is, treat officially) events that they perceive as conforming to legal definitions of serious crimes (Black, 1970; Gottfredson and Gottfredson, 1988; Gove, Hughes, and Geerkin, 1985). Also of importance in determining police response is the relationship between the victim and the offender. According to Black (1970), the more distant the relationship between victim and offender, the more likely the police are to regard the incident as criminal. This observation is consistent with the frequently cited tendency of police officers to process crimes "unofficially" when the disputants are family members (Bell, 1987).

The characteristics of victims and offenders have been shown to influence police decisions. In a study of police responses to interpersonal violence, Smith (1987) found that police officers are less likely to employ legal solutions in situations that involve African-American or female victims. In contrast, Boritch

(1992) reports that the criminal justice system deals more harshly with female offenders than male offenders, particularly those who deviate from accepted standards of feminine behavior. Violence between males is more likely to result in arrest than is violence between a male and a female, which tends to be resolved through less formal means, such as the physical separation of the disputants. Police decision making may also be influenced by the demeanor and preferences of the event participants (Smith, 1987). Thus, the police are more likely to label an event as a crime when the complainant is deferential to them or requests that they take official action (Black, 1970; Gove, Hughes, and Geerkin, 1985).

Increasingly, however, police discretion in particularly sensitive areas, such as family violence, is being removed. In most jurisdictions, police officers are now required to make an arrest when they have physical evidence that an assault has taken place, even if the victim is reluctant for them to do so. This practice was established, in part, in response to Sherman and Berk's (1984) findings that arrest is the most effective way of deterring violence among intimates and that mediative techniques do not curtail repeat offenses. Sherman reports that, in the late 1980s, more than half of the police forces across North America had in place a **mandatory charge rule** for the handling of domestic assault cases.

For some observers, removing police discretion means reducing the chances that police bias will influence decisions about the seriousness of certain violent acts. For others, it means depriving police of the opportunity to defuse situations before they become dangerous. Recent research indicates that arrest may actually heighten rather than lower the chance of violence in domestic situations (Sherman, 1992). It has also been argued that bringing individuals into an overburdened court system ill-equipped to handle their problems merely creates new problems.

THE SETTING OF CRIMINAL EVENTS

THE SOCIAL SETTING

Modernization of our society over the last century has shaped the nature of social disorder and crime in contemporary cities. Gurr (1980) has extensively studied the ways in which crime in Western societies has been shaped by four aspects of **modernization:** (1) industrialization, (2) urbanization, (3) the expression of the state's powers and resources, and (4) the humanization of interpersonal relations. Collectively, these factors have created the pressures in modern society that have led to an unprecedented rise in crime. Further, because many of these factors are difficult to change, the range of options in dealing with the growth of crime has been reduced.

Accompanying the increase in personal wealth in the late nineteenth and early twentieth centuries was a demand for the protection of private property. Moral crusades led to calls for the constraint of undesirable practices such as gambling and vagrancy. The response to demands for more social

order included devising techniques of legal criminalization, uniformed policing, and incarceration (Gurr, 1980: 36). The development of formal structures led to a transformation from the use of local action in controlling deviant
behavior to the formalization of response through legal codes and uniform
policing.

Gurr suggests that this formalization was accompanied by an increase in
humanitarianism, in which emphasis was shifted from punishment to rehabilitation. In recent years, victims rather than offenders have increasingly become
the focus of this humanitarianism, a situation that, paradoxically, has resulted
in an increased demand for harsher penalties for actions (including family violence) that previously were not included in criminal categories.

According to Gurr, the fear of crime that stems from the disorder of fast-
growing cities has resulted in increased calls for more police and for more
efficient and effective courts. The view that we are moving away from the community as the major basis of social control in society is counterbalanced by
evidence that the community still plays a crucial role in both generating and
controlling deviance. On the one hand, then, the community has become less
important as a forum of social control because the state has assumed responsibility for protecting the victim. On the other hand, the diversity of communities makes the imposition of a unitary state power difficult. This is a lesson
that police are learning in their experiments with community policing (see
Chapter 11).

To suggest that a relationship exists between criminal events and the places
in which these events occur is to imply that location involves something more
than just happenstance. In other words, place matters. Something about particular types of locations increases—or decreases—the likelihood that criminal
events will unfold. Any attempt to investigate these issues is plagued by the
fact that particular types of places are intricately linked to particular types of
activities. People who live in the center of a major city may structure their activities differently than those who live on the suburban fringe. Those of us who
do not live in the downtown core may occasionally journey there in search of
"excitement," but for rest and relaxation we head for the countryside. We
shop at malls, drink in taverns, perform occupational tasks at work, and read
or study at the library. We might ask why some of these places host more criminal events than others. Is it because certain types of people tend to be attracted
to these settings? Does the physical character of a place make criminal events
more or less likely? Are the activities associated with a particular setting more
or less likely to lead to criminal events? While these issues are discussed in
greater detail in later chapters, it is useful at this point to review some of the
empirical evidence about the locations of criminal events.

THE COMMUNITY SETTING

According to data collected by police and survey researchers, rates of many
types of crimes tend to be higher in urban centers than in rural areas (Brantingham and Brantingham, 1984; Fischer, 1976). The relationship between

crime and urbanism is generally stronger with respect to property crimes than crimes of violence.

Data from the 1992 National Crime Victimization Survey revealed that there were no significant differences in rates of violent crime victimization for residents of suburban and nonmetropolitan areas (where the rates of victimization were found to be 28 and 25 per 1,000, respectively). Residents of the central city were, however, considerably more likely to experience violent criminal victimizations (43 per 1,000). Rates of property crime were also found to be higher for residents of the central city, with those in rural areas experiencing the lowest rates of this form of victimization (U.S. Dept. of Justice, 1994a).

In urban centers, the rates of crime vary across neighborhoods (Roncek, 1981). While research into the factors that characterize high-crime neighborhoods sometimes produces conflicting evidence (Brantingham and Brantingham, 1984), much of the data indicates that these areas are likely to be poor and densely populated and to have transient populations (Cater and Jones, 1989; Flowers, 1989; Roncek, 1981; Stark, 1987).

Even in cities or neighborhoods characterized by high crime rates, most locations are crime-free. For example, while we may think of subway stations as dangerous places, data collected by Normandeau (1987) in Montreal reveals

In both popular culture and much criminological research crime tends to be regarded as a big city problem.

that most stations have relatively low rates of crime, with only a few accounting for most of the crimes that occur in the subway system. This point is more generally illustrated in Sherman, Gartin, and Buerger's (1989) study of the locations of requests for police assistance in the city of Minneapolis over a one-year period. This study revealed that relatively few "hot spots" accounted for the majority of service calls; specifically, only 3 percent of the locations in the city (addresses or street intersections) accounted for 50 percent of the 323,979 calls. With respect to predatory crimes, robberies occurred at 2.2 percent, rapes at 1.2 percent, and automobile thefts at 2.7 percent of these locations.

THE PHYSICAL SETTING

What are the characteristics of the locations of criminal events? With respect to some types of crimes, part of the answer may be found in the physical design of places or the creation of **defensible space** (Newman, 1972). In the case of a property crime, settings that offer concealment in the form of poor streetlighting, large bushes or shrubs, or hidden alleyways may make a target more attractive to an offender (Shotland and Goodstein, 1984). Similarly, a convenience store located near a vacant field may be more vulnerable to robbery than one that is located on a busy city street (Sherman, Gartin, and Buerger, 1989). Figure 2.1 shows data on the time and location of violent crimes in 1990.

In a somewhat different way, patterns of family violence may be related to some elements of physical design. Violence between husbands and wives typically occurs in private settings. The growth of single-family homes not shared with boarders, lodgers, or servants—coupled with the widespread cultural understanding that the home is a private setting closed to neighbors, friends, or even other family members, except by invitation—helps ensure the concealment of such violence (Gelles and Straus, 1988). Within the home, not all locations are equally risky. According to Gelles and Straus (1988), violence most frequently occurs in the kitchen, followed by the living room and the bedroom (Gelles and Straus, 1988), although the latter place tends to be the setting for the most violent confrontations. "A fight that erupts in the bedroom, in the early morning, constrains both parties. It is too late to stalk out of the home to a bar and too late to run to a friend or a family member. The bed and the bedroom offer no protection and there are precious few places to flee or take cover" (Gelles and Straus, 1988: 94). By contrast, the bathroom is relatively free of spousal violence in part because such rooms are small, have locks, and are understood to be places of individual privacy.

SOCIAL DOMAINS

Social domains may be thought of as major spheres of life, in which we invest most of our time and energy. In Chapters 8, 9, and 10, we focus on the three most important social domains—the family and household, leisure, and work. Each domain is distinguished by a particular location and pattern of activity (Lynch, 1987). People differ with respect to the amount of time that they spend

Figure 2.1
Time and Location of Crimes of Violence, 1990

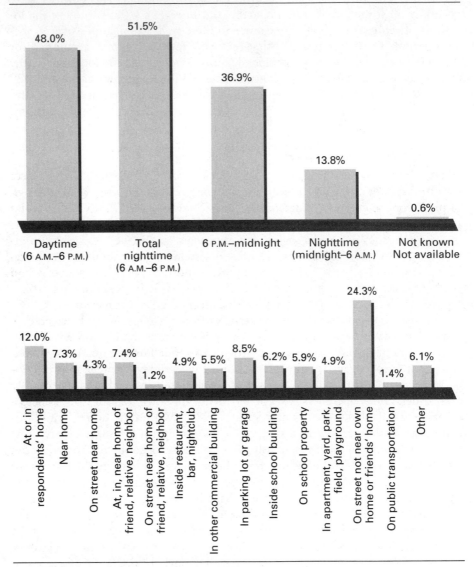

NOTE: Tables reflect rounding error.

SOURCE: U.S. Department of Justice, *Criminal Victimization in the United States, 1992. A National Crime Victimization Survey Report* (Washington, DC: U.S. Government Printing Office, 1994), pp. 73, 75.

in each of these domains. For the elderly retired person, the social domain of the household may be of greatest importance. Children spend much of their time at home, but during the teenage years, involvement in this social domain declines while involvement in the workplace and in leisure activities outside the home increases.

These social domains differ, as well, in terms of their private or public character (Fischer, 1981). The household is the most private of settings, and the people we encounter there are generally better known to us than those we encounter at work or at leisure outside the home. While we tend to think of private domains as safer places than public domains, there is increasing concern about the prevalence of criminal actions that previously were seen as private acts. The definition of privacy is changing, as are the ways in which the law and the police treat privacy. The criminal event that may once have gone undetected or untreated in the "privacy" of the home is now more likely to attract public attention and police action.

The breakdown in the taboos about intervention in private lives reflects an increased concern about the harm done in violent events involving intimates. Private affairs in the business setting are also attracting more attention, and there is an increased awareness of the need to prosecute white-collar criminals whose socioeconomic status once put them beyond the reach of the law. In addition, the private policing of private space has become more commonplace. Although the relationship between private and public policing is still an uneasy one, the surveillance that private police offer is an important component in the deterrence of property offenses and is impacting crime patterns, particularly in urban areas. Private police, however, are not subject to the same legal controls under which public police operate. For example, private security guards may evict individuals from shopping malls without any recourse to due process.

The distinctions we make between social domains may not apply with equal force to all individuals. Some people work out of their homes; others restrict their leisure activities to the household; still others may view the workplace as a leisure setting—a chance to gossip with co-workers. Despite these complications, the identification of distinct social domains helps us to clarify differences in patterns of criminal events.

The people we encounter in these social domains, the relationships we have with them, and the social activities that occur there strongly influence the kinds of criminal events that take place in a given social domain as well as the reactions to them. Victim surveys indicate that people who report that they frequently go out in the evening to bars also report higher rates of victimization (Sacco and Johnson, 1990). Moreover, observations of barroom behavior (Stoddart, 1981) and police data suggest that taverns are the site of a disproportionate amount of crime (Roncek and Pravatiner, 1989).

More generally, many types of criminal events develop in leisure settings. Much juvenile crime (including drug use, vandalism, and fighting) resembles leisure pursuits (Agnew and Peterson, 1989) and is most likely to occur when youths are engaged in unsupervised peer activities such as "hanging out" (Kennedy and Baron, 1993; Riley, 1987). Many forms of sexual assault, especially "date rape," occur in leisure environments rather than in more structured environments (DeKeseredy, 1988; Thompson, 1986). Similarly, homicides are most likely to occur when the participants are engaged in recreational pursuits in informal settings (Luckenbill, 1977).

Other types of criminal events are more closely related to nonleisure activities. For the organized criminal, crime is a form of work. For the white-collar or corporate criminal, the offending behavior may represent little more than a simple extension of his or her legitimate business practices. In other cases, a person's employment may be related to the risk of criminal victimization (Block, Felson, and Block, 1984; Linder and Koehler, 1992). For example, people who handle money, who work in an environment that is open to the general public, or who travel from one work site to another are especially vulnerable to many forms of victimization (Collins, Cox, and Langan, 1987; Mayhew, Elliott, and Dowds, 1989). It is partially because of these factors that taxi drivers, police officers, and nurses experience relatively high rates of violence (Block, Felson, and Block, 1984). In still other cases, an *absence* of activity is related to the occurrence of criminal events. With respect to breaking and entering, for instance, households that are unoccupied for long periods of time are at greater risk of victimization than are households that have higher and more regular occupancy rates (Cohen and Cantor, 1981; Waller and Okihiro, 1978).

STUDYING THE CRIMINAL EVENT

We have argued that, in studying **criminal events,** it is important to develop explanations that move beyond the motivations of offenders or the responses of victims. A more comprehensive view must consider (1) the **precursors** of the event, including the locational and situational factors that bring people together in time and space, (2) the **transactions** that indicate how the interactions among participants define the outcomes of their actions, and (3) the **aftermath** of the event, including the report to the police, their response, the harm done and the redress required, and the long-term consequences of the event in terms of public reactions and the changing of laws. Figure 2.2 shows a model of the criminal event and its key components.

HOW DO WE DEFINE IT?

The Criminal Event

The criminal event involves precursors, including the locational and situational factors that bring people together in time and space; the transaction, which indicates how the interactions among participants define the outcomes of their actions; and the aftermath of the event, including the report to the police, their response, the harm done and redress required, and the long-term consequences of the event in terms of public reactions and the changing of laws.

PRECURSORS

As criminologists, we are interested in more than just the motivation of the offender or the actions of the victims that led up to the criminal act. These elements come together in a transaction that increases the likelihood that crime will take place. Understanding criminal events as deriving from predisposing conditions helps us to separate the social behavior that is criminogenic from that

Figure 2.2
Model of the Criminal Event

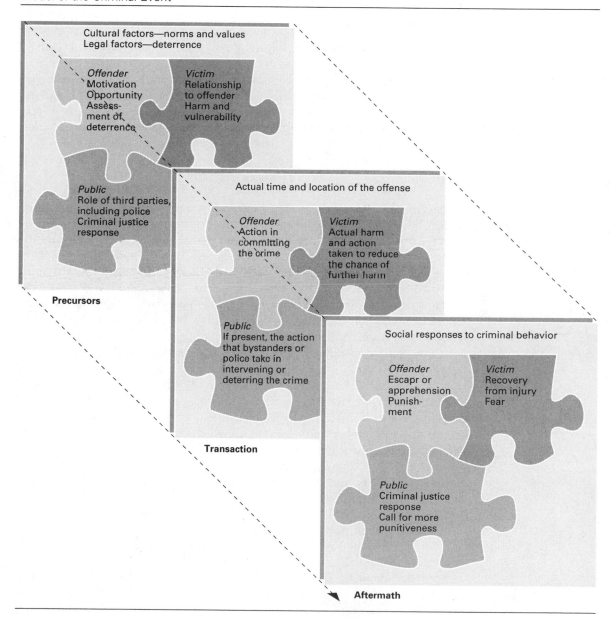

which is not. Studying the precursors of criminal events also allows us to see that, depending on circumstance, behavior that is defined or that evolves into criminality in one situation may not have the same consequences in other situations. The relationship between participants, the interpretation of the harmfulness of the acts, the anticipated responses to certain behavior, the nature of the location—all may or may not combine to create a criminal outcome.

Of course, understanding preconditions will not necessarily allow us to predict criminal outcomes with greater accuracy. The difficulties of prediction are illustrated in the recent debate over the extent to which spousal homicide could have been anticipated on the basis of previous behaviors (Sherman et al., 1991). While the predictive capability of police is low with respect to spousal homicide, it is likely very high with respect to repeat interpersonal violence.

In determining the precursors of crime, we must reconstruct criminal events using information that may be distorted by faulty memories, rationalizations, and so on. But it is exactly this process that the courts use to establish guilt or innocence. In order to reflect legal as well as social reality, criminologists must incorporate a similar process in their approaches to crime.

TRANSACTIONS

When we study the event itself, we move into an assessment of the circumstances, incidence, and frequency of certain types of crimes. As we will see in Chapter 7, different types of data sources (for example, Uniform Crime Reports, victim surveys, self-report studies) tell us about different aspects of the event, or at least provide different perspectives on such events.

We are interested in the particular groups that are affected by different types of crime. It is in this context that we are able to examine the changes in offender behavior and the extent of victimization. We are particularly interested in viewing the criminal event not in isolation but rather as it relates to social events as well as to other criminal events. Discerning trends in these events helps us understand the extent to which we need to respond to them. We also want to understand how trends in crime patterns coincide with shifts in social and economic conditions, resources for policing, and so on. The explanations that these types of analysis provide throw light on the vulnerability of certain groups to social change and the extent to which legal intervention can work to deter or alter criminal behavior.

Previously, we discussed the problems associated with defining (or not defining) certain events as criminal. Victims may not immediately appreciate that they have been subject to a crime, while offenders may rationalize their behavior as something other than criminal. The strict definition of criminality derives from the actions of the police, who certify criminality through the enactment of legal process, either in naming an event as criminal or in arresting an offender.

But what about the events that do not come to the attention of the police but that we could nevertheless define as being criminal? This hidden dimension of crime has important implications for how we define criminal events, as well as for the processes by which the police target certain victims or offenders. Criminal events, then, are dynamic not only in terms of their responsiveness to interactional factors in the environment but also in terms of the claims that are made about them by interested parties. These claims are continuously changing in response to changing political and cultural values.

THE AFTERMATH

The extent to which we can develop an integrated perspective depends strongly on the types of information about criminal events to which we have access. We are concerned not only with the actual event but also with the reactions by the police, victims, and others. In considering the aftermath of an event, we are interested in the degree to which the victim has been harmed and in the resources needed to aid in his or her recovery. We are also concerned with whether the offender feels that he or she can repeat the offense with impunity. With respect to punishment, has there been sufficient certainty, severity, or celerity to deter a repeat occurrence? These questions frame a great deal of the discussion about how we are managing our crime problems. Lending focus to this debate are the responses to different types of crime. We need to understand that our responses to criminality are a function of our perspectives in interpreting the reasons for its occurrence; moreover, these reactions will influence the types of crime that we will experience in the future.

SUMMARY
■ ■ ■

Crime is, strictly speaking, the breaking of the law. But the laws and their interpretation are an embodiment of social morality. As such, they are subject to change, as is our understanding of criminal events. Crime is a social construct that varies according to definition and response by legal authorities. It is the job of criminologists to assess how legal and moral definitions of crime coincide with the circumstances that people face and then evolve into events that demand enforcement and result in labeling individuals criminals.

The criminal event is a social event. Like all other social events, it has a beginning and an end. Criminal events are social in that they involve interaction between human beings. The nature and form of this interaction shape the course of the event, determine the stages through which it proceeds, and define how serious it is judged to be in terms of harm done. Many different types of actors are involved in these events.

The most obvious participant is the offender. Offenders tend to be young, disadvantaged males. At the same time, however, we are witnessing a growth in family violence; the major offenders in these crimes frequently are older and better-off males. Further, women are increasingly becoming involved in property crimes.

Much attention has been directed at trying to understand the motivations, as well as the group pressures, that influence the behavior of criminals. The study of offender perceptions provides an important source of information about the pressures that direct individuals to behave in certain ways. Offenders may choose to deal with their blameworthiness by rationalizing their crimes.

While the victims of crime, like offenders, tend to be young and male, other groups are heavily victimized in particular types of crime. Sexual assault and family violence is disproportionately directed against women. The nature of victims and their relationship to offenders, then, is very much a function of the type of event that has occurred and is governed by location and circumstance. Like offenders, victims may redefine the event as harmless or, at least, not criminal. Victim definitions can be very important in influencing the actions taken by criminal justice agencies in criminal events.

Bystanders and witnesses also play a role in defining and interpreting the social events that become crimes. They may defuse a violent situation or they may actually promote violence through their actions. While bystanders can be very helpful in clarifying what actually occurred during a criminal event, their accounts often prove to be inaccurate.

The police play a major role in criminal events as well. They have the power to certify an event as a crime by assessing the match between the event as they have come to understand it and their knowledge of what the law disallows. In reactive policing, the police respond to reports from citizens, who may be either victims or bystanders. In proactive policing, certain groups or communities are targeted for police attention as a way of preventing criminal events.

With respect to intervention, the police are heavily influenced by their perceptions of what they can do to reduce crime. Police use a great deal of discretion in their work, discretion that can be used negatively to discriminate against certain groups. Police discretion in family violence cases is increasingly being removed.

The police operate through the administration of the law and, although they use some discretion in applying it, the legal structure outlines clear expectations vis-à-vis personal behavior and the legal response to the breaking of these expectations. Law is a form of social control that defines individual actions on the basis of socially acceptable standards. Criminal events are social events and, as such, are governed by societal as well as legal tenets. Forms of control may also be socially based. Gossip, ridicule, and ostracism may combine with legal threats to discourage individuals from acting in a criminal manner.

One other important aspect of criminal events is the conditions under which they occur. The different dimensions of people's lives, ranging from family interaction and work to leisure-time activities, all invite different types of behavior and offer circumstances that may or may not give rise to criminal events. A comprehensive view of the criminal event must consider three key components: precursors of the crime, the transaction itself, and the aftermath.

Criminal events, like all forms of social events, are complicated affairs. This chapter has discussed their basic dimensions and, in so doing, has raised questions about who participates in these events, when and where they occur, and why they elicit particular forms of societal reaction. In order to understand a criminal event, we need to understand how each of its elements combines and interacts. We cannot address the issue of sexual assault by reducing the problem to a single question—why do some men commit sexual assaults? Instead, we need to put this question in an appropriate context that also asks why some women are more likely than others to be victimized by sexual assault, when and where such assaults are most likely to occur, and why police, lawmakers, and members of the general public think about sexual assault as they do.

QUESTIONS FOR REVIEW AND DISCUSSION
■ ■ ■

1. How do offenders see their actions relative to their victims and to the situations they find themselves in?
2. What do we mean when we say that crime is a social event that takes place in time and space?
3. What role does the legal system play at each stage of the criminal event? Is it always the same agency that deals with the precursors, the transaction, and the aftermath?
4. When does a social event become a criminal event?
5. What does it mean when we say that a criminal event takes on the character of a transaction?

PART THREE

THEORIES

To understand each of the components of the criminal event, we will review criminological theories that have been developed to explain offender motivation, social control, opportunity, and response to crime. This provides an overview of the ways in which criminologists have studied aspects of crime and builds an empirical base for the development of an integrated approach to its study.

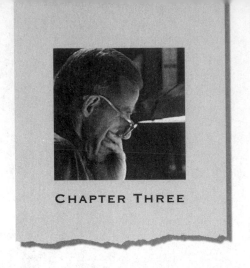

Psychosocial Conditions and Criminal Motivations

WHAT'S IN CHAPTER THREE

In this chapter, we will begin our review of the theories that have been used to explain crime. We focus on those explanations that deal with the question, Why are some people more inclined than others to behave in ways that violate the law? This involves an examination of offender motivation, including deficiencies in physiological or psychological makeup, propensities produced by troublesome social conditions, and problems that arise from the offender's commitment to cultural beliefs that condone criminal conduct.

What are criminological theories and why do we need them? In day-to-day conversation, we tend to use terms like *theory* or *theoretical* to describe something that may be interesting but is also irrelevant, unimportant, or impractical. We can dismiss what someone tells us with the retort, "While that may be true in theory, it doesn't have much to do with reality!" As students of criminology, however, we need to recognize that, far from being irrelevant, **theories** can be extremely useful and practical analytical tools.

We can understand criminological theories as generalized explanations of criminal phenomena. Our theories provide potential answers to questions about why crimes occur, why some types of people are more likely than others to be involved in crimes (as offenders or as victims), why crimes are more likely to occur in certain places and at certain times, and why agencies of social control respond to crime as they do.

Of course, criminologists are not alone in seeking answers to these questions. Angry newspaper editorials may offer seemingly reasonable accounts of why crime rates are rising. On any given Sunday morning, television preachers explain crime and associated problems in terms of evil forces at large in the world. Crime victims may ask what they did that led to the victimization. While not always recognized as such, these accounts of why and how crimes occur represent a kind of theoretical thinking. However, we expect somewhat more from criminological theories than from so many of the "folk theories" that are part of our conventional wisdom.

REQUIREMENTS OF CRIMINOLOGICAL THEORIES

First, **criminological theories** (at least of the type discussed in this book) are intended as general rather than specific explanations. Stated differently, we are usually not interested in why one particular offender committed one particular crime. Instead, theories should explain the patterns that characterize criminal phenomena in general. We want our theories to tell us, for example, why males are more likely than females to commit a violent offense, why the chances of victimization are reduced as people grow older, why big cities have higher rates of some kinds of crime than do small towns, or why crime rates shot up in the 1960s.

Second, we expect that our theories will be consistent with (and can therefore make sense out of)

WHAT ARE THEY?

Criminological Theories

Theories provide us with answers to questions about why crimes occur; why some types of people are more likely than others to be involved in crimes, whether as offenders or victims; why crimes are more likely to occur in certain places and at certain times; and why agencies of social control respond to crime as they do.

the *facts* of crime as revealed to us in the research process. The gross facts of crime, as we currently understand them, are consistent with a variety of different theoretical viewpoints. As a result, the evidence sometimes seems to support, at least partially, apparently competing views. Why, for instance, do we find higher rates of theft in bigger cities? Some sociologists have argued that large cities undermine the social controls that might discourage people from stealing (Wirth, 1938). Others have suggested that bigger cities are more likely to be home to the kinds of people (for example, young, unmarried males) who tend to steal no matter where they live (Gans, 1962). Alternatively, we might argue that the city provides a setting that accommodates an elaborate network of thieves, targets, and fences and thereby turns theft into a profitable and enduring activity (Fischer, 1975).

On the surface, each of these theories of crime and urban life might seem equally valuable since each is consistent with the general pattern of empirical data. This implies that, in order to assess the relative value of these theories, we would need more detailed empirical knowledge about the relationship between crime and urban settings. As empirical data accumulated, we would hope to discover that one of the theoretical positions better accounted for the patterns we were observing.

This brings us to a third requirement of criminological theories. Like all forms of scientific theory, they should be falsifiable. That is, our theories must be stated in terms that allow them to be tested through research so that we can discover which theories provide false accounts of the phenomena being observed. A theory that cannot be rejected no matter what we discover is of little use to us.

We should emphasize that criminological theories are not merely intellectual abstractions with no real-life implications. On the contrary, theories may be highly practical, particularly when we use them as guides in our efforts to deal with crime as a social problem. Obviously, how we understand the causes of a problem has important consequences for what actions we take to resolve it.

Throughout its history, criminology has witnessed no shortage of attempts to theorize about crime. To the uninitiated, the choice of explanations can be bewildering as theories appear to contradict or at least compete with one another. Our review focuses on several types of theoretical questions. The first question concerns the behavior of offenders. Why are some people more inclined than others to behave in ways that violate the law? This question, which has attracted the greatest amount of criminological attention, provides the subject matter for this chapter and the one that follows.

In Chapter 5, we turn to another type of theoretical question. How do we understand the situations that allow offenders to act on their propensities? As we will see, an emphasis on situations and opportunities complements the more traditional motivational theories of crime. In Chapter 6, we examine theoretical explanations of what happens after a crime takes place.

For many theorists, the explanation of crime boils down to one simple question that has spawned several complicated answers: Why do offenders do what they do? Criminologists traditionally have offered two general types of answers to this question. On the one hand, criminal behavior can be understood as the product of unique factors that **motivate** lawbreaking. This approach derives from the positivist school of thought and seeks to discover the causes of criminal conduct. On the other hand, criminal behavior can be understood as the product of **behavioral choices** that are freely and rationally made. This approach derives from the classical school of thought and sees as misguided the search for causes of criminal behavior (causes referring to those factors that drive people to act in particular ways).

These perspectives differ in terms of the prominence they accord the role of **will** in human affairs. Theories that derive from the classical school conceptualize criminal behavior as willful and purposeful. Theories that derive from the positivist school view will as a less significant characteristic of criminal behavior and seek instead to understand how social and other factors compel, or at least encourage, criminal conduct. This chapter deals with those theories that reflect the positivist tradition; theories that reflect the classical tradition are discussed in the next chapter.

Three broad subthemes may be identified. The first views criminal motivation as resulting from deficiencies in the offender's physiological or psychological makeup. The second subtheme views offenders as a product of troublesome social conditions that propel them toward crime. According to the third subtheme, motivation arises from the offender's commitment to cultural beliefs that condone criminal conduct.

SOCIOBIOLOGICAL EXPLANATIONS OF CRIMINAL MOTIVATION

GENETICS

In recent years, there has been a renewed interest in the influence of **genetics** and physiology on the creation of criminal offenders. This school of thought argues that certain individuals are more likely to commit crimes due to faulty genetic programming. In arguing that a predisposition toward criminality exists in certain individuals, some researchers have used genetic explanations of behavior (Mednick, Moffitt, and Stack, 1981) while others have focused on sociobiological or constitutional aspects of individuals (Wilson and Herrnstein, 1985). This predisposition may occur through intergenerational genetic defects or through a constitutional deficiency deriving from short time horizons (that is, the absence of long-term goals) or inadequate socialization in early childhood.

The genetic approach has been used in the effort to determine the importance of family ties or blood relations in the control of individual deportment. Violent crime, in particular, can be explained in terms of its connection with genetics. For instance, individuals with intimate family ties offer the same protection from harm as would animals to their blood connections, whereas individuals with less intimate ties (for example, adopted children) are more likely to be subject to violence from non-blood relations (for example, stepparents) (see Daly and Wilson, 1988).

Ellis (1982) provides a review of the major factors that are included in a genetic explanation of crime. Genes influence behavior through the nervous system. In any particular group of behavioral events, there may be so much genetic similarity in individual nervous systems within the human species that any differences in behavior cannot be explained by genetic variation but rather depend on forces outside the individual. This has led to a debate over the extent to which nature (genes) versus nurture (environment) influences human behavior in general and criminality in particular. The effects of nature versus nurture have been studied in four different ways: (1) general pedigree studies, (2) twin studies, (3) karyotype studies, and (4) adoption studies.

As Ellis (1982) explains, **general pedigree studies** involve establishing the extent to which people who are related also behave similarly. This approach is nonexperimental, however, because it is difficult to control the effects of common genetic background versus environmental influences. While family members share both genetic and environmental factors with their children, if parents and children are criminal it is likely due to these shared factors rather than some environmental factor they do not share. The evidence shows that 30–45 percent of individuals with criminal records had one or more parents with criminal records. But, knowing about "crime in the family" does not really enhance our ability to use genetics in explaining criminality because we are really unable to detach family biology from environmental factors (including family socialization).

The second type of nonexperimental design is **twin studies**. According to Ellis (1982), this design allows for a comparison between the two types of twinning that occur in humans. The most common twins are the result of two ova fertilized by two separate sperm. These dizygotic (DZ) twins share 50 percent of genetic programming. In contrast, if a single fertilized ovum splits very early in its development, monozygotic (MZ) twins who share 100 percent of genetic programming are formed. Twin studies show a higher level of concordance between MZ twins in their criminality than between DZ twins, leading some to conclude that the genetic commonalities are the key contributory factors. However, due to the strong similarity in their appearance, MZ twins elicit common responses from others more so than do DZ twins. This similarity in treatment, a factor in the socialization of MZ twins, may be more important in guiding their behavior than the fact that they share genetic programming.

The third type of study discussed by Ellis (1982) involves genetic karyo-types. **Karyotype studies** compare the size, shape, and number of specific chromosomes in individuals. Some researchers report that among criminal males, the Y chromosome has a higher-than-expected probability of being larger than among noncriminals. In addition, research shows that some offenders have an unusual number of chromosomes, that is, a number other than the twenty-three pairs typical of humans. XYY karyotype males, while rare among the criminal population, are still more likely to appear in groups of persons convicted of or imprisoned for a crime than among control populations. However, the research in this area suffers from small samples and inconclusive explanations; the correlations that exist are not readily interpreted as causative factors linking these karyotype differences to criminality.

The fourth design is based on **adoption studies**. As Ellis (1982) points out, we can contrast the behavior of near-birth adoptees (persons adopted by nonrelatives shortly after birth) to that of both their genetic and their adoptive parents. If the behavior is due to genetics, adoptees should more closely resemble their genetic parents (whom they have never seen) than their adoptive parents. Properly executed adoption studies offer a powerful experimental design for isolating the effects of genetic factors from the influences of socialization and other environmental effects. For example, if some individuals exhibit criminal tendencies, and the birth parents but not the adoptive parents do likewise, it is assumed that this behavior is due to genetic programming.

In the research to date, the efficacy of using *genotypes*—that is, genetic makeups—to identify likely candidates for criminal behavior is not very well established. The most credible research is provided by adoption studies, but these have, in fact, reported fairly low concordance rates between the offending patterns of identical twins who have been separated at birth and raised with different families (Mednick, Moffitt, and Stack, 1981). In evaluating the relative importance of genetic structure and environmental influences, adoption studies report little evidence that genetic differences explain differences in criminality.

Walters and White (1989) summarize the problems of genetic-based research as follows:

> *Genetic factors are undoubtedly correlated with various measures of criminality, but the large number of methodological flaws and limitations in the research should make one cautious in drawing any causal inferences at this point in time. Our review leads us to the inevitable conclusion that current genetic research on crime has been poorly designed, ambiguously reported, and exceedingly inadequate in addressing the relevant issues. (478)*

Until these deficiencies are addressed, there is no real scientific basis for arguing for (or against) the existence of a **crime gene**.

DO THEY EXIST?

Crime Genes

Until we can improve on methodological deficiencies, we have no real scientific basis for arguing for (or against) the existence of a "crime gene."

The biological approaches have also focused on the **constitutional structure** (including the body types and psychological propensities) of offenders. Having reviewed research by Garafolo (1914) on Italian convicts and studies by Sheldon (1940) on incarcerated juveniles, Wilson and Herrnstein (1985) conclude that one can detect certain physiological similarities among offenders. For example, short, muscular young males are the types most likely to appear in prison populations. According to Wilson and Herrnstein (1985), "The biological factors whose traces we see in faces, physiques, and correlation with behavior of parents and siblings are predispositions towards crime that are expressed as psychological traits and activated by circumstance" (103).

BOX 3.1 BODY TYPE AND CRIMINAL BEHAVIOR

In a famous study, researcher William Sheldon (1949) attempted to determine the relationship between physique and the tendency to engage in criminal behavior. Sheldon used a method called *somatotyping* in order to categorize three basic types of body build—*endomorphic, ectomorphic,* and *mesomorphic*—each of which, he argued, was associated with a particular type of temperament. As shown in Figure 3.1, the body types represent extreme forms; most individuals are a combination of all three types.

In comparing a sample of known delinquents with a control group of students, Sheldon maintained that delinquents were more likely to have mesomorphic physiques and the accompanying temperament, which emphasized risk taking, adventure, and physical activity.

For Discussion
Aside from the argument that might link body type to temperament, can you offer any other interpretation of Sheldon's finding that mesomorphs are disproportionately represented among known delinquents? How realistic is it to assess individuals' behavior based on their body type?

The difficulty with the constitutional approach is that knowing about **body type** doesn't tell us much about a person's propensity to act criminally; it tells us (and only if we believe the research) that some inmates happen to be short and muscular. Moreover, body typing ignores the fact that one of the most popular activities in men's prisons is weight-lifting, whereby ninety-pound weaklings turn themselves into Hulk Hogans. It also fails to consider the fact that, in a violent encounter, the less muscular combatant will tend to lose the contest and end up in the hospital, while the more muscular participant will emerge as the victor and end up in prison. Further, this approach doesn't address other important factors related to crime, including the circumstances

Figure 3.1

87

*Psychosocial
Conditions
and Criminal
Motivations*

Sheldon's Somatotypes in Relation to Physique and Temperament

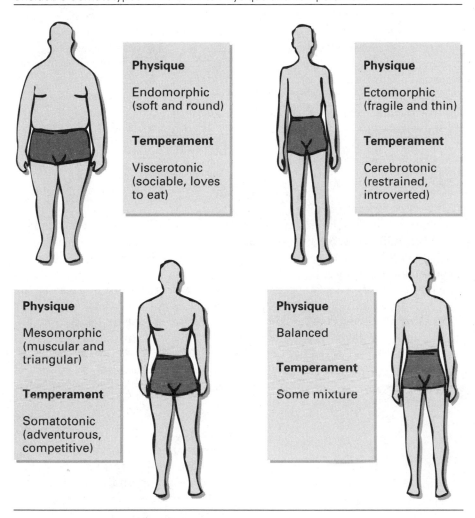

Physique

Endomorphic
(soft and round)

Temperament

Viscerotonic
(sociable, loves
to eat)

Physique

Ectomorphic
(fragile and thin)

Temperament

Cerebrotonic
(restrained,
introverted)

Physique

Mesomorphic
(muscular and
triangular)

Temperament

Somatotonic
(adventurous,
competitive)

Physique

Balanced

Temperament

Some mixture

SOURCE: Based on C. R. Bartol, *Criminal Behaviour: A Psychosocial Approach* (Englewood Cliffs, NJ: Prentice-Hall, 1980).

under which a motivated offender comes to participate in criminal activity.

In defending the constitutional approach to criminality, Wilson and Herrnstein (1985) borrow from classical criminology to argue that crime is a rational act based on a calculation of potential gain versus loss. Through this process, individuals weigh the possibilities that they will succeed in their endeavors. Individuals may discount potential costs through a process whereby immediate gratification becomes the paramount concern. This choice is not really a free choice, however, as it is predetermined by poor socialization and constitutional deficiencies. The short time horizons possessed by individuals with these deficiencies distort the way in which their decisions about benefits and costs are made. Such individuals will tend to involve themselves in criminal activity for short-term gain. According to Wilson and Herrnstein, they represent criminal types who need to be isolated and subjected to high levels of deterrence, thereby restricting their behavior and reducing the likelihood of criminality. Thus, the state's role is to set up contingencies that will reduce the benefits and increase the costs of misbehavior.

The deterministic nature of constitutional theories firmly establishes them in a positivistic framework that maintains there is little offenders can do to change their propensities to act criminally. From this perspective, we need to reduce the likelihood of criminal activity by isolating individuals who are likely to be problem offenders.

DIET

Some researchers are interested in the degree to which **diet** can affect the behavior of individuals. Strong scientific evidence supports the idea that certain individuals are more prone to hyperactivity or aggressive behavior following a sudden intake of sugar (hypoglycemia) (Dorfman, 1984). In a famous case, a San Francisco city supervisor attributed his 1978 murder of the mayor and a fellow supervisor to his diet of Twinkies and other "junk food." His lawyers were able to use what has come to be known as the **Twinkie defense** to convince a jury that their client suffered from "diminished mental capacity" and was therefore not guilty of murder.

> ## WHAT IS IT?
>
> ### *The Twinkie Defense*
>
> The Twinkie defense revolves around the argument that, due to an overconsumption of junk food, a defendant experiences diminished mental capacity and is therefore not guilty of criminal behavior.

While the idea that such dietary factors are major causes of violence seems questionable, changing dietary practices has been acknowledged to have a dramatic effect on the behavior of inmates in institutions. In a study of detention homes in California, it was established that, by revising the diets of 276 juveniles, mostly through the reduction of sugar intake via pop and junk food, antisocial behavior declined by 48 percent, incidents of theft by 77 percent, incidents of assault by 82 percent, and refusal to obey orders by 55 percent (Kinderlerhrer, 1983: 143). Similar results were obtained when supplies of orange juice were increased, a finding that has led some researchers to attribute the former negative behaviors not to excessive sugar content but rather to vitamin and nutrient deficiencies in prisoners' diets (Dorfman, 1984).

The focus on nutrients has led to research on the relationship between **trace element** patterns and a predisposition to violence. One study compared 24 pairs of violent and nonviolent brothers, while a second study matched 96 violent males of mixed age and background with 96 nonviolent males who served as a control group. The research revealed that the violent subjects fell into two groups: (1) type A's, who tested high in copper and low in sodium and potassium and who were episodically violent, and (2) type B's, who were the reverse and who displayed consistently antisocial behavior. As the type A pattern tended to fade with age, hair analysis (a procedure for tracking trace elements) could be used by parole boards to predict, on the basis of the mineral content in the subject's body, when episodic violence would likely cease (Dorfman, 1984: 46).

The applicability of these findings to offenders outside of institutions is impossible to determine. They do provide some interesting suggestions about how our lifestyle, particularly our diet, influences our actions. They do not tell us much about what situations elicit violence or about what social factors (for example, early childhood socialization, peer pressure, or fear of stigmatization) may play a role in deterring it.

The ingestion of substances other than food has attracted a great deal of attention in criminological analyses. Drugs, including alcohol, are present in many criminal events. The criminality that surrounds the illicit sale and purchase of drugs makes their use of interest to us. As with dietary factors, what is unclear is how important drugs are in providing an explanation for criminality. Their presence in criminal situations may be related but not central to the explanation of criminality. Many people use (and abuse) alcohol without becoming violent and attacking other people. Yet, as evidenced by the many bar fights that occur, alcohol sometimes appears to fuel violent attacks.

Explanations based on genetics, constitution, and diet can be summed up this way: If one accepts that crime is a cultural and social concept, defined

Misbehavior in prisons has been linked to what inmates eat.

through custom and law, it seems unlikely that such a thing as a "criminal type" or a "crime gene" exists whereby behavior is preprogrammed to deviate from this social construct or, indeed, that certain people with particular body types or diet will generally offend. These explanations, while interesting, seem to be more useful for describing the conditions of incarcerated offenders and assisting in controlling their behavior than in predicting the likelihood of criminality in the first place.

INTELLIGENCE AND CRIME

NEUROPSYCHOLOGICAL THEORY

There has been an upsurge in interest in the relationship between **IQ** and behavior (see Murray and Herrnstein, 1994). It has long been recognized in criminological research that a correlation exists between IQ and delinquency, but, as Moffitt and colleagues (1994) report, we do not know why or how low IQ influences antisocial behavior. They argue that one way to approach this issue is to look beyond IQ by applying **neuropsychological theory,** according to which, people with identical IQ scores can have very different patterns of mental strengths and weaknesses. Moffitt and colleagues claim that IQ offers limited information about which of these strengths or weaknesses influences behavior. The IQ test compresses an aggregate measure of abilities (notably **verbal skills** and spatial perception) into a single composite indicator of performance. Most neuropsychological test batteries include a standard IQ test, which measures verbal and spatial functions very accurately, but they also add more tests to cover functions such as memory, motor skills, and mental self-control. A battery of neuropsychological tests can reveal, for instance, that children with identical low IQ scores might suffer from different and relatively isolated problems such as impulsive judgment, weak language processing, poor memory, or inability to match visual information with motor actions. Each type of deficit could be more accurate than the overall IQ in predicting delinquency, but each would contribute to delinquency through a unique theoretical causal chain (Moffitt et al., 1994: 279).

LEARNING DISABILITIES

Addressing psychological dysfunction in terms of learning, Culliver and Sigler (1991) provide an extensive review of the relationship between learning disability and juvenile delinquency. **Learning disabilities** are defined as problems faced by children and youths with dyslexia, dysgraphia, aphasia, perceptual and motor deficits, poor intersensory integration, and minimal brain dysfunction. Although these disabilities are often difficult to detect, there is a strong belief that they are directly related to delinquent behavior in youths.

Culliver and Sigler report that five hypotheses have been used to study this relationship. The *school failure hypothesis* argues that academic failure results from learning disabilities and that this failure becomes self-perpetuating. As a result of their frustration, students become more aggressive and are, in turn, labeled as troublesome. Through rejection from teachers and administrators, these youths withdraw from mainstream activities and become involved in inappropriate behavior and, ultimately, delinquency. The *susceptibility hypothesis* argues that learning-disabled students have unique characteristics, such as impulsiveness, inability to anticipate future consequences, and irritability. In acting out their feelings, they are more likely to become delinquent. The *differential arrest hypothesis* posits that learning-disabled students are more likely to be apprehended by police because they are less able to conceal their activities than their non-learning-disabled peers. In addition, this hypothesis suggests that learning-disabled students cannot effectively interact with police due to poor social perception and to abrasiveness and are therefore more likely to be arrested. The *differential adjudication hypothesis* posits that delinquents with learning disabilities who are arrested and charged are more likely to be convicted of crimes due to their inability to cope with the process of criminal justice adjudication. "Moreover, learning disabled students are unable to vindicate their feelings and concerns regarding the criminal charges" (Culliver and Sigler, 1991: 125). Finally, according to the *differential disposition hypothesis*, learning-disabled delinquents face a higher chance of receiving harsher sentences than non-learning-disabled delinquents.

Culliver and Sigler report that while the potential link between learning disabilities and delinquency has generated much interest, research results "tend to create more confusion and uncertainty than fact upon which sound theories

Several hypotheses have been offered to explain the apparent relationship between learning disabilities and delinquency.

can be built and effective programs developed" (125). This same conclusion is reached by Cornwall and Bawden (1992) in their assessment of the link between reading disabilities and aggression. As Skaret and Wilgosh (1989) state, the problems with the research should lead us to deal with the effects of learning disabilities on delinquency in a different way. They state that, rather than struggling to provide definitive findings supporting a causal relationship, we should pay attention to the fact that adolescents with learning disabilities seem to be at relatively high risk for delinquency. "Sound remedial education practices, including counselling and other support systems will improve academic achievement and social skills, and *may, possibly*, lead to some reduced delinquent behavior" (Skaret and Wilgosh, 1989: 121). This is the same prescription offered by Moffitt and colleagues (1994) in their conclusions about the remedial effects of using psychoneurological testing in assessing propensity toward delinquency.

PSYCHOPATHOLOGY

Gottfredson and Hirschi (1990) focus on psychological dysfunction in their general theory of crime, which we will describe in more detail in Chapter 4. To them, the central aspect in criminal behavior (or, in fact, any imprudent behavior) is low self-control (Arneklev et al., 1993). This lack of self-control derives from ineffective childhood socialization and is manifested in personality characteristics that model the behavioral problems associated with learning disabilities or low IQ. Results of low self-control include impulsivity, preference for simple tasks, risk-seeking behavior, high need for physical activities, self-centeredness, and temper. Gottfredson and Hirschi (1990) theorize that these personality characteristics combine to lead certain individuals, when offered the opportunity, to commit crimes.

For the most heinous crimes, such as sexually motivated murders or serial murders, we often apply the label of **psychopath** to the perpetrator. According to Hickey (1991), however, the term *psychopath* is used to describe a potpourri of individuals determined by societal and medical standards to possess antisocial qualities or characteristics. He claims that the label of psychopath is used interchangeably with that of *sociopath*, and because of the generality of the term, the psychopath "often turns out to be exactly what we want him or her to be" (50).

Psychopaths are often described as aggressive, insensitive, charismatic, irresponsible, intelligent, dangerous, hedonistic, narcissistic, and antisocial. They are viewed as exceptional manipulators, capable of pretending to possess "normal" human emotions even while remorselessly carrying out their own personal agendas. They are outwardly normal but are known for their inability to maintain long-term commitment to people or programs.

Knowing that someone meets the criteria of psychopathology, however, is of little benefit in isolation from any other theoretical framework (Jeffery, 1990: 364). Jeffery suggests that we look at psychopaths in terms of a framework that emphasizes the functioning of the nervous system in times of threat. As Jeffery points out, psychopaths do not become anxious or fearful in the presence of punishment or danger because their autonomic nervous systems are not aroused by danger. Further, the inability of psychopaths to anticipate the consequences of their actions means that they make little attempt to avoid punishment or pain (Jeffery, 1990: 364).

People who fit this categorization are believed to be more dangerous than other criminals, maintaining a consistency in their criminal behavior over their lifetime. Hickey (1991) reports that psychopaths are commonly found in institutions and constitute approximately 20–30 percent of prison populations. The dilemma for criminological researchers is that the indeterminacy of the psychopathology symptomology means that people can hide these tendencies while leading "normal" lives. We know about their tendencies only when they act out their antisocial fantasies. Often, it takes some time to uncover these individuals' acts, as shown by the long crime sprees of serial murderers. For example, John Wayne Gacy, "The Killer Clown," was considered a model citizen in Des Plaines, often dressing up as Pogo the Clown to perform at children's parties and hospitals. When he was caught, the police found twenty-nine bodies in the crawl space and under the cement driveway of his house, while four other victims had been dropped into the Des Plaines River. He was caught only after one of his intended victims escaped and reported him.

SOCIAL CONDITIONS AND CRIMINAL MOTIVATION

It has been argued that, in a variety of ways, the social conditions under which people live make it difficult for them to be law-abiding. From this perspective, criminal behavior may be understood as the means by which people attempt to deal with the frustrations that characterize their lives and the problems that confront them.

FRUSTRATED AMBITIONS

People who aspire to achieve goals that they cannot realistically attain may feel pressure to behave in a criminal fashion. Such pressure is most likely to be felt by those who occupy disadvantaged positions in the social structure. Perhaps the best-known version of this argument was articulated in the late 1930s by the sociologist Robert Merton, who sought to explain how particular forms of social organization create the strains that lead to nonconformity.

Using American society as an example, Merton (1938) argued that if everyone in the society is encouraged to pursue the goal of material success, those who do not have access to the legitimate means by which success is to be achieved will be frustrated by their lack of opportunity. Those at the bottom of the social hierarchy—the poor, ethnic minorities, or recent immigrants—do not have easy access to quality education, inheritance, or other means by which the American Dream might be realized. Since success is still important to them, they must find ways of adjusting to the social strain that society imposes on them. The adjustments in many cases may involve criminal conduct.

Merton's **anomie theory** proposed that frustration and alienation develop when individuals who aspire to the economic goals of society (including upward social mobility) are not provided the means with which to achieve these goals. That is, a gap exists between expectations and opportunity. In responding to the anomie that develops due to this gap, certain adaptations occur. One such adaptation involves the use of criminal means to achieve conventional goals such as wealth. Blau and Blau (1982) argue that it is not absolute but relative deprivation that results in frustration and a sense of personal injustice, which, in turn, leads to criminal activity.

BOX 3.2 MERTON'S PARADIGM OF DEVIANT BEHAVIOR

Robert Merton (1938) argued that nonconformist behavior results when people find themselves in situations in which they are encouraged to pursue social goals that prevailing social arrangements do not allow them to achieve. While such individuals may have internalized these goals, they lack the legitimate means with which to achieve them. In such situations, individuals must adjust their behavior to accommodate the gap between the goals and the means.

Merton identified five such adaptations in the goals–means relationship:

1. *Conformity.* This adaptation involves accepting as legitimate both the goals and the means for achieving them. This is the adaptation that most people make.
2. *Innovation.* This involves accepting the goals but rejecting the means of goal attainment. For example, the person who embezzles accepts material gain as a legitimate goal but rejects the culturally prescribed means for achieving it.
3. *Ritualism.* This adaptation involves accepting the means for achieving the goal but rejecting the goal itself. Individuals who engage in ritualism simply "go through the motions" without coming any closer to the goals they supposedly seek.
4. *Retreatism.* This involves a rejection of both the means and the goals. At least in terms of what the culture prescribes, those who opt for this adaptation may be described as dropouts.
5. *Rebellion.* Like retreatism, this adaptation involves rejecting both goals and means. Rebellion differs from retreatism in that it also involves the substitution of other goals as well as other means by which they might be achieved.

Merton presented his five adaptations in schematic form as follows (where + means "accept" and − means "reject"):

	Goal	Means
Conformity	+	+
Innovation	+	−
Ritualism	−	+
Retreatism	−	−
Rebellion	−	−
	(+)	(+)

For Discussion

If high grades are a goal to be achieved, and study, essay writing, and exam taking are the means by which the goal is to be achieved, what specific forms of behavior might each of Merton's adaptations represent?

SOURCE: Based on R. K. Merton (1938), "Social Structure and Anomie," *American Sociological Review* 3: 672–682.

Consider the gangster Al Capone. Arguably, the goals to which he aspired did not differ significantly from the goals pursued by "legitimate" businesspeople. Capone sought wealth, power, and celebrity. He differed from conventional entrepreneurs with respect to the means he employed to achieve these objectives, but not with respect to the objectives themselves. Seen in this way, the behavior of gangsters, thieves, and other goal-oriented criminals is best understood as the product not of a pathological personality but of social arrangements that create a gulf between what people aspire to and what is actually available to them.

Frustrated ambition does not always manifest itself in individuals like Al Capone. It may come in more mundane forms. According to Messner (1989), criminality can be attributed to a number of factors, including race, income, and particularly unemployment. In contrast, Wilson (1983) has found that the research relating unemployment to crime is inconclusive. His explanations for criminality are consistent with the views of those who argue for frustrated ambition. His emphasis, though, is different. He claims that unemployed individuals may commit crime for any number of reasons and that it may not be the unemployment per se that causes criminality but rather the problems inherent in crime deterrence. Wilson also asserts that crime may cause unemployment. What is not evident, he argues, is whether "some people turn to crime because they are poor, some people may be poor because they have turned to crime and are not very good at it, and still other persons may have been made poor and criminal because of some common underlying factor" (126). In Wilson's view, the lower classes are less likely to be socialized to the ways of society and will thus have a greater tendency toward criminal behavior. Support from the public for targeting these groups for policing and for deterrence resides in the fact that their numbers are disproportionately represented in crime statistics (as perpetrators) and in prison populations.

At the same time, some argue that the lower classes are overrepresented in prisons because (1) the police tend to discriminate against them, (2) much of the lower-class behavior is public and therefore more likely to be open to sanction, and (3) the crimes of the poor receive more attention than the white-collar crimes of the rich (Reiman, 1990; Snider, 1992). Property crimes like embezzlement can have more detrimental effect on society than theft, breaking and entering, and other typical crimes of the poor. Notwithstanding this view, Wilson (1983: 39) believes the rise in crime is due not to poverty or racism per se but rather to a failure of individuals from the lower class to adopt behavior that is more consistent with societal norms.

STATUS DEPRIVATION

Several years after the publication of Merton's work, Albert Cohen followed a similar line in his investigation of gang delinquency among working-class juveniles. For Cohen (1955), the source of much juvenile crime was rooted in the problems experienced by disadvantaged youths who aspired to middle-class status but who were judged inadequate by a school system that dispensed status rewards on the basis of middle-class criteria. In other words, children from a working-class background typically find that, because their socialization experiences have not prepared them to compete effectively for status within the classroom, they come up short when they are assessed by the school's **middle-class measuring rod**. According to Cohen, working-class youths may experience feelings of frustration and inadequacy when they confront middle-class expectations regarding punctuality, neatness, and the need to postpone gratification.

> ### WHAT DOES IT MEAN?
>
> #### *Middle-Class Measuring Rod*
>
> Working-class youth may experience feelings of frustration and inadequacy when they confront middle-class expectations regarding punctuality, neatness, and the need to postpone gratification.

One reaction on the part of youths may be to reject the source of their problem, namely, the middle-class value system of the school. Delinquency may signal such a rejection, particularly if it celebrates standards that stand in direct opposition to those of the middle-class society. Delinquency that appears intended to offend members of conventional society rather than to achieve some specific goal may serve this purpose. For Cohen, much delinquency has an "in your face" quality precisely because it is meant to signify a rejection of middle-class values.

STRAIN AND DELINQUENCY

Richard Cloward (1959) and Lloyd Ohlin (Cloward and Ohlin, 1960) borrowed heavily from the writings of Robert Merton to demonstrate that a comprehensive theory of delinquency must explain not only why juveniles engage in delinquency but also why they engage in one type of delinquency and not another.

Like Merton, Cloward and Ohlin (1960) argued that the motivation to delinquency could be located in the discrepancy between the goals to which lower-class youths aspire and those actually available to them. Cloward and Ohlin were also influenced by Merton's view that the legitimate means to goal attainment are socially structured such that not everyone in society finds the legitimate means to conventional goals equally available. For some people, the legitimate means of obtaining success goals, such as education or a good job, are out of reach, and it is precisely this lack of legitimate opportunity that creates the pressure to deviate in the first place. Cloward and Ohlin extended Merton's theory by arguing that it is important to recognize that illegitimate means are also structured. The opportunities to be criminal are no more evenly dispersed in society than are the legitimate means to achieve success goals. Building on this logic, Cloward and Ohlin theorized that the kind of delinquent a youth becomes depends on the kinds of opportunities he or she has to be delinquent.

Cloward and Ohlin (1960) used the term **illegitimate means** to encompass two major aspects of the delinquent opportunity structure. The first is the opportunity to learn a delinquent role. As Sutherland (1947) argued, learning how to be delinquent and why it is acceptable to be delinquent are necessary precursors to being delinquent. Second, the concept of illegitimate means implies the opportunity to actually play a delinquent role. An individual can become a member of a drug network or stolen-car ring only if such organizations exist in his or her social environment. For Cloward and Ohlin, then, a central theoretical problem was to understand how particular types of community organization make particular types of delinquent opportunity structures possible. Their analysis identified three forms of delinquent opportunity structure, each of which was associated with particular types of social conditions.

The first form, the **criminal pattern**, is characterized by a rational delinquency oriented toward the pursuit of monetary objectives and exemplified by organized theft or the sale of drugs or other illicit goods or services. Delinquency of this type is most likely to emerge in lower-class neighborhoods in which a stable adult criminal world exists and in which the criminal and conformist sectors of the community are highly integrated. When such integration exists, the "cop on the beat" is willing to look the other way and the "honest" storekeeper is occasionally willing to fence stolen goods. The presence of a stable adult criminal world provides a structure for recruitment and upward mobility for juveniles who view criminality in career terms.

While neighborhoods that give rise to the criminal pattern may be described as socially organized, we expect a different pattern to emerge from neighborhoods that are characterized by a high degree of social disorganization. Socially disorganized slums lack a stable adult criminal world and thus an established criminal structure. This situation may be doubly frustrating for neighborhood youths who have already experienced the disparity between legitimate goals and legitimate opportunities. Moreover, as Shaw and McKay (1942) pointed out, these areas lack the social controls that work to contain the behavioral manifestations of this frustration. For these reasons, Cloward and Ohlin (1990) discerned in socially disorganized areas a **conflict pattern** of delinquency. The conflict pattern is characterized by gangs who express their frustration fighting over contested neighborhood turf.

Finally, Cloward and Ohlin maintained, it is unwise to assume that everyone who engages in criminal or conflict opportunities will be successful. We are not all cut out to be drug dealers or gang warriors. Cloward and Ohlin use the term *double-failures* to describe people who are unable to succeed through either legitimate or illegitimate means. Double-failures tend to become involved in a **retreatist pattern** in which delinquency is organized around the consumption of drugs.

RECENT VERSIONS OF THE STRAIN ARGUMENT

A GENERAL STRAIN THEORY

While strain theory is no longer a dominant view in criminology, there has recently been a revival of interest in the perspective. Agnew (1992), for instance, has recently proposed a **general strain theory** which extends the logic of the argument well beyond that originally proposed by Merton. According to Agnew, strain theory focuses on negative relationships with others. Negative relationships are those in which individuals are not treated the way they would like to be treated; such relationships promote anger, fear, and frustration, which may lead to delinquency.

With specific reference to juvenile offending, Agnew argues that there are three major types of strain. The first type results when we believe that others are preventing us or threatening to prevent us from achieving what we want to achieve. This type is most familiar because it is very similar to the type of strain described by Merton. The second type of strain results when we believe that others have removed or are threatening to remove what we already possess and what we value. This might include the loss of a boyfriend/girlfriend, a move out of one's neighborhood, or the death of a parent. The third type of strain results when our relationships with others cause us to experience negative life events. These might include negative relationships with teachers, abuse by parents, or bullying by peers.

As individuals attempt to cope with the negative emotions that these relationships cause them to experience, they may explore delinquent solutions. Depending on the type of strain being experienced, drug use may be a means of escape, violence may be a way to get even, or theft may allow one to acquire material goods that are not otherwise available. A test of the general strain theory (Agnew and White, 1992) found that the various types of strain had a significant effect on delinquency and that the effects were most important for adolescents who lacked self-efficacy and who had delinquent friends.

CRIME AND THE AMERICAN DREAM

Even more recently, Messner and Rosenfeld (1994) have elaborated Merton's argument in order to provide an explanation of why the United States has such high rates of serious crime relative to other industrialized nations. Like Merton, they suggest that the root of the problem is the "American Dream," which they define as "a commitment to the goal of material success to be pursued by everyone in society under conditions of open, individual competition" (1994: 69). As a result of the widespread allegiance to the American Dream, many people adopt an "anything goes" mentality as they pursue their personal goals.

According to Messner and Rosenfeld, the problems created by the American Dream are magnified because the economy and the lessons that it teaches dominate other social institutions such as the family and the school. They note, for instance, how family activities and routines are required to conform to the schedules and rewards of the labor market and that, despite much rhetoric about "family values," it is the homeowner and not the homemaker who is admired and respected. In a similar way, the school is not a setting that produces model citizens but one that teaches competition for grades as students prepare for labor force participation.

This institutional balance of power, they argue, has two important consequences. First, it allows the competitive and individualistic message of the American Dream to diffuse to other settings. Second, because the lessons of the economy override the lessons taught in other institutional environments, the social control that we expect the school or the family to exert over criminal behavior is undermined. Both conditions are conducive to high rates of crime.

CULTURE AND CRIMINAL MOTIVATION

Another major approach locates the origins of criminal motivation in the cultural worlds to which offenders have exposure. The cultural milieu in which we are socialized provides us with our ideas about what is right and wrong, moral or immoral, appropriate or inappropriate. When our socialization is successful, we internalize these views and attempt to behave in ways that conform to the cultural standards that we have learned. It follows that, if we are exposed to beliefs and ideas that support behavior that the law defines as criminal, we may be more likely to behave in criminal fashion.

As with theories that locate the sources of criminal motivation in the stress-inducing nature of social arrangements, cultural accounts present a "normalized" picture of the offender. In other words, offenders are not necessarily pathological; they merely have learned a particular set of cultural lessons. Their behavior is normal within a particular cultural context.

NORM VIOLATION

As we pointed out in Chapter 1, crime finds its origins in **norm violation**, with norms defined as a set of culturally prescribed acceptable behaviors. Are there societies in which it is possible to find complete compliance with all norms? Is it possible to have a society that is free of norm violation? Over the years, utopian communities have been depicted in literature as constituting the earthly expression of a spiritually inspired way of life. B. F. Skinner (1948) raised the possibility of developing and applying social intervention programs, such as those based on social learning theories, to design societies in which individuals will not feel the need or the inclination to deviate. In Skinner's utopian world, the motivations, needs, and aspirations of individuals are conditioned through reinforcement schedules designed to promote prosocial, nondeviant behavior. Skinner argued that, in societies in which individual interests and abilities are properly assessed and managed, there will be no need for norm violation; in other words, the individual's socialization, intended to promote his or her self-interest, will have been programmed to coincide with the collective interests of the community.

The argument against the notion that we can be free of norm violation comes from the idea, promoted by Durkheim (1964), Becker (1963), and others, that societies are always subject to norm violation due to their inevitable tendency to create outsiders and insiders. It is in the rejection of marginal individuals or outcasts that norms become defined in a way that justifies the exclusion of outsiders. Further, through this process, the legitimation of the norms for those who consider themselves insiders is reinforced by the application of sanctions against norm violators.

A key question, then, becomes, Is it true that as social morality declines, crime increases? The popular view is that much of our social fabric has been heavily rent by the rapid changes resulting from urbanization, modernization, and immigration. The breakdown of traditional communities and extended families has led to a crisis of confidence in our conventional institutions—the family, the schools, the church, and so forth. From this viewpoint, the reduction in the influence of these organizations and the increased individualization in society has diminished adherence to prosocial values. The increase in rates of divorce, unemployment, transience, and so on is accompanied by an increase in the levels of crime. The difficulty with the notion of a shared morality is that it centers on the adherence to traditional values. Rather than the loss of traditional values or the transition to a new set of norms, it is the social disorganization itself that contributes to criminality (Durkheim, 1964).

Addressing this issue in a somewhat different way, we can ask, Is there a **universal form of crime**? Cross-cultural studies have shown that, while most societies condemn murder and incest, they do not always treat these behaviors as criminal (Douglas and Waskler, 1982; Schur, 1979). Sometimes an informal mechanism exists whereby such deviation comes to be sanctioned through civil action or through the social processes of expulsion from the group or shaming (Horowitz, 1990).

As far as other types of behavior are concerned, the myriad variations in the ways in which they

DOES IT EXIST?

A Universal Form of Crime

Beyond expulsion from the group and shaming, there are myriad variations in the ways in which behavior comes to be sanctioned. Cross-cultural studies have shown that, while most societies condemn murder and incest, they do not always treat these behaviors as criminal. These variations reflect very different types of morality and lawmaking across societies.

come to be sanctioned reflect very different types of morality and lawmaking across societies. Japan has been offered as a model of the kind of society that can attribute its low crime rate to certain cultural and social constraints. Yet one must approach this comparison with care, because a great deal of the behavior in Japanese society that is dealt with informally would, in our society, probably end up being dealt with by the criminal courts. What we find across societies, then, is not always a difference in behavior but rather a difference in the societal response to behavior.

DIFFERENTIAL ASSOCIATION

Cultural approaches focus not only on norm violation as criminal behavior but also on criminal behavior that is normative. One of the early pioneers of this perspective was Edwin Sutherland, who in the 1930s proposed a cultural theory of crime that he called the **theory of differential association.** Contrary to the prevailing wisdom of his day, Sutherland (1947) maintained that crime is a learned behavior. In the process of interacting with others, whose own views support criminal conduct, one person can learn to be criminal just as another can learn to be a mechanic, a stamp collector, or a lover of classical music. According to Sutherland, the differential rate at which people associate with the carriers of criminal values determines the differential rate at which they engage in criminal conduct.

BOX 3.3 THE TENETS OF DIFFERENTIAL ASSOCIATION THEORY

Edwin Sutherland was one of the few criminologists to formulate a theory of criminality in terms of an interrelated set of propositions. The following statements refer to the process by which a particular person comes to engage in criminal behavior:

1. *Criminal behavior is learned.* This means that criminal behavior is not inherited as such.
2. *Criminal behavior is learned in interaction with other persons in a process of communication.* In many respects, this communication is verbal, but it also includes the "communication of gestures."
3. *The principal learning of criminal behavior occurs within intimate personal groups.* This means that the impersonal agencies of communication, such as movies and newspapers, play a relatively unimportant part in the genesis of criminal behavior.
4. *When criminal behavior is learned, the learning includes (a) techniques of committing the crime, which are sometimes very complicated and sometimes very simple, and (b) the specific direction of motives, drives, rationalizations, and attitudes.*
5. *The specific direction of motives and drives is learned from definitions of the legal codes as favorable or unfavorable.* In some societies, individuals are surrounded by persons who invariably define the legal codes as rules to be

observed, while in others they are surrounded by persons whose definitions are favorable to the violation of the legal codes.

6. *A person becomes delinquent because of an excess of definitions favorable to violation of law over definitions unfavorable to violation of law.* This is the principle of differential association. It refers to both criminal and anticriminal associations and has to do with counteracting forces. When persons become criminal, they do so because of contact with criminal patterns and also because of isolation from anticriminal patterns.

7. *Differential associations may vary in frequency, duration, priority, and intensity.*

8. *The process of learning criminal behavior by association with criminal and anticriminal patterns involves all of the mechanisms that are involved in any other learning.* This means that the learning of criminal behavior is not restricted to the process of imitation. A person who is seduced, for instance, learns criminal behavior by association, but this process would not ordinarily be described as imitation.

9. *While criminal behavior is an expression of general needs and values, it is not explained by those general needs and values, since noncriminal behavior is an expression of the same needs and values.* Thieves generally steal in order to secure money, but honest laborers likewise work in order to secure money. The attempts by many scholars to explain criminal behavior by general drives and values—such as the happiness principle, the striving for social status, the money motive, or frustration—have been, and must continue to be, futile, since they explain lawful behavior as completely as they explain criminal behavior.

For Discussion

Can you think of ways in which people learn criminal behavior from others? Are there particular crimes that need specialized skills to be carried out successfully?

SOURCE: Based on E. H. Sutherland, *Principles of Criminology*, 4th ed. (Chicago: J. B. Lippincott, 1947).

For Sutherland, differential association involves two important types of learning. First, one must learn actual techniques of crime commission. In some cases, these techniques are very simple and do not differ markedly from law-abiding behavior. For example, stealing a car when the owner has left the keys inside is not so different from driving one's own car. In other cases, specialized skills are required—for instance, stealing a locked car when the keys have not been left inside.

Sutherland emphasized that knowledge or technical skills alone are insufficient to explain criminal behavior. Everyone has some idea of how to commit a wide variety of crimes. And yet, while most of us could figure out how to murder or assault someone, we refrain from committing such acts. In addition to technical knowledge, one must have exposure to the "specific direction of motives, drives, rationalizations and attitudes" (Sutherland, 1939: 6). Stated differently, to behave criminally, one must learn that crime is an acceptable type of behavior. These types of learning imply the existence of cultural knowledge and beliefs that promote criminality and to which only some of us have sustained exposure. Sutherland's approach has been particularly helpful in explaining why normally law-abiding individuals take up criminal activity in their work environments. According to Sutherland (1961), white-collar crime occurs because people have learned how to commit it and because they have learned from others that it is an acceptable form of behavior.

SUBCULTURAL EXPLANATIONS OF CRIMINAL MOTIVATIONS

In complex, highly differentiated societies like our own, cultural "pockets" exist when groups of people are engaged in intensive interaction and confront common problems or share common interests. It is in this sense that we speak of subcultures of heavy-metal music fans, marathon runners, or the police. Because participants in these worlds are also participants in the larger culture shared by the rest of us, such **subcultures** are both part of and distinguishable from the larger culture. It can be argued that subcultural involvement promotes criminal behavior when the subcultural values in question are inconsistent with the conformist values enshrined in law.

Earlier in this century, Thorsten Sellin (1938) suggested that the high rates of crime among immigrant groups can be understood with reference to the culture conflict that ethnic subcultures encounter. His view acknowledged that when people migrate from one country to another, they carry with them considerable cultural baggage. We recognize this fact when we visit a restaurant in Little Italy or attend a cultural festival in Chinatown. However, this cultural baggage may also include ways of acting that, although not considered criminal in the country of origin, are defined as such in the host country. By way of illustration, Sellin (1938) tells the story of a Sicilian father in New Jersey who "killed the sixteen-year-old seducer of his daughter, expressing surprise at his arrest since he had merely defended his family honor in a traditional way" (68).

Like Sellin, anthropologist Walter Miller (1958) attempted to understand how the cultural values of a particular group can increase the likelihood of criminal conduct. Miller studied lower-class life in a large Eastern city in an effort to identify the distinct character of lower-class culture. He was particularly interested in the ways in which this subculture might relate to the delinquencies of lower-class male youths. Miller argued that life in the lower class was organized around six **focal concerns:**

1. *Trouble.* Life is a series of troublesome episodes: trouble with the police, with the welfare officer, with one's neighbors, and so on.
2. *Toughness.* "Machismo" is widely prized in lower-class areas as an interactional style.
3. *Smartness.* Not intellectual ability, but the ability to live by one's wits is valued.

4. *Excitement*. Life is best described as boring and monotonous, punctuated occasionally by thrill-seeking behavior. Excitement might include bouts of drinking or fighting.

5. *Fate*. Life is largely seen in terms of good luck and bad luck.

6. *Autonomy*. There is a general desire to be free of the control of police, landlords, welfare workers, and others who might seek to regulate life.

For Miller, these focal concerns are themselves problematic because they suggest a value orientation that is at odds with the legal code. People who live their lives in terms of these focal concerns are likely, sooner or later, to end up in trouble with the law. However, for Miller, the problem is aggravated by the fact that the type of slum areas that he describes are environments in which gangs of male adolescents are likely to form. In these gangs, he suggested, the focal concerns of the lower class are exaggerated as youths attempt to model what they understand to be adult behavior. The result is a kind of overconformity to a value scheme that promotes behavior likely to invite legal sanction.

BOX 3.4 CHICAGO GANGLAND

In a comprehensive research effort, criminologists Carolyn Rebecca Block and Richard Block (1993) examined gang homicide data over a twenty-six-year period from 1965 through 1990 and detailed information on other gang-related crime from 1987 to 1990.

Although the researchers note that forty major street gangs exist in Chicago, they focused on the four largest and most criminally active of these gangs—the Black Gangster Disciples Nation, Latin Disciples, Latin Kings, and Vice Lords. Each of these gangs was responsible for at least a thousand police-recorded incidents from 1987 to 1990. Members of the BGDN and Vice Lords are almost all African-American men while the Latin Disciples and Latin Kings are predominantly Latino men.

The major findings of this research include the following:

- Chicago's largest street gangs can be identified with most of the city's street gang crime. These four street gangs (representing about 10 percent of all street gangs and 51 percent of the estimated number of all street gang members) accounted for 69 percent of police-recorded street-gang-motivated homicides from 1987 to 1990.

- Street gangs varied in the types of activities in which they were engaged. Some specialized in incidents of expressive violence while others focused on instrumental violence. For example, the Vice Lords and BGDN were much more involved in acts of instrumental violence (such as the possession or sale of drugs), while the Latin Disciples, Latin Kings, and smaller gangs specialized in acts of expressive violence (such as turf defense). Most of the criminal activity in smaller street gangs centered on representational turf defense. The most lethal street gang hot spots were along disputed boundaries between small street gangs.

- Types of street gang crime clustered in specific neighborhoods. Street gangs specializing in instrumental violence were strongest in disrupted and declining neighborhoods. Street gangs specializing in expressive violence were strongest and most violent in relatively prosperous neighborhoods with expanding populations.
- The rate of street-gang-motivated crime in the two most dangerous Chicago communities was seventy-six times that of the two safest. However, every community area in Chicago had at least one street-gang-motivated criminal incident between 1987 and 1990.
- Most of the lethal gang-related crimes occurred in neighborhoods where street gang activity centered on turf battles, not in neighborhoods where street gang activity focused on drug offenses. Of 288 street-gang-motivated homicides from 1987 to 1990, only 8 also involved drug use or a drug-related motive.

For Discussion

Of what theoretical relevance is the finding that gang crime is spatially concentrated within urban areas?

SOURCE: Based on C. R. Block and R. Block, *Street Gang Crime in Chicago* (Washington, DC: U.S. Department of Justice, 1993).

Other theorists have applied similar logic to explain patterns of homicide and assault. Noting that much interpersonal violence is concentrated socially (among young members of the urban underclass) or regionally (in, for instance, the South), they argue that offenders (and frequently their victims) may behave as they do because they are immersed in a **subculture of violence** (Gastil, 1971; Wolfgang and Ferracuti, 1967). This subcultural orientation, it is argued, requires that some kinds of transgressions be resolved in a violent fashion. The longstanding feud between the Hatfields and McCoys is a stereotypic example of the violent subculture.

Much assaultive violence seems to originate from what many would consider to be minor or trivial altercations. An exchange that begins with a stare, a jostle, or an insult may end with one of the parties seriously injured or dead. Such patterns only make sense, subcultural theorists maintain, when we recognize the underlying powerful cultural emphasis on social honor and the need to save face. Given this emphasis, a derogatory remark made in a public setting may be enough to provoke physical retaliation.

To argue that violence, in this sense, is subcultural is to argue that it is normative. In other

WHAT DOES IT MEAN?

Subculture of Violence

A powerful cultural emphasis on social honor and the need to save face when a threat to one's honor occurs in a public setting means that a derogatory remark made about one's character may be seen as sufficient reason to engage in physical battle. To argue that violence, in this sense, is subcultural is to argue that it is "normative."

Street gangs share common values and serve to support individual members' actions, sometimes including delinquent behavior.

words, the physical defense of one's honor is not merely what one *can* do but what one *must* do to retain the respect of other cultural participants. Because the violence is normative, the person who behaves violently is unlikely to feel a sense of shame or embarrassment for doing so.

We should note that, within the context of the subculture-of-violence argument, it is the particular cultural interpretation given to an affront to character, not the affront per se, that is the source of the violence. Precisely because the cultural environments differ, a sneer is less likely to provoke trouble in a university faculty club than it is in a lower-class bar.

A weakness of the subcultural approach is that it tends to infer rather than identify independently the difference between subcultural values and subcultural behaviors. Hagan (1985) suggests further that there is little empirical evidence to suggest that groups adhere to deviant subcultures in which violence is considered an integral part of the group's functioning. Instead, the violence is more likely a consequence of situational factors such as opportunity and circumstance rather than a specific group goal.

Is Mainstream Culture Criminogenic?

Subcultural arguments generally proceed from the assumption that it is useful to distinguish between a subculture that somehow promotes criminality and a conformist mainstream culture that is reflected in criminal law. Yet not all theorists who have examined the relationship between crime and culture share this assumption. Some have attempted to argue that the so-called conformist culture may itself promote criminal behavior.

For instance, an argument can be made that violence against women finds considerable support in broad patterns of cultural belief. For many feminist writers, sexual assault and wife abuse have less to do with the subcultural orientation of a deviant minority than with pervasive cultural representations of women in mass media entertainment or advertising. When "slasher" movies, television dramas, and sexually explicit, over-the-counter magazines and videos portray women as willing or deserving victims of violence, it is not surprising that the message will be picked up and acted on by some in the society.

In a similar vein, Coleman (1987) argues that the behavior of white-collar and corporate criminals is, to an important degree, promoted by a **culture of competition** that defines wealth and success as the central goals of human action. He argues that criminal action in the support of either profit margins and bottom lines or personal success clearly reflects the influence of pervasive cultural beliefs. "[The] fear of failure is the inevitable correlate of the demand for success, and together they provide a set of powerful symbolic structures that are central to the motivation of economic behavior" (Coleman, 1987: 417).

One of the most influential statements concerning the relationship between criminal behavior and mainstream culture was provided by David Matza and Gresham Sykes (1961). Their analysis of juvenile delinquency led them to conclude that much youthful crime is better said to reflect **subterranean values** rather than subcultural values. Subterranean values are not, as subcultural values are, part of the belief system of some identifiable criminal minority.

The Pinto was known to be unsafe to drive by those who built and sold it.

Instead, they are values that are held by many in society, although they may be in conflict with other cherished values.

Matza and Sykes suggest that, while many researchers have identified such values as "disdain for work" and "search for kicks and thrills" as subcultural values of delinquency, considerable evidence indicates that these value orientations are much more widely held. Middle-class conformists and juvenile delinquents may express their disdain for work or search for kicks in very different ways, but the value orientations held by both groups appear to have much in common. Anyone who has seen *Pulp Fiction, Natural Born Killers,* or similar blockbuster movies would be hard-pressed to make the case that violence does not have a wide cultural appeal.

According to Sykes and Matza (1957) the rules of conventional society are rarely as inflexible as subcultural theories make them out to be. In fact, those who learn the lessons of mainstream culture understand that, while criminal behavior is *usually* wrong, it is not *always* wrong. Conventional morality prohibits acting criminally, but it also provides us with reasons it is sometimes all right to do so. Matza and Sykes term these culturally derived justifications of criminal conduct **techniques of neutralization** and argue that, in a very real way, they make offending possible.

Sykes and Matza (1957) identify five such neutralization techniques that are used by juvenile offenders. First, by denying responsibility, offenders express their belief that their crimes result not from ill will but from circumstances and conditions beyond their control. Second, by denying injury, offenders claim that the crime does not in fact harm others. Third, by denying the victim, offenders accept responsibility for their actions and acknowledge the harmful consequences, but suggest that victims are to blame for what happens to them. Fourth, by condemning the condemners, offenders may counteract the negative evaluations that others make of them—that is, they reject those who reject them. Finally, by appealing to higher loyalties, offenders maintain that the actions in which they engage are necessary if obligations to family and peers are to be met.

The central point of the neutralization argument is that knowledge of techniques of neutralization precedes and makes possible involvement in criminal activity. From this perspective, people are able to break the law because they define the law as irrelevant to their own be-

---

WHAT DOES IT MEAN?

Techniques of Neutralization

First, through *denial of responsibility,* offenders express their belief that their crimes result not from ill will, but rather from circumstances and conditions beyond their control. Second, through *denial of injury,* offenders reject any claim that the crime results in harm to others. Third, through *denial of the victim,* offenders accept responsibility for their actions and acknowledge the harmful consequences, but suggest that victims are to blame for what happens to them. Fourth, through *condemnation of the condemners,* offenders may counteract the negative evaluations that others might make of them—that is, they reject those who reject them. Finally, through *the appeal to higher loyalties,* offenders maintain that the actions in which they engage are necessary if obligations to family and friends are to be met.

As a "subterranean value," the search for kicks and thrills may underlie much criminal conduct. This is not restricted to behavior by kids in the lower economic classes as shown by the vandalism at the end of a football game at Harvard Stadium.

havior. Techniques of neutralization are acquired as one gains knowledge of the cultural environment to which one is exposed. Through this process of redefinition, individuals come to view criminal acts as acceptable, and this gives them the freedom to commit such acts. The redefinition of vandalism as a "harmless prank," of assault as "getting even," or of theft as "borrowing" removes the moral inhibitions that might normally prohibit these behaviors.

Subsequent research has been unable to unequivocally support Sykes and Matza's claim that neutralization precedes rather than follows involvement in crime (Agnew and Peters, 1986; Hamlin, 1988). Recent work has attempted to account for the complexities involved in neutralization processes by arguing that neutralization is a "hardening process" (Minor, 1981). In other words, over time, criminal behavior and techniques of neutralization become mutually reinforcing, such that attempts at neutralization may both precede and follow criminal involvement. As a result, a commitment to both the behavior and the cultural definition of the behavior as acceptable intensifies. Thus, the employee who steals at work may define the pilfering as a legitimate substitute for unpaid overtime or, alternatively, as a harmless activity (given that the costs are covered by insurance). The behavior that these definitions reinforce may also be self-reinforcing over time as the commitment to the act and the morality of stealing develop in a mutually supportive fashion.

SUMMARY
■ ■ ■

What causes some people to behave in criminal fashion? is a question that reflects the influence of the positivist school of criminology, which views criminal behavior as the product of causal forces working within or upon the offender. Sociobiologists have argued that the constitution of some individuals, programmed through their genetic structure, makes them more likely to commit crime. Wilson and Herrnstein claim that one can detect certain physiological similarities among offenders. In their view, offenders' constitutional deficiencies lead them to discount the costs of crime through a process whereby immediate gratification becomes a paramount concern. Such discounting can also be the consequence of physiological episodes brought about by problems with diet, drugs, alcohol, and so on.

A strong sociological tradition in criminology emphasizes social conditions as a major influence on motivations to offend. This perspective views criminal behavior as the means by which people attempt to deal with the frustrations they face in day-to-day life. The frustrated ambitions of individuals who aspire to success goals but who lack the means to achieve them result in the anomie that leads to criminal innovation. According to Merton, criminogenic conditions reside in the gap between ambition and legitimate means.

This gap can widen as a result of the economic deprivation resulting from unemployment, particularly that which affects young people. Most crime is committed by individuals in the lower socioeconomic groups, and prisons are most likely to be filled with individuals from these groups. Some criminologists have argued, however, that this is the case not necessarily because these groups are more delinquent, but rather because they are easy targets for the police, who expend more effort on street crime than white-collar crime.

The focus on frustration led criminologists to focus attention on gang delinquency among working-class juveniles. For Cohen, much juvenile crime is rooted in the difficulties experienced by disadvantaged youths who aspire to middle-class status but are judged inadequate by a school system that assigns status rewards on the basis of middle-class criteria. Rejection of this value system, in Cohen's terms, may signal delinquency.

According to cultural theorists, the criminogenic conditions that influence individual behavior emerge from the milieu in which offenders operate. There is not necessarily anything pathological about offenders; they merely may have learned a particular set of cultural lessons that, in their case, teaches them how to act criminally. Their behavior, then, is normal within a particular cultural context and explicable given that they have been thrust outside of the normal operations of society. The same process that ostracizes offenders also serves to strengthen the bonds between insiders, as sanctions are applied against norm violators.

It is possible, then, to look at criminals as outsiders who are punished for failing to conform to the explicit norms of the dominant culture. It is also possible to look upon certain criminal behavior as normative. Sutherland's differential association theory proposes that crime is learned behavior. For Sutherland, the differential rates at which criminals associate with the carriers of criminal values determine the differential rates at which they engage in criminal conduct. This perspective allows us to account for the fact that certain cultural insiders, while adhering to the law in their personal lives, commit crimes in the context of their working lives.

The idea that there may be more than one set of values in society raises the possibility that mainstream culture is itself criminogenic. Matza and Sykes argue that those who learn the lessons of mainstream culture learn that criminal behavior is usually, but not always, wrong. Some acts can be rationalized or neutralized with explanations that find their basis in the tenets of mainstream society.

QUESTIONS FOR REVIEW AND DISCUSSION
■ ■ ■

1. What types of diet are more likely to make people criminal? Is the link between poor diet and criminality a direct one?
2. Can you think of exceptions to the body-typing predictions of different crimes that are not likely to be committed by people with particular body shapes?
3. Why do you think we pay so much attention to explanations of violent behavior that emphasize "psychopathology"?
4. How is crime learned from others?
5. Why do individuals need to neutralize their feelings about the victims of their crimes?

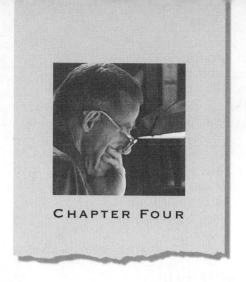

CHAPTER FOUR

Offending, Social Control, and the Law

WHAT'S IN CHAPTER FOUR

In this chapter, we will examine the ways in which informal and formal social controls influence criminal offending. Offenders may not require a distinct or unique motivation to commit crime. Rather, people may offend when social pressures that might prevent them from doing so are weak or absent. These pressures can derive from the influence of social bonds to others that restrict illegal behavior. This control may extend beyond family and friends to the community. It is here, through informal sanctions, such as shame and guilt, and through the deterrence that develops through the application of the law, that individuals are precluded from criminal behavior.

The theories discussed in the previous chapter would seem to suggest that since criminal behavior has unique characteristics, it requires unique motivations. However, by putting so much energy into trying to determine what unique types of social arrangements or cultural exposure drive crime, motivational theories risk losing sight of a basic question, namely, is motivation sufficient or necessary to explain offending? Just because individuals are moved or inclined to behave in a particular way, does this mean that they will? Motivational theories assume that it is the propensity, desire, or willingness to offend that separates offenders from nonoffenders.

Many theorists do not agree with this position, however. They argue that motivation to behave criminally is probably much more widespread than is actual criminal behavior. We can all think of occasions when lying, cheating, or stealing may have been the most effective way of achieving our goals. According to critics of motivational theories, what separates the offender from the nonoffender has less to do with the presence of motivation and more to do with the ability to act on this motivation. This position acknowledges that we are not always free to act in ways consistent with our motivations.

In this chapter, we examine approaches that focus on the ways in which informal and formal social controls influence criminal offending. The underlying significance of these perspectives is that criminal behavior may not require a distinct or unique criminal motivation. Instead, people may offend when the social pressures that might prevent them from doing so are weak or absent. Thus, criminal behavior is not so much the product of criminogenic forces as it is a rational choice made by individuals who feel no constraints about engaging in it. The emphasis on rationality, choice, and control reflects the legacy of the classical school of thought.

SOCIAL TIES AND CONFORMITY

SOCIAL CONTROLS AND THE INDIVIDUAL

It has been argued that **informal social controls** in the form of relationships that people share with others who support and promote the values of conformity are an important source of social control. Many theorists have argued, for instance, that the strength and quality of social ties that link juveniles to their (conformist) teachers, parents, and peers discourage involvement in delinquency. Strong ties to parents, for instance, make possible effective adult monitoring and supervision of juvenile leisure activity (Gottfredson and Hirschi, 1990; Wells and Rankin, 1988, 1991). Parent–child relationships characterized by caring, trust, and intimate communication offer support to adolescents who may be contemplating delinquent reactions to the problems that face them (Patterson and Dishion, 1985).

The criminologist Walter Reckless (1967) developed **containment theory** in order to try to explain how, even in areas characterized by high rates of delinquency, many youths seem to be so law-abiding. Like many of the theorists discussed in the previous chapter, Reckless recognized that many factors can "pull" and "push" people into crime—for example, they can be pulled into crime by the attraction of what they see as "easy money," or pushed by the frustration resulting from blocked opportunity. However, what interested Reckless was the fact that many more youths seem to experience these motivational pushes and pulls than engage in delinquent conduct.

Using the logic of **control theory** Reckless reasoned that youth are insulated from delinquency by **"inner"** and **"outer" containments** that constrain nonconformist behavior. *Outer containments* are those aspects of the individual's social environment that help to ensure that delinquent behavior does not occur. Most importantly, these might include the relationships with family members and the members of other primary groups. These groups set standards for individuals, teach and reinforce appropriate conduct, and provide a sense of belonging. *Inner containments* are those elements that are part of the individual's psychic makeup; for Reckless, these containments were the more important of the two. Inner containments represent the products of effective socialization and the successful internalization of rules regarding acceptable behavior. The most important element of inner containment, according to Reckless, is self-concept. Within this perspective, a "good" self-concept implies an ability to tolerate frustration, a strong sense of responsibility, and a clear orientation toward future goals. Most importantly, the containment value of self-concept implies an ability to think of one's self as a "law-abiding person." Such a view of self may prove to be an effective buffer against pressures to deviate.

WHAT ARE THEY?

Inner and Outer Containments

Inner containments represent the products of effective socialization and the successful internalization of rules regarding acceptable behavior. Outer containments are those aspects of the individual's social environment that help to ensure that delinquent behavior does not occur.

WHAT DOES IT INCLUDE?

Theory of the Bond

The first strand, *attachment*, refers to the degree to which children are sensitive to the expectations of parents or teachers. The second strand, *commitment*, refers to the size of the investment of time and energy that a youth has made to a conventional activity such as getting good grades. The third strand, *involvement*, refers to participation in the world of conformity such that little time is left for delinquency. The fourth strand, *belief*, refers to the degree to which youths believe that the conformist values of parents and teachers are worthy of respect.

THEORY OF THE BOND

The most influential statement of the relationship between social ties and social control is Travis Hirschi's **theory of the bond.** Hirschi (1969) argued that the causes of juvenile delinquency are not to be located in some type of unique delinquent motivation, but rather in the weakness of the **social bond** that links delinquent adults to the world of conformist others. Weak bonds allow individuals to formulate behavioral intentions that reflect narrow self-interest. Lying, cheating, and stealing are frequently the outcome.

For Hirschi, the bond to conformist society is composed of four distinct strands. The first strand, **attachment**, refers to the degree to which children are sensitive to the expectations of parents or teachers. Sensitivity to expectations means that the potential reactions of conformist others must be taken into account when delinquency is contemplated. If a youth cares about the views of parents or teachers, delinquency is defined as a less attractive option.

The second strand, **commitment**, refers to the amount of time and energy youths invest in a conventional activity such as obtaining good grades. The greater the investment, the less likely juveniles are to engage in behavior that jeopardizes it.

The third strand, **involvement**, refers to participation in the world of conformity—jobs to be done, projects to be undertaken, goals to be achieved, and deadlines to be met. In short, involvement in the world of conformity leaves little time for involvement in delinquency. This strand reminds us of the old adage that "idle hands are the devil's workshop."

The fourth strand is **belief**. In Hirschi's view, one need not argue, as subcultural theorists do, that delinquents are committed to a set of distinctly delinquent values. Instead, one need only argue that juveniles differ in the extent to which they believe that the conformist values of parents, teachers, or others are worthy of respect.

According to control theorists, bonds to conventional society are formed early in life.

Strong social bonds—defined by Hirschi as high levels of attachment, commitment, involvement, and belief—insulate youths against delinquent involvement. In order to explain why some youths are delinquent while others are not, we need to focus on the weakness of delinquents' bonds rather than on the factors that motivate them to behave in criminal fashion.

GENERAL THEORY OF CRIME

More recently, Travis Hirschi has elaborated his view of the relationship between social ties and delinquency and, in collaboration with Michael R. Gottfredson (1990), has proposed a **general theory of crime** applicable to all forms of crime including white-collar and organized crime. Unlike some other theorists, they argue that it is unnecessary to offer distinct explanations for distinct types of criminal conduct. This is because, despite their differences, crimes of many sorts may be defined as "acts of force or fraud undertaken in pursuit of self-interest" (Gottfredson and Hirschi, 1990: 15).

Moreover, they suggest that the acts we call crimes share many common elements:

- They provide immediate gratification of desires.
- They are exciting, risky, or thrilling.
- They provide few or meager long-term benefits.
- They require little skill or planning.
- They result in pain or discomfort for the victim.

In short, they argue, crime as a type of activity appeals to people who are impulsive, short-sighted, physical, risk-taking, and nonverbal. As pointed out in Chapter 3, Gottfredson and Hirschi use the term *low self-control* to describe this propensity and maintain that people who are attracted to crime will also be attracted to other activities (such as alcohol or drug use) that share similar elements.

What are the sources of low self-control? For Gottfredson and Hirschi, it originates in child-rearing. Child-rearing that is effective in discouraging delinquency requires that parents (1) monitor their child's activity, (2) recognize deviant behavior when it occurs, and (3) punish such behavior when it does occur. Low self-control results when this process goes awry. Parents may not care what their children do, or, even if they are concerned, they may be unable to supervise their children effectively or to punish the offending behavior.

For Gottfredson and Hirschi, low self-control is the key cause of criminality. As such, it explains why some people rather than others are likely to behave in criminal fashion. They recognize, however, the need to distinguish between criminality as a propensity and crime as a social event. Crimes occur when individuals with low self-control encounter situations and opportunities conducive to offending.

POWER CONTROL THEORY

Power control theory, which was developed by John Hagan, Ron Gillis, and John Simpson (Hagan, 1989; Hagan, Gillis, and Simpson, 1979, 1987, 1988), provides another example of the ways in which family relationships permit or discourage delinquency. Of central interest to these writers is the fact that males are much more delinquent than females. Hagan, Gillis, and Simpson attempt to explain this fact in terms of the differential ability of the family to control male and female children.

Power control theory argues that social control is stratified within the family setting. In traditional patriarchal families, which accept a cultural claim to male dominance, girls are subject to greater control than boys. In addition, mothers are assigned a greater responsibility for the control of dependent children. Two important implications follow from this position. First, the informal social control processes in which family members are involved affect female more than male family members. Mothers are more likely to be the subjects and daughters are more likely to be the objects of this control. Second, as a result of these differences, male children are considerably freer than female children to engage in a wide range of risk-taking behavior, some of which involves delinquency.

INTERACTIONAL THEORY

Terence Thornberry (1987; Thornberry et al., 1991) and colleagues have proposed an **interactional theory of delinquency** that has at its core assumptions derived from control theory. However, Thornberry attempts to link the logic of control theory to the insights derived from arguments stressing the role of cultural learning and peer influence. Like Hirschi, Thornberry argues that adolescents are at risk of engaging in delinquent behavior when they have low levels of attachment to parents, commitment to school, and belief in conventional institutions and people. Thornberry emphasizes that the weakness of the ties to conventional others does not make delinquency inevitable although it does make it more likely.

Further, Thornberry argues, it is too simplistic to assume (as many theorists seem to do) that social ties to the world of conformity are unchanging. On the contrary, they may strengthen or weaken over time in response to changing circumstances. Most notably, while weak social bonds to parents or teachers may make delinquency possible, delinquency that has already occurred may further affect these relationships. Consider the example of a youth whose weak bond to parents contributes to his or her engagement in delinquent activities. When the parents learn about the delinquency, they may react by rejecting the youth or by subjecting him or her to severe punishment. Such reactions may further undermine the relationship between child and parents, thus making delinquency an even greater possibility. In terms of illuminating the criminal event, the real strength of Thornberry's argument is that it attempts to come to terms with the dynamic and fluid character of criminality.

LIFE COURSE PERSPECTIVE

Another version of social control that pays explicit attention to change over time is the **life course perspective** formulated by Robert Sampson and John Laub (1990). These writers were interested in attempting to reconcile two contradictory sets of research findings. On the one hand, a body of research indicates that adult criminality is very strongly influenced by patterns of childhood behavior (Wilson and Herrnstein, 1985). This research suggests that because people embark on criminal paths long before adulthood, the characteristics of adults' social roles (such as unemployment) are largely irrelevant as causes of crime. On the other hand, another body of research indicates that changes in people's lives (like getting or losing a job, or getting married or having children) affect the likelihood of involvement in crime. Sampson and Laub argue that because most criminological attention is focused on the study of teenagers, researchers have not really examined how the propensity to crime does in fact change or remain stable over the life course.

Their life course perspective makes an important distinction between "trajectories" and "transitions." *Trajectories* describe the pathways on which people are located or the directions in which their lives seem to be moving. *Transitions*, however, are specific life events—like a first job or a marriage or the birth of a child—that might or might not serve to alter the trajectories. For example, a juvenile who is actively involved with delinquent peers, who lives in an abusive home, and who is failing at school might be on a criminal trajectory. However, suppose in the later teen years, the individual begins a romantic relationship with someone who is nurturing and supportive, and the two decide to get married and raise a family. After the individual develops a deep commitment to the relationship and begins to plan for and think about the future, the involvement in crime is diminished. In the life course framework, we would see the marriage as a transition that altered the individual's criminal trajectory.

For Sampson and Laub, trajectories change when transitions alter the nature and number of social bonds that help to ensure conformity. However, they argue that it is not simply the occurrence of particular life events that is likely to bring these changes about. Rather, it is the "social investment" in the institutional relationship that dictates the salience of informal social control.

SOCIAL CONTROLS AND THE COMMUNITY

Other theorists have speculated about the roles played by informal social control at the level of the local community or the neighborhood. According to Wirth (1938), the larger, the more densely populated, and the more heterogeneous a community, the more accentuated are the characteristics associated with urbanism, including isolation and social breakdown. Urbanism brings together individuals who have no sentimental or emotional ties to one another. From this emerges a spirit of competition, aggrandizement, and exploitation. To counteract this spirit, society reverts to formal controls.

People who are in frequent social contact with strangers and acquaintances also develop a reserve toward one another. The strong family and friendship ties necessary for intimate communities disappear in cities, and the result is higher levels of alienation, anomie, and delinquency. To prove the point, Wirth points out that crime rates in urban areas are higher than those in rural areas, where the informal social controls between intimates still operate.

If some urban neighborhoods more effectively constrain the delinquent inclinations of youths, then we might be able to explain why some parts of the city have higher rates of delinquency than do others. Theoretical arguments of this type were originally proposed by Clifford Shaw and Henry McKay, two sociologists associated with the University of Chicago. Shaw and McKay (1942) were interested in trying to understand why some parts of the city of Chicago had consistently high rates of crime, delinquency, and other social problems. What intrigued them was the fact that rates of delinquency remained high even when the resident population, identified at any given point in time, moved out or died and were replaced by new groups of urban residents. In other words, regardless of changes in the ethnic or demographic mix of the population residing within an area, rates of delinquency were relatively constant. For Shaw and McKay, urban variations in rates of crime are associated with the social context of urban areas rather than with the specific characteristics of the populations who live there.

According to Shaw and McKay, high-crime areas are characterized by a high degree of **social disorganization**, which may be defined as an inability on the part of area residents to achieve their common values or solve their common problems (Kornhauser, 1978). Shaw and McKay argued that areas characterized by a high level of social disorganization tend to be economically disadvantaged, to have a high rate of population turnover, and to be racially and ethnically diverse. In such areas, the informal social controls that might be expected to constrain delinquency are ineffective. As predicted by Wirth (1938), local friendship networks are less likely to develop and the level of participation in formal or voluntary organizations is low. As a result, adults in these communities may be ineffective in their attempts to supervise or control teenage peer groups that are likely to become involved in delinquency (Sampson and Groves, 1989).

We see the logic of the social disorganization argument manifested in many forms of crime prevention that attempt to re-create a sense of community in high-crime neighborhoods. Neighborhood Watch and similar programs seek to increase the level of interaction among residents and at the same time encourage them to develop a sense of responsibility for their neighbors.

Fischer (1976) argues that the city is not as disorienting—and its inhabitants not as vulnerable to social breakdown—as Wirth maintained. He points out that urban environments actually provide more opportunities for social support than do rural areas and that the ties extend beyond the boundaries of neighborhoods to stretch across the city.

According to Krohn, Lanza-Kaduce, and Akers (1984), Wirth's view of cities reflects the claim that deviant behavior results from the weakening or severing of one or more of the social bonds (Hirschi, 1969). This perspective is consistent with the arguments put forward by control theorists. Fischer's portrayal of an integrated but highly diverse urban setting offers a different view, one that emphasizes that learning deviant behavior results from (differential) association with people who provide models, definitions, and reinforcements for such behavior (Krohn, Lanza-Kaduce, and Akers, 1984: 355).

Krohn, Lanza-Kaduce, and Akers speculate that the differences in explanation provided by Wirth and Fischer revolve around the quality of the primary relationships across communities. Wellman and Leighton (1979) argue that modern cities have replaced intimate, spatially bounded communities with "liberated" communities (that is, networks of friends and acquaintances who live outside of the individuals' neighborhoods). Despite the view that the neighborhood is not essential to social support, neighborhoods that have a high degree of interaction are more likely to control crime informally through the residents' collective ability to respond to violations of the law and/or neighborhood norms (Unger and Wandersman, 1985: 143). This informal control depends, however, on the neighborhood having a consensus on values or norms, the ability to monitor behavior, and a willingness to intervene when necessary. These characteristics are generally absent in urban neighborhoods where crime is high.

While interpersonal conflict is a pervasive and inevitable feature of social life (Kennedy, 1990), most conflicts are resolved in a peaceful fashion. We might avoid the conflicting parties, give in to the demands that they make, report them to the police, or sue them. Horowitz (1990) points out that the law does not respond to all grievances in the same way. A teenager who complains that his elderly neighbors have been playing their Zamfir records too loudly will probably receive a cooler reception from the police than the elderly neighbor who complains about the volume of the teenager's Megadeth music. Similarly, argue conflict theorists, poor and minority communities are less effectively policed than are more middle-class neighborhoods, and behavior that would not be tolerated in higher-status areas is considered "normal" in areas characterized by greater social or economic disadvantage. These observations imply that teenagers or those who are socially disadvantaged may be more likely to engage in violent or other criminal forms of conflict expression. Where it is applied, the formal response through police intervention has been referred to as an "overreach" of the law, the implication being that a low tolerance is exhibited for behaviors that could be handled more effectively through informal sanctions (Morris and Hawkins, 1970).

The incidence of crime may also depend on interethnic and interracial relationships that develop in areas where groups with different backgrounds come together. The confusion and misunderstandings that arise from differences in family practice and cultural values can lead to tensions and conflicts, which can develop into criminal behavior along the lines proposed by Sellin (1938). Research by Smith (1982) suggests that many people use ethnic stereotyping as a pragmatic means of managing the dangers of urban life. These informal strategies usually entail setting up social and physical distances in order to avoid potentially harmful encounters. The avoidance of certain areas is a common strategy for coping with crime in urban centers.

In addition, Suttles (1972) found that, particularly in ethnic communities, boundaries are set by public displays of territorial marking (for example, threatened gang fights). These boundaries indicate, through spatial mechanisms, "with whom it is safe to associate" (Suttles, 1972: 161). The marking of territory plays a role in reducing neighborhood conflict by excluding those who are considered to be different or undesirable. Conflict with people outside of the neighborhood takes on a symbolic character of protectiveness of the turf.

In disorganized areas, people are less likely to know their neighbors or to be interested in their welfare. The high level of cultural distance between different groups inhabiting the area and the rapid turnover of population mitigates against the development of a strong sense of community spirit. It is more difficult to monitor the behavior of others in the neighborhood when we do not recognize them and thus do not know whether they have a right to be there

(Stark, 1987). Under such circumstances, we are not only less likely to fail to recognize people but also less likely to recognize their property; thus, stolen property that is carried around the neighborhood by a stranger, or even by someone we know, is unlikely to be identified (Felson, 1986). In contrast, in small, tightly knit communities in which the residents know one another both culturally and personally, we expect that informal community control will operate more effectively.

Areas high in social disorganization are characterized by many forms of disorder. Disorganization can be countered by programs that seek to control deviant behavior by involving the community.

Many of the social institutions that might be expected to control the behavior of youthful offenders are also less effective in socially disorganized areas. Formal social controls in the form of churches and schools, for instance, may not enjoy a high level of community support, in which case their social control functions may be undermined (Stark, 1987). In well-integrated areas, we might expect that community organizations will form in response to the problem of local crime or delinquency. However, when the level of social disorganization is high, voluntary groups formed to address community problems are less likely to develop.

In a recent restatement of the social disorganization perspective, Bursik and Grasmick (1993) distinguish three types of social controls that are rendered less effective in areas characterized by high levels of social disorganization. The first type of control functions at the "private" level. These are the types of controls that are associated with the family, the friendship group, or other groups with which one has an intimate association. The second type is "parochial" control and represents the effects of broader patterns of interpersonal association. Such controls are exerted by local schools, stores, churches, or voluntary organizations. The third type is "public" or external control. This refers to the ability of the local community to mobilize sources of control that originate beyond its boundaries. Local communities will not be equally successful in their attempts to get the urban bureaucracy to allocate funds to neighborhood projects or to get the police to take neighborhood problems seriously.

Bursik and Grasmick argue that when such controls are operating, they discourage crime by discouraging both criminal motivation and the opportunities for crime. They also note that these controls do not emerge instantaneously. Instead, they emerge slowly as residents associate with one another and establish relationships over time. Factors that contribute to residential instability undermine the processes that lead to effective community controls and therefore make higher rates of crime and delinquency more likely.

THE POWER OF LAW: THE DETERRENCE DOCTRINE

SPECIFIC AND GENERAL DETERRENCE

Laws threaten penalties for their violation, and deterrence theories are concerned with the ways in which these threats are communicated to potential offenders. More specifically, deterrence theories attempt to determine how the reaction to the threat of penalties decreases the likelihood of offending. **Specific or special deterrence** refers to the ways in which individuals are deterred, through punishment, from offending or re-offending. For example, suppose you break into a house, are apprehended, and then are sentenced to prison for a period of time. If the prison term discourages you from committing another such crime, we might say that it is a special deterrent. According to the principle of **general deterrence**, individuals are deterred from breaking the law when they see others who have done so receive punishment. Thus, in our house-breaking example, friends who witness the punishment that you receive for having broken the law will desist from breaking and entering.

The success of specific and general deterrence is based on three properties of legal threats. The first such property is the **severity** of the penalty. Does the law threaten prison or a fine? Are offenders likely to be sentenced if they are caught, or are they likely to be released with a warning? The criminal code clearly states the punishment attached to each crime, and sentencing guidelines are set for judges to apply in the cases that come before them.

It is assumed that all individuals in society are aware of the law's prescriptions about punishment and are deterred in direct proportion to the escalating threat of this punishment. Thus, it should be widely understood that the most severe punishments are reserved for the most serious crimes. For example, the death penalty is reserved solely for the crime of homicide, and only for certain severe types of homicide at that. Theft and other property crimes are punished less severely, and again, within the category of theft, harsher sentences are reserved for more serious crimes (generally measured according to the specific dollar value of the stolen property). Sentencing guidelines on both the state and federal level may change fairly often, presumably reflecting changes in our sense of the seriousness of various offenses.

> **WHAT DOES IT MEAN?**
>
> ### *Specific vs. General Deterrence*
>
> Specific deterrence refers to the ways in which individuals are deterred from offending or re-offending by receiving punishment. In the case of general deterrence, individuals who see offenders receiving punishment will be deterred from breaking the law themselves.

The second property of legal threats is the **certainty** of punishment. Regardless of what the law threatens, how likely is it that an offender will be apprehended and sentenced? A large number of research studies have argued that, with respect to possible deterrent effects, certainty is a more important characteristic of legal penalties than is severity. In other words, a high likelihood of being punished is more important than being punished in a specified manner.

Certainty of apprehension and conviction is clearly influenced by factors that relate to the reporting of crime. As we saw in Chapter 1, the majority of the crimes that are known to the police were brought to their attention by the public. For various reasons, however, many crimes go unreported. Further, many crimes that *are* reported remain unsolved. In both cases, the offender "gets away" with the crime. The rational offender calculates the certainty of risk and then acts on this calculation: When risk of apprehension and conviction is high, the crime is less likely to occur.

The third property of legal threats is the **celerity (swiftness)** of punishment (Clark, 1988). When justice is delayed, there may be a perception either that the punishment is unfair or that it will have a diminished impact on the offender. Concern has also been raised that delayed justice may unfairly stigmatize an individual who is in fact innocent. Court backlogs that lead to delays of a year or more in hearing cases have led some to argue that the cases should be dismissed without the determination of guilt or innocence. The message conveyed by such dismissals would be that the criminal justice system is unable to handle cases swiftly and that this circumstance casts doubts on the likelihood of them handling them at all.

LEGAL VS. INFORMAL SANCTIONS

Some researchers suggest that, in emphasizing the importance of penalty characteristics, deterrence theories have adopted too narrow a view of how legal threats discourage crime. Williams and Hawkins (1986) assert that the deterrent effects of legal sanctions may be supplemented by at least three types of sanctions: (1) commitment costs, (2) attachment costs, and (3) stigma of arrest.

Commitment costs refer to the possibility that arrest may jeopardize people's investments in some legitimate activity. The greater a person's investment in some conformist line of activity, the more he or she will be discouraged from offending by a belief that arrest might threaten that investment. Commitment costs may include concerns about future employment or educational prospects. **Attachment costs** refer to the costs associated with the loss of valued relationships with friends or family members. The belief that arrest will weaken these ties may make arrest a fearsome prospect. Finally, the **stigma of arrest** relates to the belief that apprehension by the police may harm one's reputation. It is important to distinguish this fear that others will learn about one's arrest from the fear that they will learn that one has committed the act. Williams and Hawkins point out, for example, that a lower stigma generally is associated with driving while impaired than with being arrested for this action. In the case of homicide, however, the stigma associated with arrest for the act may not be much greater than the stigma associated with the commission of the act. In general, Williams and Hawkins argue that because attachment costs, commitment costs, and the stigma of arrest are forms of informal social control that are activated by formal controls, they should be viewed as part of the deterrence process.

An illustration of how this mix of legal and informal sanctions can work is provided by recent research on the contribution of arrest to the reduction of repeat wife assault. Dutton and colleagues (1992) examined data that compared results from a general population sample with those from a group of arrested and convicted wife assaulters who were undergoing treatment in a court-mandated program. Respondents were asked to express their views of the likelihood (certainty) of specific legal and social sanctions, assuming they were to assault their wives. They were also asked to judge the severity of the punishment that would follow such an assault. Police arrest was among the legal sanctions offered. The social sanctions included police being called, the partner leaving the relationship, disapproval of friends and family, and loss of self-respect.

The arrested assaulters reported a greater degree of confidence than those in the general samples that an arrest would occur if an assault took place. Interestingly, the general and treatment samples had similar responses to the question relating to the loss of self-respect. In terms of severity of punishment, the two samples were high with respect to all factors. Thus, deterrence appears to be a function not only of the arrest but also of the social consequence of the arrest.

To test this theory further, responses made by assaulters before they entered the treatment program were compared with those made at the end of the treatment about a year later. Not only was there an increase in the perceived severity of arrest and conviction, but it was accompanied by a substantial increase in the judgment of the perceived severity of losing one's partner or facing social disapproval. Disclosure of these events, which are often kept private, can "be a first step toward generating informal sanctions from friends and family toward the assaultive male and an empowering support network for the victim. Because arrest makes disclosure more likely, that informal side effect of arrest could serve to reduce recidivism" (Dutton et al., 1992: 124). Here we have a case of legal sanction (arrest) and informal sanction (social disapproval) working together to increase deterrence.

Arguments about the deterrent properties of legal sanctions do not assume that potential offenders are accurately informed about the risks they face. How accurate their perceptions are is itself an empirical question of considerable scope (Henshel and Silverman, 1975). We can suggest, however, that, in terms of whether an individual will offend, what the law actually threatens is less significant than what people *believe* the law threatens.

SITUATIONAL DETERRENCE

Criminologist Maurice Cusson (1993) has criticized deterrence theory and research for its failure to address the specific character of the situations in which crimes occur. A typical research project might ask respondents to indicate how likely it is that they will be apprehended if they attempt to steal a car. Too often, however, the context of the automobile theft is not specified. Obviously, how risky one perceives car theft to be depends greatly on the specific circumstances under which the theft is attempted. Although study respondents may make certain assumptions in order to provide an answer to the researcher's question, the answers may have little to do with the actual assessment of risks that an individual makes in any specific situation.

In addition, Cusson notes, while researchers ask survey subjects to calmly assess the risks of apprehension, this research ignores the emotional character of the deterrence process. Deterrence, he argues, is not about the cold and rational calculation of risks but about fear. A burglar who breaks into a house may rationally believe that the chances of getting caught are low but may panic when he hears a noise. Fear can override rational calculation and make the deterrence process look quite different in reality than it appears in theory. For these reasons, Cusson suggests the need to consider deterrence as a situational factor. **Situational deterrence** emphasizes the ways in which the offender's fear of apprehension is related to the specific circumstances of the criminal event.

According to Cusson, potential offenders face two types of danger in the precriminal situation. The first type is immediate: The robber worries that the victim may fight back or be armed while the burglar worries that a barking dog might bite. The second type of danger refers to subsequent harm that is signaled by some element in the precriminal situation. Thus, the television monitor in the convenience store about to be robbed does not threaten the robber directly but may eventually if it leads to the robber's apprehension.

Cusson notes that the risks facing offenders prior to or during the commission of the offense do not guarantee that the offender will be deterred. Offenders differ in terms of the level of courage that they can muster in particular situations and also in terms of their ability to manage the fear they do experience. In addition, some crimes (such as joyriding or vandalism) may be more attractive precisely because they involve an element of danger.

The value of Cusson's analysis is that it forces us to recognize that deterrence effects are not embodied solely in abstract legal threats but also in the risks that offenders understand themselves to be facing in the settings in which criminal events actually occur.

AMBIVALENCE ABOUT CRIME AND DETERRENCE STRATEGIES

Clearly, deterrence arguments figure quite prominently in many public policy debates. Despite the perception that there is widespread consensus over the need to crack down on crime, public attitudes toward crime and its prevention suggest a strong degree of **ambivalence**, which has many sources. First, the public is concerned that the law is not adequately enforced (Currie, 1985). Research suggests that the public feels that the law generally reflects their values (Tyler, 1990) and that they obey the law because they believe it to be right. At the same time, however, they are critical of the way in which justice is currently being dispensed. Many believe that the law favors the rich and the powerful and that the legal process is too slow. The system as a whole is seen as ineffective in deterring serious crime, particularly in terms of the punishment that is administered (Brillon, 1985).

There is no consensus in the research literature, however, concerning the effectiveness of punishment in reducing criminal behavior. Cook (1977) concludes from his review of the research on deterrent effects (including the impact of capital punishment on the eradication of violent crime) that little persuasive evidence has been produced concerning the size, or even the existence, of the deterrence mechanism. The lack of strong support in the research literature undermines proposals for strict punishment regimens, especially if they are contrary to our views of what is humane and just.

Second, as Braithwaite (1989) points out, confusion develops over what is perceived as a conflict between crime control and respect for civil liberties. Some express concern that too much informal social control impedes individual freedom—neighbors spying on neighbors can be a real threat to personal privacy. However, punishment delivered by formal agents without the shaming that comes from informal social sanctions is ineffective. If the risk of arrest is perceived as low and the severity of punishment minimal, individuals may still be prevented from committing a crime by the stigmatizing reactions of others for being involved in crime.

A third problem that contributes to ambivalence about crime is the lack of consensus over the viability of expensive and seemingly ineffective incarceration (Miller and Anderson, 1986). At the same time, we are uncomfortable with leaving reintegration to the community. Few communities are ready to receive criminals as they begin their transition to "normal" life. In fact, there have been recent efforts by some communities to actively block the return of released offenders, particularly those who were imprisoned for sex offenses. While offenders need to be reintegrated into society and kept from reoffending, there is limited effort by communities to take this job over from formal agencies.

A fourth and final factor contributing to the ambivalence about crime is the general awe with which we regard it. While the reality of violent criminality is usually horrific, its depiction in the media is titillating, thrilling, and addictive. Promoting prosocial behavior in a society in which criminals are often depicted as folk heroes is no easy task (Phelps, 1983). While Skipper (1985) suggests that the folk hero syndrome is on the decline, there still exists in our society a residual belief that the criminal should be admired for expressing some degree of resistance to convention.

North American ambivalence about the application of deterrence strategies is in sharp contrast to the Chinese government's actions subsequent to the army's move to destroy the "democracy movement" through the Tiananmen Square massacre in June of 1989. The show trials and rapid executions gave witness to the ferocity of Chinese justice, and yet they conformed very neatly to the principles outlined in the deterrence doctrine: that there be quick, certain, and severe punishment that incapacitates the offender and discourages others from following the same route.

What is interesting about the Chinese experience is that the democracy movement flourished at all, given the knowledge that draconian steps almost certainly would be used to effect its downfall. This fact underlines the role of the offender's perception about the nature of the crime being committed, the chances of getting away with it, and the likelihood of punishment if apprehended. In the Chinese case, there appeared to be a widespread belief that the democracy movement derived its moral strength from public support and contributed to some new form of ambivalence about punishment (*New York Times Magazine*, 1989). The movement was further justified through its exposure of abuses of power on the part of government officials. The failure of the democracy movement can be summed up with the truism that, without the instruments of power, it is difficult to effect change. The power to sanction remained in the hands of the government, which used this power to criminalize its critics. Time will tell how effective the punishment has been in deterring further dissent. In the short term at least, it has been very effective in purging "criminal" elements from China's political scene.

Like deterrence theories, rational choice theories view the offender in a way that suggests clear links with the classical tradition. However, **rational choice theories** take a somewhat broader perspective than do deterrence theories. While these theories recognize the role that legal threats play in deterring offending, they argue that other factors such as the potential gains that might be derived from the commission of a crime and the ease with which it can be committed are also important.

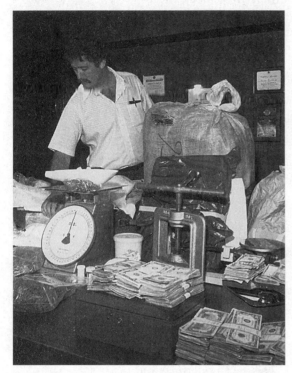

Rational choice theories emphasize the rewards associated with many types of offending.

The increasing popularity of rational choice theory can be seen at least in part as a product of the dissatisfaction of many criminologists with more traditional motivational theories (Fattah, 1993). Theories that emphasize strain or cultural learning, for instance, are seen as creating a false distinction between criminal and noncriminal activity. Rational choice theories argue that both types of behavior seem to be oriented toward the same kinds of ends (for example, money, self-gratification); therefore, criminal behavior may not require a unique motivation (Cornish and Clarke, 1986). In addition, traditional motivational theories really only explain why some people might be predisposed to commit crimes, not why or how crimes are committed. Because crimes are events that occur in specific places at specific times, motivational theories may be faulted for their inattention to the situational context of criminal events.

Rational choice theories focus on offenders' actions based on perceived benefits rather than on some precipitating social or psychological factors (Clarke and Felson, 1993). Moreover, as offenders seek benefits and attempt to avoid losses, they make decisions and choices that can be understood as reflecting rational thought. Therefore, the rational choice theorist argues that, rather than study what broad social factors (strain or cultural values) might influence offending behavior, it makes more sense to study how offenders make these decisions. There are actually two broad types of decisions that invite attention.

COMMITTING A CRIME

One type of decision relates to the commission of particular crimes. How do burglars decide in which neighborhood they will look for targets? How do they decide which house to break into? How do they decide what to do if they see a window sticker indicating that the home is protected by an alarm system? The answers to such questions allow rational choice theorists to develop an understanding of criminal events and the role that offenders play in such events (Tunnell, 1992). Obviously, when compared to many traditional theories of motivation, rational choice theory is interested in the situational character of crime (Birkbeck and LaFree, 1993).

In attempting to answer questions about offenders' decisions, rational choice theories do not assume that offenders operate in purely rational fashion. Instead, offenders usually employ a "limited rationality." In other words, they may inaccurately perceive the benefits of committing a particular crime, lack the time to weigh the possible outcomes, or have access to limited information with which to make the decision.

Contrary to some of the other theories discussed in this and the previous chapter, rational choice theorists argue that because specific situational factors are so important and because offender decision making varies across situations, it makes little sense to try to develop a generic theory of crime. The choices that must be made when an offender is deciding whether to rob a convenience store will be very different from the choices that will be made if an offender is deciding whether to steal a car or defraud a bank (Clarke, 1992).

THE CRIMINAL CAREER

The other major issue of interest to rational choice theorists relates to the **criminal career**. How do offenders decide to get involved in crime? How and when do they decide to give up a life of crime? The notion that crime may be thought of in career terms is widely shared both inside and outside of criminological literature. The true-crime section of any bookstore usually carries several titles that detail the exploits of the "professional thief," "professional robber," or "contract killer." Such books promise a look into a world of crime that, at least superficially, seems to be organized in ways that reflect the occupational structure of the "legitimate" work world. In some fundamental sense, these offenders view crime as their job. They have acquired the technical skills they need to perform this job, and they derive their livelihood principally from successful job performance. Just how superficial are comparisons between crime and legitimate work? Does it make sense to conceptualize criminal involvement in career terms?

BOX 4.1 ROBBERS AND ROBBERY

Robbery is probably the type of violent crime that most people associate with the "career criminal." Thomas Gabor and Andre Normandeau undertook detailed interviews with thirty-nine convicted robbers, all but one of whom were serving sentences in the Montreal area. The study revealed the following:

- The offenders were male, and most were under 30 years of age, had no more than a secondary school education, and came from a blue-collar background.

- Their self-reported criminality was far in excess of that reported in their files.
- The offenders were motivated to rob by the fact that robbery is a fast and direct way to obtain money compared to the less lucrative and more complicated acts of breaking and entering and fraud.
- Unemployment, the need for drugs, and criminal associates were among the precipitating factors.
- Most of the subjects began their careers committing other crimes, such as auto theft or breaking and entering, before advancing to robbery.
- Early success at armed robbery allows the offender to gain confidence and to develop and refine "professional skills."
- As they aged, several offenders experienced increasing fear of prison sentences—a change motivated in part by their negative experiences in previous periods of incarceration and by the knowledge that successive sentences were likely to be longer.

For Discussion

In your view, what skills are important to a successful career in robbery? Why does robbery figure so prominently in urbanites' fear of crime?

SOURCE: Based on T. Gabor and A. Normandeau (1989), "Armed Robbery: Highlights of a Canadian Study," *Canadian Police College Journal* 13(4): 273–282.

THE CONCEPT OF CAREER

A useful place to begin this discussion is with a brief consideration of the concept of "career" itself. In occupational terms, the concept of career denotes "the sequence of movements from one position to another in an occupational system made by any individual who works in that system" (Becker, 1963: 24). This definition is consistent with popular usage. We think of a work career as beginning at some specific point in time and continuing until death, retirement, or a voluntary or forced career change. Over the course of the career, we can identify movement through various stages (which, in the context of formal organizations, we call promotions). Each stage brings with it new responsibilities and additional rewards and provides the individual with the skills, knowledge, or experience he or she needs to advance to successive stages.

The relative success that characterizes career movement is dependent on several "career contingencies." The occupational system may, for instance, allow for little career advancement, or the individual may lack the training that would allow movement beyond a certain occupational level. Contingencies include any factors on which career success depends. Within the setting of a business or other organizational bureaucracy, a useful metaphor is a high-rise building. Each floor represents a career stage, and the career itself may be understood as the elevator that carries people upward or, in unfortunate cases, downward. Clearly, the career concept has more general applicability. Think of your college or university career as having begun when you started your postsecondary education. As your career takes you through several well-defined stages, your success will be judged in large part by the grades you receive. However, your success will depend on career contingencies such as the types of examinations used to judge performance, the restrictions placed on program enrollment, and your abilities as a student.

How valuable is the career concept in the study of crime? Although there is a long history of research and theory that attempts to link the study of offending to the study of careers (Letkemann, 1973; Miller, 1978), criminologists debate whether this is a worthwhile exercise. Some criminologists maintain that the career concept is useful in understanding the relative degree of involvement of offenders in criminal activity. From this point of view, every offender may be said to have a criminal career. The use of the term *career* in this context does not necessarily mean that crime provides the offender's major source of livelihood. The individual who commits only one crime early in adolescence may have a short career in contrast to the person who engages in serious crime throughout his or her life. By focusing on criminal careers, we are encouraged to ask why offenders' careers develop as they do. While the "criminal career" is not a theory in and of itself, it is seen as a useful way of organizing what we know about crime.

Moreover, it is argued, the career concept encourages us to ask questions we would not otherwise be prompted to ask (Blumstein, Cohen, and Farrington, 1988a, 1988b). The first has to do with entry into a criminal career, which is sometimes called "onset." Here we might ask what sorts of factors encourage movement into a criminal career. Or we might try to discover the ages at which people typically begin criminal careers. The second question has to do with the degree of career productivity, which, in the context of legitimate work, might be called the "level of success." During the duration of the career, how many crimes do offenders commit, and what contingencies affect the relative success of criminal careers? Finally, we might ask about what is called "desistance." How and why do offenders end their criminal careers?

Advocates of the career concept argue that, for theoretical reasons, it is important to distinguish questions about onset from questions about frequency and desistance, since factors that affect one aspect of the career may be unrelated to another (Blumstein, Cohen, and Farrington, 1988a). For instance, some of the apparently confusing findings about the relationship between crime and unemployment might become more comprehensible if we recognize that unemployment may not be related to onset, productivity, and desistance in the same ways. For example, the level of unemployment might not be expected to affect the onset of criminal careers that people typically begin in their teenage years, before they are eligible to enter the adult labor force. Once a criminal career has begun, the availability of legitimate work may affect the timing of desistance. An individual may abandon a criminal career if offered more profitable legitimate work. Conversely, although most people end their criminal careers before middle age, desistance may be delayed if the rate of unemployment decreases the likelihood of securing a legitimate job. In general, the career concept suggests that it may be misguided to try to find simple and direct effects between familiar criminogenic concepts and rates of crime. Factors such as employment may affect different career aspects in different ways; and a factor that is important at one point of a career may have no causal significance at a later point.

THE CAREER CRIMINAL

Perhaps the most interesting findings to emerge from the research on criminal careers are those that relate to "career criminals," that is, offenders who commit crimes at a very high rate. The extreme differences in the rates at which individuals offend were first documented in a cohort study undertaken by Wolfgang, Figlio, and Sellin (1972). The researchers attempted to examine the offending patterns of all males born in Philadelphia in 1945 for the period up to their eighteenth birthdays in 1963. The study identified 627 career criminals who, while they constituted only 6 percent of the original cohort and 18 percent of the delinquents, were responsible for more than half of all the crime engaged in by cohort members. More importantly, perhaps, these career criminals were responsible for 71 percent of the murders, 73 percent of the rapes, and 82 percent of the robberies.

Later studies support the view that small numbers of offenders account for large numbers of crime. A longitudinal study in England, known as the Cambridge Study of Delinquent Development, found that about 6 percent of a sample of 411 boys accounted for about 50 percent of all criminal convictions (Farrington, 1989). In a study by the Rand Corporation of offenders in California, Michigan, and Texas prisons, the most active 10 percent of all inmates who had committed robbery reported committing at least 58 robberies per year, while the most active 10 percent of burglars reported committing 187 or more burglaries per year (Chaiken and Chaiken, 1982).

However, contrary to what we might expect, this research also shows that offenders whose careers are characterized by high rates of offending seldom specialize in only one type of crime (U.S. Dept. of Justice, 1988; Visher, 1991); instead, they tend to commit a variety of violent and property crimes (Kempf, 1987). The research into career criminals also shows that there is general stability in levels of offense seriousness over the course of a career. It does not appear, for instance, that the longer offenders offend, the more likely they are to move from one type of crime to another type that requires more technical skill or knowledge.

These findings regarding levels of offense seriousness and the tendency of so-called career criminals not to specialize in particular types of crimes have led some criminologists to be very critical of the career approach to offending. Gottfredson and Hirschi (1986, 1988, 1990) question whether there is anything of value to be gained from examining criminal careers. The concept of a career, they argue, usually assumes some notion of specialization and career progress; and yet, the available evidence undermines the validity of such assumptions.

Gottfredson and Hirschi also contend that it is fruitless to search for the unique factors that explain desistance from criminal careers since all offenders—irrespective of the types of offenses in which they engage or the rates at which they engage in them—become less productive as they age. To argue that different factors explain different career elements is also misleading, according to Gottfredson and Hirschi, since most of the factors in which career researchers are interested (such as unemployment) are only weakly related to crime. For these authors, the tendency to engage in crime is highly stable for all offenders and is related to a low level of self-control.

In a somewhat different way, Luckenbill and Best (1981) also question the value of the career concept as a way of understanding crime and other types of nonconformity. They maintain that the analogy between legitimate and deviant careers is very limited, in large part because legitimate careers must be understood in the context of organizational settings while criminal careers emerge in much less structured settings. Criminal careers are not formed in response to institutional requirements that "spell out the career's positions, pathways for mobility, and rewards, while authorities enforce these rules and ensure the career's security" (Luckenbill and Best, 1981: 197). By contrast, those who are involved in deviant careers are not able to draw on such institutional resources. Moreover, they risk the possibility of social control sanctions and exploitation by deviant associates, and their rewards from deviance are uncertain. Luckenbill and Best (1981) express the differences between legitimate and deviant careers as follows:

> *Riding escalators between floors may be an effective metaphor for respectable organizational careers, but it fails to capture the character of deviant careers. A more appropriate image is a walk in the woods. Here some people take the pathways marked by their predecessors, while others strike out on their own. Some walk slowly, exploring before moving further, but others run, caught up in the action. Some have a destination in mind and proceed purposefully; others view the trip as an experience and enjoy it for its own sake. Even those intent on reaching a destination may stray from the path; they may try a shortcut or they may lose sight of a familiar landmark, get lost and find it necessary to backtrack. Without a rigid organizational structure, deviant careers can develop in many different ways. (201)*

While the debate about the value of the career approach to understanding criminality is unresolved (Dechenes, 1990; Gibbons, 1988; Greenberg, 1992; Langan, 1983; Walker, 1989), comparisons between the legitimate and the illegitimate worlds of work are particularly illuminating with respect to particular types of crime. One such type is known as "enterprise crime," which is discussed in Chapter 10.

SUMMARY
■ ■ ■

Critics of motivation theories argue that many people contemplate breaking the law but do not. Formal and informal social controls prevent them from acting in (sometimes) rational but criminal ways. Hirschi argues that delinquency emerges when controls diminish through the weakening of the social bonds that link adolescents to conformist others. Strong social bonds, which are based on high levels of attachment, commitment, involvement, and belief and which are built into the socialization that individuals experience at home and at school, insulate youths from delinquent involvement. These bonds are subject to pressure from changes in the ways in which families function. They are also influenced by the degree of social disorganization experienced in communities, disorganization that can lead to weakening social ties and increased levels of criminality.

The purpose of deterrence strategies is to communicate to individuals the threat that punishment will follow delinquent acts. If the law is not imposed in a quick, certain, and severe way, deterrence does not result. But deterrence depends on many factors, including the fear of punishment, the perception of risk, and so on. It has been suggested that what the law actually threatens is less relevant to the decision to offend than what people believe it threatens. Perceptions of deterrence are also affected by the widespread public ambivalence concerning the likelihood and efficacy of punishment.

Some criminals may be looked upon as making rational choices to be involved in crime, weighing the benefits of crime involvement against the costs of apprehension. This may mean that certain individuals are more likely to live a life of crime. Career criminals follow a path toward heavy involvement in crime. Even if they are not actually following crime as a career, there is evidence that a small number of individuals commit a disproportionate amount of crime.

QUESTIONS FOR REVIEW AND DISCUSSION
■ ■ ■

1. What factors do you think would help to strengthen the social bonds between parents and children? Which ones weaken these bonds?
2. How effective are various legal and informal sanctions in deterring crime? Is the threat of jail the only form of punishment that is effective in stopping crime?
3. If crime is so profitable, why don't we all commit crimes?
4. If most crime is committed by a small number of people, why can't we simply focus on that small group and make sure that they are constrained from acting in criminal ways?
5. What is likely to stop a "career criminal" from continuing his or her life of crime?

Opportunities, Lifestyles, and Situations

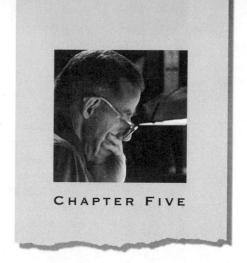

CHAPTER FIVE

WHAT'S IN CHAPTER FIVE

In this chapter, we will focus on the role that opportunities, lifestyles, and situations play in the commission of crimes. Some criminologists have argued that criminal activity is dictated not only by the presence of motivated offenders but also by the array of opportunities that are afforded them to commit crime. These opportunities may come from lifestyles or "routine activities" that follow delinquent patterns. Risky lifestyles may end in higher levels of victimization, as well. When these crimes happen, they may be viewed as "situated transactions" that occur at a particular time and place.

KEY TERMS

lifestyle exposure theories

routine activities theories

capable guardianship

hot spots

victim precipitation

situated transaction

The fact that offenders are ready and willing to engage in criminal conduct, either because of their personalities, background, or views of the law, does not in and of itself explain the occurrence of criminal events. Potential offenders must encounter opportunities that allow these criminal inclinations to be given expression. This is no less true of crime than of anything else. An inclination to learn the saxophone, go to graduate school, or become a skydiver does not ensure that these things will happen. In such cases, as in the case of criminal events, it is useful to consider how opportunities allow individuals to act on their inclinations.

OPPORTUNITY THEORIES AND VICTIMIZATION

LIFESTYLE EXPOSURE

As discussed in Chapter 3, Cloward and Ohlin's analysis of criminal behavior extended the range of relevant theoretical questions beyond the search for motivational factors. Their theory alerts us to the fact that it is not enough to explain why people might be motivated to break the law, since answers to this question generally do not explain why some laws and not others end up being broken. It is also necessary to understand how criminal inclinations are channeled by the opportunities to be criminal to which people have access.

Since the late 1970s, the study of criminal opportunities has been dominated by researchers interested in the study of victimization events. Known as **lifestyle exposure** or **routine activities theories**, these explanations focus on how variations in levels of crime from place to place or over time are related to variations in the opportunities to commit crime rather than to variations in the numbers of people who are motivated to commit crimes or who feel that they will be rewarded by this action.

The lifestyle exposure theory of criminal victimization was formally developed by Michael Hindelang, Michael Gottfredson, and James Garofalo in their 1978 book, *Victims of Personal Crime*. Their theory, which was grounded in the data of victimization surveys, sought to explain what it is about being male, young, single, or poor that increases the chances of being victimized.

The linchpin of their argument is the concept of lifestyle. In general terms, *lifestyle* refers to the patterned ways in which people distribute their time and energies across a range of activities. We have no trouble recognizing that the lifestyle of a teenage male differs quite markedly from the lifestyle of an elderly female. Such differences relate to how and where time is spent, with whom one associates, and what type of leisure pursuits one enjoys. These lifestyle differences are not merely a matter of personal choice; they also reflect the social roles one is required to play and the various types of social constraints to which one is subject.

Routine activities theory is used to explain why some people rather than others become victims of crime. However, people sometimes experience criminal victimization more than once. Researchers James R. Lasley and Leslie Rosenbaum used data from a victimization survey (the British Crime Survey) to try to determine if routine activities were related to the occurrence of multiple victimizations.

The analysis of the relationship between two lifestyle indicators—weekend nights out and alcohol use—and single and multiple personal victimization rates is presented in Table 5.1. These data suggest that as weekend nights spent outside the home and alcohol use increase, so does the risk of becoming a multiple victim of crime.

Table 5.1
Weekend Nights Out, Alcohol Use, and Victimization
(per 10,000 victims)

	Single Victims	Multiple Victims
Nights out		
0	7,890	2,110
1	7,090	2,910
2	6,160	3,840
Alcohol use		
Abstainer	7,830	2,170
Infrequent	7,440	2,560
Occasional	7,380	2,620
Moderate	7,150	2,850
High	5,980	4,020

For Discussion
What would you expect to be some of the other characteristics of multiple victims of personal crime? What do these data suggest about the usefulness of lifestyle variables in efforts to explain multiple victimization?

SOURCE: Based on J. R. Lasley and J. L. Rosenbaum (1988), "Routine Activities and Multiple Personal Victimization," *Sociology and Social Research* 73(1): 47–50.

Where and how people spend their time is related to their risk of victimization. While the number of evening activities in which people engage outside the home increases their chances of becoming a crime victim, research suggests that crimes are more likely to occur in some places, at some times, and in the course of some activities than in others. The data in Table 5.2, drawn from the 1992 National Crime Victimization Survey, illustrate variations in the place and time in which five serious criminal events are likely to occur.

Hindelang, Gottfredson, and Garofalo (1978: 251–264) offer the following eight propositions about victimization that summarize the link between

Table 5.2

Distribution of Crime Occurrence by Place, Time, and Victim Activity, 1992

Place of Occurrence	Rape	Robbery	Aggra-vated Assault	Larceny w/ Contact	Motor Vehicle Theft
At respondent's home	16%	10%	10%	1%	<1%
Near home	8	5	8	3	21
On street near home	5	6	6	3	22
At/in/near friend/relative/ neighbor's home	14	3	9	4	3
On street near friend/relative/ neighbor's home	0	1	2	0	4
In restaurant/bar/club	0	1	4	8	—
In other commercial building	2	3	6	15	<1
In parking lot/garage	7	14	8	3	35
In school building	7	3	2	5	
On school property	1	1	6	3	<1
In apartment yard/park/field/ playground	9	6	5	2	0
On street, not near own/ friend's home	26	40	28	32	13
On public transportation	0	3	1	10	0
Other	7	5	6	11	2

Time of Occurrence	Rape	Robbery	Aggra-vated Assault	Larceny w/ Contact	Motor Vehicle Theft
Daytime (6 A.M.–6 P.M.)	40%	40%	43%	63%	21%
Nighttime (6 P.M.–midnight)	60	59	57	35	69
Unknown/unavailable	0	2	0	2	11

Victim's Activity	Rape	Robbery	Aggra-vated Assault	Larceny w/ Contact	Motor Vehicle Theft
Working or on duty	6%	5%	12%	0%	11%
Going to or from work	12	9	8	14	2
Going to or from school	0	3	4	2	<1
Going to or from other	19	24	13	15	1
Shopping or running errand	0	11	4	26	3
Attending school	3	3	4	5	1
Leisure away from home	32	28	29	31	15
Sleeping	12	1	3	2	44
Other activity at home	12	10	17	1	13
Other	6	5	7	5	3
Don't know	0	1	<1	0	6
Unavailable	0	<1	0	0	1

SOURCE: U.S. Department of Justice, *Criminal Victimization in the United States, 1992* (Washington, DC: U.S. Government Printing Office, 1994a).

lifestyle and key demographic variables such as age, sex, marital status, family income, and race:

1. The more time individuals spend in public places (especially at night), the more likely they are to be victimized.
2. Following certain lifestyles makes individuals more likely to frequent public places.
3. The interactions that individuals maintain tend to be with persons who share their lifestyles.
4. The probability that individuals will be victims increases according to the extent to which victims and offenders belong to the same demographic categories.
5. The proportion of time individuals spend in places where there are a large number of nonfamily members varies according to lifestyle.
6. The chances that individuals will be victims of crime (particularly theft) increase in conjunction with the amount of time they spend among nonfamily members.
7. Differences in lifestyles relate to individuals' ability to isolate themselves from those with offender characteristics.
8. Variations in lifestyles influence the convenience, desirability, and ease of victimizing individuals.

Lifestyle theories maintain that differences in victimization risk are related to patterns of leisure and nonleisure activity.

Rates of personal victimization are relatively high for young minority males because these individuals tend to associate with people who are likely to offend (that is, other young minority males) and because they tend to frequent places (for example, bars) where offending often occurs. An elderly female, by contrast, is likely to associate with other elderly females (whose level of offending is very low) and to avoid high-risk settings. Lifestyle in a sense structures victimization opportunities. In explaining empirical variations in levels of personal crime, Hindelang and colleagues advance these opportunity structures, not offender motivation, as a central theoretical issue.

BOX 5.2 WARNING: SMOKING MAY BE HAZARDOUS TO YOUR HEALTH

Opportunity theories of victimization attempt to understand how particular elements of lifestyle increase exposure to the risk of criminal victimization. Several studies have shown that as alcohol consumption or the frequency of visiting bars increases, so does the risk of becoming a victim. Perhaps somewhat less obviously, University of California researcher Ichiro Tanioka has published evidence suggesting that victimization rates are higher for smokers.

The data for Tanioka's study came from the 1978 and 1983 General Social Surveys. Among the questions asked of respondents were whether they had ever been "punched or beaten by another person" and whether they smoke. Because the tendency to become a crime victim and the tendency to smoke are related to other social characteristics, Tanioka included in his analysis measures of age, sex, marital status, urban residence, employment status, and frequency of bar attendance.

The analysis revealed that, independent of the effects of the other variables included in the study, smoking had a significant effect on the risk of assaults. Overall, 32.3 percent of smokers had experienced an assault, compared to 17 percent of nonsmokers. However, the relationship was even stronger for single females aged 18–49, among whom 43.5 percent were victimized, compared to 20 percent of nonsmokers.

This is not to suggest that smoking is a *cause* of victimization in any simple sense. What is more likely is that a measure of smoking indexes certain other lifestyle preferences (unmeasured in the survey) that are more directly related to victimization risk.

For Discussion
How do you account for Tanioka's findings on the relationship between smoking and victimization? Can you think of any other types of noncriminal deviance that may be linked to crime victimization?

SOURCE: Based on I. Tanioka (1986), "Evidence Links Smoking to Violent Crime Victimization," *Sociology and Social Research* 71(1): 58ff.

Cohen and Felson (1979) note that traditional motivational theories in criminology are unable to explain the dramatic increase in many forms of crime that occurred in Western nations in the post–World War II period. Many of the explanatory factors (for example, poverty, unemployment, size of inner-city population) indicated trends suggesting that crime rates should have been falling during this period rather than climbing. How, then, could the problem of rising crime rates be reconceptualized?

According to Cohen and Felson, the presence of a motivated offender is only one component necessary to the completion of assaults, sexual assaults, homicides, breaking and enterings, or other "direct-contact predatory violations." For such crimes to occur, two other conditions must be met. First, there must be a "suitable target" against which the criminal motivation can be directed (for example, homes to break into, people to assault, and goods to steal). Second, there must be an "absence of **capable guardianship**," meaning that the motivated offender must meet the suitable target in the absence of anything (or anyone) that might prevent the crime from occurring.

Cohen and Felson suggest that variations in levels of crime are determined not only by the numbers of people willing to commit crimes but also by the numbers of suitable targets and by the levels of guardianship that are routinely exercised over these targets. Even if the numbers of suitable targets and the levels of guardianship remain unchanged, higher crime rates can be expected if the tempos and rhythms of social life affect the rate at which motivated offenders encounter suitable targets in the absence of capable guardianship. For Cohen and Felson, illegal activities must be understood as behaviors that depend on, and feed off, the "routine activities" of the population. "Although the fox finds each hare one by one, the fox population varies with the hare population upon which it feeds" (Felson, 1987: 914). As the structure of the routine activities changes, so does the frequency at which crimes occur.

> **WHAT DOES IT INCLUDE?**
>
> ### *Routine Activities Theory*
>
> First, there must be a motivated offender. A suitable target against which the criminal motivation may be directed must also be available. Third, there must be an absence of capable guardianship.

How do these insights inform our theoretical understanding of why crime rates changed as they did after World War II? Cohen and Felson argue that changes in patterns of routine activities substantially altered levels of target suitability and guardianship and the rates at which these elements and motivated offenders came together in time and space. This period witnessed a broad shift in the locus of routine activities. In increasingly large numbers, women whose lives had revolved around the household entered or returned to the paid labor force or school. In addition, vacation periods became longer and travel became cheaper, so that holidays were more likely to be spent away from home. Even the frequency with which people dined at restaurants increased and gave rise to a booming fast-food industry. At the same time, divorce rates increased and people who were single were waiting longer before getting married. Both changes pointed to a significant rise in the number of smaller, single-person households and further contributed to the likelihood that leisure interests previously pursued at home would now be pursued elsewhere, among nonfamily members.

Not coincidentally, this period also witnessed "a revolution in small durable product design" (Cohen and Felson, 1979: 500). A general increase in the standard of living combined with technological advancement to produce a wide range of lightweight, durable consumer goods. Demand for tape recorders, television sets, and stereo equipment increased, as it later did for products like personal computers, CD players, and VCRs (Felson, 1994).

These changes, according to Cohen and Felson, exerted a profound impact on the rates of direct-contact predatory crimes. Through their effects on target suitability and guardianship levels, they provided greater criminal opportunities and pushed crime rates upward. The shift in routine activities away from the home exposed increasingly large numbers of people to criminal dangers from which they previously had been insulated. Moreover, in greater numbers, they left their homes unoccupied for increasing periods of time and thus deprived of capable guardianship. At the same time that guardianship was being lowered, homes were being stocked with larger numbers of highly desirable durable consumer goods that were easy to steal, carry, and sell or use. As guardianship declined, target suitability increased. One need not agonize over the question of criminal motivation, Cohen and Felson conclude, in order to understand an increase in crime over the period.

The typical modern American home has many things that a thief would want to steal.

Fraud may be defined as the attempt to use deceit or falsehood in order to gain goods, services, or financial gain without legitimate rights. As with other types of crime, levels of fraud depend on the availability of criminal opportunities. For example, in a 1985 study by the Bureau of Justice Statistics examining rates of electronic funds transfer (EFT) fraud, ATM fraud was found to be less common and less costly than credit card fraud loss. Table 5.3 shows key data from the study. The study's authors suggest that differences in the levels of sophistication associated with the technology governing the use of ATM cards and credit cards and/or in the levels of organization related to each type of bank fraud may account for the discrepancies:

> One possible explanation for these differences is that organized fraud, especially card counterfeiting operations, does not appear to be a problem in the ATM industry at this time. Additionally, more lenient withdrawal limits and a greater inability to control "hot-carded" transactions [situations in which a stolen card is identified by the bank and its use is frozen] may result in higher credit card losses. (U.S. Dept. of Justice, 1985: 3)

Table 5.3
ATM and Credit Card Fraud Costs, 1983

	ATM Fraud Loss Ratios	*Credit Card Fraud Loss Ratios*
Loss per transaction	$0.031	$0.081
Loss per $1,000 of transaction volume	0.321	1.590
Total estimate of ATM fraud	$70–100 million	
Total estimate of credit card fraud	$561 million	

NOTE: Data regarding the total volume of ATM fraud was extrapolated from a sample of 2,707 ATM fraud incidents. The data are median estimates of the total amount of ATM fraud. Credit card fraud estimates were reported by VISA and by the Nilson Report (Report No. 347, Los Angeles, CA, January 1985).

SOURCE: Based on U.S. Department of Justice, *Electronic Fund Transfer Fraud* (Washington, DC: Bureau of Justice Statistics, 1985).

For Discussion
Are there other technological innovations that invite criminal activity, and what can we do to stop these crimes?

Newman (1972) borrows from the ideas of opportunity theory in arguing that the most effective way to reduce crime is to redesign public and private spaces in such a way that opportunities for crime are removed. The "defensible space" concept proposes that one can "harden" targets by installing locks or by improving surveillance, such that the criminal is deterred from committing the crime, either for fear of detection or simply because the target has been made inaccessible. The operators of 7-Eleven convenience stores redesigned their premises under the direction of Ray D. Johnson, who had served twenty-five years for robbery and burglary in the California state penitentiary system. The insights provided by a former perpetrator led to a design that removed the chance of concealment:

> *To allow clear sightlines from the street into the store, they moved cash registers up front and removed all advertising from the front windows. They also put bright floodlights outside the entrance, forcing potential robbers to perform where any passerby could look in and see.*
>
> *They also installed special cash drawers that make it impossible to get at more than $10 every two minutes. This gives the would-be robber the choice of getting away with very little cash, waiting "onstage" to make the payoff worthwhile or simply going elsewhere. (Krupat and Kubzansky, 1987: 60)*

The incidence of robberies in the redesigned 7-Eleven stores was 30 percent lower than that in the stores that had not been redesigned.

In a similar vein, Sherman, Gartin, and Buerger (1989) identify high-crime areas known as **hot spots**. These places may be public (taverns) or private (households that are frequently reported for family disturbances). The authors' prescription is to minimize or eliminate the crime at these hot spots by increasing police surveillance or by removing them altogether. The idea that crime will be deterred through defensible space or through targeting hot spots supports the theory that offenders are motivated by opportunity. However, removing these opportunities will not necessarily reduce the desire to commit a crime—it may simply displace it to some other location. For example, police spend a great deal of time moving street prostitutes from certain areas only to have them reappear in other parts of town.

Over the past several years, a large body of research has grown up around the questions raised by opportunity theories of victimization (Cohen, Kluegel, and Land, 1981; Kennedy and Forde, 1990; Maxfield, 1987; Miethe, Stafford, and Long, 1987; Skogan and Maxfield, 1981). In a very basic way, the ideas generated by this research have re-oriented criminologists' thinking about the causes of crime. Opportunity theories have provided an additional piece to the puzzle as to why and where criminal events occur. A major limitation of these theories is that they pay little attention to the nature of the offender's motivation or to the relationship between offender and victim. Opportunity theories assume that probabilities of offending can be worked out on the basis of a set of conditions relating to opportunities. We believe that to the notion of opportunity must be added questions about the characteristics of offender motivation.

One way to fight theft in commercial establishments is through the use of surveillance that includes mirrors to help keep track of customers in store aisles who would otherwise be out of sight of store employees.

CRIME AS INTERACTIONS

An important theoretical question in the study of criminal situations relates to the manner in which these events unfold over time. They are set in motion by offenders who are inclined to make use of available criminal opportunities. In order to explain why they follow a particular course of action, it is necessary to raise questions about the specific behavioral choices that offenders, victims, and others make in the situational contexts in which they find themselves. In particular, it is important to understand how the choices that each participant makes influence the choices made by others. Victims and offenders act and react, and in so doing, they exert mutual influence. Stated differently, crimes have an interactional character: What any one participant does depends on what others do. Although interactional dynamics have not attracted as much attention as issues like offender motivation, a general appreciation of how criminologists attempt to understand these interactions is necessary.

One of the concepts most frequently employed in the study of crime dynamics is that of **victim precipitation,** according to which the opportunity for crime is created by some action of the victim. In an early and influential study of 588 criminal homicides in the city of Philadelphia, the sociologist Marvin Wolfgang (1958) reported that, in about one-quarter of these cases, the victims could be said to have precipitated their own murder. In such cases, Wolfgang noted, it was the eventual victim who, frequently under the influence of alcohol, was the first to brandish a weapon or to threaten deadly force. The eventual offender, fearing for his or her own safety, either intentionally or unintentionally reacted to the threat in a way that proved fatal for the victim. In a stereotypical case, an altercation between two individuals at a bar escalates to the point at which one of the parties produces a gun or a knife or a broken bottle and says to the other party, "I'm going to kill you." The other party responds with haste and force, and suddenly the person who uttered the threat is lying dead on the barroom floor.

> ## WHAT DOES IT MEAN?
>
> ### *Victim Precipitation*
>
> This occurs when the opportunity for crime is created by some action of the victim.

The concept of victim precipitation encourages us to understand the outcome of a crime situation as the joint product of the behaviors of the offender and the victim rather than simply the offender's motivation. In the case of the barroom encounter, the killing can be said to result not from the killer's actions but from the killer–killed interaction. It is important to point out that what people might *intend* their words or their actions to mean in cases of this type is much less important than *how they are interpreted* by others engaged in the interaction. The person who brandishes a broken beer bottle and threatens death to a disputant may be expressing mere bravado rather than serious intent to harm the other party. To the disputant, however, whose judgment is clouded by alcohol and who believes the threat to be real, other interpretations of the situation are well out of reach. With respect to such cases, we have little trouble understanding the explanatory value of the concept of victim precipitation. The homicide would probably not have occurred, we can conclude, if the victim had not initially behaved in an aggressive fashion; thus, the victim was an active contributor to his or her own violent demise.

Problematic from a theoretical standpoint is the degree to which the explanatory logic of victim precipitation is generalizable to other types of events. Is it reasonable, for instance, to argue that crimes such as robbery, theft, or sexual assault can also be victim precipitated? In these types of events, does it make sense to argue that victims actively contribute to their own victimization?

Amir (1971) concluded from a study of over 600 rape cases in the city of Philadelphia that about one case in five was victim precipitated. Amir classified rapes as victim precipitated if the victim "actually, or so it was deemed, agreed to sexual relations but retracted before the actual act or did not react strongly enough when the suggestion was made to the offender" (266).

While we might be inclined to agree that victims who initially threaten their offenders in some sense precipitate a homicide, we would not agree that victims who initially consent to sexual relations precipitate rape if they subsequently change their minds. For one thing, the assumption in the latter case seems to be that the female rather than the male is responsible for the level of male sexual arousal and that if that arousal is not satisfied, the female must bear the violent consequences. In addition, it seems to imply that a subsequent decision not to engage in sex, when there has been some initial agreement to do so, is appropriately understood as precipitous of violence. Finally, homicide and sexual assault differ in a fundamental way that is obscured by the haphazard application of the concept of victim precipitation. The types of homicides described by Wolfgang involve events in which victims threaten their offenders with deadly force and are repaid in kind. In the cases of rape described by Amir, the victim is not behaving in a threatening or aggressive fashion, and the violence exhibited by the offender cannot be understood as "payment in kind."

Amir's study illustrates a serious concern that many people have with the concept of victim precipitation—that it is difficult to separate the moral dimensions of the concept from its explanatory dimensions. The claim that victims precipitate victimization seems uncomfortably close to the suggestion that victims should be *blamed* for their victimization. For many criminologists, victim blaming should be avoided at all costs (Timmer and Norman, 1984). At the same time, most people can express some degree of empathy for the battered wife who, after years of being subjected to violence, kills her abusive husband. To call a killing of this type victim precipitated does not usually elicit a charge of victim blaming.

For some criminologists, the solution is to recognize that crude attempts to sort crimes into precipitated and unprecipitated categories are doomed to failure. Victims and offenders may contribute to the unfolding of a criminal event in a variety of ways, and thus a broader taxonomy of victim and offender roles is necessary (Fattah, 1991; Karmen, 1990). Another solution involves recognizing that, in many cases, it is not appropriate to speak of victim or offender roles, since doing so minimizes our understanding of the ways in which the circumstances of events themselves determine who shall bear what label. In other words, there is a need to move beyond the study of victim precipitation to "the full round of interaction," which involves not only the eventual victims and offenders but also other event participants (Luckenbill, 1984).

THE SITUATED TRANSACTION

Goffman (1963) defines a **situated transaction** as a process of interaction that involves two or more individuals. If we are to understand criminal events as situated transactions, we need to emphasize the study of what goes on between the participants rather than what any one of them does. According to Goffman

(1959), human behavior is acted out as though part of a theatrical performance. What's important in the interaction is the impression that the actor gives to others. Based on this impression, which generally involves the playing out of a particular role in specific situations, individuals extract information about others in the interaction. When enough information is obtained for each individual to define the situation to his or her satisfaction, the roles can be properly acted out (Martin, Mutchnik, and Austin, 1990: 332). With these definitions in hand, individuals are able to sustain and complete a number of transactions throughout their daily lives. These transactions do not always have positive outcomes, however.

Luckenbill (1977) utilized an approach that draws on symbolic interactionism in analyzing seventy homicides that occurred in California. Like other researchers, Luckenbill reported that these murders tended to occur in informal settings and generally involved people who knew each other. What distinguishes his approach, however, is his view of homicide as a product of the situated transaction rather than as a product of the behavior of individual participants. For Luckenbill, situated transactions should be viewed as "character contests" in which efforts on the part of the disputants to "save face" result in deadly combat.

> ## WHAT DOES IT MEAN?
>
> ### *Situated Transaction*
>
> This refers to a process of interaction involving two or more individuals that lasts as long as they find themselves in one another's presence.

BOX 5.4 STAGES IN THE SITUATED TRANSACTION

David Luckenbill has argued that homicide can be understood as a situated transaction. It is a "transaction" in that "an offender, victim and possibly an audience engage in an interchange which leaves the victim dead" and it is "situated" in that the "participants interact in a common physical territory" (1977: 196). Based on analysis of seventy homicide events in a California county, Luckenbill argued that these incidents typically move through six stages:

- *Stage 1:* The opening move in the transaction is an action undertaken by the (eventual) victim and defined by the (eventual) offender as an offense to "face." For example, the victim says, "Get lost" or "What are you staring at?"
- *Stage 2:* The offender interprets the victim's words or actions as personally offensive.
- *Stage 3:* The offender makes an opening move in salvaging "face" or protecting "honor"—in short, the offender retaliates verbally or physically.
- *Stage 4:* The victim responds in an aggressive manner, and the actions suggest a working agreement that the situation is one suited to violent resolution. By cheering or heckling, onlookers may encourage the movement toward violence. They may also block a convenient exit for one or both parties or prevent others from breaking up the fight.

- *Stage 5:* There is a physical interchange, typically brief and precise.
- *Stage 6:* The brief battle is over, and at this point, the offender flees or remains at the scene, either voluntarily or as a result of force applied by bystanders.

For Discussion

Many people view homicide as nothing more than the acts of a murderous individual. What sort of revision of this view does Luckenbill's analysis require? What role do various types of "crime facilitators" (such as drugs, alcohol, or weapons) play in this process?

SOURCE: Based on D. Luckenbill (1977), "Criminal Homicide as a Situated Transaction," *Social Problems* 25: 176–186.

This perspective on criminal events is not meant to imply that situated transactions are restricted to one type of crime. The kinds of transactions that result in acquaintance rapes differ from those that result in homicides. Even in the case of homicides, important differences characterize the nature of the situated transaction (Williams and Flewelling, 1988). For example, it is incorrect to argue that the victims of mass murderers or serial killers are combatants who are committed to battle. (This is not to deny, however, that these crimes, too, have situational dynamics.)

In many cases, the complexities of transactions blur in our minds whatever a priori distinctions we might wish to make between victims and offenders. How useful is it for us to say that individuals are of a certain "criminal type" when we know that their behavior can be affected to such a large extent by the situations they face and the roles they believe they must play in completing the transaction? It is the course of action that, to a large degree, determines the identity of the eventual victim and offender. We do not (as we do in cases of victim precipitation) look to the victim for the causes of the violence, but rather to the victim–offender exchange. With respect to the homicides described by Luckenbill, it should be clear that, up until the moment of battle, either party might have pulled out of the exchange or responded differently, resulting in quite different consequences. Questions about who should have done what (and when) to prevent the violence are likely to elicit more than one answer from interested observers.

According to Sampson and Lauritsen (1990), the difficulties that we have in identifying offender and victim in many criminal events derive from the fact that the likelihood of victimization increases the more frequent one's contact or association with members of demographic groups that contain a disproportionate share of offenders. In this matrix, the dynamics of the situation, using Luckenbill's approach, make it likely that victims and offenders will be drawn from the same group, a view consistent with Hindelang, Gottfredson, and Garofalo's (1978) proposal that those with common lifestyles are more likely to be victimized by one another.

The research on victim–offender interactions challenges many of the stereotypes that are inherent in other theoretical approaches. With respect to motivational theories, for instance, we are sometimes led to argue that crimes occur only because criminals are determined to commit them. Theories that focus only on opportunity, if not carefully interpreted, seem to suggest that crimes occur because motivated offenders find the opportunities to translate their inclinations into action.

In contrast, interactional theories suggest that more than motivation and opportunity are needed to understand why and how crime occurs. Crimes are the outcome of social exchanges between people who find themselves in specific circumstances and must make quick decisions about how they should respond to each other's behavior. A robbery does not occur merely because an offender with an inclination to rob encounters an opportunity conducive to robbery. The potential victim may resist in ways that turn a potential robbery into an attempted murder. The potential victim of an attempted breaking and entering may "overreact" by killing the offender. Victims of property crimes contribute to the interaction through the steps they take—or don't take—to protect their property; their actions, or lack thereof, send a message to the potential offender about the risks of trying to steal the property. Victims are not, therefore, merely passive objects of an offender's predatory desires; nor are they necessarily active contributors to their own victimization. They are, however, key event participants whose actions shape and constrain event outcomes.

Similar comments apply to other participants. The study of homicide by Luckenbill, for instance, revealed that the role of bystanders in situated transactions should not be minimized. He found that the presence of bystanders and the actions they took shaped the course of the transaction. In the early stages, they sometimes increased the likelihood of mortal battle by encouraging the offender to interpret an offensive remark as requiring a firm response, while in the later stages, they sometimes supplied a weapon or blocked the exit of the potential victim. Of course, just as bystanders may facilitate the occurrence of a crime, they may also prevent crimes or transform one type of crime into another. A bystander who has the presence of mind to call "911" upon witnessing an assault or who is familiar with cardiopulmonary resuscitation (CPR) may prevent an assault from becoming a murder.

SUMMARY
■ ■ ■

The pressure to behave in a criminal fashion is not sufficient to explain why people commit one type of crime and not another. Using a routine activities approach, researchers explain variations in levels of crime across places and over time based less on variations in the numbers of individuals motivated to commit crime than on variations in the opportunities to commit crime. The concept of opportunities revolves around the notion that some individuals have certain lifestyles or follow certain routines that make them vulnerable to criminal victimization. This lifestyle exposure, coupled with the presence of motivated offenders and the absence of capable guardians, makes becoming a victim of crime more likely. Changing routines, hardening targets through architectural change, and attacking hot spots (places where crime is most prevalent) all entail removing the opportunity to commit crime.

When crimes do occur, they take on a dynamic character that involves choices by offenders, victims, and others, all of which affect the outcome. Crimes can thus be said to have an interactional character; what any one participant does depends on what others do. An important consideration in this equation is the role played by the victim, who, together with the offender and other main players, comes to be involved in what is called a situated transaction. In such transactions, the characteristics of the individuals involved in an interaction come to define the direction that a crime will take. In the early stages of these interactions, it is often difficult to predict the eventual victim and offender. It is the actions that occur that more clearly define these roles. Depending on the actions of third parties, harm and guilt are clearly worked out only after the fact.

Interactional approaches suggest, then, that crimes are the outcome of social exchanges between people who find themselves in specific circumstances and who must make quick decisions about how they should respond to one another's behavior. Their responses determine the outcomes. These outcomes are not always predictable in that they can be affected by many factors in the situation. Interactional approaches help us to determine the effectiveness of various strategies that are used by victims or police in deterring or preventing crime.

QUESTIONS FOR REVIEW AND DISCUSSION
■ ■ ■

1. Why do you think that young males are more likely to live risky lifestyles than any other group?
2. What do you think will be the major change in the future in lifestyles that will make individuals in society more vulnerable to crime? Less vulnerable?
3. Are there steps that can be taken to reduce the likelihood that individuals who confront one another in interaction will escalate this dispute to violence?
4. The police play an important role as third parties in defining behavior as criminal or noncriminal. What are the pluses and minuses of police using more discretion in deciding what should be treated criminally and what should be treated as a dispute that can be solved by the disputants themselves?
5. Are we likely to see a drop in crime as young people who follow risky routines become older and less likely to be involved in these types of behavior?

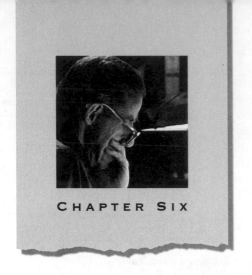

Crime's Aftermath: The Consequences of Criminal Events

KEY TERMS

fear of crime

vulnerability conversion

avoidance behavior

Neighborhood Watch

costs of victimization

labeling theory

secondary deviance

incivility

claimsmaking

valence issues

moral panic

WHAT'S IN CHAPTER SIX

In this chapter, we will review the theories that deal with the aftermath of the criminal event. This includes a review of the costs of victimization, the labeling of offenders, and the consequences for the public including enhanced fear of crime. We will examine, in addition, the extreme forms of reaction to crime—moral panics—whereby the public responds in an intense fashion to the threat of criminal acts. These reactions have an important effect on the ways in which we come to define the crime problem through the action of claimsmakers in setting out our agenda for responding to criminal events.

This chapter is concerned with what happens in the aftermath of the criminal event. The issues, theories, and research discussed remind us that, for analytical purposes, it makes little sense to say that criminal events end when the thief flees the scene or when the victim of homicide falls to the floor. The ways in which event participants and the rest of us respond to the event are as much a part of the event as the commission of the crime itself.

Several of the questions addressed in this chapter relate to the experiences of offenders and victims. How do offenders who are apprehended contend with the criminal status accorded them? What sorts of costs does crime present to victims? How do victims cope with these losses, and why do some manage better than others?

Our interest must not be confined to event participants, however. Criminal events elicit responses from many individuals and groups in society. As we will see, the **fear of crime** is regarded as a pervasive problem—particularly in large urban areas. Obviously, the aftermath of criminal events must be seen, to some extent, as an outcome of the event transaction as well as the wider social context within which these events occur. The level of injury experienced by a victim of violence, for instance, will be related to decisions made by the victim to resist an offender and decisions by the offender to actively overcome that resistance (Kleck and Sayles, 1990; Ziegenhagen and Brosnan, 1985). A "random" murder that is given sensationalist treatment by the mass media will elicit more public fear than a murder involving drinking partners (Liska and Baccaglini, 1990). And an offender who is caught selling illegal drugs when society is in a state of panic about drug crimes can expect less sympathy than an offender who is apprehended during a period when the level of concern is lower.

PROBLEMS WITH COST MEASUREMENT

Any attempt to discuss the consequences crimes have for victims or the ways in which they attempt to cope with these effects is beset by some rather serious research problems. Perhaps the most notable can be termed the "specification problem" (Fattah and Sacco, 1989). In short, it is not always clear how we are to determine what should and what should not be considered an effect of crime.

BOX 6.1 THE COSTS OF VICTIMIZATION

According to the results of the National Crime Victimization Survey (NCVS), the direct cost to victims of crime was $17.6 billion in 1992. The crimes covered by the survey are rape, robbery, assault, personal and household theft, burglary, and motor vehicle theft.

With respect to the crimes that involved loss, pertinent data include the following:

- About 12 percent of personal crimes and 24 percent of household crimes involved economic losses of $500 or more.
- Lost property was not recovered in 89 percent of personal crimes and 85 percent of household crimes.
- For crimes of violence involving injuries in which medical expenses were known, 65 percent involved costs of $250 or more.
- About 8 percent of all victims lost time from work as a result of a crime of violence, and 6 percent as a result of a household crime.

For Discussion

What types of costs of crime are not likely to be measured adequately in surveys of this type?

SOURCE: Based on P. A. Klaus, *Crime Data Brief: The Costs of Crime to Victims* (Washington DC: U.S. Department of Justice, 1994).

Of course, specification is not always a problem. With respect to financial loss, it is obvious that the economic costs sustained when someone steals a purse from a victim equals the replacement price of the purse and its contents. But suppose the victim reacts to the theft by deciding to install deadbolt locks and to take taxis rather than walk to evening destinations. Suppose as well that she decides that instead of carrying cash she will write checks for her purchases in the future. Should the costs of the locks, the taxi fares, and checking charges be considered an economic cost of the crime? The nature of the problem becomes even more apparent when we recognize that financial losses are perhaps the easiest to calculate, given that there is a convenient standard of measurement.

With respect to physical injury, if a victim sustains a broken bone, the injury clearly should be considered a consequence of the crime. But if stress resulting from the crime aggravates a pre-existing health condition, is it correct to say that the incident resulted in physical harm even though there are no apparent physical injuries? The problems with efforts to assess the costs of crime for victims emerge logically from the types of research methods that are used. Most typically, information about victimization outcomes, like other information about victims, comes from victim surveys or from specialized samples of crime victims.

Two general strategies can be used to investigate the ways in which victims are affected by crime. First, survey respondents can be asked directly about the losses that they experienced. These questions, like all questions that ask people to report on past events, are subject to errors as a result of faulty memory, dishonesty, and misunderstanding (Skogan, 1986). Usually, these questions focus on the most obvious losses to the victim, such as injury or stolen or damaged goods. While these questions are useful, they focus attention only on what happens during or immediately after the event but reveal little about what hap-

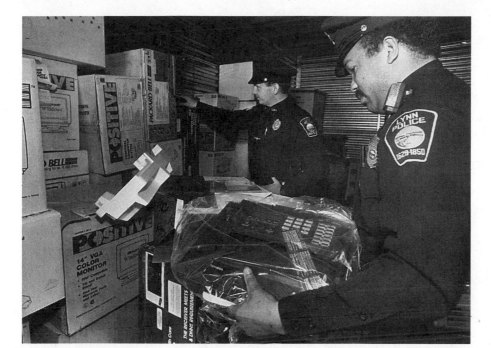

Property loss is one of the most obvious and most easily measurable consequences of crime.

pens to the victim over the longer term. In the case of the NCVS, for example, respondents are asked about victimization events that occurred during the six-month period preceding the survey; therefore, our knowledge about problems that emerge later is minimal.

Respondents might also be asked about how they changed or limited their behavior in response to the victimization. These questions require that respondents not only recall accurately when their behavior changed but also understand the causes of their behavior. However, criminologist Gwynne Nettler (1984) warns that research of this type is likely to confuse the causes of action with the reasons people give for their actions.

A second research strategy is to allow the researcher rather than the survey respondents to make judgments about the effects of the victimization experience. For instance, suppose we are interested in trying to determine whether the victim's involvement in a criminal event increased feelings of anger. Rather than asking victims directly if they are angry about the experience, we might compare victims and nonvictims in terms of the responses they give to more general questions about feelings of anger. If we discover that victims are more angry than nonvictims, we might conclude that the victimization experience is responsible for some of the difference. While this is standard social scientific practice, the results may not be clear since we probably asked the questions about victimization and about feelings of anger in the same interview. As a result, it is impossible to determine what is the cause and what is the effect. While it is reasonable to argue that victimization results in feelings of anger, it may be just as reasonable to argue that people who have an angry demeanor are more likely to become victims of crime. The costs of crime for victims are generally considered to fall under four major categories: financial, physical, emotional, and behavioral.

VICTIM OUTCOMES: THE CONSEQUENCES OF VICTIMIZATION

FINANCIAL CONSEQUENCES

As stated, financial costs are among the most obvious costs associated with victimization. As with all types of costs, these may be direct or indirect. The direct costs involve the value of the property stolen or damaged as well as any costs associated with medical care. Indirect financial costs may reflect lost work time, child care costs, or expensive lifestyle changes.

Data from the 1992 NCVS (U.S. Dept. of Justice, 1994a) provide some indication of the levels of economic loss sustained by victims. The survey found that 71 percent of all personal crimes reported resulted in some economic loss through theft or damage. This included 97 percent of all personal crimes of theft and 23 percent of all crimes of violence. In the case of household crimes, 91 percent resulted in an economic loss as a result of property taken or damaged.

In the case of personal crimes, the size of the loss was less than $50 in more than one-third of all cases. About 12 percent of victims of personal crimes had associated losses of $500 or more. With respect to household crimes, about one-quarter of victims had losses of less than $50, but about the same proportion had losses of $500 or more. Not surprisingly, motor vehicle thefts and burglaries were most likely to result in the largest losses.

In addition, victims recovered none of their property in about 90 percent of the personal crimes and about 84 percent of the household crimes. Victims of motor vehicle theft were somewhat more fortunate in that about 42 percent got their vehicles back and about 30 percent got some back (in the form of automobile parts).

An analysis of twenty years of NCVS data revealed that victims incurred medical expenses in 10 percent of all violent victimizations (Zawitz et al., 1993). In those cases for which victims knew the dollar amount, the medical expenses exceeded $250 in almost three-fifths of the cases. Moreover, victims were not covered by health insurance or were ineligible to apply for public health benefits in 34 percent of the incidents that resulted in injury. This was most likely to be a problem for low-income victims, who would have been least able to shoulder the costs associated with their medical care.

The analysis of NCVS data collected between 1973 and 1991 indicate that during this period, 36.6 million people were injured as a result of violent crime and that about one in six received serious injuries (Zawitz et al., 1993). Of the victims of violent crime who were injured, 84 percent received bruises, cuts, scratches, or other minor injuries. More serious injuries occur with lesser frequency. Among those who were victimized by violent crime between 1973 and 1991, 1 percent received gunshot wounds, 4 percent received knife wounds, and 7 percent suffered broken bones or had teeth knocked out.

The findings from the 1992 NCVS provide some indication that women are more likely to be injured in robberies than are men (U.S. Dept. of Justice, 1994a). In addition, the survey found that assault victims were more likely to receive physical injuries from an offender who was known to them than were victims who were assaulted by a stranger. Of the injured victims who received medical care, about six in ten received care in an emergency room and about four in ten received in-patient care.

While victimization studies are quite useful in telling us about the direct injuries incurred from criminal victimization, they tell us relatively little about longer-term effects. Although not evident in surveys of this sort, the injuries

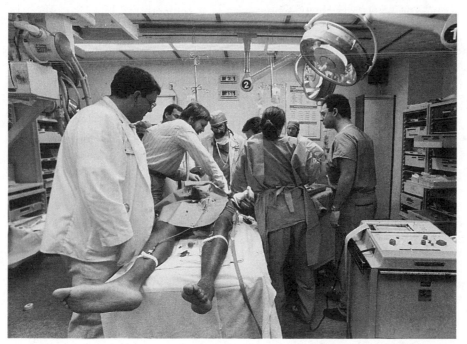

The physical consequences of crime may include immediate injury or the worsening of existing health conditions.

that result from physical encounters can lead to a worsening of existing health problems, and when mobility is restricted, the victim may be less able or even unable to exercise or to meet nutritional requirements.

EMOTIONAL CONSEQUENCES

Victims can experience a variety of emotional reactions to crime, from the mild to the extreme. These reactions may include shock, mistrust, sleeplessness, anger, stress, depression, and a diminished capacity to enjoy life events (Burt and Katz, 1985; Mayhew et al., 1993). Victims may also express a sense of guilt because they blame themselves for what has happened (Mayhew et al., 1993).

One of the most significant effects that has been associated with victimization is an increase in fear of crime (Skogan, 1987; Smith and Hill, 1991; Wirtz and Harrell, 1987). Serious crimes, especially crimes of violence, may result in a **vulnerability conversion** (Lejeune and Alex, 1973) as victims develop a sudden understanding that they are more susceptible to the dangers of life than they thought.

Janoff-Bulman and Frieze (1983) maintain that serious criminal victimization is stressful in large part because it is unusual, and unlike more routine stressors, it does not trigger well-developed coping mechanisms. Such events, they argue, make evident people's "psychological baggage" and suggest a need to question not only their assumptions of invulnerability but also other assumptions that underlie their day-to-day existence.

One such assumption is that "the world is meaningful." Most of us prefer to go through life believing that things happen for a reason, that good things happen to good people and that bad things happen to bad people. In general, it is comforting to think that, all things considered, the world makes sense. We can hold these beliefs because we also believe that we can exercise a certain amount of control over what happens to us. A serious, random act of crime, however, can challenge this assumption. In the aftermath of such an event, the world appears to make less sense—we have become victims of misfortune even though we may have tried hard to keep ourselves safe.

Criminal victimization may also undermine an individual's positive self-concept. Victims may develop feelings of weakness and helplessness and believe that they could have done more than they did to prevent themselves from being victimized. Traditionally, society has reinforced this view by holding victims responsible for what has happened to them.

It is not only violent interpersonal crimes that have emotional consequences. Burglary is one type of crime against property that can invite a strong response (Hough, 1985; Smith and Hill, 1991), in part because it can be viewed as a crime with the potential for violence. Even though victims are typically away from home when the offense occurs, they are forced to contemplate what might have happened had they been at home. In addition, because a burglary could threaten violence against other members of the household, each member of the household may feel concern not only for his or her own personal safety but also for the well-being of other family members. Finally, because burglary is a crime that represents an invasion of privacy and, in many cases, involves theft of or damage to objects that might have sentimental value, the emotional response may be severe (Hough, 1985).

Ironically, it has often been argued that victims' psychological distress can be magnified by social and criminal justice agencies charged with the responsibility of helping victims (Rosenbaum, 1987). In particular, the police have sometimes been accused of failing to provide victims with the emotional support they require and often expect (Carter, 1985; Skogan and Wycoff, 1987). Victims may feel that the police are not doing enough to help them or to recover stolen property. When property is recovered, they may wonder why it is not returned to them more promptly.

To some extent, victim discontent with the police reflects the routine nature of police work. Some victims of even minor crimes expect a rapid response when they telephone the police. For the dispatcher overwhelmed by calls for service, however, a minor crime may be assigned very low priority. As a result, the victim feels let down by the police. In a similar way, victims who know with certainty that they have been victimized might expect that the police officer who arrives on the scene will accept their version of the story at face value and then engage in hot pursuit of the offender. For the police officer, the situation may be more ambiguous, and it may be necessary to ask questions before sense can be made of the event. In addition, the officer's experience suggests that "hot pursuit" is pointless because the offender is unlikely to be found in this way—if at all.

In general, much of the research on emotional reactions to victimization seems to indicate that when symptoms occur, they are likely to erode slowly over time (Burt and Katz, 1985; Hough, 1985). However, some evidence also suggests that symptoms sometimes persist or even re-emerge months after the incident (Sales et al., 1984). Such findings imply that the recovery process may not be as linear as is sometimes believed.

BEHAVIORAL CONSEQUENCES

Some of the behavioral effects that result from victimization are directly related to physical injuries or economic losses. Victims may need to take time off from work, for instance, because medical care is required or because property must be repaired or replaced. The 1992 NCVS found that victims lost time from work in about 8 percent of violent victimizations, 4 percent of personal thefts, and 6 percent of household crimes (U.S. Dept. of Justice, 1994a). About 35 percent of the victims of personal crimes who lost time from work were away less than a day, while 9 percent were away for eleven days or more.

Victims exhibit a variety of behavioral reactions to crime, many of which are intended to make them safer. A common response is **avoidance behavior**, by which victims seek to distance themselves from the kinds of people or situations that they perceive as dangerous (DuBow et al., 1979). In extreme cases, this may involve changing residences or neighborhoods (Burt and Katz, 1985).

Police departments deploy victim services units to help victims deal with the consequences of crime.

Victims might also try to increase home protection by installing new locks or an alarm system or personal protection through the purchase of a gun or enrollment in a self-defense course. An important irony revealed in research is that, while victims often engage in these behaviors, they may be less likely than others to believe that they are safer because they do so (Lurigio, 1987).

Victims also seek help from others. As we saw in Chapter 1, a common (although less common than many think) response is to contact the police. Victims appear most likely to do this when they see some practical or tangible reason to do so. However, even before they contact the police, victims often contact friends or family members in order to ask their opinions about what should be done. The victim might be unsure, in some cases, whether the event is in fact a crime or whether it is serious enough to warrant police intervention. These friends or family members can help clarify matters by reminding the victim of standards against which the event can be judged (Ruback et al., 1984).

This information-seeking behavior has two important implications. First, it helps to explain why, according to some research, victims often wait well over an hour after an incident before notifying the police (Greenberg et al., 1982). Second, it demonstrates that the victim's decision is not necessarily an individual one but rather reflects the social influence of others to whom the victim has access immediately following the crime (Ruback et al., 1984).

Over the longer term, victims might engage in some form of collective participation (DuBow et al., 1979). The most obvious form of such participation might be membership in some community crime prevention group such as a

Neighborhood Watch (Rosenbaum, 1988). Alternatively, victims may get involved in one of the many generic or more specialized victims' groups that have proliferated in recent decades.

A common reaction is to tell others the story of the crime (Wachs, 1988). Lejeune and Alex (1973) reported that this was a near-universal tendency in their sample of mugging victims. They observed as well that the interest of the victim in telling the story seems to be matched by an interest on the part of others in hearing it. Telling the story of one's victimization might have important therapeutic value. When others react in supportive ways or tell similar stories, the victim may find it easier to make sense of the event and to put it into some broader perspective.

The behavioral reactions of victims can be easily overstated because most people are familiar with someone who has responded to crime in perhaps an extreme manner. However, in general, most victims do not seem to react to the crime by making major or basic lifestyle changes (Hindelang et al., 1978). Because our lifestyles are a product of our family responsibilities and occupational commitments, they are not changed easily.

Although there is a tendency in the criminological literature to think about such changes as **costs of victimization** that limit behavior, there may be some benefits. As Skogan (1987) states, when people change their behavior in other circumstances in response to negative experiences, we call this "learning." To the degree that such changes do make people less vulnerable without dramatically affecting the quality of life, they may be beneficial.

COPING WITH THE COSTS OF VICTIMIZATION

Victims differ in their ability to cope with the costs of criminal victimization due to a number of factors (Resick, 1987; Sales et al., 1984; Skogan, 1987). Victims who are isolated from supportive others may find it more difficult to manage the stresses associated with crime than will those whose families and friends are able to lend emotional or practical assistance. People with more economic resources may find it less difficult to absorb economic losses or to replace stolen or damaged property. Also important are prior psychological functioning and previous victim history. Individuals who are already suffering from depression may respond to criminal victimization more negatively, as might those who have already been victimized by crime.

One way in which victims attempt to cope with the costs of victimization is by engaging in a re-evaluation of the event (Taylor et al., 1983). In so doing, victims redefine the situation to make it less threatening to their self-esteem or to their future plans. In short, victims are being attentive to various cultural adages that advise us to "look on the bright side." Taylor and colleagues suggest that victims achieve this end through a series of evaluative strategies. They may, for instance, compare themselves with less fortunate others. Provided one chooses the criteria for comparison carefully, one can always find examples of people who have lost more or suffered more. Alternatively, despite suffering or loss, victims might try to discover some way in which the event was beneficial.

In this respect, the victim might say, "I sure learned my lesson" or "I won't ever get myself into that situation again."

Agnew (1985) suggests that this process resembles the neutralization process that Matza and Sykes (1961) described in their explanation of why offenders commit crime. However, rather than convincing themselves, as offenders do, that a particular criminal act is not really wrong, victims try to convince themselves that particular acts of victimization are not really harmful. Victims may, for instance, invoke a "denial of injury" in order to minimize the harm caused. Or they may articulate a "denial of responsibility" to minimize the guilt or shame that accompanies self-blame. These neutralizations, claims Agnew, allow victims to avoid feelings of fear or other negative emotions that sometimes accompany criminal victimization.

OFFENDER OUTCOMES: SOCIAL STIGMA AND LABELING

In a simple way, a victim's loss is often an offender's gain. Losing cash or property in a theft or losing a physical encounter can translate into wins for the offender. Of course, the offender risks apprehension and punishment, but as we have seen in previous chapters, these risks are often slight. Proponents of punishment or rehabilitation contend that if offenders are apprehended, the criminal justice system may play an important role in discouraging further offending. A school of thought known as **labeling theory** proposes a markedly different view of how the frustration created by particular forms of social arrangements may motivate criminal behavior (Becker, 1963; Gibbs, 1966; Kitsuse, 1962; Rubington and Weinberg, 1987). Labeling theorists maintain that the social response to minor and sporadic criminal acts may create conditions that increase the likelihood of more serious patterns of criminality.

Labeling theorists place great emphasis on the ways in which the responses of the police and the criminal justice system to people identified as offenders create problems for those who must bear the label of "criminal." Such a label can be understood as a form of stigma that makes it difficult for those on whom it has been imposed to lead normal lives. The person who is labeled a criminal, thief, delinquent, or troublemaker may find it difficult to obtain employment or to maintain friendships with others, who tend to react to the powerful emotional content of the label. People who have been labeled may be frustrated by their

WHAT IS IT?

Labeling

A label can be understood as a form of stigma that makes life difficult for those on whom it has been imposed to lead normal lives. The person who is labeled a criminal, thief, delinquent, or troublemaker may find it difficult to obtain employment or to maintain friendships with others. People who have been labeled may be frustrated by their personal circumstances. Increasingly, legitimate associations may become less available, and illegitimate associations more so.

personal circumstances, or they may view as hypocritical the response of those who condemn their conduct. Increasingly, legitimate associations may become less available, and illegitimate associations more so.

Labeling theorists argue that the effects of societal reactions have important implications for the ways in which labeled people see themselves. Feedback that consistently provides the message that one is a disreputable person may eventually lead to acceptance of that definition. The effect of these labeling processes, then, may be to create a criminal self-identity, that is, **secondary deviance** (Lemert, 1951). The problems created by the labeling process increase the likelihood that the labeled person will develop a stable pattern of criminal behavior. What labeling theory describes to us is a kind of self-fulfilling prophecy in that people who are treated as though they were beyond redemption will come to act as if they were. Thus, while the police and other criminal justice agencies intend to reduce involvement in crime, they very often have the opposite effect.

Criminologists have criticized the labeling approach for redirecting attention from the individual onto the agencies of social control and for failing to develop a body of supporting empirical evidence (Gove, 1975; Sagarin, 1975; Wellford, 1975).

SOCIAL OUTCOMES: INDIVIDUAL, ORGANIZATIONAL, AND GOVERNMENTAL RESPONSES

Crimes have implications not only for those who are directly involved but also for others who have only secondhand knowledge of these events. The ways in which members of the general public, government officials, and various private interests respond to crime invite criminological investigation.

PUBLIC FEAR OF CRIME

Since the early 1970s, researchers have been interested in the study of public reactions to crime. Much of this research has been organized around the study of the fear of crime. While surveys suggest that serious crime is a statistically rare event, the fear of becoming the victim of such a crime is much more pervasive. The notion that fear of crime may have become as serious a problem as crime itself has been taken up by journalists, and the media have covered the issue extensively in recent years.

WHAT IS THE FEAR OF CRIME?

Despite the fact that the term **fear of crime** is widely used in the popular and social scientific literature, there is relatively little agreement regarding its meaning; both *fear* and *crime* are complicated terms. Common usage of the term *fear* suggests an emotional or physiological reaction. We recognize that we are afraid when our mouths are dry, our hearts begin to pump, and the blood drains out of our faces. This, however, is not the way in which the term is typically employed by criminologists who do research in this area. After all, criminologists rarely have access to people when they are actually afraid.

Most research on the fear of crime comes from surveys (often victimization surveys) in which members of the public are asked about their beliefs or perceptions regarding crime. As a result, fear is usually treated as an attitude or a perception rather than as an emotion. In addition, we most often treat fear as a personal rather than an altruistic matter in that we ask people about their worries regarding their own safety or the safety of their property. Warr (1991) argues, however, that people often are fearful not for their own safety but for the safety of other family members. Parents, for instance, may express less fear if asked about their own safety but more fear if asked about the safety of their children.

Skogan (1993) argues that the research literature indicates at least four distinct meanings of fear. The first meaning, *concern*, focuses on the extent to which people understand crime to be a serious problem in their communities. Concern is a judgment that people make about the frequency and seriousness of crime in the local environment. Using this definition, it is possible for a person to be concerned about crime without being personally fearful (Furstenberg, 1971).

A second definition of fear emphasizes *risk*. Research that uses this type of definition employs questions asking respondents how likely they think it is that they will become victims of crime at some point in the future. While this definition does not include an explicit emotional dimension, the assumption is that people who perceive their chances of being a victim of crime to be high will be more afraid.

Third, fear may be understood in terms of a *threat*. This definition stresses the potential for harm that people believe crime holds for them. Respondents to surveys are frequently asked, for instance, "How safe do you or would you feel walking alone in your neighborhood at night? Would you say that you feel very safe, reasonably safe, somewhat unsafe, or very unsafe?" Questions of this sort ask people how likely they think it is that they would be harmed if they were to expose themselves to risk.

Finally, fear may be defined in terms of *behavior*. People may be asked not how they feel about their safety or how likely they think they are to be subject to harm, but about what they do (or say they do) in response to crime. Respondents may be asked, for example, whether they engage in "avoidance behavior" or about the other precautions they take to protect themselves from crime.

BOX 6.2 PRISON PRECAUTIONS

165

The fear of crime is usually considered a problem that affects the residents of particular neighborhoods. However, for obvious reasons, fear is also a problem in prisons, although there has been relatively little research into this topic.

One researcher who has investigated the problem is Richard McCorkle, who undertook a study of victimization, fear, and precautionary behavior among the (male) inmates of Tennessee State Prison. Three hundred inmates completed questionnaires about crime and reactions to crime in the institution. In addition, twenty-five face-to-face interviews were conducted with prison inmates.

The study revealed that older inmates who were more socially isolated tended to report using more passive, avoidance techniques (such as steering clear of certain areas of the prison or spending more time in their cell) to reduce the risk of victimization. On the other hand, younger inmates who had long histories of institutionalization were more likely to try to reduce their risks by engaging in more aggressive precautionary behaviors (such as keeping a weapon handy or lifting weights).

McCorkle notes that all inmates are likely to use both types of strategies at various points in their incarceration. Even the toughest inmate, for instance, might try to avoid troublesome members of the prison population prior to a parole hearing in the hope of gaining early release. Correspondingly, the more passive inmate may behave aggressively if confronted with a dire threat that is not alleviated by less aggressive action. Still, McCorkle concluded, "The general orientation and response to perceived threats, be it passive or aggressive, probably remains consistent over the course of the incarceration experience."

For Discussion

Compared to life on the outside, what types of limitations does prison life place on the ability of people to cope with the fear of victimization? Are the problems described by McCorkle likely to manifest themselves in the same way in women's prisons?

SOURCE: Based on R. C. McCorkle (1992), "Personal Precautions to Violence in Prisons," *Criminal Justice and Behavior* 14: 160–173.

It is not only the concept of fear but also the concept of crime that is problematic in this research. While it is rarely stated explicitly, the kinds of crime to which reference is made are those of a direct predatory nature. Respondents are usually asked about how much they worry about crimes like robbery or burglary or about their feelings of safety on neighborhood streets. They are less frequently asked about how much they fear corporate crimes or violence in the family (Warr and Stafford, 1983).

PATTERNS IN FEAR

The term *public fear of crime* encourages the view that fear is a problem evenly shared by all members of society. As in the case of other social problems, however, the burden of fear falls more heavily on the shoulders of some than others. We can identify two broad sets of factors that have been shown to be related to differences in the fear of crime. One set of factors suggests characteristics of individuals, and the other involves the characteristics of their social environments.

Both sets of factors are important to a comprehensive understanding of fear of crime. The individual-level factors—gender, age, and socioeconomic or minority status—are often interpreted as measures of social and physical vulnerability. They explain why some people (women, the aged, the poor, racial minorities) might feel they are particularly susceptible to criminal victimization or less able to cope with the consequences of any victimization that does occur. In contrast, the environmental factors can be understood as describing dangers in the environment itself. When crime rates are higher, when public order is tenuous, and when people learn about local crime by talking to friends and neighbors, they define their environments as less safe.

INDIVIDUAL-LEVEL FACTORS

GENDER

Of all the factors that have been shown to be related to fear of crime, the strongest effects are associated with gender. Overall, women are much more likely to express anxiety about crime than are men (Garofalo, 1981; LaGrange and Ferraro, 1989; Skogan and Maxfield, 1981). For one thing, women are more likely both to be and to perceive themselves as smaller than and less physically capable than the typical male offender (Gordon and Riger, 1989). These physical differences are, of course, reinforced by the traditional gender-role socialization that encourages females to think of themselves as vulnerable to a variety of forms of danger and discourages the development of assertive methods for dealing with threatening behavior (Sacco, 1990).

Another important factor explaining the higher levels of fear among women is the specific fear of rape (Gordon and Riger, 1989). Although men are unlikely to express concern about the possibility of sexual victimization, this crime seems to be at the core of much of the concern that women express for their personal safety. Warr (1985) argues that, compared to many other crimes, women see rape as both serious in its consequences and frequent in its occurrence. This tendency to estimate the risks of rape as relatively high and the consequences as relatively severe has a significant impact on women's fear.

In addition, claims Warr, rape can be thought of as a "perceptually contemporaneous offense." In other words, it is a crime that can occur not only as an isolated act but also in connection with other crimes such as robbery or burglary. For women, the association of these crimes with sexual danger makes them even more fear-provoking.

AGE

It is widely believed that fear of crime is a particular problem for the elderly. Several studies do show that despite their lower victimization rates, older people express greater concern for their personal safety (Baldassare, 1986;

Garofalo, 1981; Skogan and Maxfield, 1981; Yin, 1980). The high level of fear has come to be regarded as reflecting reality by journalists, policymakers, and many social scientists (Cook and Skogan, 1990; Fattah and Sacco, 1989).

Arguments about the high level of fear among the elderly suggest important parallels with the case of women. Older people, it can be argued, possess lower levels of physical efficacy and fewer physical resources with which to cope with the threat of crime or the consequences of victimization (Yin, 1980).

Despite the popularity of the claim regarding high levels of fear among the elderly, it has been challenged by many researchers (Moeller, 1989; Yin, 1982). LaGrange and Ferraro (1987) argue that researchers who have found that fear increases in old age tend to measure fear by asking questions about feelings of safety while on the street alone at night. They maintain that while older people are more likely to give answers indicating anxiety about their personal safety, this question really has nothing to do with the day-to-day lives of most older Americans. For a variety of reasons relating to health, finances, and general lifestyle, older people do not typically find themselves walking alone on the street at night. This means that the answers are more hypothetical than descriptive of the everyday realities of the elderly.

Many institutions have developed ways to combat personal victimization.

RACE AND INCOME

Studies show that personal safety is a greater problem for low-income individuals and for African-Americans (Baumer, 1978; Skogan and Maxfield, 1981). While the differences are not as great as in the case of gender, they are significant.

Two factors might be advanced to explain these relationships. First, in the context of American society, income and race are indicators of access to resources. Economic and racial minorities may be less able to take taxis, install alarm systems, or take other measures that might make them feel safer. Second, in many American cities, there are very clear patterns of racial and economic segregation, and many neighborhoods with large numbers of low-income or minority residents are also neighborhoods with very high rates of crime. This means that measures of race and income, at the individual level, are related to fear because they are "proxy" measures for neighborhood of residence.

ENVIRONMENTAL FACTORS

We are more likely to feel anxious about our personal safety in some settings than others. Warr (1990) has shown that people are more afraid of crime when they are alone, when they are in a novel setting, and when it is dark. An awareness of environmental factors alerts us to the fact that fear is not just a sociopsychological characteristic that some people have and other people do not have but also a response to the social contexts in which we find ourselves.

In general, the fear of crime is a more significant problem in big cities than in small towns (Baumer, 1978; Garofalo, 1981; Moeller, 1989). The simple explanation for this is that big cities have higher crime rates, and the greater fear of urbanites is a rational response to the reality of big-city crime.

While this is probably true, it is not necessarily the whole story. The urban sociologist Claude Fischer (1981) has suggested that fear is a more significant problem in cities because the "public world of city life" routinely presents residents with situations that increase their feelings of insecurity. As we travel through urban public places, we are likely to encounter people who are strangers not only in the personal sense but also in a cultural sense. Because cities are hotbeds of lifestyle innovation, Fischer argues, we always run the risk of finding ourselves on the street, in an elevator, or on a subway platform with people whose style of dress or public behavior strikes us as weird or threatening. While many of the strangers we encounter are not criminals or delinquents, our unfamiliarity with groups whose lifestyles differ dramatically from our own may undermine our sense of security in cities.

BOX 6.3 COMMUNITY DISORDER

Researchers such as R. LaGrange and colleagues (1992) and Wesley Skogan (1990) argue that public concern about disorder is usually gauged by asking survey respondents to indicate how serious a problem they perceive each of several different types of problems to be in their own neighborhoods. The types of disorders about which people are typically asked include the following:

- Trash and litter lying around
- Dogs barking loudly or being a nuisance
- Inconsiderate or disruptive behavior
- Graffiti on sidewalks and walls
- Vacant houses and unkept lots
- Unsupervised youths
- Noisy neighbors
- People drunk or high on drugs in public
- Abandoned car parts lying around
- Kids or adults trespassing in people's yards

For Discussion

Are any of these things a problem in your neighborhood, and if so, do they have anything to do with the way you feel about the neighborhood? Given that many of these problems seem to have little to do with crime or criminal justice (in the narrow sense), who should be responsible for controlling them?

SOURCES: Based on R. L. LaGrange, K. F. Ferraro, and M. Supancic (1992), "Perceived Risk and Fear of Crime: Role of Social and Physical Incivilities," *Journal of Research in Crime and Delinquency* 29(3): 311–334; W. G. Skogan, *Disorder and Decline: Crime and the Spiral of Decline in American Neighborhoods* (New York: Free Press, 1990b).

Within communities, levels of fear vary from one neighborhood to another. Again, some of the difference is due to differences in crime rates (Miethe and Lee, 1984). Residents who live in neighborhoods where the levels of crime are higher are more likely to be concerned about their personal safety and the safety of their property than are people who live in neighborhoods with lower crime rates.

However, levels of neighborhood fear are also affected by what some writers have called "social disorder" or **incivility** (Baumer, 1987; Bursik and Grasmick, 1993; LaGrange et al., 1992; Skogan, 1990). These terms refer to those low-level breaches of the social order that, while not strictly criminal, in many cases seem to be related to a sense of unease. Incivilities are usually considered to be of two types. Physical incivilities include conditions such as abandoned buildings, unkempt residences, and strewn trash and litter. Social incivilities include public drinking or drug use, panhandlers, and groups of noisy youths. In a study of reactions to disorder in forty neighborhoods, Skogan (1990) found that although disorder tends to be a problem where crime is also a problem, its effects on levels of fear supplement the effects exerted by the local crime rate.

> ### WHAT ARE THEY?
>
> ### *Incivilities*
>
> Incivilities include physical conditions, such as abandoned buildings, unkempt residences, and strewn trash and litter, and social conditions, such as public drinking or drug use, panhandlers, and groups of noisy youths.

Why does social disorder promote fear of crime? A dominant interpretation stresses the role that disorder plays in signaling to people the breakdown of local social controls. People may read signs of incivility as indicating that in this neighborhood people don't care very much about themselves or their community. In effect, the message is that neighborhoods that can tolerate conditions like these can also tolerate more serious threats to person or property.

THE INFORMATION ENVIRONMENT

Fear of crime is a reaction to what we experience as well as what we see and hear. However, since fear is more pervasive than crime itself, it makes sense to ask what role various information sources play in the promotion of crime-related anxieties.

It seems reasonable to argue that the mass media must be an important factor in promoting fear of crime. After all, as we saw in Chapter 1, crime figures prominently in both news and entertainment media, and Americans are avid consumers of mass media.

Despite the apparent logic of this argument, researchers have had trouble documenting the existence of a clear and unambiguous relationship between people's media diets and their fear of crime (Cumberbatch and Beardsworth, 1976; Doob and MacDonald, 1976; Sacco, 1995; Skogan and Maxfield, 1981). Some of the problem relates to limitations of the research. For instance, it is not always easy to determine what people learn from the mass media and what they learn from other sources (Doob, 1982). This is because most of us not only watch television news or read newspapers but also talk to friends or neighbors about what we hear and read.

Even when these limitations are taken into account, however, the effects of media on fear of crime are not as strong as we might expect them to be. It is, after all, too simplistic to argue that people respond in a predetermined way to media messages about crime. Individuals approach the media with their own predispositions, personal histories, and beliefs about media credibility, all of which affect their interpretations of the information they receive (O'Keefe, 1984; Schlesinger et al., 1992).

Although we are heavy consumers of media content, what we learn does not necessarily have much relevance to our judgments about our personal safety. Rather, we seem to learn these kinds of lessons far more effectively from other sources. The relevant research indicates the news about crime that moves through interpersonal channels in the form of gossip and rumor may be more likely to induce fear than the news that comes to us in broadcast or print form (Baumer, 1987; Bursik and Grasmick, 1993; Skogan and Maxfield, 1981). When we learn about crime by talking to our neighbors, for instance, we learn about victims of whom we might have some personal knowledge. In these cases, we cannot dismiss what we hear by telling ourselves that the victims are nameless and faceless and that they live somewhere else.

In comparison, the average crime story that we read about in the newspaper is stripped of much of its emotional content and is likely to involve victims who are much more anonymous. Moreover, the typical media crime story provides us with so little information about victims, offenders, or the circumstances of the crime that we learn relatively little that will help us assess the risks in our neighborhoods, our workplaces, or anywhere else our daily routines take us (Gordon and Riger, 1989). Most crime news is "nonlocal" in character and thus not relevant to the judgments we need to make about the threats we face in local environments. Consistent with this view is the finding reported by some researchers that news coverage is likely to affect fear when the media give prominent treatment to random violent crimes that occur locally (Heath, 1984; Liska and Baccaglini, 1990).

COMMUNITY REACTIONS

How do individuals' reactions to crime have implications for the communities in which they live? Theorists have provided two general answers to this question. The first, derived from the writings of the famous French sociologist Emile Durkheim, suggests that public reactions to crime can make important contributions to the cohesion and stability of social life: "Crime brings together upright consciences and concentrates them. We have only to notice what happens, particularly in a small town, when some moral scandal has just been committed. [People] stop each other on the street, they visit each other, they seek to come together to talk of the event and to wax indignant in common" (Durkheim, 1933: 102).

From this view, crime is thought to shock our sentiments and reaffirm our commitment to the common values that the crime violates. Our communal opposition to crime unites us. We might speak out against crime, be more vigilant in the exercise of informal social control, join a concerned citizens' group, or support the toughening of laws intended to control crime. The overall effect described by this view is one of social integration and a strengthening of social control whereby crime rates may decline or at least stabilize.

In sharp contrast, others have suggested that because crime generates fear, it is more likely to drive people apart than to bring them together (Conklin, 1975; DiIulio, 1989). John Conklin argues that when people are less afraid of crime, they are more likely to trust others and to think positively about their communities and less likely to restrict their activities and reduce their social interaction with other community members. In contrast, when levels of fear are high, people are more likely to stay home at night and less likely to get to know or to be interested in their neighbors. Some might even be tempted to flee the community for a safer haven. Overall, then, crime does not build communities up as the Durkheimian model contends, but rather undermines communities by weakening interpersonal ties.

This view implies that public reactions to crime weaken informal social controls. When the streets are empty and neighbors cease to care what happens to one another, potential offenders may feel freer to take advantage of criminal opportunities.

BOX 6.4 CAN CRIME CAUSE CRIME?

Some researchers have argued that public reactions to rising crime rates can amplify subsequent crime-rate increases. The central mechanism in this process is the breakdown of informal social control at the community level. Lynne Goodstein and Lance Shotland (1982) have described the processes by which crime rates spiral upward as follows.

The cycle begins with actual increases in the crime rate or with the occurrence of one or several particularly noteworthy crimes. Such crimes might include an unsolved murder or a series of sexual assaults for which an offender has not been apprehended.

In the next stage, information about these crimes and the threats that they pose to other members of the community is disseminated widely. People learn via the mass media or rumor networks that crimes are increasing and/or even they might be at risk.

As the information circulates, people begin to fear for their safety. This fear causes them to withdraw from community life. They stay home at night rather than go out and report that their enjoyment of the community has declined.

As people withdraw from the community, the delicate web of social relations begins to break down, as do the various informal social controls that regulate conduct. Thus, as the streets become less populated, they are subject to less control because citizen surveillance of them is reduced.

As the levels of community control decline, the levels of crime may be expected to rise; and as the levels of crime continue to rise, the cycle begins to repeat itself.

Goodstein and Shotland's argument is consistent with the theoretical view that crime is made more likely by the absence of controls that check it. As the authors note, empirical evidence supports each of the individual linkages just described. What is less clear, however, is the validity of the overall model, which has not been rigorously tested in its entirety.

For Discussion

Are there ways in which fear of crime has changed the ways in which you go to work or to school?

SOURCE: Based on L. Goodstein and R. L. Shotland (1982), "The Crime Causes Crime Model: A Critical Review of the Relationship Between Fear of Crime, Bystander Surveillance, and Changes in the Crime Rate," *Victimology* 5(2–4): 133–151.

Research evidence supports both points of view. In general, however, arguments about the ways in which crime drives people apart seem to have more empirical validity than arguments about the ways in which it brings them together (Skogan, 1981, 1990). We should note, too, that the two arguments are not necessarily inconsistent with each other. Using data collected in six Atlanta neighborhoods, for instance, Gates and Rohe (1987) distinguished three types of reactions to crime—avoidance, protection, and collective action. They found that each type of reaction was related to a different combination of factors. Avoidance behavior (avoiding places or people in the neighborhood) was found to be related to local crime rates and the fear of crime. Protective behavior (such as taking a self-defense course or obtaining a gun or watchdog) was more closely related to levels of neighboring and the amount of control that respondents felt they could exert in the local area. Finally, collective reactions (such as involvement in local crime prevention efforts) were related to both sets of factors.

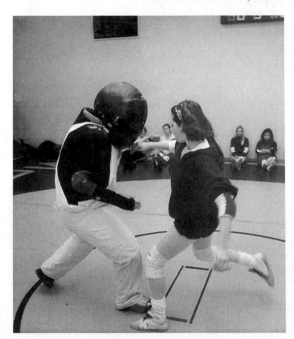

The fear of crime may prompt a variety of protective measures.

In an interesting reanalysis of this issue, Liska and Warner (1991) used the routine activities theory of Cohen and Felson (1979) to suggest why elements of both arguments are useful. In short, they contend that the Durkheimian view is correct in claiming that the effect of public reactions to crime is to reassert social controls in ways that stabilize crime rates or push them down. However, their view of the process by which this happens is closer to the position taken by Conklin than the one advanced by Durkheim.

As discussed in the previous chapter, the routine activities theory emphasizes the role that opportunities play in the commission of crime. Social patterns that separate people from their property and from their family members increase the opportunities for crime. Liska and Warner agree that public reactions to predatory crimes (like robbery) keep people at home and away from strangers. While this reduces their sense of community, it also allows them to exert greater guardianship over their persons and property. As this happens, opportunities for crime are decreased and greater control of crime is achieved.

CLAIMSMAKING

Fear can enhance the public's concerns about crime. How they react may be determined by the actions of the special interest groups that lobby for attention to be paid to these problems. Some writers refer to the processes by which laws are passed or legal reforms are initiated as claimsmaking (Best, 1990; Spector and Kitsuse, 1977). In the **claimsmaking** process, groups offer assertions about the existence of some problem that requires a policy solution. They then attempt to gain public support for these claims and to attract the attention of public officials and the mass media. Becker (1963) describes the claimsmaker as a "moral entrepreneur" who is best exemplified by the crusading reformer. According to Becker, there is "some evil which profoundly disturbs" these reformers, who believe that "nothing can be right in the world until rules are made to correct it" (147–148).

> ### WHAT DOES IT MEAN?
>
> #### *Claimsmaker*
>
> The claimsmaker is a "moral entrepreneur," best exemplified by the crusading reformer who believes that rules must be formulated to combat the evil in the world.

In the early stages, the claims may reflect a narrow set of relatively private interests (Pfuhl, 1986; Ross and Staines, 1972). Claimsmakers may regard themselves as representing those who have been victimized by some condition or who feel directly threatened by it (Weeks et al., 1986). However, claims may also be issued by state agencies seeking to expand their mandates or by professional groups seeking to enhance their status. It has been argued, for example, that marijuana laws find their origin not in widespread public concern about drug use, but in the claimsmaking activities of the Federal Bureau of Narcotics (Becker, 1963; Reasons, 1976). More recently, researchers have suggested that the pressure for the passage of computer crime laws has largely resulted from the crusading efforts of computer crime "experts" who, in publicizing the issue, were able to gain recognition for themselves and their work (Hollinger and Lanza-Kaduce, 1988).

Best (1990) asserts that, with regards to legislative and other policy-making bodies, claimsmakers may be described as being either insiders or outsiders. Insiders include political lobbyists, representatives of powerful professional organizations, and members of government, all of whom have relatively direct access to those who make public policy. By contrast, outsiders have no such direct access and must rely to a greater extent on taking their message directly to the general public. In so doing, outsiders hope to enlist members in their cause.

Spector and Kitsuse (1977) offer a four-stage model of the claimsmaking process. In stage 1, groups attempt to argue that some condition is harmful and that public action (perhaps the passage of new laws) is necessary. In stage 2, the problem is recognized by some official agency; the result may be an official investigation (for example, congressional hearings). Stage 3 is characterized by the re-emergence of claims and demands, either by the original group or by others who express dissatisfaction with the official response to the problem. Stage 4 involves a rejection by claimsmakers of the official response (or lack of response) to the problem. Spector and Kitsuse acknowledge that this "natural history" model may not precisely describe all efforts to mobilize the public response to crime or other social problems. The manner in which any specific claimsmaking process unfolds will depend on several factors, two of which require particular attention.

The first involves the amount of opposition that claimsmakers encounter in their attempts to convince the public and policymakers that a particular type of remedy is necessary. In other words, some kinds of claimsmaking are more adversarial than others. Issues that do not have this adversarial quality are sometimes referred to as **valence issues**. Child abuse, crimes against the elderly, and computer crime are valence issues in that most people would readily agree that they are problems requiring public intervention. By contrast, efforts by claimsmakers to organize public support for interventions directed against abortion or pornography are frequently met by resistance or by counterdefinitions of what the problem really is (Ross and Staines, 1972).

A second factor affecting the fate of claimsmaking is the wider social context in which this process unfolds. Prevailing social values and beliefs may at any time facilitate or hinder claimsmaking. Based on an analysis of a large number of case studies of criminalization, Hagan (1980) argues that successful claimsmakers are usually able to make effective appeals to dominant cultural values. For example, it has been argued that the social problem of crime against the elderly emerged in the 1970s because there existed a "ripe issue climate" in which rising crime, the needs of crime victims, and the needs of the elderly were already seen as important problems.

While criminalization is clearly a form of claimsmaking, the passage of a law is not always enough to satisfy the claimsmakers. Much contemporary claimsmaking about crime is directed toward changing the ways in which behavior that has already been criminalized is treated within the criminal justice system. The recognition in recent years of crimes against women, victims' rights, impaired driving, and crimes against the elderly as problems requiring more vigorous enforcement or innovative approaches attests to the validity of this observation.

In general, an understanding of responses to crime as the product of claimsmaking, conflict, and power (rather than of social consensus) alerts us to the biases of these responses. Such arguments cast serious doubt on the value of approaches that characterize the law as a neutral arbiter that can be understood without reference to the societies that produced it.

Cook and Skogan (1990) explore the claimsmaking process in their analysis of the rise and fall of the issue of crime against the elderly mentioned earlier. They show that between 1970 and 1978, crime against the elderly emerged as a significant political issue. It received attention from the news media as well as academics, elderly interest groups, and congressional committees. They suggest that the issue came to prominence when it did because it brought together into one neat package three important themes—rising crime rates, the rights of victims, and the aging of the population. The salience of these issues meant that the promotion of the problem of crime against the elderly was broad-based. In addition, the issue was not divisive in that the claim that crime against the elderly was a problem did not invite organized opposition.

Although these convergent voices put the issue of crime against the elderly on the public agenda, Cook and Skogan note that by decade's end interest in the issue had declined dramatically. They suggest that five major factors account for this.

First, there was a breakdown of the early consensus about the problem. Early in the decade, when research evidence was lacking, it was easy to argue that the elderly experienced very high rates of victimization. As the information from victimization studies began to accumulate, however, this became an untenable position. Survey after survey showed that older Americans had the lowest and not the highest rate of victimization.

Second, efforts to reformulate the problem were unsuccessful. Some advocates tried to argue that even though the elderly had low rates of victimization, they suffered more than others when they were victimized. This claim was also not supported by available research evidence. A further reformulation defined the problem in terms of fear of crime rather than crime itself, but this was a redefinition that moved the problem further away from the concerns of policymakers.

Third, the issue of crime against the elderly was not seen as central to the mandate of any particular federal agency. Those agencies that might have had an enduring interest in the problem (the Law Enforcement Assistance Administration and the Administration on Aging) were familiar with the results of the surveys showing that the problem was less serious than was being claimed. In addition, over the decade, these agencies developed other priorities, which reduced the motivation to address the problem.

Fourth, a cohesive policy community failed to develop. In this respect, there existed little agreement about how the problem should be addressed or whether feasible solutions could ever be developed.

Finally, there was a significant decline in media attention. Although, as we have seen, the media has considerable interest in stories about crime, the research showing that elderly crime rates were low made coverage of the issue more complicated and, from the viewpoint of commercial media, less interesting.

In general, public reactions to crime can be characterized as subtle and routine (Hindelang et al., 1978). Typically, crime dominates neither our personal nor our public agendas. Sometimes, however, the media, the government, and members of the general public respond to crime in a much more intense fashion. The sociologist Stanley Cohen (1972) used the term **moral panic** to describe these kinds of episodes. Goode and Ben-Yehuda (1994) explain:

> *During the moral panic, the behavior of some members of a society is thought to be so problematic to others, the evil they do, or are thought to do is felt to be so wounding to the substance and fabric of the body social that serious steps must be taken to control the behavior, punish the perpetrators and repair the damage. The threat this evil presumably poses is felt to represent a crisis for that society: something must be done about it and something must be done now; if steps are not taken immediately, or soon, we will suffer even graver consequences. The sentiment generated or stirred up by this threat can be referred to as a kind of fever; it can be characterized by heightened emotion, fear, dread, anxiety, hostility and a strong feeling of righteousness. (31)*

According to Goode and Ben-Yehuda, moral panics can be recognized by several distinguishing characteristics:

- A heightened concern over some behavior or the group that is thought to be responsible for it
- An increase in hostility toward the individuals in question
- A substantial or widespread consensus regarding the seriousness and the nature of the problem
- A public reaction that seems to be out of proportion to the size of the problem
- A volatile character such that panics emerge and subside rather suddenly

In recent years, we have witnessed several episodes that could be described in these terms. The social response to illegal drugs (Reinerman and Levine, 1989), serial killers (Jenkins, 1994), and child abduction (Best, 1988) provide illustrations of this concept.

One clear example of moral panic that has attracted the attention of several researchers is the satanic crime scare that emerged as a visible public issue in the 1980s (Best et al., 1991; Victor, 1993). Late in the decade, it was argued on several fronts that the United States was in the midst of a serious crime wave resulting from the conspiratorial actions of thousands of satanic cult members. The allegations included claims about the molestation of children in day-care centers, the satanic involvement of serial killers such as the "Son of Sam," the use of fantasy role-playing games to recruit teen satanists, graveyard desecrations, the covert actions of business leaders active in satanic worship, and police and government cover-ups of evidence that could expose the conspiracy (Best et al., 1991; Jenkins, 1992; Jenkins and Meier-Katkin, 1992; Victor, 1993).

The claims were promoted in several ways by several groups. The bizarre and sensationalist nature of the claims made them an attractive topic for afternoon talk shows and other "tabloid television" programs as well as for "legitimate" news organizations. A watershed event in this respect was the 1988 broadcast of a television special on satanic crime, hosted by Geraldo Rivera. The media fascination with these allegations was reinforced by a developing therapeutic community that claimed to have uncovered clinical evidence of the effects of satanic abuse and that promised effective treatment. In addition, many police departments developed units to fight occult crime, and the policing of satanic activity became a new law enforcement specialization (Hicks, 1991).

> ### WHAT IS IT?
> #### *A Moral Panic*
> During a moral panic, the behavior of some members of a society is seen as so problematic, evil, or harmful to the society it becomes a social imperative to control the behavior, punish the offenders, and repair the damage.

Careful analyses of these claims have shown that they lack substance (Bromley, 1991). Supporting "evidence" was at best ambiguous and at worst nonexistent. Moreover, the claims frequently defied logic and strained credibility. Still, the overriding belief that satanists often pose as "respectable" members of society allowed those caught up in the panic to discount critics—because, of course, they could be satanic conspirators as well.

According to Jenkins and Meier-Katkin (1992), the roots of the satanic crime issue can be located in the political concerns of the fundamentalist religious right. They argue that the issue was framed and promoted in a way that reflected the concerns of Christian fundamentalists at a time when this movement was undergoing a rapid expansion.

More generally, Goode and Ben-Yehuda (1994) maintain that three types of theories have been used to explain the development of moral panics. The first, the *grassroots model,* views these panics as originating in the mood of the general public. The concern that is expressed by mass media or politicians is seen as a reaction to public sentiment rather than as a cause of it.

A second theory, the *elite-engineered model,* argues that moral panics represent the deliberate attempt on the part of the economic or political elite to promote public concern about some issue that does not involve their interests. In this way, the moral panic is seen as a form of consciousness manipulation that diverts attention away from the real social problems, solution of which might undermine elite interests.

The third approach, which is also the most commonly used perspective in the study of moral panics, is *interest-group theory.* Unlike the elite-engineered model, this perspective does not see the power or resources that create moral panics as narrowly concentrated in the hands of a small group. Instead, power is understood as more diffuse and more pluralistic. The implication is that moral panics may be set in motion by the actions of politicians, crusading journalists, or professional associations.

Goode and Ben-Yehuda argue that while the elite-engineered model does not seem to explain most moral panics, the other two perspectives are of greater value—particularly when they are used in combination. This is because the grassroots model allows us to see what fears and concerns are available as the raw materials for moral panics, and the interest-group model allows us to understand how these raw materials are intensified and mobilized.

SUMMARY
■ ■ ■

The costs of victimization include financial, physical, emotional, and behavioral consequences, and the ability to adjust depends on a number of factors. Victims who are alone may find it more difficult to manage the stresses associated with crime than will those whose families and friends are able to lend emotional or practical assistance. People with more economic resources may find it less difficult to absorb economic losses or to replace stolen or damaged property. Also important are prior psychological functioning and previous victim history. Individuals who are already suffering from depression may respond to criminal victimization more negatively, as might those who have already been victimized by crime.

A further consequence of criminality is the social stigma attached to the offender. Labeling theorists emphasize the ways in which the responses of the police and the criminal justice system to people identified as offenders create problems for those who must bear the label of "criminal." Such a label can be understood as a form of stigma that makes it difficult for those people to lead normal lives. Individuals who are labeled a criminal, thief, delinquent, or troublemaker may find it difficult to obtain employment or to maintain friendships with others, who tend to react to the powerful emotional content of the label. People who have been labeled may be frustrated by their personal circumstances, or they may view as hypocritical the response of those who condemn their conduct. Increasingly, legitimate associations may become less available and illegitimate associations more so. Feedback that consistently provides the message that one is disreputable may eventually cause that person to accept that definition. The effect of these labeling processes, then, may be to create a criminal self-identity, or secondary deviance. The problems created by the labeling process increase the likelihood that the labeled person will develop a stable pattern of criminal behavior.

Fear of crime may also increase in the aftermath of crime. The research literature indicates at least four distinct meanings of fear. First, fear may mean "concern," a judgment that people make about the frequency and seriousness of crime in the local environment without necessarily being personally fearful. Second, fear may be equated with "risk," or how likely people think it is that they will become victims of crime at some point in the future. Third, fear may be understood as "threat," stressing the potential for harm that people believe crime holds for them. Finally, fear may be defined as "behavior," such that the focus is on what people do (or say they do) in response to crime, including avoidance behavior or other precautions taken to protect themselves from crime.

In response to the costs of victimization and the rise in fear, the public discussion of crime may be fueled by special interest groups pushing for increased police and criminal justice system interventions. These "claimsmakers" seek to get certain issues and problems on the forefront of the public agenda. Moral panic represents an extreme response, whereby there is an intense reaction to crime problems and strident calls for action, even in cases where the crimes being committed are few in number and not widely threatening to the public.

QUESTIONS FOR REVIEW AND DISCUSSION
■ ■ ■

1. Are there ways in which we can properly compensate crime victims for their losses? Should the offenders be involved in this process?
2. Can we use the label of offender in a positive way to help us rehabilitate offenders back into the community, or is it the case that once people offend they cannot be expected to behave normally again?
3. Is the fear of crime a realistic assessment of the risk of crime or a reflection of an overreaction to crime?
4. Do you agree that people should not change their behavior in response to their fear of crime? Does not changing behavior raise their chances of being victims, or does it keep the chances of victimization the same?
5. Can you identify different moral panics that have occurred and explain what the reactions to these panics have been?

RESEARCH

METHODS

Understanding criminal events depends on obtaining accurate data of the frequency and extent of crime occurrence. Drawing from reports from police, victims, and offenders, we are able to comprehend more fully how crime evolves and how it affects all parts of society.

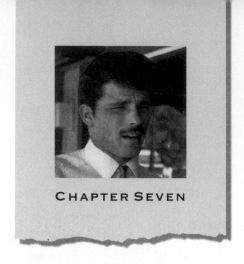

Researching Criminal Events

WHAT'S IN CHAPTER SEVEN

In this chapter, we discuss the major types of information about crime to which criminologists have access. Our discussion includes not only a description of these data sources but also a critical evaluation of their various advantages and disadvantages. We begin by addressing two very general types of crime information—observations and reports. We then discuss specific sources of crime data, including police, victim, and offender reports. We conclude with a discussion of crime rates.

In the previous chapters, we detailed some of the major ways in which modern criminologists think about and attempt to explain criminal events. In so doing, we raised several significant questions about why particular types of events occur, when and where they occur, why they unfold as they do, and why some people are more likely than others to be involved in events, either as offenders or victims. This chapter takes up a related issue—how are the questions raised by criminological theory to be answered?

In assessing the validity of dominant explanations of criminal events, criminologists do not rely on idle speculation. Rather, they seek to determine the extent to which these explanations are consistent with the empirical evidence that describes these events. In other words, they have more confidence in a given theory if it is able to organize and make sense of the **"facts of crime"** as revealed by research data. This means, of course, that we need to concern ourselves with the quality of crime data. We begin by addressing two very general types of crime information—observations and reports.

HOW ARE THEY USED?

Observations and Reports

Without question, most criminological research proceeds through the use of reports rather than observations.

OBSERVING CRIME

DIRECT OBSERVATION IN NATURALISTIC SETTINGS

At first glance, the study of criminal events might seem a relatively straightforward matter. If researchers wish to investigate criminal events, why do they not just position themselves so as to observe these events directly?

Observation could be accomplished in several ways. The researcher might (1) covertly observe a setting in which criminal events are known to occur with some frequency, (2) attempt to gain access to police or private security surveillance videotapes in order to monitor the action in a high-crime setting (Surette, 1992), (3) associate with people who engage in offending behavior in order to observe their actions and the actions of those with whom they interact, or (4) obtain permission from the local police to join patrol officers for tours of duty on city streets (Black and Reiss, 1967; Ericson, 1982; Ferraro, 1989).

Although such methods of learning about crime events would seem to have an obvious advantage in that they allow researchers direct access to the types of information in which they are interested, they have serious limitations. First, they may not be very efficient because, statistically speaking, crimes are relatively rare events (O'Brien, 1986). Even if one conscientiously observes a high-crime setting, criminal events will occur only infrequently. Similarly, even if one associates with chronic offenders, it will become obvious that much of their time is spent in crime-free activity. Thus, researchers would have to expend a considerable amount of time and energy to amass a sufficient number of observations to allow something meaningful to be said about offenders or offending.

A second problem with direct observation is that criminal behavior is usually secretive behavior. Therefore, those who are engaged in such conduct generally will do whatever they can to ensure that external observers (including criminologists) will not have as good a view as they might like.

A third problem relates to the ethics of this method of data gathering. We should be concerned about the legal and moral obligations of the researcher who observes a crime in progress. We also should be leery of modes of data collection that involve researchers covertly observing people who are going about their business or misrepresenting their real purposes to people who take them into their confidence.

Finally, the data yielded by these methods of direct observation are limited with respect to the types of questions they can address. In general, while they may allow us to observe criminal events, they do not necessarily tell us much about why the events occur where they do or why some people are more likely than others to be event participants. For example, systematic observation of a high-crime subway platform might provide an opportunity to witness a number of minor thefts or assaults. However, such observations will not tell us how this subway platform differs from others where the crime rate is much lower. Similarly, observations (by whatever means) of juvenile misconduct tell us very little about why some juveniles engage in law-violating behavior while others

Citizen interest in crime problems mobilizes the community to get involved in finding solutions.

do not. And while police ride-alongs might increase the researcher's exposure to particular types of events, they do so in a way that is subject to numerous limitations. As we have mentioned in previous chapters, the police generally become involved in criminal events after receiving requests from citizens for police assistance. Thus, while police ride-alongs may do much to increase our understanding of the role of police in criminal events, they do relatively little to facilitate our direct observations of what transpires before police assistance is sought.

In sum, observation alone generally does not tell us much about how offenders, victims, or other event participants perceive their own actions or the actions of others. We cannot glean from observation why the offenders act as they do, how they perceive their victims, why they are willing to risk punishment, or what they believe the rewards of their actions to be. Answers to such questions can only be inferred from observing the event.

EXPERIMENTAL OBSERVATION

A second observational approach involves the use of **experimentation.** Rather than waiting for things to happen, the researcher interested in exploring some aspects of criminal events arranges for them to happen. Experimentation allows for controlled observation of behavior. Also, by varying experimental conditions, researchers can study the relationship between different conditions and event outcomes (Steffensmeier and Terry, 1973).

For example, Shotland and Straw (1976) designed an experiment intended to shed light on how bystanders respond when a man attacks a woman. Subjects in the experiment were told that they were taking part in an "attitude study." Each subject was directed to a separate room where a questionnaire was to be completed. Shortly after beginning work, the subject heard a loud verbal argument between a man and a woman in the hallway. After approximately fifteen seconds of heated discussion, the man physically attacked the woman, violently shaking her while she struggled, resisting and screaming. The screams were loud piercing shrieks, interspersed with pleas to "get away from me" (Shotland and Straw, 1976: 991). What the experimental subjects did not know was that the assailant and the victim were drama students who were confederates of the researchers. Shotland and Straw's study revealed that subjects were more likely to intervene when they believed that the attack involved strangers rather than a married couple.

Tracy and Fox (1989) designed an experiment investigating automobile insurance fraud, a type of white-collar crime that does not frequently come to the attention of law enforcement officials. The researchers were interested in discovering whether automobile repair shops tend to give higher estimates for body work on insured vehicles. In order to investigate this issue, drivers who were confederates of the researchers presented assigned cars to randomly selected body shops across the state of Massachusetts. The analysis, which took the amount of damage and several other variables into account, revealed that, on average, estimates for insured vehicles were 32.5 percent higher than estimates for uninsured vehicles, a difference that the researcher concluded was unrelated to the extent of the damage, the sex of the driver, or the location of the body shop.

As these examples illustrate, experiments may provide a valuable means for answering some types of questions about criminal events. Still, experiments present some major problems, and their use by criminologists has been limited. Most of the experimental work has not focused on what many consider to be the vital roles in criminal events—offender and victim. Instead, as in the case of the Shotland and Straw study, experiments have been used to study the reactions of witnesses or bystanders to contrived situations (Farrington et al., 1993; Frinell, Dahlstrom, and Johnson, 1980; Shotland and Goodstein, 1984).

Experiments that seek to entice people into criminal conduct or that feign the victimization of unsuspecting experimental subjects pose obvious ethical dilemmas. In some circumstances, such experiments place not only the study subjects but also the researchers or their confederates at risk of physical or emotional harm.

Field experiments can also be used to assess the impact that criminal justice programs have in reducing the incidence of crime. Two well-known studies are the Kansas City patrol study conducted by Kelling and colleagues (1974) and the Minneapolis domestic violence experiment administered by Sherman and Berk (1984). Both studies involved predetermining the police intervention that would take place in different targeted areas of the city and then assessing its impact on crime.

Kelling divided Kansas City into sectors and, with the cooperation of the chief of police, allocated different types of patrol strategies to each sector. As part of the research design, Kelling tried to ensure that similar types of neighborhoods received different patrol tactics. The police then adopted three strategies: high-visibility patrol, low levels of patrol, and standard patrol levels. In analyzing the results, Kelling and his associates discovered that police patrol strategies had little effect on crime rates or fear of crime in the targeted areas. The areas that received high levels of police patrol were perceived as no more safe than those receiving lower levels. There was also little difference in the measured levels of crime.

Sherman and Berk's study was also based on a field experiment design. Its purpose was to reveal whether differences in how the police treat wife assaulters are associated with differences in the likelihood that these assaulters will re-offend. The study was restricted to cases of "simple" assault (assaults without serious injury). Each time the officers involved in the experiment encountered such a case, they were to follow experimenters' instructions, which involved a "random" choice among three forms of case processing: arrest, advice (which could include informal mediation), and an order to the suspect to leave the premises for eight hours. The behavior of the suspect was tracked for six months after the incident in order to determine if different forms of treatment resulted in different levels of re-offending. The researchers concluded that arrested suspects are less likely to engage in subsequent violence against their partners.

Interestingly, in replications of Sherman and Berk's study attempting to fine-tune the original methodology, several studies yielded results opposite to those reported by Sherman and Berk, particularly that arrest led to higher levels of subsequent domestic violence among the unemployed than among the employed. Sherman (1992) attributes the discrepancy in findings to the increased precision of the testing that was used in the replications and to the differences in the demographic characteristics of the cities that were studied. He argues that it is exactly this ability to replicate and refine findings that makes the experimental approach so valuable as a means of guiding policy decisions using social science research.

While field experiments have indeed influenced policing strategies and shaped our understanding of crime incidence, they require a great deal of cooperation from the police. Concerns have also been raised about the ethics of shifting police resources as part of a research design, which may end up endangering people. Experimenters might attempt to deal with safety or ethical issues by developing experiments that do not involve engagement in real criminal events but that approximate processes that are common to these events. Such an approach characterizes much of the research into the effect of violence in the media on behavior. Typically, the researcher exposes experimental subjects to a film or video depicting violence and then observes whether they behave in an aggressive fashion afterward. With children, the measure of aggression may involve aggressive play; with adults, it may involve the willingness of test subjects to behave punitively toward a confederate of the experimenter (Bandura, Ross, and Ross, 1963; Malamuth, 1983).

While such field experiments may pose no real danger to those who participate in them, critics charge that, because the experimental situations are artificial, they tell us very little about real-life criminals (Surette, 1992). The essence of this charge is that there is a huge difference between the willingness to behave "violently" in an experiment—when such violence is encouraged and does no real harm to anyone—and the types of criminal violence that concern the criminal justice system and so many members of the general public.

REPORTING CRIME

THE CRIME FUNNEL

The data most frequently used by criminologists interested in the study of criminal events come not from direct observation but from the reports of those who have direct knowledge of the event, principally the police, victims, and offenders. Criminal justice system agencies besides the police, such as courts and prisons, can be important sources of information about criminal events. After all, such agencies are in the "crime business" and keep records of people who are arrested, cases that go to trial, and the number of people incarcerated.

If our interest centers on the criminal event, the data made available by the various criminal agencies differ in terms of their value. In part, this is because different agencies have different needs and therefore do not all collect the same type of information. Of equal importance is the fact that criminal justice agencies are connected to one another in a "volume-reducing system" (Reiss, 1986a). In other words, there is a high level of attrition as cases travel through the various stages of the criminal justice system. Not all criminal events that come to the attention of the police result in an arrest, not all arrests result in a trial, and not all trials result in a conviction. Some writers have described this attrition process as a **"crime funnel"** (Silverman, Teevan, and Sacco, 1991). For example, according to government estimates, in the early 1990s:

- About 54 percent of all burglaries were reported to the police (U.S. Dept. of Justice, 1994b).
- Of the burglaries that were reported to police, about 13 percent were cleared by an arrest (U.S. Dept. of Justice, 1994a).
- Of the burglary cases that were brought to trial, about 68% resulted in a conviction (U.S. Dept. of Justice, 1993).

In a similar vein, Dutton (1987) argues that, as cases of wife assault move through the criminal justice system, a "winnowing process" occurs. The probability of wife assault being detected by the justice system is about 6.5 percent. Once detected, the probability of arrest is about 21.2 percent. Given these contingencies, offenders in cases of wife assault he studied had only a 0.38 percent chance of being punished by the courts.

POLICE REPORTS

For the purpose of studying criminal events, the data contained in police records are quantitatively and qualitatively superior to those maintained by the courts or correctional agencies. In a quantitative sense, police data encompass a larger number of criminal events. In a qualitative sense, police data are not directly subject to the various sorting procedures whereby cases may later be processed out of the system in a nonrandom manner.

Police crime data are based on criminal events about which police have knowledge. You will recall, however, that any measure of "crimes known to the police" cannot be expected to be synonymous with all crimes that occur, because many crimes, especially less serious ones, are not reported to the police. The data discussed in Chapter 1 indicate that as much as 50 percent of the crime reported by victims to survey interviewers is not reported to the police. You will also recall that proactive policing results in the discovery of relatively few crimes. Thus, the types and numbers of crimes about which the police have knowledge depend primarily on the reporting behavior of members of the general public.

Further, not all of the criminal events that come to the attention of the police become part of the official record. A call from a citizen who reports a crime to the police may not lead to a car being dispatched, and no subsequent action may be taken (Gilsinan, 1989). Even when the police do show up at the scene, they may decide to treat the matter unofficially or as something other than a crime.

Some types of event characteristics increase the likelihood that a crime will be recorded (Gove, Hughes, and Geerken, 1985). Events with elements that suggest a high degree of legal seriousness are more likely to be recorded as crimes (Gottfredson and Gottfredson, 1988). In addition, when strong physical evidence or compelling testimony indicates that a crime has occurred, the event is more likely to enter the official record. An event also is more likely to be treated as a crime when the person who makes the complaint to the police urges that official action be taken (Black, 1971).

Recording rates relate not only to the characteristics of the event but also to the characteristics of the policing agency. Specifically, highly professional police departments are more likely to officially record crimes (Gove, Hughes, and Geerken, 1985), in part because these departments tend to make greater use of crime data in developing departmental priorities and deploying resources. Highly professional departments also rely to a greater extent on existing official records in the processing of citizen complaints, which means that there is a stronger incentive at all departmental levels to "write up" a larger number of police–citizen interactions (Skogan, 1977).

The descriptions of events that are officially labeled as crimes by an investigating officer may undergo significant changes as they move through the internal bureaucracy of the police department. As information travels from the line officer through the communications section to the records division, offenses may be shifted from one category to another, downgraded, or ignored (Skogan, 1977). Thus, the amount of crime recorded by the police department is affected by the internal organization of the police department and by the bureaucratic procedures by which information is processed (McClearly, Nienstedt, and Erven, 1982).

THE UNIFORM CRIME REPORTING SYSTEM

Police crime data are collected and processed as part of what is known as the **Uniform Crime Reporting system (UCR)**. Since 1930, the UCR has primarily provided annual reports of the nature and amount of seven "index offenses"—homicide, assault, robbery, rape, burglary, larceny, and motor vehicle theft. In 1979, arson was added to the list of index offenses, by congressional mandate. These offenses were selected for study because of (1) their seriousness, (2) their pervasiveness, (3) their frequency, and (4) their likelihood of being reported to the police.

The UCR is basically a survey in which individual police departments across the country report crime information, in a standardized way, to the Federal Bureau of Investigation (FBI). The FBI then collates the information provided by each participating agency and publishes the data in *Crime in*

> **WHAT IS IT?**
>
> ### Uniform Crime Reports
>
> Police crime data are collected and processed as part of the FBI's Uniform Crime Reporting system (UCR), which provides police departments with a consistent set of procedures for collecting relevant information about crimes that come to the attention of the police.

the United States each year. Information about crimes is reported in an aggregate form in the UCR, with data available on a national, state, city, county, and even college campus level. The UCR currently provides no unaggregated reports of single crime incidents.

In addition to information regarding the index offenses, the UCR also provides (1) detailed information on arrest rates (including limited data on arrests for over twenty other offenses), (2) demographic information on people arrested (for example, age, race, and sex), (3) information about law enforcement officers (including how many officers are employed in a community, how many officers are killed or injured in the line of duty, and the like), and (4) details about homicide events (including data such as victim–offender relationships, weapon used, and circumstances of the event).

The UCR also compiles statistics on the percentage of crimes reported to the police that are "cleared by arrest." Clearance status refers to a judgment made by the police as to whether they can identify at least one of the offenders involved in the offense. Table 7.1 provides clearance rates for the index crimes (excluding arson) for 1993. Violent crimes have higher clearance rates than do nonviolent or property crimes, probably in part because violent crimes are more likely to be perpetrated by someone known to the victim, and hence are easier for the police to "solve."

Even though the UCR is undeniably the most complete source of data on crimes reported to the police in the United States, several methodological criticisms of the UCR data have been raised:

- Reports made to the FBI are voluntary and vary in accuracy and completeness.
- Not all agencies submit reports.
- The FBI uses estimates in total crime projections.
- In situations in which there are multiple offenses by one person, only the most serious is reported.
- For some crimes, each act is counted as a single offense, while for others this is not the case (for example, the robbery of six people in a bar would count as one robbery, whereas assault of these six people would be counted as six assaults).
- Uncompleted acts are counted together with completed ones.
- The reports are filled out by busy police officers and are subject to all of the clerical problems that one might expect to find with any reported data set (Savitz, 1982).

In an effort to address the problems and to improve the quality and usefulness of UCR data, the FBI began to redesign the program in the early 1980s. The result has been the development of the National Incidence-Based Reporting System (NIBRS). Currently in the process of being implemented in all fifty states, NIBRS will provide for the collection of data for twenty-two categories of crime. For acts within each category, data will be collected on the type of crime, victims and offenders, property involved, and arrests/outcomes. All of

Table 7.1
Offenses Known to the Police Cleared by Arrest, 1993

Type of Offense	Number Reported	Percent Cleared by Arrest
Violent crime	1,772,279	44.2%
Murder	22,697	65.6
Rape	84,624	52.8
Assault	1,036,626	55.5
Robbery	628,332	23.5
Property crime	11,091,352	17.4
Burglary	2,562,566	13.1
Larceny	7,068,072	19.8
Motor vehicle theft	1,460,714	13.6
Total index crime	12,863,631	21.2

SOURCE: U.S. Department of Justice, *Crime in the United States, 1993* (Washington, D.C.: U.S. Department of Justice, 1994).

this information is available in police records; NIBRS will simply allow the FBI to collect and distribute this information on a national level.

When NIBRS has been fully phased in, the FBI will continue to publish aggregated accounts of crime consistent with the current form and content of the UCR. In addition, however, they will also be able to make available to government officials, researchers, policymakers, and other interested parties a wealth of additional information regarding crimes known to the police.

VICTIM REPORTS

Reports from victims of crimes are a second major source of information about criminal events. Victims may be asked to describe what transpired during the event, how they reacted, whether the police were summoned, and what physical or psychological costs they may have sustained as a result of the incident. Data from crime victims are usually collected via **victimization surveys**—large-scale studies that ask individuals about their experiences with crime victimization. While many researchers employ some sort of victimization survey in attempts to learn about the ways in which individuals experience crime, the National Crime Victimization Survey (NCVS) is the most extensive—and arguably the most important—victimization survey. When the Bureau of Justice Statistics began collecting these data in 1972, one of the chief purposes of the survey was to obtain reliable information about crimes that were *not* reported to the police (and hence would not be counted in the UCR) through asking individuals about their personal experiences with victimization.

The NCVS is largely (although not entirely) a telephone survey. Interviews are conducted with all members over the age of 12 of a random representative sample of U.S. households. In 1992, for example, about 166,000 people residing in 84,000 households were interviewed. A household stays in the NCVS sample for a total of three years, during which time seven interviews are conducted (usually one every six months). Initial interviews are conducted face to face with a Bureau of Justice Statistics interviewer, while subsequent interviews are generally conducted over the phone. The NCVS has consistently obtained a response rate of about 95 percent, an impressive completion rate for research of this type.

BOX 7.1 VICTIMIZATION IN SPECIAL POPULATIONS

Sometimes, victimization surveys are carried out with special populations. Victim surveys that focus on family violence or crime in schools are examples of such studies. In 1988, the National Incidence Studies of Missing, Abducted, Runaway, and Thrownaway Children (NISMART) was conducted with a random sample of U.S. households in order to gather information about the experiences of American children with abduction, running away, and related experiences of being lost or missing. Telephone surveys with the caregivers for more than 20,000 children were conducted, and police records were studied, in order to ascertain how many children experienced such events. Table 7.2 summarizes the results. One of the findings of the study was that while stranger abductions of children are perhaps perceived as being one of the greatest dangers to children, American youth are actually much more likely to be "missing" due to other causes.

Table 7.2
NISMART Survey Results, 1988

Type of Event	Estimated Number of Children Affected	Estimated Rate per 1,000 Children Aged 0–17
Family abduction	354,100	5.61
Nonfamily abduction	4,600	0.07
Attempted nonfamily abduction	114,600	1.80
Runaways	446,700	7.08
Thrownaways	112,600	1.79
Lost, injured, otherwise missing children	438,200	6.95

SOURCE: David Finkelhor, Gerald T. Hotaling, and Andrea Sedlak, *Missing, Abducted, Runaway, and Thrownaway Children in America: First Report* (Washington, D.C.: U.S. Department of Justice, Office of Juvenile Justice and Delinquency Prevention, 1990).

For Discussion
How do these results compare to what the media describe as the problem of missing children? How might interviews with caregivers (rather than the children themselves) lead to research errors?

BOX 7.2 EXCERPTS FROM THE NCVS

HOUSEHOLD SCREEN QUESTIONS

36. Now I'd like to ask some questions about crime. They refer only to the last 6 months— between _____ 1, 19___ and _____, 19___. During the last 6 months, did anyone break into or somehow illegally get into your (apartment/home), garage, or another building on your property?
☐ Yes—How many times? _____
☐ No

37. (Other than the incident(s) just mentioned) Did you find a door jimmied, a lock forced, or any other signs of an ATTEMPTED break in?
☐ Yes—How many times? _____
☐ No

38. Was anything at all stolen that is kept outside your home, or happened to be left out, such as a bicycle, a garden hose, or lawn furniture? (other than any incidents already mentioned)
☐ Yes—How many times? _____
☐ No

39. Did anyone take something belonging to you or to any member of this household, from a place where you or they were temporarily staying, such as a friend's or relative's home, a hotel or motel, or a vacation home?
☐ Yes—How many times? _____
☐ No

40. What was the TOTAL number of motor vehicles (cars, trucks, motorcycles, etc.) owned by you or any other member of this household during the last 6 months? Include those you no longer own.
511
0 ☐ None— SKIP to 43
1 ☐ 1
2 ☐ 2
3 ☐ 3
4 ☐ 4 or more

41. Did anyone steal, TRY to steal, or use (it/any of them) without permission?
☐ Yes—How many times? _____
☐ No

42. Did anyone steal, or TRY to steal, parts attached to (it/any of them), such as a battery, hubcaps, tape-deck, etc.?
☐ Yes—How many times? _____
☐ No

INDIVIDUAL SCREEN QUESTIONS

43. The following questions refer only to things that happened to YOU during the last 6 months— between _____ 1, 19___ and _____, 19___. Did you have your (pocket picked/purse snatched)?
☐ Yes—How many times? _____
☐ No

44. Did anyone take something (else) directly from you by using force, such as by a stickup, mugging or threat?
☐ Yes—How many times? _____
☐ No

45. Did anyone TRY to rob you by using force or threatening to harm you? (other than any incidents already mentioned)
☐ Yes—How many times? _____
☐ No

46. Did anyone beat you up, attack you or hit you with something, such as a rock or bottle? (other than any incidents already mentioned)
☐ Yes—How many times? _____
☐ No

47. Were you knifed, shot at, or attacked with some other weapon by anyone at all? (other than any incidents already mentioned)
☐ Yes—How many times? _____
☐ No

48. Did anyone THREATEN to beat you up or THREATEN you with a knife, gun, or some other weapon, NOT including telephone threats? (other than any incidents already mentioned)
☐ Yes—How many times? _____
☐ No

49. Did anyone TRY to attack you in some other way? (other than any incidents already mentioned)
☐ Yes—How many times? _____
☐ No

50. During the last 6 months, did anyone steal things that belonged to you from inside ANY car or truck, such as packages or clothing?
☐ Yes—How many times? _____
☐ No

51. Was anything stolen from you while you were away from home, for instance at work, in a theater or restaurant, or while traveling?
☐ Yes—How many times? _____
☐ No

52. (Other than any incidents you've already mentioned) Was anything (else) at all stolen from you during the last 6 months?
☐ Yes—How many times? _____
☐ No

53. Did you find any evidence that someone ATTEMPTED to steal something that belonged to you? (other than any incidents already mentioned)
☐ Yes—How many times? _____
☐ No

54. Did you call the police during the last 6 months to report something that happened to YOU which you thought was a crime? (Do not count any calls made to the police concerning the incidents you have just told me about.)
512
☐ No—SKIP to 55
☐ Yes—What happened?

CHECK ITEM C: Look at 54. Was HHLD member 12+ attacked or threatened, or was something stolen or an attempt made to steal something that belonged to him/her?
☐ Yes—How many times? _____
☐ No

55. Did anything happen to YOU during the last 6 months which you thought was a crime, but did NOT report to the police? (other than any incidents already mentioned)
513
☐ No—SKIP to Check Item E
☐ Yes—What happened?

CHECK ITEM D: Look at 55. Was HHLD member 12+ attacked or threatened, or was something stolen or an attempt made to steal something that belonged to him/her?
☐ Yes—How many times? _____
☐ No

CHECK ITEM E: Who besides the respondent was present when screen questions were asked? (If telephone interview, mark box 1 only.)
514
1 ☐ Telephone interview—Go to Check Item F
Personal interview—Mark all that apply.
2 ☐ No one besides respondent present
3 ☐ Respondent's spouse
4 ☐ HHLD member(s) 12+, not spouse
5 ☐ HHLD member(s) under 12
6 ☐ Nonhousehold member(s)
7 ☐ Someone was present—Can't say who
8 ☐ Don't know if someone else present

CHECK ITEM F: If self-response interview, SKIP to Check Item G
Did the person for whom this interview was taken help the proxy respondent answer any screen questions?
515
1 ☐ Yes
2 ☐ No
3 ☐ Person for whom interview taken not present

CHECK ITEM G: Do any of the screen questions contain any entries for "How many times?"
☐ Yes—Fill Crime Incident Reports.
☐ No—Interview next HHLD member. End interview if last respondent.

For Discussion

Why might people be reluctant to answer some of these questions? Can you think of situations in which people might answer yes to these questions even though no crime occurred? How would you answer this questionnaire?

The NCVS asks about experiences with the following criminal events: rape, robbery, assault, burglary, personal and household larceny, and motor vehicle theft. It includes no questions about commercial burglary or robbery or about victimless crimes like drug use or prostitution. NCVS respondents who report that they have been victimized in some way are also asked about whether they reported the crime to the police (and why or why not) and about perceived characteristics of the offender (including whether the offender was a family member, acquaintance, or stranger), the extent of injuries and the need for medical treatment, the amount of financial loss, and the time and place in which the crime occurred. This information provides both a valuable portrait of victimization experiences and a rich complement to UCR crime data.

As valuable as they are, the NCVS data, like the UCR data, have been subject to methodological criticisms. Chief among these are the following:

- Certain crimes are thought to be undercounted (for example, domestic violence offenses).
- Undercounting may result because people forget things that happened to them, a phenomenon especially likely if the crime was a relatively minor one or, perhaps worse, if the individual is particularly accustomed to being victimized.
- People may forget or misrepresent the time frame of their experiences and report crimes that are actually outside of the time reference of the study, hence inflating incidence rates.
- Like the UCR, the NCVS records only the most serious offense committed during a criminal event in which more than one law was broken.
- Respondents may lie to please the interviewer (that is, respondents may fabricate crimes in order to provide data).

Like the UCR, the NCVS also has undergone revision in recent years in order to strengthen the quality of the data collected. Perhaps most notable among recent changes in the NCVS have been the revisions of "screener questions" designed to elicit more information about experiences of sexual assault and of domestic violence. In 1992, the new questions were used for half of the sample, and in 1993, the entire NCVS sample received the revised version of the interview.

In general, claims about the value of victim reports of crime derive from several assumed advantages of the research approach. First, it is frequently argued that because victimization surveys collect information directly from victims of crime, they can tell us about crimes that have not been reported to the police (Fattah, 1991). In so doing, victimization surveys provide a more valid estimate of the actual crime rate.

Second, because victimization surveys use samples drawn from the general population, data are collected from both victims and nonvictims over a given period. This allows researchers to compare the two groups and to analyze which social and demographic groups face the greatest risks of victimization as well as how these risks are affected by particular kinds of lifestyle behaviors such as drinking alcohol or living alone. These data can inform the development of theoretical models that link victim involvement in criminal events to factors of this type (Hindelang, Gottfredson, and Garafalo, 1978; Laub, 1987). These models were discussed in Chapter 5.

Finally, victimization survey approaches permit an investigation of the consequences of victimization and the ways victims cope with these consequences. These data shed light on the types of questions raised in Chapter 6.

OFFENDER REPORTS

Interviews with offenders can give us important insights into their behavior, attitudes, and motivations. We might learn why they commit the type of offenses that they commit, how they feel about their victims, and how they assess their risk of being apprehended by the criminal justice system (Bennett and Wright, 1984).

REPORTS FROM KNOWN OFFENDERS

Perhaps the most obvious form of offender report makes use of data gathered from a sample of known offenders such as prison inmates or those who have been convicted of an offense and are awaiting sentence (Baunach, 1990). Surveys of this type can shed light on a range of subjects, including the use of weapons by offenders (Wright and Rossi, 1986) and the characteristics of offenders' victims (Innes and Greenfeld, 1990). Understanding such subjects gives us useful insights into how offenders regard their own actions as well as those of other event participants.

BOX 7.3 PRISONERS AND THEIR VICTIMS

Most of what we know about the victims of crime is derived from victim surveys or from the records of policing agencies. However, it is also possible to learn about victims by surveying those who have offended against them.

In interviews with a nationally representative sample of over 13,000 prisoners, for instance, the 1986 Survey of Inmates in State Correctional Facilities collected information about violent offenders and their victims. The findings of this survey included the following:

- Violent offenders did not differ from nonviolent offenders in terms of sex, ethnicity, age, marital status, or education. However, violent offenders were more likely to be African-American (51 percent) than were nonviolent offenders (42 percent).
- About one in four violent offenders was imprisoned for an offense that led to a victim's death. Nearly one-half of the violent female inmates had killed their victim.
- Of all violent offenders, 59 percent reported not knowing their victim, 24 percent said they knew the victim very well or as an acquaintance, 10 percent said the victim was a relative, and 7 percent described the victim as an "intimate."

- More than one-half of violent offenders reported that the victim or victims were male.
- Violent offenders with the most extensive criminal histories were most likely to have victimized a stranger.
- About one-quarter of the women serving time for a violent offense said that the victim was a spouse or a relative.
- Over two-thirds of the violent inmates reported that either they or their victims were using alcohol or drugs at the time of the crime.

For Discussion

What special problems are we likely to encounter when we do research on prison populations and when we try to interpret the results of such research?

SOURCE: Based on C. A. Innes and L. A. Greenfeld, Bureau of Justice Statistics special report, "Violent State Prisoners and Their Victims" (Washington, D.C.: Office of Justice Programs, 1990).

One major concern with surveys of known offenders relates to the generalizability of the findings (Flowers, 1989). Given that many offenders are not captured and that many of those who are captured are not convicted or sentenced, what we learn in interviews with convicted offenders may not be representative of the larger offender population.

As discussed in Chapter 1, early studies on criminals focused on their physiological characteristics. Research conducted by Cesare Lombroso in the nineteenth century included measures of cranial structure. From his research on criminals, Lombroso developed profiles for identifying "criminal types" in the general population. Despite the limitations inherent in using a "captive" population to study crime, this is a popular form of research, primarily because it is relatively inexpensive and offers an accessible study population.

PARTICIPANT-OBSERVATION

Participant-observation provides another means by which information may be gathered from known offenders. As a research strategy, **participant-observation** moves beyond the use of a structured interview as the researcher attempts to develop more intimate associations with the people being studied (Wright and Bennett, 1990). The researcher gathers offender accounts by informally participating in and observing the social world of the offender.

This approach rests on the assumption that formal interviews with offenders yield very limited research data. Researchers may find it very difficult to gain access to members of "outlaw" motorcycle gangs, organized-crime groups, and professional thieves through conventional means (Ianni and

> ### WHAT IS IT?
>
> #### Participant-Observation Study
>
> Participant-observation requires the researcher to gather offender accounts by informally participating in and observing the social world of the offender.

Reuss-Ianni, 1972; Wolf, 1991). However, if researchers are able to cultivate informal relationships with offenders, they may be able to penetrate their social world and thereby learn much that would be invisible to an outside researcher. Studies of street gangs, such as those done by Stephen Baron on punks, provide insights into life on the street that could not be gleaned in police statistics or victim surveys (see Baron, 1989; Kennedy and Baron, 1992). Chambliss (1975), a proponent of this method of urban ethnography, argues that the data on organized crime and professional theft as well as other presumably difficult-to-study events are much more available than we usually think. "All we really have to do is get out of our offices and onto the streets. The data are there; the problem is that too often the sociologist is not" (39).

SELF-REPORT STUDIES

Self-report studies predate victimization surveys, having become popular during the 1950s and 1960s. Like victimization surveys, **self-report studies** gather data from the members of some large population. However, instead of being asked about their involvement as victims in criminal events, respondents are asked about their involvement as offenders. Like victimization surveys, self-report studies are intended to uncover crimes that have not been reported to the police (as well as to elucidate those that have). Also like victimization surveys, self-report studies allow the sample to be broken up into respondents who have and who have not been involved in criminal events over a specified period. This allows the researcher to compare offenders and nonoffenders in terms of social and lifestyle characteristics that might be useful in testing explanations of criminality.

> ### WHAT IS IT?
> #### *Self-Report Study*
> Instead of being asked about their involvement in criminal events as victims, respondents are asked about their involvement as offenders, in order to uncover crimes that have not been reported to the police (as well as those that have).

Self-report research has most frequently been used in the study of juvenile crime, although there is nothing in the approach that prevents it from being applied to the study of adults (Laub, 1987) or to "nontraditional" offenses such as computer crime. The emphasis on juveniles has largely been a matter of convenience in that juveniles, in the context of the school classroom, represent a captive audience for the researcher (Chilton, 1991). Once a sample of respondents has been selected, the data about self-reported delinquency are collected in one of two ways (O'Brien, 1985). Some researchers use a questionnaire that includes a checklist of delinquent acts. Subjects are asked to indicate whether they have committed each of the acts and, if so, how frequently, over a given period. Alternatively, researchers may ask respondents about their delinquent conduct in face-to-face interviews. Each approach has its advantages. The questionnaire makes it easier to assure the respondents of anonymity. The interview, however, allows for more detailed questioning about the circumstances surrounding the delinquent conduct (Gold, 1970).

Box 7.4 Measuring Self-Reported Computer Crime

How adequate are the data of official agencies, victim surveys, or self-report offender surveys in revealing the extent of computer crime? In theory, at least, each approach should be as applicable to the study of computer crime as it is to any other type of crime. However, our experience with these data sources is not so extensive as to allow definitive judgments to be made about their relative value.

Official data relating to computer crime seem to share many of the same problems with data relating to more traditional offending (Taber, 1980). The more routine problems of victim nonreporting and selective enforcement, however, are complicated by uncertainties about how computer crime should be defined (Bequai, 1987). The literature also indicates that researchers who attempt to survey organizations that are victimized by computer crime face serious difficulties with respect to sampling and data access.

While researchers have made only very limited use of self-report offender surveys, Sacco and Zureik (1990) provide some indication of how such a survey might proceed. These researchers undertook a survey of anonymous student respondents who were enrolled in computing courses at a medium-sized university. Respondents were asked to complete a twenty-two-page questionnaire that dealt with a variety of computing behaviors, attitudes, and perceptions. A total of 202 questionnaires were distributed in class to students who were enrolled in courses required for a major in computing science and other applied science disciplines. The sample spanned the usual four years of undergraduate instruction. Slightly more than 50 percent (105) of the participating students completed and returned the questionnaire.

In one section of the questionnaire, respondents were asked to indicate whether, during the previous year, they had engaged in any of five specific types of computer misbehavior. The most frequently reported behavior was the unauthorized copying of copyrighted material for personal use (62 percent). The least frequently reported behavior was the unauthorized use of a program that was the property of a time-share system (5 percent). Equal portions (15 percent) reported that they had rummaged through discarded printout "for interesting program listings" or had used an unauthorized password. Twenty-nine percent indicated that they had used a program in such a way that they avoided being charged for its use.

For Discussion

How would reports of computer crime differ from reports of violent crime? What problems are likely to characterize "official" and victimization data relating to computer crime?

THE LIMITATIONS OF CRIME REPORTS

Much of what we know about criminal events is based on the reports provided by offenders, victims, and the police. In addressing the limitations of these data, two issues require consideration: (1) the type of event that is captured by each method of data collection, and (2) the perspective brought to bear on those events that are captured.

WHAT TYPE OF EVENT?

Each of the methods that we have discussed in this section is somewhat restricted in terms of the kinds of criminal events it illuminates. Victimization surveys usually ask respondents only about those events that have a direct and immediate victim (Reiss, 1986b). Because they are household surveys, they tend to exclude crimes that victimize businesses or the wider community (for example, vandalism of public property). Victimization surveys also exclude victims to whom access is limited, including children, the homeless, and residents of psychiatric or other institutions (Weis, 1989).

Self-report studies have been used primarily to obtain information about the "common delinquencies" of youth. They have been criticized for excluding the more serious, but less frequently occurring, types of delinquency (such as extreme forms of violence) while emphasizing nonserious forms of behavior (such as "cutting classes" or "disobeying parents") (Braithwaite, 1981; Elliott and Ageton, 1980; Gove, Hughes, and Geerken, 1985; Hindelang, Hirschi, and Weis, 1981). When students in criminology classes are asked to demonstrate with a show of hands whether they have committed any of the "crimes" listed in the self-report questionnaires, a large number always respond in the affirmative. Even political leaders have admitted to experimenting with marijuana as youths. A loose interpretation of these data, then, can make everyone a criminal (Figlio, 1990).

The police reports that form the basis of the UCR are in some ways the most comprehensive data source. Unlike victimization surveys, the UCR includes crimes without direct victims, as well as crimes committed against businesses, the community, and those individuals who are unlikely to appear in surveys (Reiss, 1986b). A limitation of the UCR system is that the data it collects are based only on those crimes that the police know about.

WHOSE PERSPECTIVE?

The issue of perspective is central to any attempt to make proper use of crime report data. Each method offers a limited perspective since it elicits information from only some types of event participants. As we saw in Chapter 2, event participants' understanding of criminal events may differ quite markedly. We expect, therefore, that their reports will reflect these differences.

Victimization data rely on victims' perceptions of criminal events. As such, their quality is subject to whatever distortions, intentional or unintentional, characterize these perceptions. The accuracy of respondents' reports also is subject to numerous compromises. For example, respondents may fail to disclose experiences in which the researcher is interested (Skogan, 1986). If someone is victimized during the course of an illegal activity, he or she may not want to tell the researcher about it. If the event is of minor significance, it may be forgotten by the time of the interview; this may be a particular problem when the reference period about which the respondent is asked is very long.

The opposite problem involves what is called **telescoping** (Skogan, 1986). In this case, crimes the victim regards as significant life events may be reported as having occurred during the reference period when, in fact, they actually occurred at an earlier point in time. Telescoping is most likely to be a problem in the study of serious violent crimes.

> ## WHAT DOES IT MEAN?
>
> ### *Telescoping*
>
> Research problem whereby crimes that the victim regards as significant life events—especially serious violent crimes—may be brought forward in time, such that the respondent reports them as having occurred during the reference period when they actually occurred at an earlier point in time.

In many cases of serious victimization, the victim may be discouraged from reporting the event to a researcher. This may be true, for instance, in cases of family violence when the victim feels ashamed or embarrassed or believes that reporting the event may put him or her at risk. This may be a particular problem with sexual assaults or crimes involving strangers.

Victims' perspectives are limited in other ways as well. If respondents cannot or do not define an event as a crime, they are unlikely to tell a researcher about it (Block and Block, 1984). In some cases, people may be victimized but not realize it—many forms of fraud are intended to accomplish precisely this outcome. Similarly, if a purse is stolen but the victim believes that she has lost it, she will not report it to a researcher who asks her a question about theft. Much of the criminal harm that is perpetrated by corporations and governments is not readily apparent, even to those who are directly affected; as a result, victims may have no idea that they have been victimized (Walklate, 1989).

Respondents are also likely to differ in their views as to what level of violation constitutes a crime (Gove, Hughes, and Geerkan, 1985). Some studies show, for instance, that the reporting of assault victimization is more likely among highly educated people. Such a finding is most reasonably interpreted in terms of class differences in the definition of injury or in the willingness to tolerate violence rather than in terms of the greater threats of criminal violence faced by more highly educated respondents (Skogan, 1990a).

Self-report studies allow us to understand criminal events from the perspective of the offender. Yet offenders who have the most to hide may be least willing to participate in the research (O'Brien, 1985). Moreover, some offenders may exaggerate their wrongdoing (perhaps as a show of bravado), while others may be reluctant to admit to involvement in criminal activity (Wright and Bennett, 1990). When the latter do report, they may be more willing to admit to trivial rather than serious offenses (Jupp, 1989).

In the case of the UCR system, the organizational perspective of policing agencies determines the rules for data collection. Administrative or political pressure may dictate that the policing of certain kinds of criminal events (for example, impaired driving) be emphasized over others (for example, "soft" drug use) (Jackson, 1990; O'Brien, 1985; Schneider and Wieresma, 1990). Police practices, public tolerance for particular kinds of behavior, and the needs of the agency for particular kinds of data all influence the ways in which data are collected (Savitz, 1978).

Reiss (1986a) argues that the perspective implicit in police data offers a distinct advantage over self-report and victimization data. Whereas the latter two data sources reflect the view of highly self-interested parties, police data allow for a more balanced picture. Police reports of criminal events are based on a wider variety of information sources, including victims, offenders, bystanders, and witnesses. In addition, police data normally are collected closer in time to the actual event than is the case with victim or offender surveys. As a result, police data are less likely to be influenced by the selective effects of memory.

In a similar vein, Gove, Hughes, and Geerken (1985) suggest that, in comparison with other data sources, official statistics provide more rigorous criteria for the definition of criminal events. They argue that victimization surveys give us only the victim's perspective, which is insufficient in determining whether a crime has in fact occurred. In order to make this judgment, we also need to know the offender's intention, the circumstances surrounding the event, and the condition of the victim (Mayhew, Elliot, and Dowds, 1989).

Criminal events that are recorded in official statistics have passed through two filters. First, they have been judged sufficiently serious to be worth reporting to the police. Second, they have been certified by the police as serious events deserving of criminal justice intervention. According to Gove, Hughes, and Geerken (1985), the reports contained in the UCR provide a good indicator of "the extent to which citizens feel injured, frightened, and financially hurt by a criminal act" (489).

These different perspectives have very important implications for how criminal events are understood. If, for example, an individual gets into a fistfight

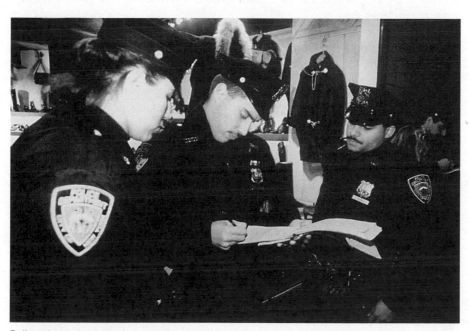

Police play an important role in documenting what happens when a crime occurs.

with a drinking companion, the event might be understood differently within the context of different data collection systems. If the individual is asked in a victimization survey whether anyone has hit him or threatened to hit him, and he responds honestly, he is likely to be counted as a victim. If he is asked in a self-report survey whether he has hit anyone, and he answers honestly, he is likely to be counted as an offender. If the police are summoned, they may, because of the circumstances and the relationship between the parties, screen the event out so that it never enters the official record.

We do not necessarily expect reports from different event participants to tell us the same things. Victimization surveys and UCR data may disagree because they employ different criteria in determining the types of events that are to be included (Block and Block, 1984; Blumstein, Cohen, and Rosenfeld, 1992; Booth, Johnson, and Choldin, 1977; Gove, Hughes, and Geerken, 1985; Menard and Covey, 1988; O'Brien, 1985, 1986). Thus, if researchers undertook a victimization survey in a given community and then compared the survey rates to the UCR rates for that same community, several sources of variation would be apparent. While the UCR measures would encompass crimes committed against businesses, institutionalized persons, and individuals who do not have a permanent residence, the victim survey would probably omit such crimes. The UCR rates would include crimes committed within the policing jurisdiction, irrespective of victims' place of residence. Thus, the UCR might include crimes committed against tourists who were visiting the community as well as crimes against commuters who work in the community but live elsewhere. By contrast, the victimization study, because it usually involves a household survey, would restrict attention to crimes committed against community residents, regardless of whether the crime occurred in the local community or elsewhere.

Similarly, the descriptions of offenders that emerge from police reports of crimes serious enough to have passed through citizen and police filters cannot be expected to concur with offender profiles that emerge from self-report studies that focus on nonserious delinquency (Hindelang, Hirschi, and Weis, 1981; West and Farrington, 1977).

Although for decades criminologists have engaged in an intense debate about the relative value of specific crime measures, clearly no single data source is sufficient to answer all of the questions we might have about crime events (Jackson, 1990; Menard and Covey, 1988). Because our data sources tell us different things, it does not really make sense to think about one data source as *better* than another. While subsequent chapters will make extensive use of data derived from these sources, it is important that these data always be approached cautiously and critically, as the discussion of the measurement of women's victimization illustrates.

MEASURING WOMEN'S VICTIMIZATION

One of the most consistent findings to emerge from the UCR and victimization surveys is that men are more likely than women to experience certain kinds of victimization (Sacco, 1990; Wilson, 1985). By most measures, men are more likely to be the victims of homicide, serious assault, and robbery; and although sexual assault is more likely to victimize women than men, the data also indicate that sexual assaults occur less frequently than do the other offenses routinely investigated by victimization researchers.

These findings have implications that extend well beyond a narrow concern with crime measurement on the part of academic researchers. They strongly influence the ways in which the public agenda is formulated, and they tend to legitimize the activities of some but not other social problems claimsmakers. Feminist social critics who attempt to raise public awareness of the problem of crime against women are frequently opposed by those who claim that women's fear of victimization is not rooted in reality, but rather suggests a nonrational reaction to a world that threatens men more than it does women (Sacco, 1990). In response, some feminist researchers have generated research findings that provide estimates of female victimization that are wildly at odds with the data yielded by more traditional measures (Gilbert, 1991).

PATTERNS OF FEMALE VICTIMIZATION

These observations point to a need to understand the patterns of female victimization revealed by the UCR and by victimization surveys. The logical starting point in such an exercise is to determine areas of agreement across methodological approaches to women's victimization. Two such patterns are consistently reported by the advocates of both traditional and more critical research approaches (DeKeseredy and Hinch, 1991; Gartner and McCarthy, 1991; Riger, 1981; Stanko, 1985, 1990; Timrots and Rand, 1987; Wilson, 1985). The first pattern concerns the fact that women are more likely than men to be victimized by people they know or with whom they have some ongoing relationship. The second, related pattern suggests that women have a greater tendency than men to be victimized in private (most notably the home) rather than public settings.

These patterns are clearly exemplified by gender differences in homicide victimization, with women more likely than men to be killed by a family member. For example, in the five-year period between 1980 and 1984, 42 percent of all female homicide victims were killed by a family member (someone related by blood, marriage, or adoption), while only 17 percent of male victims were murdered by family (Straus and Williams, 1988). During the same period, about two-thirds of the victims of spousal/partner homicide were women (Browne, 1987).

DOMESTIC AND SEXUAL ASSAULT

The two types of assault that we most closely associate with the victimization of women—domestic assault and sexual assault—also illustrate the private and intimate character of female victimization. In order to understand why official data and victimization surveys portray female victimization as they do, we need to assess how adequately these measures investigate crimes that are committed in private places and that involve offenders and victims who are in intimate relationships.

As we have discussed, many women who are abused in the context of marital relationships do not define what is happening to them as criminal (Kantor and Straus, 1987). Several cultural factors encourage these women to view such incidents as normal and to blame themselves for the violence (Ferraro and Johnson, 1983). Even the fact that a woman phones the police to report an attack by a spouse does not necessarily mean that she defines the event in criminal terms; her action may have less to do with "reporting a crime" than with trying to obtain immediate assistance in order to prevent injury. And even if women do define such events as crimes, they may choose not to phone the police for a variety of reasons (Kantor and Straus, 1987). They may perceive that taking such action places them at greater risk, or they may be concerned that the police or other criminal justice agents will not take them seriously.

As we have seen, the appearance of the police at the scene of a domestic violence incident does not always mean that the event will be counted as a crime. If there is no clear evidence of physical harm, the police may engage in mediation by attempting to cool the parties down, listening to their respective accounts, or issuing stern warnings (Bell, 1987; Kantor and Straus, 1987). The victim may be given information or advice or referrals rather than treated like a complainant in a criminal matter.

In many domestic disputes, the law may be viewed by the police as a means for dealing with the disorderly situation that confronts them rather than as a means for addressing the problem of wife assault (Gondolf and McFerron, 1989). The consequence of this is that, in many cases, no legal action is taken, because the situation is not seen as warranting a legal response. Even those cases that do involve a legal resolution do not necessarily require that official note be taken of the fact that a woman has been victimized.

As we pointed out in Chapter 1, some jurisdictions have attempted to reduce the use of police discretion in the handling of domestic assaults by passing laws that make arrest mandatory in these cases. However, such laws do not completely remove the discretionary decision making in which police engage. In one jurisdiction, police arrested an abuser in only 18 percent of the cases in which arrest was possible, despite the existence of a presumptive arrest law (Ferraro, 1989).

Victims of sexual assault, like victims of domestic violence, may be reluctant to apply a criminal label if the offender is an acquaintance. Using national victimization data, Lizotte (1985) reports that factors which make a strong case for prosecution are closely related to women's reporting decisions regarding rape. Thus, women are less likely to report an incident to the police when they are unmarried, when the offender is not a stranger, and when the offender has a right to be in the location in which the offense occurs. As a result, the UCR measures sexual assaults for which the legal evidence is relatively clear but that are not necessarily typical of women's sexual victimization.

While it is often claimed that victimization surveys broaden the search for incidents of women's victimization, this technique also clearly excludes many types of events. Most notably, these studies undercount crimes that involve intimates—precisely the types of crimes that disproportionately victimize women. Moreover, victimization surveys usually ignore victimization in the form of obscene phone calls, exhibitionism, and sexual harassment in the workplace (Gillespie and Leffler, 1987; Hanmer and Saunders, 1984; Junger, 1987; Stanko, 1985).

RECENT RESEARCH INNOVATIONS

Several recent research innovations reflect attempts to provide a more valid assessment of women's victimization. Much research in the area of family violence, for instance, has made use of measures based on something other than traditional legal categories. The most frequently used measure, developed by Murray Straus and Richard Gelles, is known as the **Conflict Tactics Scale (CTS).** CTS items are ranked in order of increasing seriousness. Items A–J describe nonviolent means of conflict resolution (such as use of verbal skills), while items K–S describe the kinds of violent acts that constitute wife abuse. In order to investigate such abuse, husbands or wives may be asked how frequently they or their partners use each of these strategies in conflict situations. In one sense, the CTS may be understood as an approach that combines victimization and self-report measures.

BOX 7.5 THE CONFLICT TACTICS SCALE

Q35. No matter how well a couple get along, there are times when they disagree, get annoyed with the other person, or just have spats or fights because they're in a bad mood or tired or for some other reason. They also use many different ways of trying to settle their differences. I'm going to read some things that you and your (spouse/partner) might do when you have an argument. I would like you to tell me how many times (Once, Twice, 3–5 Times, 6–10 Times, 11–20 Times, or More than 20 times) in the past 12 months you (READ ITEM).

Q36. Thinking back over the last 12 months you've been together, was there ever an occasion when (your spouse/partner) (READ ITEM)? Tell me how often (he/she) . . .

Q37. (IF EITHER "NEVER" OR "DON'T KNOW" ON ITEM FOR BOTH Q35 *AND* Q36, ASK Q37 FOR THAT ITEM) Has it *ever* happened?

|---|---|---|
Q35. Respondent In Past Year	Q36. Spouse In	Q37.
1—Once	1—Once	
2—Twice	2—Twice	
3—3–5 Times	3—3–5 Times	
4—6–10 Times	4—6–10 Times	
5—11–20 Times	5—11–20 Times	
6—More than 20	6—More than 20	1—Yes
0—Never	0—Never	0—No
(don't read)	(don't read)	

A. Discussed an issue calmly	1 2 3 4 5 6 0	1 2 3 4 5 6 0	1 0
B. Got information to back up your/his/her side of things	1 2 3 4 5 6 0	1 2 3 4 5 6 0	1 0
C. Brought in, or tried to bring in, someone to help settle things	1 2 3 4 5 6 0	1 2 3 4 5 6 0	1 0
D. Insulted or swore at him/her/you	1 2 3 4 5 6 0	1 2 3 4 5 6 0	1 0
E. Sulked or refused to talk about an issue	1 2 3 4 5 6 0	1 2 3 4 5 6 0	1 0
F. Stomped out of the room or house or yard	1 2 3 4 5 6 0	1 2 3 4 5 6 0	1 0
G. Cried	1 2 3 4 5 6 0	1 2 3 4 5 6 0	1 0
H. Did or said something to spite him/her/you	1 2 3 4 5 6 0	1 2 3 4 5 6 0	1 0
I. Threatened to hit or throw something at him/her/you	1 2 3 4 5 6 0	1 2 3 4 5 6 0	1 0
J. Threw or smashed or hit or kicked something	1 2 3 4 5 6 0	1 2 3 4 5 6 0	1 0
K. Threw something at him/her/you	1 2 3 4 5 6 0	1 2 3 4 5 6 0	1 0
L. Pushed, grabbed, or shoved him/her/you	1 2 3 4 5 6 0	1 2 3 4 5 6 0	1 0
M. Slapped him/her/you	1 2 3 4 5 6 0	1 2 3 4 5 6 0	1 0
N. Kicked, bit, or hit him/her/you with a fist	1 2 3 4 5 6 0	1 2 3 4 5 6 0	1 0
O. Hit or tried to hit him/her/you with something	1 2 3 4 5 6 0	1 2 3 4 5 6 0	1 0
P. Beat him/her/you up	1 2 3 4 5 6 0	1 2 3 4 5 6 0	1 0
Q. Choked him/her/you	1 2 3 4 5 6 0	1 2 3 4 5 6 0	1 0
R. Threatened him/her/you with a knife or gun	1 2 3 4 5 6 0	1 2 3 4 5 6 0	1 0
S. Used a knife or fired a gun	1 2 3 4 5 6 0	1 2 3 4 5 6 0	1 0

For Discussion

How accurate do you think the responses to these questions will be? What do you think may be missing from the survey?

SOURCE: Murray A. Straus and Richard J. Gelles, *Physical Violence in American Families: Risk Factors and Adaptations to Violence in 8,145 Families* (New Brunswick, N.J.: Transaction, 1990).

Although the CTS has been widely used, it has been criticized for ignoring both the consequences and the context of violent behavior (DeKeseredy and Hinch, 1991). For example, the scale is unable to distinguish between a situation in which a husband offensively strikes his wife, causing serious physical injury, and a situation in which a wife defensively strikes her husband and causes no injury.

Obviously, claims about the low rates of crime experienced by women must be assessed with extreme caution. This is not because the research is done in a careless or unsophisticated fashion, but because all research approaches are subject to inherent limitations.

The form in which we most frequently encounter reports of criminal events is the crime rate, a measure that is widely used in criminology. Although journalists and politicians, among others, frequently issue declarations about rates of crime, we are seldom encouraged to think critically about what crime rate measures really are.

THE NATURE OF CRIME RATES

What are **crime rates**? As defined by Nettler (1984), "A rate compares events during a specified time against some base of other events, conditions or people. It takes the form $(m/P)k$, where m is a measure of some occurrence, P is a population count (or tally of some other condition of interest), and k is a constant" (47).

BOX 7.6 CALCULATING CRIME RATES

In order to calculate a crime rate, three quantities are required. The first is a count of the number of crimes. In the expression $(m/P)k$, this is the quantity m. National Crime Victimization Survey data reveal that in 1992 there were 18,831,980 personal crimes committed against people over the age of 12.

Next, we need a measure of the population that could be involved in these crimes. This "at risk" population is signified by the quantity P. Using census data, we can estimate that the U.S. population over age 12 in 1992 was 206,414,480.

Finally, we need a constant, k, such as 1,000, which will allow us to express the number of crimes that occur per k members of the population.

Putting all of the above together, we can calculate the rate of personal crime per 1,000 Americans aged 12 or over in 1992 as follows:

$$\frac{18,831,980}{206,414,480} \times 1,000 = 91.2$$

For Discussion
Why do we need to use crime rates for comparison instead of just using actual amounts of crime? What might be some sources of error in this particular crime rate?

As this definition suggests, computing crime rates is a fairly straightforward matter. First, we develop some estimate of the numerator (m)— some count of criminal events. We have already discussed the major forms of such counts— crimes recorded by the police or reported in victimization surveys or self-report studies. Next, we select a measure of the denominator (P). This is generally thought of as a measure of the population that is exposed to the events, or is at risk of being involved in the events, as offenders or victims (Reiss, 1986a). Finally, the number we obtain when we divide the number of criminal events (m) by the measure of exposure or risk (P) is multiplied by some constant (k), so that the rate can be expressed per k units of exposure. The selection of the constant is largely arbitrary, but rates are traditionally expressed per 1,000 or per 100,000 units of exposure.

SOME USES OF CRIME RATES

In subsequent chapters, we will make extensive use of crime rates in our investigation of criminal event patterns. By analyzing these rates, we can assess the value of particular theoretical arguments about how and why these events occur. Crime rates are also used by noncriminologists for a variety of other purposes. One of the most popular is as a "social barometer" that indexes the quality of life (Bottomley and Pease, 1986). Thus, just as the gross national product is employed as an indicator of our collective economic well-being, crime rates are frequently read as indicators of our social well-being (Waller, 1982).

At a personal level, we may factor information about crime rates into our decisions about whether we will buy a home in a particular neighborhood, vacation in a particular locale, or allow our children to attend a particular school.

Crime rates also are used to assess the effectiveness of community-based crime prevention programs such as Neighborhood Watch and Operation Identification as well as a large number of other criminal justice interventions (Rosenbaum, 1988). And, as we have discussed, changes in crime rates are frequently used to evaluate the quality of police services.

Claimsmaking activities often include organized efforts to produce and publicize crime rate data that are said to document the issues to which the claimsmakers wish to draw attention (Best, 1988; Bottomley and Coleman, 1981). According to Gilbert (1991), such efforts "embody less an effort at scientific understanding than an attempt to persuade the public that a problem is vastly larger than is commonly recognized" (63). Best (1988) and Hotaling and Finkelhor (1990) have written about how "advocacy numbers" have been used in defining the problem of missing children. They suggest that "guesstimates" of the number of children abducted by strangers have greatly overestimated the prevalence of the problem. Best maintains that the use of crime data for political purposes generally proceeds from three basic assumptions: (1) Big numbers are better than small numbers, (2) official numbers are better than unofficial numbers, and (3) big official numbers are best of all. As a result, data collection agencies, official or otherwise, may experience more pressure to keep numbers high than to keep them accurate (Reuter, 1984a).

Crime rates provide an important standard by which we are able to compare the relative extent of crime incidence across jurisdictions and across groups. In this context, they have been offered as a way of measuring individual risk of crime victimization.

Annual victimization rates are important measures in that they tell us how many people (or how many households in a particular area) have been victimized by crime. Often, we use these rates to estimate our own risks of victimization. As an alternative measure, we can calculate lifetime chances of victimization. Using these rates, we ask, "What are my chances of experiencing this kind of victimization during my lifetime?"

Using a variety of data sources, Michael R. Rand was able to estimate the lifetime risks of homicide victimization as well as other forms of criminal and noncriminal misfortune (see Table 7.3).

Table 7.3
Annual and Lifetime Chances of Various Criminal and Noncriminal Events

Event	Annual Chance	Lifetime Chance
Homicide	1 in 10,200	1 in 151.0
Violent crime	1 in 32	1 in 1.2
Rape (females only)	1 in 714	1 in 12.5
Robbery	1 in 179	1 in 3.3
Assault	1 in 40	1 in 1.4
Personal theft	1 in 16	1 in 1.0
Accidental death	1 in 2,681	1 in 38
Heart disease death	1 in 338	1 in 4.0

For Discussion

How closely do you think these statistical estimates correspond to media images and public perceptions of these risks? How do you think these risks vary across gender, class, and racial groups?

SOURCE: M. R. Rand, "Life Chances of Becoming a Victim of Homicide," in C. R. Block and R. L. Block (eds.), *Questions and Answers in Lethal and Non-Lethal Violence: Proceedings of the Second Annual Workshop of the Homicide Research Working Group* (Washington, D.C.: U.S. Department of Justice, 1993).

CRIME RATES AS MEASURES OF RISK

In most of the cases just described, we are interested in crime rate measures because we interpret them as measures of risk. When we are told that the homicide rate per 100,000 people is four times higher in the United States than in Canada, for example, we are led to understand that, when the differences in population sizes are taken into account, the risk of homicide is much greater south of the border than north of it. Similarly, when we are told that the neighborhood to which we are thinking of moving has a much higher crime rate than the neighborhood in which we currently live, we may want to reconsider our decision.

How adequate are crime rates as measures of risk? Our answer to this question depends on how much confidence we have in the numbers that are used in the calculation of the crime rate. We have already discussed the many problems that confound our tallies of criminal events (that is, the numerator m of the crime rate equation). However, we also should be concerned about crime rate denominators (P).

In selecting a crime rate denominator, the usual practice is to use the total population residing within the jurisdiction in which the count of events has taken place. Such measures are usually referred to as **"crude" crime rates** because they provide only a very general assessment of the level of risk (Silverman, Teevan, and Sacco, 1991). They do not take account of the demographic characteristics of the population or the empirical fact that different segments of the population are involved in criminal events with different levels of frequency. This problem is sometimes countered through the use of a denominator that better reflects the population at risk. In **age-specific crime rates,** the base number for calculating the rate might include only those individuals aged 18–24. However, the difficulties inherent in determining a number that accurately reflects particular subpopulations sometimes leaves such rates open to charges of inaccuracy.

HOW DO THEY DIFFER?

Crude vs. Age-Specific Crime Rates

Crude crime rates make use of a denominator that consists of the total population residing within the jurisdiction in which the count of events has taken place; age-specific crime rates make use of a denominator that better reflects the population at risk, such as individuals aged 18–24.

Nonetheless, we can reasonably argue that a more refined measure would take account of the differential risks faced by distinct segments of the population. Thus, since most of the crimes counted in crime and victimization rates involve young males, it may make more sense to standardize the level of risk in terms of the proportion of young males in the population rather than in terms of the total population. This is because a shift in the size of this segment of the population will exert a more significant effect on the overall rate than will shifts in other segments of the population, for instance, elderly women.

Not only the demographic composition but also the location of communities may be relevant to an understanding of crime rates (Gibbs and Erikson, 1976; Stafford and Gibbs, 1980). The concept of **ecological position** refers to geographic and economic relationships that link the community for which the rate is being calculated to nearby communities. Given their responsibility to patrol specific neighborhoods, the police have always been interested in ecological factors. However, until recently, they have not had the ability to do a quick and detailed analysis that considers not only changes in crime rates across neighborhoods but also other factors that may change, such as age composition. With the development of high-powered computers and large-scale data-processing packages that offer analysis on a geographic basis, the police now have the resources to do ecological analyses quickly, thereby enhancing their ability to respond to changes in neighborhoods.

Ecological analyses are relevant in explaining why two communities may have populations of similar size and demographic composition but differing crime rates. Community A, for example, may be a considerable distance from neighboring communities such that the residents of these other communities do not commute to Community A, either for employment or for recreational purposes. In other words, the members of the neighboring communities are not regularly available as offenders or victims in Community A. When the official crime rate of Community A is calculated in terms of the population residing within Community A, most of the at-risk population will be taken into account.

By contrast, Community B may be a "central city" within a larger metropolitan area. Members of neighboring communities may travel to and spend most of their working days in Community B. In addition, residents of these satellite communities may regularly attend cultural events or shop in the central city. If the residents of the satellite communities commit crimes or are victimized as they visit Community B, these crimes may be counted in the official crime rate of the central city. However, because these individuals are not residents of Community B, they are not counted in the denominator. If we fail to account for the differences in the ecological positions of Community A and Community B, we may be at a loss to explain why the latter community has a generally higher crime rate.

At a more basic level, we can reasonably ask whether population measures are adequate indicators of risk in the calculation of crime rates. Population measures give some indication of the numbers of people who expose themselves to risks (of offending or victimization), but they do not tell us about the frequency with which this exposure takes place. Populations may differ not only with respect to demographic structure but also with re-

Public concern about crime attracts strong political interest. Governor Wilson of California signs the bill to implement the new "three strikes and you are out" bill that incarcerates three-time offenders for life.

spect to members' potential for victimization. For example, a community in which people regularly spend a great deal of time engaged in evening activities outside the home may have a very different rate for some types of crimes than a community in which most people stay at home most of the time. The risky lifestyles that characterize the former community make its members more vulnerable to victimization (Kennedy and Forde, 1990).

For these reasons, many sociologists have argued in recent years that we need to measure risk more directly (Balkin, 1979; Fattah and Sacco, 1989; Lindquist and Duke, 1982; Stafford and Galle, 1984). For instance, it has been suggested that the elderly may have lower rates of victimization because their level of exposure to victimization risk is lower; if their victimization rates were to be adjusted for differential exposure, they might more closely approximate those of younger people (Lindquist and Duke, 1982). Efforts to examine such hypotheses have met with only limited success (Clarke et al., 1985; Fattah and Sacco, 1989). Any comprehensive investigation of these issues must await considerable refinement in how the concept of "exposure" is defined for research purposes.

SUMMARY
■ ■ ■

Research data are indispensable to the understanding of criminal events. They allow for the testing of theoretical ideas, they help us chart the dimensions of criminal events for policy purposes, and they provide us with indicators of the quality of life. While data about criminal events may derive from many different sources, they tend to be generated by one of two basic investigative strategies: observations and reports.

Criminal events may be directly observed either in naturalistic settings or in the context of field or laboratory experimentation. While much can be learned about criminal events by waiting for them to happen (as in the former case) or by making them happen (as in the latter case), most contemporary research depends on information revealed by reports about crime.

The most widely used of such reports come from those who are most active in criminal events: police, victims, and offenders. The data collected by the police through the Uniform Crime Reporting system describe a wide range of crimes and provide a continuous national record. Recent revisions to the UCR survey are likely to increase the value of these data for both academic and policy purposes. The major limitation of these data relates to the fact any police-based information system can tell us only about crimes that come to the attention of the police in the first place. A significant number of crimes that the police do not learn about are not included in the UCR system.

Surveys of victims and offenders are intended to illuminate those crimes that are not recorded by the police. Despite the valuable information they provide, these surveys are subject to all of the problems that characterize any type of survey. Victims and offenders are not always as accessible as we would like them to be, and we cannot always be sure that they will not, intentionally or unintentionally, distort the truth in response to questions about their involvement in criminal events.

The problems associated with these major sources of crime data—police, victim, and offender reports—do not suggest a lack of knowledge or awareness on the part of those who collect the data. Rather, they alert us to the fact that any attempt to investigate complex social phenomena is fraught with inherent difficulties. The ways in which crime data construct our statistical images of crimes against women illustrate this fact.

We have also seen that no single data source is likely to answer all of the questions that we have about criminal events. Our major data sources tell us quite different things, because they are likely to capture different types of events and to bring different perspectives to bear on these events. For this reason, it is unproductive to engage in endless debates about the superiority of one data source over another. To a considerable extent, the usefulness of any data source depends on how well it helps us to address particular questions.

We should not dismiss crime data just because our data sources are flawed and less comprehensive than we would like. A great deal can be learned from a judicious use of crime data. Although we know that our data are problematic, in many cases we also know *how* they are problematic. Frequently, the errors that characterize our efforts at data collection are not random, but systematic; knowing the sources and consequences of these systematic errors makes data more valuable than they might otherwise be.

QUESTIONS FOR REVIEW AND DISCUSSION
■ ■ ■

1. How useful are crime rates as a measure of our "quality of life"?
2. The UCR crime data often figure prominently in press reports of crime trends. What does the informed news consumer need to know about these rates?
3. What types of data collection problems do victimization studies and offender self-report studies share in common?
4. What are some of the more important ethical problems confronting criminological researchers?
5. Why is it too simplistic to claim that victimization surveys or self-report studies of offending are "better" than the UCR?
6. Do the major forms of crime measurement support or dispute the popular notion that there are "lies, damned lies and statistics"?

DOMAINS OF CRIME

CRIME INVOLVES DIFFERENT ASPECTS OF OUR LIVES. THREE MAJOR "CRIME DOMAINS" CAN BE USED TO HIGHLIGHT HOW THE WAY WE LIVE AFFECTS THE TYPES OF CRIME THAT WE FACE. THESE DOMAINS INCLUDE FAMILY AND HOUSEHOLD, LEISURE, AND WORK.

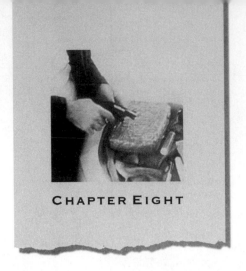

The Family and the Household

WHAT'S IN CHAPTER EIGHT

In this chapter, we focus on crime at the family level. Our interest in criminal events in the family and household domains centers on two substantive issues. The first issue is family violence. How do we make sense of the ways in which family members victimize each other? The second issue is crime against the household. Many types of property crime can be understood as crimes in which the household unit is the victim.

In Part Three, we presented the different theoretical perspectives that criminologists have used to explain criminal behavior and the evolution of criminal events. Part Five focuses attention on the ways in which criminal events cluster in particular social domains. Chapters 9 and 10 are concerned with the leisure and work domains. In this chapter, we analyze the domain of the family and the household.

In these chapters, we present crime events in an integrated fashion, reviewing what we know from current research about offenders, victims, the circumstances under which these events occur, and so on. As we proceed, we will alert you to the relevant theories that best explain the aspect of the event that we are examining. Some theories, particularly those that focus on motivation, work better in providing a framework for precursors. The transactions are generally best understood from opportunity perspectives, while the aftermath can be analyzed using insights drawn from theories about reactions to crime.

Throughout these chapters, we encourage you to think about the research findings being discussed using the theories that we have reviewed. The theories provide us with a road map to guide us through the details of research findings, helping us to identify commonalities in social behavior and to provide an understanding of the complexities of social interaction. We begin with a description of the family and household domain.

THE FAMILY AND THE HOUSEHOLD

In general, we understand the **family** as comprising any relatively enduring pattern of social relationships through which domestic life is organized (Miller, 1990). Customarily, the family is distinguished from other intimate groupings in that relationships are based on kinship. However, what we consider to be a family is as much a matter of cultural definition as social organization. For instance, our cultural view of the family as a unit of procreation leads many people to define a family in which the father is absent as a "broken" home (Wells and Rankin, 1986).

The **household** is generally understood as comprising the social and physical setting within which family life is organized. Many surveys (such as those used in the census) lead us to equate families with households, but in doing so, they may distort the empirical reality of family relations. Family relations in many cases extend beyond any particular household. Husbands and wives who are separated, for instance, usually maintain separate households, although (perhaps because of dependent children) family relations may be sustained.

A wealth of demographic data reveals that the American family has changed a great deal in recent years. For example:

- People are waiting longer to marry. In 1991, the average age of first marriage was 26.3 for men and 24.1 for women. In the mid-1950s, on average, men were married at age 22.5 and women at age 20.1 (U.S. Bureau of the Census, 1992).
- Couples are living longer, and enjoying a better standard of living after their children leave home, than ever before (Glick, 1990).
- Participation of women in the labor force has increased dramatically over the last several years. In 1960, 19 percent of married mothers with children under age 6 worked outside the home. In 1989, 58 percent of these women were in the labor force (U.S. Bureau of the Census, 1991c).
- The total fertility rate (that is, the number of children born to the average woman) has declined. In 1955, the fertility rate was 3.6. In 1990, it had fallen to 2.0 (Population Reference Bureau, 1992; U.S. Bureau of the Census, 1989).
- The proportion of people living in common-law relationships tripled between 1970 and 1982. The number of people living together without being married has increased more gradually since then (U.S. Bureau of the Census, 1983; U.S. Bureau of the Census, 1991b).
- Increasingly large numbers of elderly people are living alone (U.S. Bureau of the Census, 1991a).
- The number of single-parent families has greatly increased. In 1960, 9 percent of children under age 18 lived with only one parent. In 1990, about 25 percent of children lived in a single-parent household (O'Hare et al., 1991).
- Rates of divorce have increased markedly. Some demographers have predicted that in the future, up to two-thirds of first marriages will end in divorce (Castro, Martin, and Bumpass, 1989).
- More and more people are living alone. In 1970, 17 percent of households contained only one person. By 1993, this number had risen to 24.5 percent (U.S. Bureau of the Census, 1994).
- Increasing numbers of families, and especially men, are homeless.

BOX 8.1 CRIME AND HOMELESSNESS

A common assumption is that the homeless are responsible for much urban crime, and the presence of homeless people is frequently an important factor in public fear. How criminal are the homeless? Researchers David A. Snow, Susan G. Baker, and Leon Anderson attempted to answer this question by tracking a random sample of homeless males through the police department records of a large south-western city over a twenty-seven-month period from January 1983 to March 1985. Their analysis revealed the following:

- With respect to more serious crimes of violence, the arrest rates for the homeless were either lower than or not significantly different from those of the nonhomeless.
- The homeless had higher rates with respect to property crimes—especially burglary and theft. However, many of the burglaries involved breaking into warehouses or abandoned buildings to find places to sleep, and the thefts frequently involve shoplifting for food, cigarettes, or other items that can be sold on the street.
- Arrest rates for crimes were much higher among the homeless than the non-homeless. In particular, the homeless experienced high rates of arrest for public drinking.

The researchers also found that the risks of criminal behavior were higher for those who had spent more time on the street and that the mentally ill homeless were more likely to be arrested than the non-mentally ill.

For Discussion

In your view, what is the relationship between the social condition of homelessness and the types of crimes in which the homeless engage? What are some of the difficulties researchers are likely to experience when they attempt to study crime and victimization among homeless populations?

SOURCE: Based on D. A. Snow, S. G. Baker, and L. Anderson (1989), "Criminality and Homeless Men: An Empirical Assessment," *Social Problems* 36(5): 532–49.

The American family, then, is changing. We are witnessing a move away from the conventional single-family unit to variations that include single parents, multiple singles, and lone individuals. These varying structures make social relations within families different from what we would have expected in the past. In addition, as growing numbers of households have come to be occupied by the elderly, this group's dependence on their children is increasing.

Reflecting the change in family social relations are the significant changes that the physical setting of households has undergone (Hasell and Peatross, 1990). In the layout of the typical suburban home, formal dining rooms have been replaced by family rooms or TV rooms. Master bedrooms have increased in size and have walk-in closets and attached bathrooms, both of which make it easier for couples rather than individuals to get ready for work in the morning. Similarly, kitchens are larger so that adults in a hurry can jointly engage in meal preparation. All such changes have important implications for the types of criminal events that occur in the family domain, as well as for the rate at which they occur.

The cultural tendency to idealize the family as the most intimate and nurturing of social groups traditionally has discouraged research into the extent to which violence is a part of family life (Miller, 1990). Consequently, the recognition of **family violence** as a social problem has occurred only very gradually, and in distinct stages, consistent with the evolution of claimsmaking, which we reviewed in Chapter 6. In the 1960s, the problem of child abuse emerged as a policy and research issue (Best, 1990; Nelson, 1984; Pfohl, 1977). In the 1970s, wife abuse moved onto the agendas of researchers and criminal justice professionals (Loseke, 1989; Tierney, 1982). In the 1980s, elder abuse came to be recognized as a form of family violence requiring attention (Crystal, 1988). Criminologists have begun to research and theorize about other forms of family violence as well, including sibling violence (Pagelow, 1989) and adolescent violence toward parents (Agnew and Huguley, 1989).

Until recently, it was widely believed that the police could do little about the problem of violence within the family. However, revelations about the pervasiveness of family violence have focused attention on the structure and dynamics of family life and on the need for involvement by criminal justice and other social agencies.

PRECURSORS

Any discussion of the preconditions of family violence must begin with a critical look at the social organization of family life, which may be said to contain within it the seeds out of which violent episodes grow.

CHARACTERISTICS OF FAMILIES

Interpersonal conflict theory has been used to shed light on how families run into the kinds of problems that lead to interpersonal violence. The following proposals draw on the insights provided by Gelles and Straus (1988). First, family life provides the social setting for omnipresent conflict. Family members spend a great deal of time with one another, and their interactions cut across a wide number of dimensions, ranging from decisions about how money will be spent to who will spend it; from where vacations will be spent to how to pay for them; from who will prepare dinner to what that dinner will consist of. The frequency of those interactions, coupled with their often intense nature, sets the stage for conflict. In addition, because the family is a heterogeneous social grouping—including within it males and females and people of different ages—it also provides the context for the playing out of gender or generational conflicts that have societal origins. Because family members usually know one another so well, they are aware of each other's weaknesses and vulnerabilities. Such intimate knowledge facilitates the escalation of conflicts into violent exchanges.

Second, family life is private life. What happens between family members frequently takes place behind closed doors. The private character of family life reflects a consensus view that families are different from other social groupings. The privacy of the family has structured the ways in which the police and the courts have responded to intrafamily violence. Neighbors, friends, or co-workers may not know about violence that occurs between family members, and even if they do know about it, they may regard it as none of their business. Moreover, the view that violence in the home is a family matter may be shared by the victims of violence. All such factors reinforce the low visibility of violent conflict in the home and suggest the extent to which it is immune to many of the informal social controls that regulate such behavior among nonintimates. Those who take a feminist perspective argue that concerns for the privacy of the home simply shield the abuser from the sanctions of the criminal justice system. Such concerns, they argue, reflect a bias toward maintaining power relationships in families that favor men while ignoring the injustices perpetrated against women.

Third, cultural attitudes toward family violence are highly ambivalent. In the family, unlike in the workplace or other more formal settings, physical violence continues to be tolerated. This is most evident with respect to the spanking of children (Steinmetz, 1986). A majority of parents believe that under certain conditions, it is perfectly appropriate for one family member to use physical force against another family member. This is not to suggest that spanking is necessarily abusive (although it well may be), but rather that rules

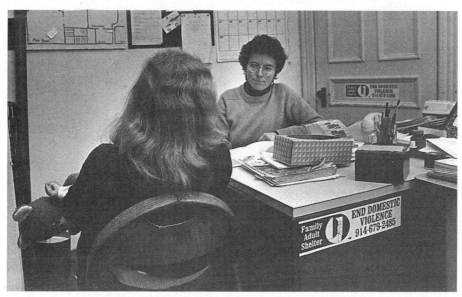

Women shelters provide safe havens for women escaping violent partners.

about violence in the home differ from rules about violence in other social domains. Nor does the tolerance of physical violence extend to dependent children alone. In the recent past, violent behavior by husbands against wives was tolerated much the way parental violence toward children currently is viewed. Most people still continue to regard violence among siblings as normal and natural and, despite obvious physical consequences, not really a form of violence at all.

Fourth, the family is a hierarchical institution. This means that some family members have more power than others. Obviously, parents are more powerful than children. As power control theory would predict, in traditional patriarchal family structures, which are characterized by the presence of an adult male authority figure, the husband is assumed to have the right to make decisions that are binding on other family members (Hagan, Gillis, and Simpson, 1985; Kalmuss and Straus, 1990). Such authority relations, which are recognized by law, create a situation that allows those with more power to behave with relative impunity toward those who have less power. In addition, the widespread support for existing authority relations allows those with power to believe that they have a right to expect compliance from those who are less powerful. Violence may be understood as one effective way in which such compliance is gained.

INEQUALITY IN FAMILY RELATIONS

As we have said, consensus views of the family have been challenged by those who see that the inequality in family relations renders some people more vulnerable than others to intrafamily violence. Our tendency to categorize the major forms of family violence as "wife assault," "child abuse," and "elder abuse" reflects this fact. The consequences of this "hierarchy of family violence" rest most heavily on the shoulders of women, who have historically been economically dependent on men (Davis, 1988). Not surprisingly, as both children and adults, females face greater risks of violence than do males. Victimization surveys typically show that women comprise between 80 and 90 percent of victims of spousal violence (Harlow, 1991; Klaus and Rand, 1984). According to data from the National Crime Victimization Survey, about 92 percent of the victims of "intimate" assaults between 1987 and 1991 were women. Almost 30 percent of the total assault victimizations reported by women were either at the hands of spouses, ex-spouses, or boyfriends. By contrast, less than 2 percent of all reported male assaults occurred in the context of these intimate relationships (Bachman, 1994).

Studies that use the Conflict Tactics Scale, which we introduced in Chapter 7, have presented findings suggesting that, in the context of the family, women are as violent as men. This has led some observers to argue that we need to focus attention on the "battered husband" as well as the battered wife (Steinmetz, 1977–78). However, these studies provide counts of violent acts that do not clarify the context, motives, or consequences associated with the violence (DeKeseredy and Hinch, 1991). As Saunders (1989) notes, by most measures of victimization—who initiates the violence, who uses violence offensively rather than defensively, and who is injured most—there is little question that women are more frequently victimized.

In the case of children, patterns of violence also reflect patterns of inequality and dependency. Family assaults—by both parents and siblings—are alarmingly common for all children, and especially for the very young. The first National Family Violence Survey (1975), for example, found an estimated rate of severe violence perpetrated on children by their parents of 142 per 1,000 (a rate considerably greater than that for partner violence), and a rate of severe violence among siblings of 530 per 1,000 children (Straus and Gelles, 1990a). An estimated 70 percent of homicide victimizations of children are perpetrated by parents (about 23 percent) or other family members (about 44 percent). The younger the child homicide victim, the greater the likelihood that he or she will be murdered by a family member, in his or her own home (Jason, 1983). Likewise, children are much more likely to be abducted by family members (at a rate of 2.6 per 1,000 children) than by strangers or nonfamily members (where the victimization rate has been estimated at between .05 and .07 per 1,000 children) (Finkelhor, Hotaling, and Sedlak, 1990). Another form of abuse that reflects hierarchy and dependency relationships is elder abuse, the victims of which may be infirm and reliant on a spouse or adult/child caregiver for the basic necessities of life (Pillemer and Finkelhor, 1988; Quinn and Tomita, 1986; but see Pillemer, 1985).

ISOLATION AND ECONOMIC STRESS

Conflict, privacy, ambivalent attitudes about violence, and inequality are not the only factors that contribute to the occurrence of violence in the family. When families are isolated from the wider community of kin, friends, and neighbors, the negative effects of privacy may be increased (Straus, 1990b). Under such conditions, those who behave violently may become increasingly insensitive to prevailing community standards regarding appropriate conduct. Further, they and their victims may lose or find less accessible the social supports that could be crucial in ending or preventing violence or in mediating the conflicts that lead to violence.

Conditions of economic stress may also contribute to violent conduct. As strain theories would predict, a husband or father who is out of work may use violence to compensate for the feelings of inadequacy that the perceived failure to play the breadwinner role may promote (Frieze and Browne, 1989). This interpretation is consistent with the widely reported finding that rates of family violence are generally higher among lower-income groups (Klaus and Rand, 1984; Schwartz, 1988; Steinmetz, 1986; Straus and Smith, 1990). Strain may also arise from noneconomic sources such as illness or the death of a loved one. In the case of child abuse or elder abuse, strain may originate from the demands of the caregiving experience itself (Fattah and Sacco, 1989).

How frequent are violent events within the family? For reasons discussed in Chapter 7, victimization surveys typically provide low estimates of levels of family violence. Between 1987 and 1991, however, the National Crime Victimization Survey found that 5.4 of every 1,000 American women had been assaulted by someone with whom they were in an intimate relationship and that another 1.1 of every 1,000 women had been assaulted by "other relatives" (Bachman, 1994). Recall, however, that victimization studies like the NCVS can tell us only about those violent events that women label as criminal and are willing to report to a survey interviewer. Recall, too, that the NCVS, partly in recognition of this fact, has recently been revised, with new questions designed to garner more information about domestic assault.

Studies that have used the Conflict Tactics Scale provide estimates of wife assault suggesting that the problem is far from uncommon. The National Family Violence Surveys, conducted in 1975 and again in 1985 using a random sample of the U.S. population, found that 38 of every 1,000 couples experienced "severe" husband-to-wife violence in 1975. The rate for 1985 was similar—30 of every 1,000 couples were found to have experienced such violence (Straus and Gelles, 1990b). Table 8.1 lists data from the 1975 and 1985 National Family Violence Surveys regarding rates of specific violent acts reported by American couples.

While we know that the rate of homicide victimization for adults is slightly more than two-and-one-half times the victimization rate for children (aged 0–17) (U.S. Dept. of Justice, 1994), we lack information about other forms of violence toward children (Finkelhor and Dzuiba-Leatherman, 1993).

Table 8.1
Husband-to-Wife Violence in the United States, 1975 and 1985

	Rate per 1,000 Families	
Violent Act	*1975*	*1985*
"Minor"		
Threw something	28	28
Pushed/grabbed/shoved	107	93
Slapped	51	29
"Severe"		
Kicked/bit/hit with fist	24	15
Hit, tried to hit with object	22	17
Beat up	11	8
Threatened with gun/knife	4	4
Used gun/knife	3	2

SOURCE: Murray A. Straus and Richard Gelles (1990), "Societal Change and Change in Family Violence from 1975–1985 As Revealed by Two National Surveys." In Murray A. Straus and Richard Gelles (eds.), *Physical Violence in American Families: Risk Factors and Adaptations to Violence in 8,145 Families* (New Brunswick, N.J.: Transaction, 1990).

Box 8.2 Child Maltreatment

According to the U.S. Department of Justice Office of Juvenile Justice and Delinquency Prevention, in 1992, child protective services agencies nationwide received
an estimated 1.9 million reports of child abuse and neglect involving an estimated
2.9 million children. In 41 percent of these reports, subsequent investigation substantiated or indicated the maltreatment. Even worse, as Figure 8.1 indicates, these
rates have been climbing steadily since the mid-1970s.

Figure 8.1
Child Maltreatment Reports per 1,000 Children

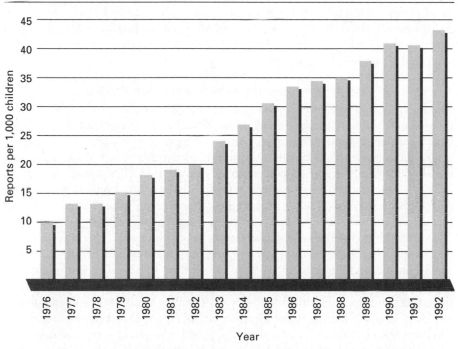

SOURCE: National Center on Child Abuse and Neglect, *Child Maltreatment 1992: Reports from the States to the National
Center on Child Abuse and Neglect* (1994).

For Discussion

Do these increasing rates indicate real increases in child maltreatment or increases
in the willingness of people to report maltreatment when it does occur? How would
you design a research study to determine which type of factor better explains the
increase?

SOURCE: Based on B. Allen-Hagen, M. Sickmund, and H. N. Snyder, *Juveniles and Violence:
Juvenile Offending and Victimization* (Washington, D.C.: U.S. Department of Justice, 1994).

As discussed previously in this chapter, part of the problem in generating such data concerns the widespread attitude that some types of violence against children, such as spanking, are permissible. For instance, Straus and Gelles (1990a) report that, according to the 1975 and 1985 National Family Violence Surveys, over 90 percent of parents said that they had hit their children. Further, the rates are quite high with respect to severe violence, which includes hitting the child with an object; 11 out of every 100 parents reported hitting a child in a way that probably fits most people's definition of abuse.

Research on violent events involving elderly victims is still in the very early stages in this country. One study by Karl Pillemer and David Finkelhor (Pillemer and Finkelhor, 1988) investigated the extent of elder abuse among a sample of 2,020 elderly residents of Boston. The study, which defined elder abuse as physical violence, verbal aggression, and neglect, found that the rate of overall mistreatment was 32 per 1,000 elderly persons. In all, 20 per 1,000 had experienced physical violence, 11 per 1,000 had experienced verbal aggression, and 7 per 1,000 had experienced neglect.

LOCATION AND TIMING OF FAMILY VIOLENCE

The location and timing of violent events in general reflect the importance of the precursors discussed previously. Most violent events involving family members occur in the home. About 86 percent of spousal homicides, for example, occur in the home of the victim. Only about 20 percent of homicides involving non-family members occur in the victim's household (U.S. Dept. of Justice, 1994b). The reason for this pattern is fairly obvious: The home is where family members are most likely to confront each other and where privacy allows these events to develop.

Intrafamily violence is most likely to erupt in the evening or late at night. Arguments that begin in the early evening may turn violent if they are unresolved as the night wears on (Gelles and Straus, 1988). The late-night and early-morning hours bring with them a reduction in the options available to the parties in the conflict through which the matter could be resolved without violence. It is too late to call a family member or to leave the house in order to visit a friend. Stressful events that fuel tensions or challenge parental or patriarchal authority increase the likelihood of a violent episode involving children. Despite the attention paid to the physical mistreatment of very young children by parents, it appears that much violence is directed against teenage children whose various forms of adolescent rebellion may be viewed as requiring strict physical discipline (Pagelow, 1989).

BOX 8.3 THE CIRCUMSTANCES OF FAMILY MURDER

The United States has over 3,000 counties, but according to the Department of Justice, more than one-half of all murders occur in just 75 of them. A survey of murder cases disposed in 1988 in the courts of large urban counties allows for a comparison of the characteristics of family and nonfamily murders. The study covered disposed charges against nearly 10,000 murder defendants, whose murder cases accounted for over 8,000 victims. As Table 8.2 illustrates, there are some interesting differences between family and nonfamily murders.

Table 8.2
Selected Characteristics of Murder Victims and Defendants, 1988

	Alcohol Use at Time of Murder	History of Mental Illness	Unemployed	Homeless
Victims				
All	47.4%	0.5%	13.8%	1.1%
Nonfamily	50.9	0.4	15.8	1.3
Family	32.7	0.9	7.4	0.2
Spouse	49.6	1.5	12.8	0.5
Offspring	5.7	1.3	0	0
Parent	25.4	0	4.4	0
Sibling	34.9	0	17.7	0
Defendants				
All	64.4%	4.3%	35.3%	1.6%
Nonfamily	68.0	2.7	36.6	1.7
Family	47.6	14.3	29.1	1.2
Spouse	54.4	12.3	25.0	1.6
Offspring	29.8	15.8	28.9	0
Parent	28.4	25.1	33.6	2.3
Sibling	53.9	17.3	34.9	3.3

For Discussion
According to these data, what roles do alcohol, mental illness, unemployment, and homelessness play in family and nonfamily murders? What types of theoretical interpretations can we make of these factors?

SOURCE: Based on J. M. Dawson and P. A. Langan, *Murder in Families* (Washington, D.C.: U.S. Department of Justice, 1994).

On some occasions, the factors that contribute to the likelihood of a violent event come into sharp relief. Gelles and Straus (1988) note that violent events occur with higher-than-usual frequency during the Christmas or Easter holidays. At these times, the sources of both economic and noneconomic stress may be especially pronounced. Family members spend more time than usual together and may entertain unrealistically positive expectations about how others will behave. In addition, family celebrations may involve drinking alcohol, which can facilitate the movement toward violence.

BOX 8.4 THE SUPER BOWL MYTH

Shortly before the 1993 Super Bowl, television and newspapers carried stories of research purporting to show that Super Bowl Sunday is the day of the year on which women face the greatest risk of domestic violence. The claim, which was actively promoted by a coalition of media watchdog and antiviolence organizations, was said to be empirically supported by research that provided unequivocal evidence of the Super Bowl effect.

The press actively promoted the story and provided a forum for a variety of "experts" who explained that the spectacle of the Super Bowl includes scantily clad cheerleaders, the legitimate use of physical violence, and highly paid, successful athletes with whom the male viewer at home might compare himself unfavorably. In short, Super Bowl Sunday should show the effects of a national celebration of machismo.

Although most of the press coverage was uncritical, a *Washington Post* writer, Ken Ringle, checked out the sources for the story. He found that the empirical evidence that supposedly provided support for the claim was lacking and that some of the experts who had been cited in the publicity wave that preceded the game had been misquoted. Moreover, those shelters and hotlines that monitored their calls for assistance very closely on Super Bowl Sunday in 1993 reported no variation in the number of calls received.

Despite the lack of evidence to support the claim that a widely watched sports spectacle produces dramatic increases in wife assault, the myth of the Super Bowl effect, like many criminological myths, continues to be widely quoted as fact.

For Discussion

In your opinion, why did this story receive the attention that it did? In other words, why did it appear to suggest that the hype surrounding Super Bowl Sunday would have the effects that advocates said that it had?

SOURCE: Based on C. H. Sommers, *Who Stole Feminism?* (New York: Simon and Schuster, 1994).

PATTERNS OF FAMILY VIOLENCE

Perhaps the most distinctive characteristic of family violence events is their repetitive and cyclical character. In contrast to forms of victimization that result from a chance encounter between victim and offender, the intimate relationships in which family members are involved increase the probability that violent events will re-occur or escalate. Minor acts of violence may be self-reinforcing when those who engage in them come to see violence as an effective means of achieving compliance and when the use of violence carries few sanctions (Feld and Straus, 1990). While most victims try to resist the physical violence, their resistance is more likely to be passive (reasoning with the offender, trying to get help) than active (Harlow, 1991; Klaus and Rand, 1984). Silverman and Kennedy (1993) note that most spousal homicides are not the result of a sudden "blow up," but rather represent the culmination of serial violence, which is fueled by drugs and alcohol, a lack of problem-solving skills, and the effects of longstanding quarrels and antagonisms. Many cases of family violence escalate into more serious forms of victimization. At a minimum, the physical violence that does occur is probably part of a much larger pattern that involves a variety of forms of emotional and psychological mistreatment.

The violent events in a household may take on the character of routine activities (low-level conflict) that escalate to violence. The opportunities for this violence are facilitated by the privacy of the home, which protects the offenders from detection and provides them with objects with which to vent their anger. The violence is likely to be repeated (the opportunities for victimization rarely change) at least until the victim decides to flee or seek outside help.

THE AFTERMATH

Family violence may result in severe physical consequences, and even death. In fact, some evidence suggests that violence in the home is more likely than other types of violent episodes to result in injury (Harlow, 1991; Klaus and Rand, 1984). This finding may be explained by the repetitive character of family violence and by the relatively limited ability of victims to escape such violent encounters.

SHORT- AND LONG-TERM CONSEQUENCES OF FAMILY VIOLENCE

Violence has emotional and psychological as well as physical effects. Victims of violence in the home, like other victims of violence, experience many forms of fear, trauma, and stress (Wirtz and Harrell, 1987). Indeed, violence in the home may be more likely than other forms of violence to produce these consequences (Gelles and Straus, 1990). Violence may be more threatening if it occurs in environments that individuals have defined as "safe" (Burgess, Holmstrom, and McCausland, 1977). In addition, being victimized by an intimate may produce greater stress since the victim has to cope with the fact that the violence has been at the hands of a trusted individual (Sales, Baum, and Shore, 1984).

Despite the seriousness of their injuries, victims may decline to seek medical aid so as to avoid having to explain to others the sources of the injury. The stigma of being a victim may also keep many from seeking help. Even when they do seek help, they may encounter emergency room personnel who are less than sympathetic. According to Kurz (1987), some ER personnel describe abused wives as "AOBs" (alcohol on breath) and as troublesome people who deserve the predicament in which they find themselves.

Victims of family violence may, for similar reasons, decline to report the incident to the police (Klaus and Rand, 1984). For many female victims of spousal abuse, calling the police is a last resort, even when the violence is severe (Kantor and Straus, 1987). Victimization surveys suggest that the victim's fear that the offender will retaliate through violence against the victim (and possibly against dependent children) figures largely in the decision not to report. The victim may also have concerns about how an arrest may lead to a loss of financial support (Steinman, 1992).

In the past, police have been reluctant to intervene in family situations or, when they did intervene, to remove the offender (most often the husband) from the situation to "cool off." Increasingly, however, the police are taking steps to invoke the law as it applies to family violence. Williams and Hawkins (1986) argue that applying sanctions to offenders may deter future offending. As was pointed out in our review of deterrence theories in Chapter 4, research has shown that there is a considerable stigma associated with arrest (Dutton et al., 1992).

There is also a strong sentiment among victim groups that more must be done to help victims of family violence. The number of safe houses is considered inadequate to meet the needs of women who feel at risk. At a more basic level, some claim, it is unfair that women have to flee their homes for safety's sake. Browne and Williams (1989) attribute the 25 percent reduction in female-perpetrated spousal homicide in the United States since 1980 to the fact that the public is more aware of the difficulties women face when dealing with violent spouses. Accompanying this awareness has been an increase in the resources available to women victims—resources that have enabled them to escape their partner's violence rather than suffer alone or respond with violence themselves.

Providing resources such as shelters is helpful in managing the more serious forms of violence, but the day-to-day problems that people encounter most often do not come to the attention of the authorities. Many of these problems are, however, known to neighbors, friends, and others. We are becoming increasingly aware of situations of serial violence, eventually resulting in homicide, in which outsiders knew of the conflict over a long period but were either reluctant to intervene or were not taken seriously by authorities when they attempted to do so.

BOX 8.5 FAMILY VIOLENCE

In recent years, several cases of family victimization have captured public attention. One of the most notorious involved the murder of 6-year-old Lisa Steinberg by her adoptive father, Joel Steinberg.

The homicide, which took place in New York City on November 2, 1987, represented the culmination of a pattern of escalating abuse. When paramedics arrived at the location of the fatal assault—the Steinberg apartment—they discovered a shocking scene: walls smeared with blood and urine; drug paraphernalia scattered everywhere; floors covered with broken televisions, VCRs, and other electronic equipment; Lisa's 16-month-old adoptive brother tied to a urine-soaked crib; and Steinberg's common-law wife, Hedda Nussbaum, showing signs of severe physical and psychological abuse.

This case attracted attention for several reasons. One of the more obvious was the apparent respectability of the people involved. Steinberg presented himself as a lawyer (although it was subsequently discovered that he had obtained his license to practice fraudulently), and Nussbaum was an editor of children's books. Their social status suggested the extent to which abuse cuts across class lines.

In addition, the subsequent investigation revealed that, although neighbors, teachers, and others had reported their suspicions about child abuse in the Steinberg home to child welfare agencies, no action was taken. The case thus signaled to many the inadequacy of child protective services.

These factors, combined with the history of wife and child abuse in the Steinberg household, galvanized public opinion about the case. Steinberg became for a brief time the most hated man in New York, if not in the United States. Edward Koch, the mayor of New York, called him a "monster" and said that he should be "boiled in oil." Hundreds attended the funeral and visited the site of Lisa's victimization. At his trial, Steinberg was fined $5,000 and sentenced to the maximum prison term allowed by law.

The publicity that accompanied the Steinberg case significantly increased public awareness about the problem of child abuse.

For Discussion

Why do you think that family violence is so difficult to detect? In your view, is this a typical or an atypical case of family violence?

One very important issue being considered by researchers interested in the aftermath of family violence is the way in which violent behavior by one family member promotes violent behavior on the part of others. The fact that courts are becoming increasingly willing to accept the psychological consequences of violence as a defense for killing indicates that we cannot always rely on the notion of rational behavior when judging why people act as they do. Arguments about acts performed in the "heat of passion" have always been recognized when one partner kills another in a jealous rage. However, the idea that violence begets violence is only now being viewed as contributing to a condition that may constitute a justifiable defense.

FAMILY VIOLENCE AND DELINQUENCY

In a related way, it has been argued that the use of physical violence against children may increase the risk that they will themselves behave in either violent or nonviolent criminal ways. Although physical punishment may induce conformity in children in the short run, over the longer term it may create the very problems it is intended to prevent (Straus, 1991). Some delinquency researchers, including Wells and Rankin (1986, 1991), have emphasized the importance of the broken home as a cause of delinquency. However, the quality of family interaction, not the fact that a home is legally broken, may be the key issue in the study of delinquency.

How does physical violence against children increase the risks of their delinquency? Several types of effects may derive from such violence. First, social control theorists have argued that the bonds between juveniles and their parents (and other conformist models) provide a certain insulation against involvement in delinquency. A high degree of parental attachment means that the parent is better able to teach the positive social skills that facilitate an individual's success in the workplace or at school (Currie, 1985; Patterson and Dishion, 1985). Obviously, parental abuse may weaken this bond and lessen the degree of juvenile sensitivity to parental expectations of appropriate behavior (Rankin and Wells, 1990).

Second, if a parent is abusive, the child or adolescent may seek to avoid contact. To the extent that delinquency is prevented by the ability of the parent to monitor and supervise the behavior of children, delinquency in such situations may be expected to increase, as predicted by control theory (Gottfredson and Hirschi, 1990; Thornberry, 1987).

Third, violent delinquency may be a form of acting out on the part of the child (Agnew, 1985). Children may run away from home or engage in other "escape crimes." Their resulting homelessness, combined with a lack of labor market skills, may increase the likelihood that they will make use of whatever delinquent or criminal opportunities present themselves in order to support themselves (McCarthy and Hagan, 1991). In addition, they may behave violently toward classmates or other acquaintances as a way of expressing their frustration about the abusive home situation.

Fourth, growing up in a violent home may provide children with lessons in the use of violence as a means of achieving goals and controlling others (Peek, Fischer, and Kidwell, 1985). A child who witnesses spousal violence may come to see it as a legitimate way of resolving conflict (Fagan and Wexler, 1987; McCord, 1991). According to Hotaling, Straus, and Lincoln (1990) homes in which child assault or spousal assault occurs have higher rates of sibling violence and higher rates of violence by the dependent children against children outside of the home.

CRIMES AGAINST THE HOUSEHOLD

Crimes against the household are very common in the United States. In 1992, data from the National Crime Victimization Survey showed that about 44 percent of the nearly 33 million victimizations uncovered were in the category of **household crimes** (defined in the NCVS as burglary, household larceny, and motor vehicle theft) (U.S. Dept. of Justice, 1994). Table 8.3 lists data comparing the rates of violent, property, and household crimes as found in the NCVS for 1992. Rates of victimization reported for household crime were far greater than those for either crimes of violence or those of theft.

Table 8.3
Violent, Theft, and Household Crimes in the United States, 1992

Type of Crime	Rate per 1,000*	Percentage of All Crimes
Violent crimes	32.1	19.7%
Rape	0.7	0.4
Robbery	5.9	3.6
Assault	25.5	15.6
Theft crimes	59.2	36.3
Personal larceny, contact	2.3	1.4
Personal larceny, no contact	56.8	34.8
Household crimes	152.2	44.0
Burglary	48.9	14.1
Household larceny	83.2	24.1
Motor vehicle theft	20.1	5.8

*For violent and theft crimes, rates are per 1,000 individuals. For household crimes, rates are per 1,000 households.

SOURCE: U.S. Department of Justice, *Criminal Victimization in the United States, 1992* (NCJ-145125) (Washington, D.C.: U.S. Department of Justice, Bureau of Justice Statistics, 1994).

PRECURSORS

The routine activities theory of predatory crime, which was described in Chapter 5, explains such crimes in terms of how offenders encounter opportunities for offending. With modern lifestyles forcing people to spend long periods outside of the home working or pursuing leisure activities, the household may remain unoccupied and unguarded, enhancing its appeal as a target for crime.

Not all households are equally likely to be victimized. The patterns of household victimization as revealed by victimization surveys and UCR data suggest that opportunities for property crimes are structured. Location of households raises the likelihood of victimization: The more urbanized the household, the higher the rates of household crime (Cohen and Cantor, 1981; Maguire and Bennett, 1982). For example, the 1992 National Crime Victimization Survey revealed that household larceny occurred at a rate of 114.5 per 1,000 households in urban areas, while the rates for suburban and nonmetropolitan areas were 72.4 and 61.6 per 1,000, respectively (U.S. Dept. of Justice, 1994). Likewise, the UCR reported burglary rates of 1,182 per 100,000 individuals in metropolitan areas, compared with rural burglary rates of 633 per 100,000 (U.S. Dept. of Justice, 1994). This discrepancy in rates might be explained by the fact that formal and informal social controls are less effective in urban centers. Alternatively, larger cities may provide a fertile breeding ground for criminal subcultures that provide an intricate network for the distribution of stolen goods (Fischer, 1976).

Not all urban neighborhoods face the same risk of household crime. Residents of socially disadvantaged areas may face greater risks than do those who reside in more affluent areas (Evans, 1989; Maguire and Bennett, 1982). Low-income areas may have many characteristics that increase the risks of household crime. Lower income may translate into fewer precautions taken to protect the household—particularly when such precautions involve the use of limited discretionary income. Low-income areas also contain a disproportionate number of single-parent households, leaving children with generally lower levels of adult supervision (Maxfield, 1987; Smith and Jarjoura, 1989). Mixed land use in these areas may mean the presence of bars and stores that bring a large number of strangers through the neighborhood. Under such conditions, it may be more difficult to know who does and who does not belong in an area (Lynch and Cantor, 1992). Finally, the greater degrees of residential instability and social heterogeneity in poor areas may undermine the development of collective community sentiments and thereby diminish effective informal social control at the local level (Smith and Jarjoura, 1988, 1989). In other words, as people become less tied to one another, they have less reason to worry about what others think and to conform to their expectations.

The fact that poor *areas* have higher rates of household victimization than more affluent ones does not necessarily mean that poorer *households* have higher rates of victimization than their more affluent counterparts (Maguire and Bennett, 1982). In fact, several studies have shown that the risk of many forms of household victimization increases with household income (Cohen and Cantor, 1981; Cohen, Kluegel, and Land, 1981). This may be because offenders choose the more affluent targets in less affluent areas or the wealthier homes located near such areas (Waller and Okihiro, 1978). Data from the National Crime Victimization Survey showed that in 1992, households with income less than $7,500 reported burglary rates of 71.3 per 1,000. Households with income of $50,000 or more were burglarized at a rate of 43.6 per 1,000 (U.S. Dept. of Justice, 1994).

Victimization research also suggests that some types of housing structures are more susceptible to various forms of household crime than are others (Massey, Krohn, and Bonati, 1989). Most susceptible are those dwellings that offer the thief or the burglar easy access or that provide cover during the commission of the crime. Thus, the risk of breaking and entering is higher when a housing structure offers multiple points of entry, when doors or windows are covered by trees or shrubs, when the house is located on a corner or near a major route that allows easy escape, or when neighbors' houses do not directly overlook the target (Bennett and Wright, 1984; Evans, 1989).

Studies in which burglars themselves have served as informants have also provided information regarding what types of household settings are likely to be "high risk" for this type of victimization. In a study with one hundred convicted burglars, for example, Reppetto (1974) found that the burglars were able to identify several characteristics that made a household a more (or less) attractive target: ease of access, appearance of affluence, inconspicuous setting, isolation of the neighborhood, absence of police patrols, and lack of surveillance by neighbors.

Burglary trends also seem to vary somewhat by time of day. Many studies have found burglaries are quite likely to occur when houses are empty, often

Changing lifestyles have meant that people spend most of the day away from their homes, leaving them unoccupied and unguarded.

during daylight hours (Evans, 1989; Hough, 1987; Miethe, Stafford, and Long, 1987; Rengert and Wasilchick, 1985). Data from the 1992 National Crime Victimization Survey showed that among the burglaries for which the time of occurrence was known (67.8 percent of the total), about 55 percent occurred during daylight hours (U.S. Dept. of Justice, 1994).

The rhythms and tempos of family life affect the risk of household crime in other ways. A good deal of traffic in and out of the home is an expected characteristic of large families. Doors are more likely to be left open or unlocked, and property may not always be put away, which makes such homes an attractive target for thieves (Smith and Jarjoura, 1989). The summer months, which bring warm temperatures, open windows, and houses vacated by vacationers, may also increase the opportunities for household crime (Sacco and Johnson, 1990; Waller and Okihiro, 1978).

TRANSACTIONS

While we may think about opportunities for crime as an objective feature of the social environment (an open door invites theft), the situation is more complicated than this. Criminal opportunities also have a subjective quality. For criminal events to occur, a potential offender must define the open door as an opportunity for theft. While one person might see the large shrubs blocking a residential window as nothing more than interesting landscaping, another might see this shrubbery as providing cover during a robbery attempt.

What are the characteristics of the property offender? Like many other types of predatory offenders, these individuals tend disproportionately to be young males, many of whom come from socially disadvantaged backgrounds (Maguire and Bennett, 1982; U.S. Dept. of Justice, 1994; Waller and Okihiro, 1978). Data from the 1993 Uniform Crime Reports, for example, indicate that 74 percent of those arrested for all index property offenses (burglary, larceny, motor vehicle theft, and arson) were males, 33 percent of those arrested were under age 18, and 65 percent of those arrested were under age 30. Similar patterns are discernible in examining data for burglary (with 90 percent of arrestees male and 69 percent under age 30) or motor vehicle theft (with 88 percent of arrestees male and 75 percent under age 30) (U.S. Dept. of Justice, 1994).

PROFESSIONAL VS. AMATEUR THIEVES

It is useful to distinguish between two broad types of property offenders (Evans, 1989). On the one hand, there is the professional offender, who is sometimes characterized as the "good burglar" (Shover, 1973, 1983) and as the "elite of the criminal world" (Cromwell, Olson, and Avary, 1991). They have a considerable degree of technical competence and are connected to a network of other thieves and tipsters as well as fences to whom the stolen property is sold. Professional thieves think of themselves as "specialists" and understand their offending in occupational terms; they speak of pulling a "job" or "working" a particular area (Maguire and Bennett, 1982). The crimes in which they engage are generally said to reflect careful planning that involves a rational assessment of the specific risks and benefits.

The professional offender usually figures very prominently in media portrayals of household crime and police rhetoric about the typical offender. However, several researchers argue that popular images of the cool, calculating, highly specialized, and rational property offender may be exaggerated. According to Cromwell, Olson, and Avary (1991), much of what we know about such offenders comes from interviews with offenders or ex-offenders who may engage in **rational reconstruction**. In other words, in recalling their crimes, they suggest that far more planning took place than was actually the case. While professionals sometimes are said to seek opportunities for crime, Cromwell and his colleagues maintain that these offenders do not so much seek opportunities as develop a special sensitivity to the opportunities they happen to encounter.

Hough (1987) suggests that, despite the activities of some unspecified number of professional household thieves, these individuals are probably responsible for only a minority of the crimes revealed in victimization surveys. This speculation is supported by the fact that such surveys generally uncover large numbers of crimes that point to amateurish offenders with little technical knowledge or experience (Felson, 1994). Many household crimes are committed by unsophisticated offenders, the majority of whom are probably juveniles. These **occasional offenders** commit crimes when opportunities or situational inducements present themselves (Evans, 1989). Property crimes such as theft and breaking and entering (irrespective of the level of professionalism of the offender) are motivated by instrumental needs (Bennett and Wright, 1984). These crimes do not reflect expressive needs like anger or revenge, but rather are prompted by a desire on the part of the offender to obtain the property of the victim.

Engagement in household theft, as well as movement out of this type of crime with advancing age, can be understood in terms of control theory. Household theft is a crime that easily resists detection (Maguire and Bennett, 1982). Offenders learn from their own and others' experiences that the chances of getting caught in the commission of any particular crime are very slim (Bennett and Wright, 1984). They also recognize, however, that if they become known to the police as thieves and they fail to vary their method of crime commission, their chances of getting caught become greater over time, thus reducing the attractiveness of this form of crime (Cromwell, Olson, and Avary, 1991). While the professional thief may be said to have a lengthy criminal career, a substantial number of juvenile offenders commit crimes only rarely, and do so with even less frequency as they get older (Shover, 1983). The number of repeat offenders as measured by the recidivism rate for burglary is higher than that for many other crimes, but many juvenile offenders do not repeat the crime at all (Maguire and Bennett, 1982).

As events, crimes against the household can be relatively uncomplicated affairs. An opportunistic thief may pass a house and notice some item of value lying unguarded on the front lawn or in the driveway (Lynch and Cantor, 1992). Seeing no one about, the thief will grab the item and continue on his or her way. Similarly, under cover of darkness in the early hours of the morning, the thief may happen upon an unlocked car and steal either its contents or the car itself.

The crime of breaking and entering varies in terms of how much planning it requires. In a large number of these events, young offenders target a house not far from their own residence (Brantingham and Brantingham, 1984; Cohen and Cantor, 1981; Hough, 1987). The proximity of the target may reflect two distinct considerations: (1) offenders' relatively limited mobility (they may be too young to drive) and (2) offenders' direct knowledge of both the contents and routine activities of the households they encounter in the course of their own routine activities. In such cases, entry may be "child's play" (Maguire and Bennett, 1982). The offender tests the door and, if it is open, enters the house. (According to the National Crime Victimization Survey, almost half—46 percent—of the household burglaries reported by victims in 1992 did not involve forcible entry [U.S. Dept. of Justice, 1994]). The thief moves through the house quickly, more interested in getting in and out with something of value than with the wanton destruction of property (Maguire and Bennett, 1982; Waller and Okihiro, 1978). The items stolen may include money, alcohol, and light electronic goods such as portable TV sets or VCRs.

The more professional burglar may select a target more carefully. The selection process may include several stages as the offender makes decisions about which neighborhood, which block in the neighborhood, and which house on the block will be victimized (Taylor and Gottfredson, 1986). Relationships may be cultivated with "tipsters" who can provide information about vacant homes and potentially large "scores" (Shover, 1973). Some tipsters may be "fences" who are attempting to boost their inventory, while others may be thieves who for some reason are unable to undertake the crime themselves. Additionally, thieves may, in the course of their regular travels through the neighborhood, be attentive to homes that appear empty or that promise easy entry. Waiting at a traffic light may provide potential burglars with the opportunity to view potential targets without attracting attention (Cromwell, Olson, and Avary, 1991).

RISK, EASE OF ENTRY, AND REWARD

Irrespective of the level of professionalism, burglars who are intent on breaking and entering must consider three questions: (1) Can they get away with the crime (risk)? (2) Can they commit the crime without great difficulty (ease)? and (3) Can they get anything out of it (reward)? (Bennett, 1989). Of these three factors, the first (degree of risk) is probably the most important (Bennett and Wright, 1984). Homes that provide cover from surveillance by other homes present the offender with fewer risks. The mere presence of passersby may not influence the decision to offend, since thieves are concerned not about being seen but about being seen *and* reported (Cromwell, Olson, and Avary, 1991).

The occupancy of the household may be the most important aspect of risk. The presence of a car in the driveway or signs of movement or activity in the house may encourage the potential offender to look elsewhere (Bennett, 1989). Some offenders may engage in more sophisticated **occupancy probes** in order to establish whether the household is vacant.

BOX 8.6 OCCUPANCY PROBES

In their interviews with burglars, P. F. Cromwell and colleagues discovered that these offenders use several imaginative methods to determine whether anyone is home:

- If working as part of a team, the most "presentable" burglar knocks on the door or rings the doorbell. If someone answers, the burglar asks for directions or for a nonexistent person.
- The burglar rings the doorbell and, if someone answers, claims that his or her car broke down and that he or she needs to use the phone. If the resident refuses, the burglar may leave without attracting suspicion. If the resident consents, the burglar may have an opportunity to check out the merchandise in the home as well as whatever security measures may exist.
- The burglar telephones the residence to be broken into from a nearby phone. The burglar then returns to the residence. If he or she can hear the telephone ringing, it is unlikely that anyone is at home.

- The burglar targets a house next to a residence that has a "for sale" sign on the front lawn. Posing as a buyer, the burglar can examine the target household from the vantage point of the sale property.

One informant in the Cromwell et al. study would dress in a tracksuit, jog to the front door of the target household, remove a piece of mail from the potential victim's mailbox, and ring the doorbell. If anyone answered, he would say that he found the letter and was returning it. The tracksuit explained why a stranger might be ringing a doorbell in the neighborhood, while the apparently neighborly gesture suggested that the burglar was a good citizen and therefore above suspicion.

For Discussion

What do you think is the most effective deterrent to occupancy probes? Why is occupancy so important to the potential burglar?

SOURCE: Based on P. F. Cromwell, J. N. Olson, and D. W. Avary, *Breaking and Entering: An Ethnographic Analysis of Burglary* (Newbury Park, Calif.: Sage, 1991).

An occupied home is to be avoided not only because of the risk of detection but also because of a concern on the part of the offender that, if someone is home, the crime of breaking and entering could escalate into a more serious offense. Some researchers (Kennedy and Silverman 1990; Maxfield, 1990) have observed that, although a rare occurrence, there is a higher-than-expected number of homicides involving elderly victims in their homes. This may be due to the fact that the elderly occupy households that appear uninhabited during the day. The burglar surprised by an unexpected encounter may strike out against the elderly person, with fatal consequences. The occurrence of such unpremeditated homicides, coupled with uncompleted burglaries due to the presence of the householder, suggests that offenders may not be quite as adept at assessing occupancy as is sometimes thought (Hough, 1987).

The second factor (ease of entry) concerns the relative difficulty burglars encounter in attempting to enter the residence. In general, this factor cannot be assessed until the offense is underway (Bennett and Wright, 1984). In many cases, it is a simple matter to break a door or a window; even the presence of special locks and security hardware may not serve as a strong deterrent (Lynch and Cantor, 1992; Maguire and Bennett, 1982). However, while many professional burglars report that they can, if required, deal effectively with alarms or watchdogs, they also report that the large number of households that are unprotected by such measures makes attempted burglary of protected homes unnecessary (Maguire and Bennett, 1982).

The final factor (the potential reward) is probably the least important consideration. Offenders who engage in breaking and entering may be unable to determine before the commission of the crime whether anything of value is to be gained (Lynch and Cantor, 1992; Miethe and Meier, 1990). As noted previously, information from a tipster may decrease uncertainty, and higher-

Tools of the burglar's trade.

status households may hold the promise of greater rewards. However, in most situations, the thief can be relatively certain that something of value will be collected in the course of the crime (Cromwell, Olsen, and Avary, 1991).

THE AFTERMATH

Data from the 1992 National Crime Victimization Survey indicate that almost 98 percent of the household crimes reported resulted in some economic/ monetary loss; about 24 percent of all household crimes resulted in loss of money or property valued in excess of $500 (see Figure 8.2). Perhaps not surprisingly, completed motor vehicle theft was the crime most likely to result in a loss greater than $500 (93 percent), while household larceny was least likely to involve monetary loss this great (about 10 percent) (U.S. Dept. of Justice, 1994). Some of the net loss for property crimes may be mitigated by either recovery or insurance. Members of lower-income groups, who are less likely to have insurance, generally experience the greatest net loss for household crimes.

Such figures provide only a partial picture of the impact of household crime. Incidents of illegal entry that escalate into assaults, robberies, sexual assaults, or homicides have very direct and immediate physical consequences (Warr, 1988). Because incidents of this type are relatively rare, and because household crimes generally involve rather small net losses, these crimes are sometimes assumed to have little psychological impact on victims. Such is not the case, especially with respect to breaking and entering. Many victims—particularly women—

Figure 8.2
Economic Costs of Household Crime, 1992

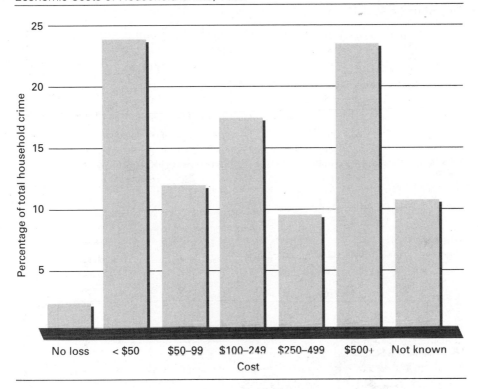

may be badly shaken by the event (Maguire and Bennett, 1982). Victims may experience feelings of vulnerability, concern that the offender will return, and fear of being alone, even in situations that are not directly related to household crime. They may also experience long-term sleeping disorders or require tranquilizers for an extended period. Maguire and Bennett (1982) report that, in a sample of British burglary victims, negative effects were reported by 65 percent of the victims four to six weeks after the crime.

Like other criminal events, many crimes against the household are not reported to the police. Data from the National Crime Victimization Survey indicate that in 1992, about 41 percent of all household crimes were reported (54 percent of burglaries, 26 percent of household larcenies, and 75 percent of motor vehicle thefts). Respondents who said that they had reported their victimizations were most likely to cite "a desire to recover property" as the reason (26 percent of respondents gave this reason). The single most common reason for not reporting household crimes was because the stolen property was recovered or the offender was unsuccessful in his or her attempts (30 percent) (U.S. Dept. of Justice, 1994).

BOX 8.7 BURGLARY

Data from the 1992 National Crime Victimization Survey reveal the following:

- About 4 percent of all households experienced one or more of the 4.8 million household burglaries that occurred in 1992.
- When the time of the crime was known, victims reported that one-half of the burglaries took place between 6 A.M. and 6 P.M.
- Almost 3 in 10 burglaries resulted in losses of $500 or more.
- Some economic loss, including property damage, resulted in 86 percent of all burglaries and about 95 percent of all forcible-entry burglaries.
- The direct cost to burglary victims was $4.2 billion.
- Overall, about one-half of all burglaries were reported to the police.

As Figure 8.3 shows, according to NCVS data, rates of burglary have been declining over the past two decades.

Figure 8.3
Rates of Household Burglary, 1973–1992

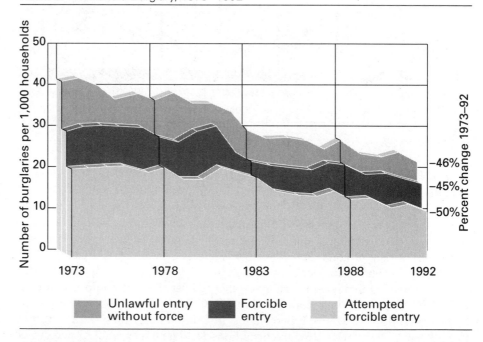

For Discussion

How can we account for the apparent decline in burglary rates in recent years?

SOURCE: M. W. Zawitz, et al., *Highlights from 20 Years of Surveying Crime Victims: The National Crime Victimization Survey, 1973–92* (Washington, D.C.: U.S. Department of Justice, 1993).

Crimes against the household also indicate that it is *what happens to the victim* rather than *who the victim is* that determines whether an event will be reported (Evans, 1989). In other words, the likelihood of reporting is not very strongly related to the social and demographic characteristics of victims. Instead, the crime is more likely to be reported when it has characteristics that might be interpreted as indicators of greater seriousness, such as when there is evidence of forced entry or malicious destruction and when the loss is relatively high (Waller and Okihiro, 1978). Thus, unreported household crimes, at least in the legal context, are generally less serious than those that come to the attention of the police (Maguire and Bennett, 1982).

Victims who report household crime do so with the hope that the police will be able to apprehend the offender and recover the stolen property. At a minimum, victims expect that the police will undertake an investigation and treat them with some sympathy (Maguire and Bennett, 1982). In the aftermath of household crime, victims may seek the assistance of a friend, neighbor, or landlord in addition to, or instead of, the police. When losses are substantial, victims may seek compensation through private insurance.

Reported household crimes carry with them a low certainty of arrest. The low clearance rates for such crimes results from the fact that, by the time they are reported to the police, the perpetrator is long gone. In addition, unlike in the typical crime of violence, there is no immediate suspect (Maguire and Bennett, 1982).

In the aftermath of the crime, offenders are probably less concerned with arrest than with the uses to which the stolen merchandise might be put. Cash or alcohol may be used for "partying." Although some stolen merchandise may be kept and used by the offender, there is a limit to how much loot one can put to personal use. Retaining too many stolen goods may also increase the risk of arrest.

Much of what is stolen may be converted into cash through the sale of merchandise. Although a substantial market exists for stolen goods, particularly lightweight electronic goods, offenders recoup a relatively small amount from each item. Some stolen goods are sold directly to private buyers for their own use. Such people may see this exchange not as a criminal activity but as "good business." Their reasoning may be, "It was already stolen and if I don't buy it someone else will" (Cromwell, Olson, and Avary, 1991). Merchandise is also sold to "fences," who purchase the items for the purpose of resale. Some fences are businesspersons who do not have a criminal record, while others are ex-thieves (Maguire and Bennett, 1982).

One popular public response to the increase in property crime has been to make homes less vulnerable to attack. "Target-hardening" activities include installing deadbolt locks and bars on windows, purchasing alarms and watchdogs, and developing programs (such as Neighborhood Watch) that increase the surveillance of property. Such forms of protection are becoming a routine part of architectural design, with notions of "defensible space" governing how many residential areas are constructed (Newman, 1972).

Violent events within families can be partially attributed to the values that our society places on family privacy. Feminist researchers see family violence as reflecting the differential power within families, whereby men use violence against women and children as a form of control over their actions (Simpson, 1989: 611).

For a more complete understanding of family violence, we must also consider the stresses placed on families, the reluctance of victims to report the violence, the modeling of parental behavior in managing conflict and anger, the breakdown of social control mechanisms that restrain interpersonal violence, and the paucity of deterrence strategies. The discovery in recent years of the extent of family violence, coupled with changes in societal values, has been influential in defining violent events within families as criminal events. Changes in the laws and in the police enforcement of those laws have come increasingly to reinforce such a definition.

Property crime is a booming business. The target of most of this crime is the household, which is filled with portable appliances that can be easily transported and resold. Much property crime is opportunistic in nature, involving the presence of a thief at a place and time in which property is unguarded and easy to steal. A good deal of the property crime committed by youthful offenders falls into this category. The more complicated crime of breaking and entering, which often requires considerable planning and technical expertise, tends to be committed by professional burglars, who not only take the time to plan the event but also ensure that the merchandise can be disposed of after the fact. Sometimes, due to a miscalculation on the part of the offender, residents may be unexpectedly encountered in the course of a household burglary; the consequences—especially for elderly victims—can be fatal.

Many property crimes are not reported to the police. People who do not report may feel either that there is little that the police can do to solve the crime or that the crime is not serious enough to warrant such action. Increasingly, homeowners are engaging in target-hardening activities intended to discourage both opportunistic and professional burglars.

There is increased interest in dealing with crimes that both occur in and are directed toward the household. Intrafamily violence is attracting a great deal of public concern, and there have been demands that more action (in the form of education and changes in the law) be taken to reduce the likelihood that such violence will occur. Attempts have been made to give victims of family violence greater protection under the law and to provide them with safe havens, as well as to treat offenders. (We will examine these actions in greater detail in Chapter 11.) As our review of family violence has shown, it is important to consider different theoretical approaches to the problem. New perspectives that draw attention to such things as power differentials in the family have become increasingly effective in providing us with explanations of family violence and in suggesting ways in which we should respond to it.

There are many different views about why people are motivated to commit property crimes as well. Obviously, not everyone who is given the opportunity to steal does so. Depending on your view of human behavior, you might assume that people will steal if they know they won't get caught (social control), if they see others doing the same thing (cultural influence), or if they feel pressured by social circumstances (strain). All of these explanations of motivation rely on the idea that the offender has the opportunity (and some skills) to commit the crime and little fear of apprehension. Limiting opportunities should provide the most effective means of reducing this type of crime.

QUESTIONS FOR REVIEW AND DISCUSSION
■ ■ ■

1. Why has there been so much resistance to the claim that family violence is a serious problem?
2. How can we use strain theory to explain wife assault?
3. Many people would argue that sibling violence is normal and that this kind of violence is very different from the kinds of violence that we label "wife assault" or "child abuse." Do you agree with this statement? Why or why not?
4. Recently, many notorious court cases have revolved around family violence issues (for example, the Lorena Bobbit and O. J. Simpson cases). Is the high level of media attention devoted to these cases a good thing or a bad thing in your opinion?
5. Marcus Felson has argued that over the past few decades, the decrease in levels of household occupancy and the proliferation of "lightweight durable consumer goods" has resulted in a "deskilling of crime." How valid is this proposition with respect to crimes against the household?
6. With respect to your own residence, how might a potential thief or burglar make decisions about "risk," "ease," and "reward"?

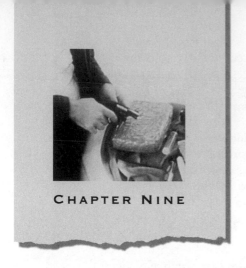

Leisure

WHAT'S IN CHAPTER NINE

In this chapter, we look at the social domain of leisure to examine the nature of crime that takes place when people pursue recreation and leisure activities. Here, we examine the view that leisure actually acts as a corrupter of youth and makes social control difficult. The contexts in which leisure-based criminal events take place include the street and bars, dating relationships, and vacation travel.

In this chapter, we discuss a second social domain that is significant to the study of criminal events—the leisure domain. As we will see, the relationship between leisure and crime has several interesting dimensions. People who are "at leisure" seem to be particularly susceptible to the risk of many different types of criminal victimization. Moreover, many types of offending—particularly juvenile offending—are themselves forms of leisure. Our language reflects this fact when, for instance, we describe illegal drug use as "recreational drug use" or when we describe stealing a car to use for fun as "joyriding." The leisure preferences of young people may also be seen as a cause of crime. This is evident in periodic scares in our society about the criminogenic effects of violent television, popular music, fantasy role-playing games, and video games.

We will also see that certain leisure settings, such as bars and sports complexes, are frequently scenes of crime and victimization. The street is also a likely location for crime victimization, as we begin to adopt lifestyles that take us away from our homes and into public areas in search of leisure pursuits. We begin our review of the relationship between leisure and criminal activities with a discussion of the concept of leisure.

WHAT IS LEISURE?

Leisure may be defined in a variety of ways (Wilson, 1980). Frequently, we use the term in an objective way to describe the "spare time" or "free time" that is left over after paid work or other obligations (such as child care) have been taken care of (Iso-Ahola, 1980). However, leisure has a subjective as well as objective character. In other words, leisure is not just free time, but rather free time that is used in a particular way—usually for play or recreation. Leisure activity may be regarded as intrinsically satisfying in that it contains its own rewards (Roberts, 1983). In addition, we usually assume that leisure activities are freely chosen and that leisure interaction occurs among peers. By contrast, family- or work-related activities tend to be less voluntaristic and to be characterized by authority relations that are enforced by law or custom.

Like other scarce resources, leisure time is unequally distributed (Wilson, 1980). Teenagers and the elderly tend to have more leisure time than young parents or middle-aged individuals. And because household tasks and child-care responsibilities reduce free time, men generally have more leisure time than women. People also differ with respect to their leisure preferences and the resources they have to pursue them. Those in higher-income groups are more likely to frequent restaurants, while young people are more likely to go to bars, movies, or video arcades (Provenzo, 1991). The elderly are less likely to go out in the evening for leisure of any kind (Golant, 1984); elderly people who do engage in leisure outside the home tend to visit friends or to go to the mall.

The amount of leisure time that people have available to them and the uses to which they put it are important elements of what we refer to as lifestyle, a concept introduced in Chapter 5. Moreover, the leisure content of people's lifestyles has important implications for the kinds of criminal events in which they are involved, whether as offenders or victims. Opportunity theories are particularly attentive to the linkage between lifestyle and crime.

PRECURSORS

What does leisure have to do with the timing, location, and relative involvement of particular types of people in particular types of criminal events? There are two answers to this question. One stresses the ways in which specific types of leisure activities motivate offenders toward or free them from constraints against offending. The other suggests that leisure activities and settings facilitate encounters between offenders and potential victims. These perspectives are not contradictory, but they do differ in their fundamental emphases. While the former is offender-centered, the latter is opportunity-centered.

LEISURE AS A CORRUPTER

Arguments about the corrupting influences of leisure have typically been made with respect to the youthful offender. Throughout this century, every major form of youth leisure preference has been characterized by interest groups as a corrupter of young people. Feature films, rock and roll, rap and heavy metal

There continues to be controversy over the negative effects that violent television programs have on children's behavior.

music, video games, comic books, and Saturday morning cartoons have all, at one time or another, been accused of weakening youthful inhibitions, providing negative role models, destroying childhood, and disrupting the bonds between adolescents and adult authority figures (Best, 1990; Gray, 1989; Tanner, 1992).

Literally hundreds of studies have investigated the potentially negative effects of television violence, and the issue has been the focus of attention from the general public as well as blue-ribbon presidential panels. The argument that television violence has some causal relationship with real-life violence would seem to be supported by much anecdotal evidence (in the form of so-called copycat crimes, for example) and by common sense. We know that television is a powerful persuader; otherwise, advertisers would not spend so much money buying commercial time in order to convince consumers to purchase their products. We also know that television is a violent medium and that young people (who are most likely to behave violently) have high levels of exposure to such content.

BOX 9.1 IS TV TO BLAME FOR VIOLENCE?

Television sets were found in fewer than 15 percent of America's homes in 1950. They were found in 93 percent of our homes in 1990. In that period, the number of murders per year in the United States increased from 7,942 to 21,860; the murder rate per 100,000 population approximately doubled—from 5.3 to 10.2.

Is there a cause-and-effect relationship in these numbers?

"The average American preschooler," Brandon Centerwall of the University of Washington reports, "watches more than 27 hours of television per week. This might not be bad if these young children understood what they were watching. But they don't. Up through the ages of 3 and 4, most children are unable to distinguish fact from fantasy on TV and remain unable to do so despite adult coaching. In the minds of young children, television is a source of entirely factual information . . . [about] how the world works. There are no limits to their credulity. . . . An Indiana school board had to issue an advisory to young children that . . . there is no such thing as Teenage Mutant Ninja Turtles. Children had been crawling down storm drains looking for them."

Gene Lees, author, composer and cultural critic, writes that the National Coalition on Television Violence estimates that "by the age of 18, the average American young person has witnessed 200,000 acts of violence on television, including 40,000 murders." He quotes from a report of the Council on Scientific Affairs of the American Medical Association: "Over the past decade the messages portrayed by certain types of rock music . . . may present a real threat to the physical health and well-being of especially vulnerable children and adolescents. . . . Lyrics promoting drug and alcohol use, sexual exploitation, bigotry and racism are combined with rhythms and intensities that appeal to youth. Physicians should know about [these] potentially destructive themes. . . . Members of the entertainment industry . . . should exercise greater responsibility in presenting [such] music to young people."

A majority of Americans, a *Times-Mirror* poll reported last month, "feels its entertainment television is too violent, and believes this situation is getting worse. . . . A strong and growing majority believes that this is harmful to society. . . . Most feel that we as a society have become desensitized to violence as a result of seeing it so frequently on television and in movies. . . . There is . . . a significant level of concern among parents about the pictures that their children are seeing and the words they are hearing."

This deluge of violent images is augmented constantly by books, films, magazines and newspapers. It thus becomes both fair and necessary to inquire whether the media, in the name of commerce, are promoting the current epidemic of murder, rape and violence in other forms that afflicts our society in the last years of the 20th century.

Centerwall, writing in the current issue of the *Public Interest,* believes the evidence assembled by various academicians is conclusive and indicates that "if, hypothetically, television technology had never been developed, there would be 10,000 fewer homicides each year in the United States, 70,000 fewer rapes and 700,000 fewer injurious assaults. Violent crime would be half what it is."

He bases this conclusion on several studies. Some of them involved children living in remote areas of Canada. In one village, five years after television was introduced the rate of aggression among the children increased by 160 percent. In two other villages without television during the same period, aggression rates among children were unchanged. A similar finding came out of a study of Indian communities in northern Manitoba: There was "a positive relationship between exposure [to television violence] and physical aggression."

Centerwall says the same effects are seen on whole populations. Because of a historical accident, South Africa had no television prior to 1975. So, Centerwall compared homicide rates among whites in that country from 1945 to 1975 with the rates among whites in the United States and Canada. During those 30 years the U.S. homicide rate increased by 93 percent, the Canadian rate by 92 percent. The rate among South Africans (who have no traditions of pacifism and non-violence) declined in the same period by 7 percent. He was unable to find any economic, political or social factor other than television to explain these different results.

Other "experts" have arrived at other conclusions. An NBC report published in 1982 found that among 2,400 schoolchildren studied, no connection could be established between television violence and childhood behavior. And even in studies that reach an opposite conclusion, the increase in violence attributed to television is ordinarily slight. But Centerwall maintains that even small increases are significant: "If exposure to television causes [only] 8 percent of the population to shift from below-average aggression to above-average aggression, it follows that the homicide rate will double. The findings of the NBC study and the doubling of the homicide rate are two sides of the same coin."

There is a dilemma here for the media. On the one hand we argue that what we do is important not only in shaping how people think about things but in shaping their behavior. The television industry, for example, has claimed—legitimately, I suspect—that by exposing Americans to the racial violence and brutality inflicted on blacks in the South, the civil rights movement was advanced significantly.

On the other hand, we have a tendency to dismiss or minimize radical conclusions of the Centerwall variety as the chatter of nervous nellies or as unwarranted threats to our liberties. If his thesis is correct, the implications could be serious. Should Congress through new laws or an invigorated FCC set broadcasting standards to cull programs with violent themes? Would other media—newspapers or films, for example—be targeted for censorship or "guidelines" under a finding that violence has become a threat to the "national security"? Would new "sin" taxes be levied to effectively put out of business the Arnold Schwarzeneggers and Rambos of television and the silver screen?

The *Times-Mirror* poll does not suggest that mobs are in a mood to storm the network studios or tar and feather Clint Eastwood for making our days. But there is a lot of real concern, and it's something the media, if they are responsive to the marketplace, will take to heart.

For Discussion

How can we control the amount of violence depicted in the media? Would there be popular support for or resistance to this control? How has the proliferation of VCRs changed the debate about television violence?

SOURCE: Richard Harwood, "Is TV to Blame for Violence?" *Washington Post,* 17 April 1993, p. A23.

BOX 9.2 THE CONCERN ABOUT YOUTH CRIME

Much of the concern about leisure as the corrupter of youth is fueled by perceptions of rising rates of youth violence. According to the Uniform Crime Reports (U.S. Dept. of Justice, 1994d) 17 percent of the 11,046,849 arrests made in 1993 were of juveniles (persons under the age of 18). Juveniles accounted for 18 percent of the arrests for violent index crimes (homicide, rape, robbery, and assault) and 33 percent of the arrests for property index crimes (burglary, larceny, and motor vehicle theft).

The majority of arrests of juveniles in 1993 were for property crime. Index property crime offenses comprised almost 30 percent of juvenile arrests in 1993; only about 6 percent of the youths arrested in 1993 were charged with violent index offenses (see Figure 9.1).

Although juveniles have much higher levels of involvement in property than in violent offenses, their rate of involvement in serious violent crimes is increasing rapidly. For example, between 1985 and 1993, the juvenile homicide arrest rate increased 134 percent, while the murder arrest rate for adults rose by only 8 percent. In addition, the juvenile arrest rate for index property offenses is actually higher than the arrest rate for adults. Changes in the involvement of youth in property crimes have been less marked across time—between 1985 and 1993, the juvenile arrest rate for index property offenses actually fell by about 5 percent (see Figure 9.2).

Figure 9.1
Juvenile Arrests by Type of Offense, 1993

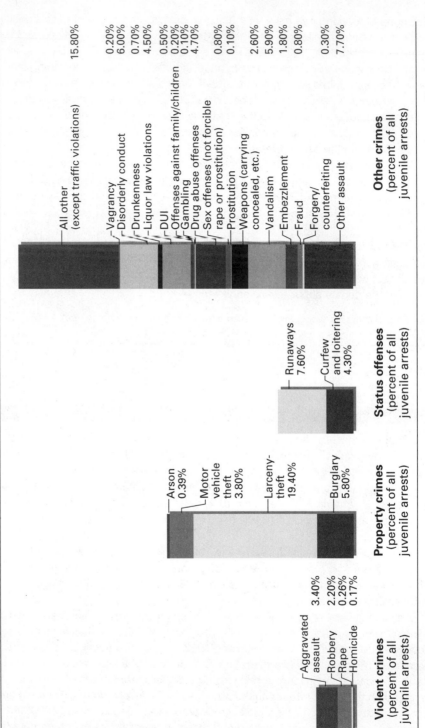

All other
(except traffic violations) — 15.80%

Vagrancy — 0.20%
Disorderly conduct — 6.00%
Drunkenness — 0.70%
Liquor law violations — 4.50%
DUI — 0.50%
Offenses against family/children — 0.20%
Gambling — 0.10%
Drug abuse offenses — 4.70%
Sex offenses (not forcible
rape or prostitution) — 0.80%
Prostitution — 0.10%
Weapons (carrying
concealed, etc.) — 2.60%
Vandalism — 5.90%
Embezzlement — 1.80%
Fraud — 0.80%
Forgery/
counterfeiting — 0.30%
Other assault — 7.70%

Other crimes
(percent of all
juvenile arrests)

Runaways
7.60%

Curfew
and loitering
4.30%

Status offenses
(percent of all
juvenile arrests)

Arson
0.39%

Motor
vehicle
theft
3.80%

Larceny-
theft
19.40%

Burglary
5.80%

Property crimes
(percent of all
juvenile arrests)

Aggravated
assault — 3.40%
Robbery — 2.20%
Rape — 0.26%
Homicide — 0.17%

Violent crimes
(percent of all
juvenile arrests)

SOURCE: Uniform Crime Reports, 1993.

Figure 9.2
Adult vs. Juvenile Arrest Rates, 1985–1993

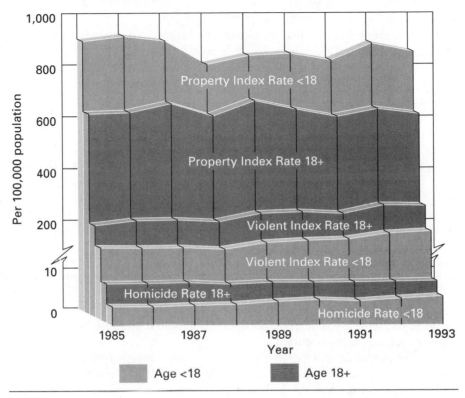

SOURCES: Uniform Crime Reports, 1985–1993; and U.S. Bureau of the Census, *Statistical Abstracts of the United States* (Washington, D.C.: Government Printing Office).

For Discussion
Is juvenile crime as serious as adult crime? Should we begin to treat the two in the same way?

However, despite anecdotal evidence and commonsense notions, the nature and significance of the effects of televised violence are unclear. The effects of television violence on criminal motivation are likely limited by several factors. First, UCR data indicate that violent crimes comprise a small proportion of total crime. Therefore, unless we want to argue that violent portrayals affect nonviolent crime in some as yet undetermined fashion, the amount of crime that could be causally linked to violent content is going to be limited, even if the effects on violence are substantial. In fact, some researchers have suggested that the real effects of television may be on property rather than violent crimes (Hennigen et al., 1982). The basis for this argument is that the media emphasis on consumerism raises expectations about the amounts of material goods to which people think they are entitled (Surette, 1992). The link between television and property crime has not, however, received sufficient research attention to warrant firm conclusions.

Second, given that criminal motivation is a complex issue, whatever effects media exposure produces must be understood in the context of many other factors that encourage or restrain offending. The amount of variation attributable to media exposure is likely to be smaller than many observers would argue. Some researchers claim that 5–10 percent of the difference between violent and nonviolent behavior may be attributed to exposure to media violence (Surette, 1992). Whether this means that television violence is a relatively important or unimportant factor in real-life violence remains unresolved.

Third, while many research experiments have been able to show that exposure to violent content in the laboratory setting triggers violent arousal, the same effects are not necessarily produced by media exposure in the real world. In laboratory experiments, subjects may be encouraged to behave violently (or at least not discouraged from doing so); by contrast, violent behavior in most social contexts is discouraged. Also, the ways in which violence is measured in the lab (for example, the willingness of children to play with violent toys or of subjects to administer a harmless electrical shock to another person) may not have much to do with the willingness of people to beat, assault, rob, or kill others. Studies that attempt to link television violence to aggressive behavior in real-life settings have frequently been less successful than those that try to find these effects in the laboratory.

As the preceding discussion suggests, the relationship between television violence and criminal violence is more complicated, and perhaps less substantial, than we sometimes think. Much of the research supports the view that television violence may influence the behavior of a pool of at-risk individuals who may be particularly susceptible to its effects. In other words, television violence may be most likely to affect the behavior of individuals already predisposed to behave aggressively. Unfortunately, we lack detailed knowledge of the size of this at-risk pool or of the factors that put them at risk. The effect of media violence may be not to cause interpersonal aggression in any direct way, but rather to reinforce pre-existing tendencies or to shape them in particular ways. In the case of copycat crimes, for instance, media violence may not motivate someone to commit a crime, but it may affect *how* that person commits a crime.

In many cases, the effects of television (or movie) violence may be short-term. Anyone who has ever left a movie theater feeling excited or energized may intuitively understand the nature of this temporary arousal. We also know that such effects tend to dissipate rather quickly as we return to the family, work, or school responsibilities that structure our lives. Thus, whether people behave violently subsequent to such arousal may have as much to do with the situations and circumstances in which they find themselves as with their level of arousal. It is also important to note, though, that we know relatively less about the long-term effects of high levels of violent content in media on cultural beliefs and social practices.

The work of sociologist David Phillips (1983) illustrates how some of the effects might work. In a number of studies, Phillips has shown that media portrayals of homicide or suicide may exert temporary effects on the rates of such behavior. In the case of homicide, for instance, Phillips studied what happened to homicide rates after highly publicized prize fights. These media events are particularly interesting because they involve violence that is both widely publicized and generally condoned rather than condemned. In a careful assessment of homicide trends, Phillips was able to show that in the few days immediately following a highly publicized fight, homicide rates increased by about 12 percent and that such effects could not be attributed to seasonal, monthly, or other temporal patterns.

Much of the rancorous public debate about television violence has recently begun to find a parallel expression in debates about video games. Not only is the content of these games typically violent, but, because they are interactive, it is argued that they may be more likely than television viewing to produce delinquency. While we have not yet amassed a significant body of research on the subject of the criminogenic influences of video games, thus far, concerns about the effects of these games on serious criminal offending seem to be overstated (Ellis, 1984; Provenzo, 1991).

Debates about the corrupting influence of popular culture are not restricted to juveniles. Public alarm about the effects of pornography on sex crimes reflects concerns similar to those voiced by the critics of television violence. Yet, in a similar way, attempting to draw direct causal links between violent pornography (for example, "slasher" movies that combine sexual scenes with violent ones) and sex crimes ignores the complexity of the issue. A large body of experimental literature suggests that exposure to such pornography promotes negative attitudes toward women, a greater acceptance of rape myths (for example, that rape victims are to blame for what happens to them), and a decreased sensitivity toward female victims of violence (Malamuth, 1983; Malamuth and Donnerstein, 1984). Yet, as in the case of television violence, the effects of violent pornography on perpetrators of sex crimes may be most evident in men who are already predisposed to behave violently toward women.

LEISURE AND FREEDOM FROM SOCIAL CONTROL

In the case of juveniles, it is sometimes argued that patterns of leisure activity increase the likelihood that crimes will occur by freeing youth from the social controls that might be expected to check or restrain delinquent conduct. This position builds on the arguments suggested in the theories presented in Chapter 4.

Juvenile leisure is most frequently pursued out of the sight of parents or teachers and in the presence of peers (Agnew and Peterson, 1989). The modern video arcade, like the pool hall of an earlier era, is off limits to adults. "Hanging out" at the video arcade or mall or on the street corner may provide the behavioral freedom that makes group delinquency possible (Lotz, Poole, and Regoli, 1985). A study by Riley (1987) of juvenile crime in England and Wales found that offenders and nonoffenders engaged in different types of leisure activities. Nonoffenders generally spent more time with parents and around the home, while offenders were more likely to spend their time in peer activities away from home. In addition, offenders were more often out in the evening, were expected home later, and were more likely to spend their money on youth-oriented amusements. Such leisure activities remove some of the obstacles to delinquency by lessening the chances of apprehension and by providing exposure to behavioral contexts that facilitate delinquent action.

By contrast, leisure activities organized by adults or leisure time spent with parents may be expected to decrease the possibilities of delinquency by strengthening social bonds and thereby rendering delinquency less attractive (Agnew, 1985; Messner and Blau, 1987). One study found that, while "hanging out" and social activities such as dating and partying were associated with higher levels of delinquent involvement, organized leisure was associated with lower levels of delinquent involvement (Agnew and Peterson, 1989). The researchers also reported, however, that it is not sufficient for youths to be engaged in "positive" leisure for a decrease in delinquency to occur—they also must enjoy the activity. In other words, coercive leisure cannot be expected to bring about a decrease in offending behavior.

The role of leisure in the development or the freeing of delinquent motivation may have more to do with the behavior of males than of females (Riley, 1987). In part, as power control theory has argued, this is because female adolescents have traditionally been subject to higher levels of control, which restrict their leisure options (Hagan, Gillis, and Simpson, 1985; Singer and Levine, 1988). These gender differences may be rooted in patterns of family socialization. As we saw in Chapter 4, while risk-taking behavior is encouraged in male children, female children are generally subjected to significantly greater degrees of parental control. Gender differences in delinquent leisure may reflect these patterned gender differences in risk taking and control.

LEISURE ACTIVITIES AND OPPORTUNITIES

Leisure activities provide important occasions for criminal events of various types, as evidenced by the times and places at which crimes occur. A large number of personal victimizations occur during the evenings and on weekends when most people are "at rest," when they have dropped their more serious work roles, and when the formal social controls of the school and the workplace are not operative (Luckenbill, 1977). Personal victimizations also occur disproportionately in leisure settings—informal contexts that host a wide range of activities such as drinking or gambling, dancing and playing games. In a study of high school youth in Tucson, Arizona, Jensen and Brownfield (1986) found partying, cruising, and visiting bars—in general, the social pursuit of fun—to be significantly related to victimization risk.

Bars are good examples of such **permissive environs.** Not only are bars themselves the site of large numbers of criminal events, but so are the blocks on

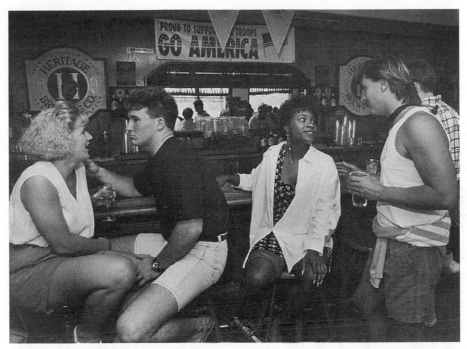

Bars are the location where young adults socialize. They are also frequently the location of crimes against the person, such as assault.

which they are located (Roncek and Maier, 1991; Roncek and Pravatiner, 1989). There are many reasons for this. Bars do most of their business in the evenings when people are freed from many of the social controls that structure their working days. Bars also deal in cash and liquor, which are easily stolen and easily used by the offender. Further, bars tend to place no real restrictions on who can enter, and they are particularly popular among young people. Finally, for many people, the consumption of alcohol increases the probability of interpersonal conflicts and impairs judgments about the scale of these conflicts.

More generally, activities that bring people out of their homes in the evening increase the likelihood of personal and household crime (Kennedy and Forde, 1990). Messner and Blau (1987) found that the volume of leisure activity in the home (indexed by levels of reported television viewing) is related to lower rates of victimization, while the volume of leisure activity outside of the home (indexed by the number of sports and theatrical facilities) is related to higher rates of victimization.

A similar pattern has repeatedly been revealed by victimization surveys. Violent and household victimization increase as evening activities outside of the home increase, and this relationship is independent of marital status, employment status, and age (Gottfredson, 1984). Going out on weekends increases these risks more than going out during the week, while engaging in leisure pursuits increases risk more than does going to work or to school (Gottfredson, 1984; Lasley and Rosenbaum, 1988; Smith, 1982). The American National Crime Survey data indicate that about 30 percent of violent or theft victimizations occur while people are taking part in a leisure activity away from home, compared to about 11 percent when people are at work and about 2 percent while they are asleep (U.S. Dept. of Justice, 1994a).

In general, leisure can be part of a **risky lifestyle** that has dangerous consequences (Kennedy and Forde, 1990). Some types of leisure are clearly riskier than others. Young single males are more likely than others to go to bars where, as we have seen, the risks are higher. By contrast, elderly people are less likely to leave their homes for leisure in the evening; when they do, they are less likely to come into contact with potential offenders.

Several studies suggest that forms of leisure that are themselves criminal may pose particularly high victimization risks (Gottfredson, 1984; Jensen and Brownfield, 1986; Lauritsen, Sampson, and Laub, 1991; Sampson and Lauritsen, 1990). This is partially because offenders make good victims—they may be unlikely to call the police and, if they do, may be likely to have difficulty establishing their credibility.

TRANSACTIONS

The content of criminal events varies across leisure settings and activities. Criminologists have focused particular attention on the street, bars, dating, and tourism.

THE STREET

For many youths, the street is itself a leisure setting. For others, it is the route that they take from one setting to another or from these settings to their homes. Criminal events in the street seem to support the argument of opportunity theorists that people are victims of routines that leave them vulnerable to offenders. In fact, research indicates that, despite the horror stories from inner-city areas where people of all ages are vulnerable to crime, the group that is most likely to be involved in these "risky" routines on the street are young males. Their behavior tends to be more public than that of most other groups, and they frequent the street to a greater degree than others.

YOUNG MALES

As stated previously, the groups most vulnerable to assaults in public places are young, unmarried males who frequent bars, go to movies, go out to work, and spend time out of the house walking or driving around. This lifestyle creates exposure to risk. While violent crime may be spontaneous, its targets tend to be people who are in places that are conducive to violent conflict. This observation does not account for the motivation behind violent crime, but it does explain the high levels of victimization among particular groups based on their exposure to certain settings and activities. Kennedy and Forde (1990) report a similar pattern for robberies: Young, unmarried males who frequent bars and who are out walking or driving around are more likely to be victims of this crime.

The behavior of young males who just hang around on the street is often seen as criminogenic. According to Skogan and Maxfield (1981), urban residents are most afraid of run-down urban areas where teenagers are hanging around on street corners. Even if the loitering is harmless and the individuals who engage in it never become involved in crime, the street is seen as a dangerous place.

If these youths are loosely attached to one another, those whom they encounter in street situations are likely to be acquaintances and the chances of violence tend to be low. When individuals are more closely affiliated, as in a gang, the chance of violence increases, although, as Kennedy and Baron (1993) report, violence may not be a routine outcome of activity by gangs on the street. Much of the crime engaged in by gangs actually occurs when they come into contact with other gangs. Minor theft and robbery certainly occurs, but not to the extent that the public believes. In addition, the view that gangs pursue violence for violence's sake, as would be predicted by the subculture-of-violence theory, is not substantiated by the research.

The same individuals on the street who represent potential offenders can also be victims. Young men in risky areas can easily become targets of assaults and robberies. When alcohol or drugs are involved, spontaneous conflicts may arise between individuals who are complete strangers to one another. Motivation in the violence that occurs between young males, whether in gangs or not, may simply be based on tests of character (Luckenhill, 1977).

Although women may be present in street environments, they are less likely to become involved in conflicts directly, even though they may act as third parties in escalating or defusing the conflict. Women alone tend to avoid those areas they perceive as risky (particularly the street) or situations that may lead to violence or loss of property. Of course, women can be targets of theft just as easily as men—purse snatching is all too common. Nonetheless, street crime appears to be predominantly the domain of young men, both as offenders and victims.

The precursors of assaults or robberies may depend on conflict styles that vary according to the individual personality and the social situation that individuals confront (Hocker and Wilmot, 1985: 38). Hocker and Wilmot assume that people develop patterned responses to conflict. Decisions about response style are based on past experience and learning—by observing others' behavior and by trying out different responses.

Third parties also play an important role in the conflict escalation or de-escalation. Young boys often jokingly exhort their friends to physically restrain them when they are confronting a foe. The opponent is advised, "You're lucky he's holding me back, or you'd be sorry!" While this type of posturing, which is facilitated by third parties, may work to dissipate conflict, it may also have the opposite effect. The joking may become serious, and third parties may promote the conflict instead of acting to reduce its outbreak. However, even when one participant lands a blow that, in legal terms, might be considered criminal assault it is probably not viewed as such by the parties involved. There is likely too much confusion over the identities of the instigator and the victim. Only when physical harm that requires medical assistance is inflicted do these situations lead to the involvement of a formal third party (i.e., the police).

Kennedy and Baron (1993) found that members of punk gangs would absorb a great deal of verbal abuse but become involved in a fight only when they felt they needed to protect themselves, not when they felt that backing down would make them look foolish. This finding suggests not that the members of punk gangs were unprepared for the violence or that they would just walk away if attacked, but rather that the crime in which they engaged was more likely to be characterized by spontaneous outbursts of violence than by conscious, planned events (Gottfredson and Hirschi, 1990).

VANDALISM

As discussed in Chapter 6, people's attitudes toward city streets may be affected not only by the presence of gangs but by graffiti and other signs of vandalism and decay. When people see these signs, in addition to the patterns of movement around them, their fears tend be awakened. While **vandalism** is not a criminal event in conventional terms (that is, an event in which at least two parties are involved in a criminal action), we can still view it in event terms. Vandalism differs from other criminal events in that there is a time delay between the offense and the victimization.

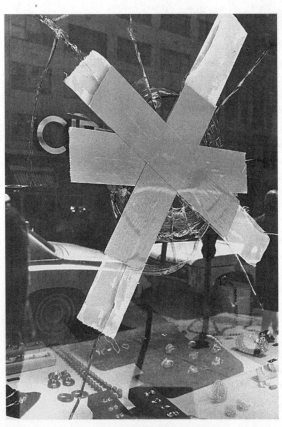

Vandalism is a growing problem in our society.

Criminologists have focused greater attention on the consequences rather than causes of vandalism. Skogan (1990b) and Wilson and Kelling (1983) identify vandalism as a major contributor to the public's declining sense of security in their neighborhoods. Wilson and Kelling argue that disorder and crime are inextricably linked in a kind of developmental sequence. Wilson (1983: 78) notes that social psychologists and police officers tend to agree that if a building window is broken and left unrepaired, the remaining windows will soon be damaged. Vandalism occurs more frequently in areas in which surveillance is low. In generating what Wilson calls "untended" behavior, vandalism leads to a breakdown of community controls and the degeneration of the neighborhood into one that may become criminogenic. The fear that accompanies this degradation may discourage people from routinely using the streets or providing informal surveillance as a way of constraining disorderly behavior. As vandalism increases and the neighborhood continues its decline, residents may move to safer, more congenial environments.

While abandoned buildings appear to be the most frequent targets of vandalism, we are witnessing the growth of public vandalism, which involves tagging (writing graffiti) on walls, public vehicles, or whatever else is available. Graffiti-filled trains and stations have long been the scourge of New York public transit and have created the impression of a dangerous system, even though there are fewer incidents of crime on the subway than on the streets of New York. The New York City transportation department has taken extreme steps (discussed later in this chapter) to ban all graffiti on its subway trains. Similar strategies have been used in other cities as well.

While most tagging takes place at night, when there is little possibility of detection, graffiti writers are becoming bolder and are sometimes recognized for their skills at leaving their mark in daylight hours. This bravado may be the natural response of taggers who have come to see themselves as artists; to most people, however, graffiti is nothing more than simple vandalism.

What motivates most vandalism? Thrill seeking and the fact that it doesn't appear to harm anyone are probably significant causative factors. And notwithstanding the efforts made to curtail it in many cities, vandalism is almost impossible to detect and deter.

BARS

Bars (taverns, lounges, and so on) are places people go to relax, meet friends, listen to music, and drink. Although most bars escape the frenzied aggressiveness that may lead to crime, some attract it. In these locations, where alcohol and drugs mix with loud music and bravado, violence often erupts. Bar owners are increasingly concerned about this violence but often are confused about what to do to reduce it. They hire private guardians (bouncers) to remove the most raucous of their clients, but sometimes the actions of bouncers incite more violence. When one asks college or university criminology students where they would go to find a fight on any given night, they can easily list two or three notorious bars in town in which violence occurs with regularity. Apparently, these places attract a clientele that tends to be more aggressive than average, a conclusion that supports the subculture-of-violence perspective.

Criminal events that occur in bars generally consist of minor assaults, particularly between young males. These events may also involve vandalism (breaking windows, chairs, and tables). Events that involve interpersonal conflict may conclude without violence, with the protagonists walking away or being pulled away from one another. When there is escalation, violence may erupt. As a member of a band that has played for student gatherings told the authors, a crowd that is docile throughout an entire gig may suddenly become violent when the band finishes its last set. It is, he said, almost as if they can now hear one another speak and don't like what is being said! The jostling and shoving that may occur in these situations may be seen by all parties as harmless, but violence may ensue if the aggressiveness accelerates. While this description suggests that the event is spontaneous, the idea that certain bars attract this type of problem implies that some individuals go there in search of trouble. Luckenbill's (1977) characterization of the "character contest," discussed in Chapter 5, would seem to apply to such situations. The jostling and shoving that precedes a fight might be combined with insults and threats. When the fight breaks out, those around the combatants may add fuel to it by offering encouragement or by joining in.

DATING VIOLENCE

According to popular thinking, adolescent dating is a context for innocent exploration, while violence is a feature of conflict-ridden and constricting marital relationships (Sugarman and Hotaling, 1989). However, in recent years, dating violence has been recognized as existing in some unknown proportion of dating relationships. The efforts of researchers to estimate levels of dating violence are fraught with the same difficulties that characterize attempts to understand violence in families; as a result, estimates of the size of the problem are highly variable. While the term **dating violence,** or courtship violence, has no precise meaning, it generally refers to various forms of sexually and nonsexually assaultive behaviors (Thompson, 1986). In dating behavior, as in marital relationships, women rather than men typically are the victims of violence (DeKeseredy, 1988; DeKeseredy and Hinch, 1991).

Most of the contemporary discussion about dating violence has focused on the subject of date rape. Because such rapes occur in a social context in which consensual sex is a possibility, until recently, the tendency has been to view date rape as something other than "real rape" (Bechhofer and Parrot, 1991). This has led to a victim-blaming strategy, as well as to a widespread willingness to dismiss the injury or trauma experienced by victims. A more realistic appraisal links date rape to culturally supported dating rituals that reflect patriarchal assumptions about male power and privilege (Muehlenhard and Linton, 1987). Research suggests that male sexual aggression is more likely when males exert greater control over the dating process—that is, when they control the initiation of dating, assume responsibility for expenses and transportation, and choose the dating activity (Harney and Muehlenhard, 1991).

BOX 9.3 DATING VIOLENCE

While the empirical study of violence in marital relationships dates back twenty or more years now, researchers were somewhat slower to recognize that much violence also occurs between individuals who are dating but not yet married. One such study designed to identify levels of violence existing between dating couples was conducted by researchers Peter Burke, Jan Stets, and Maureen Pirog-Good in 1986. The researchers surveyed 505 students enrolled in upper-level courses at a large midwestern university, asking them questions about their involvement as both victims and perpetrators in a number of violent actions with their dating partner(s). Respondents were asked to report how many times in the previous year they had engaged in both physical and sexual abuse. "Mild" physical abuse was defined as any of the following: threw something at the partner; pushed, grabbed, or shoved the partner; or slapped or spanked the partner. "Severe" physical violence was defined as kicked, bit, or hit the partner with a fist; hit or tried to hit the partner with something; beat up the partner; threatened the partner with a gun or knife; or used a gun or knife on the partner. All sexual abuse incidents were defined as being against the partner's (or one's own) will. Mild sexual abuse involved breast fondling or genital fondling. "Severe" sexual abuse was defined as attempted intercourse that was not successful or intercourse.

Table 9.1 shows the average number of times, along with the range (that is, the high and low values for all respondents), that men and women in the study reported having experienced physical or sexual violence in dating relationships in the past year.

Table 9.1
Incidence of Physical and Sexual Abuse Among Dating Partners

Action	Males		Females	
	Range	Mean	Range	Mean
Inflict Sexual Abuse				
Mild	0–104	5.1	0–120	1.7
Severe	0–64	2.5	0–60	1.2
Inflict Physical Abuse				
Mild	0–23	0.4	0–47	1.0
Severe	0–38	0.3	0–65	0.6
Sustain Sexual Abuse				
Mild	0–67	0.8	0–120	1.8
Severe	0–64	0.9	0–63	2.1
Sustain Physical Abuse				
Mild	0–61	0.8	0–84	1.1
Severe	0–74	0.4	0–25	0.2

For Discussion

How are factors that cause dating and marital violence similar or different? What kinds of policies might colleges and universities adopt to control dating violence?

SOURCE: Based on Peter Burke, Jan E. Stets, and Maureen A. Pirog-Good, "Gender Identity, Self-Esteem, and Physical and Sexual Abuse in Dating Relationships." In Jan Stets and Maureen Pirog-Good (eds.), *Violence in Dating Relationships*, pp. 72–93 (New York: Praeger, 1989).

Male control may translate into sexual aggression in two distinct ways. First, many men may interpret a woman's willingness to allow the male to make decisions about where they will go on a date, what they will do, and who will pay for it as a sign of interest in sexual activity (Johnson, Palileo, and Gray, 1982). Such men might reason that if women don't object to coming back to their room or accompanying them to a secluded spot, they must be interested in sex, even if they say otherwise. In particular, a woman's heavy consumption of alcohol may be interpreted by the male as a sign of sexual interest (Benson, Charlton, and Goodhart, 1992; Muehlenhard and Linton, 1987).

Second, to the extent that the male controls the circumstances of dating, he controls the opportunities for offending. When he controls transportation, for instance, he can effectively impede the ability of the female to escape a situation in which sexual assault is likely. The woman who is in an isolated spot with a sexually aggressive male may be reluctant to leave the car because she has been warned that even greater dangers confront women who are not protected by male companions. Not surprisingly, date rapes typically occur in the home of the offender, inside an automobile, or in some other isolated location (Harney and Muehlenhard, 1991). These two consequences of male control—misinterpretation of sexual interest and the creation of opportunity—frequently work in concert. For example, "parking" combines privacy, which provides the opportunity for sexual aggression, with the likelihood that the male will overestimate the female's willingness to engage in sexual relations (Muehlenhard and Linton, 1987).

In courtship violence, like marital violence, violence is supported by the patriarchal belief that the use of force by men against women is legitimate (Lloyd, Koval, and Cale, 1989). Women who are assaulted by boyfriends frequently cite jealousy or attempts to terminate the relationship as the precipitating factors. Ironically, such dating violence may be viewed as a sign of love by either or both parties. According to Sugarman and Hotaling (1989), assaultive violence in dating relationships is most likely to occur on weekends, in both private (the residence of one of the partners) or relatively public (an automobile or out of doors) settings.

TOURISM

It is impossible to ignore the growing importance of tourism in our society. Large amounts of money are spent on tourist attractions, and people are allocating increased amounts of their disposable income to travel. Despite the growing awareness that tourists are not immune to crime, however, hotels and travel agencies have been slow to warn tourists about potentially dangerous areas. Tourists tend to be easy targets for the pickpocket or the robber. Nor is it just the property that tourists take with them that is at risk. One scam involves thieves reading the identification tags of departing travelers and then going to their homes to burglarize their now unoccupied homes!

Victimization of travelers is hardly a recent phenomenon. In the Middle Ages, castles were built in the south of France to protect pilgrims who traveled through areas inhabited by thieves and robbers. And although modern tourism has left the impression that tourists are not likely to be victims, they *are*, and they need to take precautions to protect themselves. As tourists become increasingly aware of their vulnerability, many once-popular tourist destinations are finding that the visitors are staying away.

BOX 9.4 RESPONSES TO TOURIST-DIRECTED CRIME

Crime is not a significant danger for North American visitors to most of the Caribbean and the Bahamas, according to officials in Ottawa and Washington, but travellers should note that safety varies by island. And normal precautions are recommended throughout the region.

On most islands, petty street crime is not uncommon.

"Normal precautions" for travellers generally include not walking alone on unfamiliar, deserted streets at night; being alert to potential pickpockets or purse snatchers, particularly in crowded places and on public transportation; not carrying large amounts of cash; keeping car doors locked; not leaving valuables unattended; and, in general, looking over your shoulder.

But on some islands, safety conditions are more severe. In Jamaica, although the government has recently taken steps, including increased police patrols and better training for hotel security personnel, to enhance tourist safety, officials concede that crime remains a problem, particularly in the Kingston area.

The U.S. State Department, for instance, warns that "persons out walking after dark or who take other than licensed taxicabs are at particular risk. There is sporadic gang violence in inner-city Kingston."

Some parts of the city "are also, on occasion, subject to a curfew."

Despite Kingston's problems, Jamaica is still considered generally safe—if you do not mind the hordes of street hawkers selling soft drugs. Among the safest lodgings, according to independent observers, are the self-contained resorts, which offer a high degree of security. Many provide escorted group tours of Jamaica's cities and countryside for visitors who enjoy venturing beyond their hotel.

Although Barbados is generally considered a safe destination, "street crime, sometimes involving assault," was mentioned in a recent U.S. State Department crime note. Barbados Tourism representatives acknowledged that violent incidents have occurred in "crowded inner-city parts of Bridgetown" (the capital) and in the city's outskirts to the south and east, where a lot of the country nightspots are located; and where tourists who drink are easy targets.

As in other resort destinations, cruise ship passengers are viewed as easier targets than hotel guests since it assumed that their stay will be brief and they won't stick around to testify against thieves. Cruise passengers planning to explore the island (or other islands) independently might be wise to avoid "telltale" tourist clothes—T-shirts with the cruise line logo, fancy cruisewear—when disembarking.

Safety statistics have been improving in St. Martin, where a "serious crime problem" was reported in 1990. Tourism officials say that both sides of the island have since increased their police forces significantly, and new officers are being trained. Back roads that were totally dark have now been lighted; and lighting has been upgraded along the main connecting Lowlands Road. Petty crime last year was down 32 percent.

Far more severe is the security situation in Haiti, no longer popular among tourists due largely to the country's political instability and a current trade embargo.

"Foreigners are at risk from increased criminal attacks, particularly in the urban areas," according to the Bureau of Consular Affairs in Washington. What makes Canadians and Americans targets is "their relative affluence."

But no place is immune. Even among some of the safest islands, population destinations like Antigua and Barbados, "petty street crime occurs, but is unusual" and "valuables left on the beach are subject to theft," the U.S. State Department says.

For Discussion

Why are tourists thought to be particularly vulnerable to many types of crime? How can we make tourists less vulnerable to criminal activity?

SOURCE: Elizabeth Wissner-Gross, "Emphasize Safety in the Caribbean as Anywhere Else," *The Toronto Star,* 30 January 1993, p. F7.

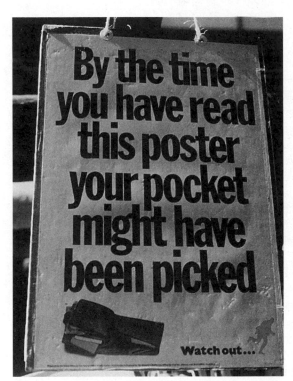

Being on holiday doesn't protect you from becoming a victim of crime.

Major outbreaks of violence against tourists receive widespread media attention, which may also consist of advice to tourists about special precautions they can take to protect themselves. Attacks on foreign tourists in parts of East Africa and Egypt recently have led to a worldwide alert to avoid these areas. Canadians have recently received highly publicized warnings about travel in Florida—a very popular destination for families and the elderly. Also, travel agencies and tour groups now steer clients away from areas they consider dangerous. The governments of many countries issue warnings to their nationals to avoid certain areas, particularly those characterized by a pattern of violence and robbery against tourists or a great deal of political instability; in the latter situation, travelers may become a target of local anger and frustration. Some countries are responding to crime against tourists by developing programs that enhance security in resort areas and that educate travelers about the hazards they may encounter in certain areas. Tourist-directed crime would seem to be best explained by opportunity theorists, who see tourists as vulnerable targets in areas where surveillance may be low and precautions more difficult to take.

The tourist is more likely to be a victim of theft or robbery than of personal attack. Most commonly, luggage is stolen or pockets are picked. As thieves develop sophisticated techniques for picking or jimmying locks, they increasingly are preying on autos as well. In one scam, the car thief drives along a beach road that is not too crowded and checks out the parked cars. If there are signs of an attractive target (for example, a foreign license plate or a rental car), and if the owner(s) is nowhere to be seen (and thus presumably down at the beach), the thief parks behind the car, approaches the car, and breaks through the lock (with special tools, this can be accomplished fairly easily). Then the thief quickly searches the car and exits with whatever loot he finds. Slashing a tire prevents the victim from attempting pursuit.

Tourists may also run into problems simply because they do not understand the local customs or language. In one case, a 16-year-old Japanese exchange student was shot and killed in a Louisiana neighborhood because he did not understand the warning "Freeze!" The youth had been looking for a Halloween party and did not stop when he was accosted by Rodney Peairs, who said that he had felt that his life had been threatened by the costumed youth. Peairs was acquitted under a Louisiana law that allows citizens to use deadly weapons to protect themselves. In response to the student's tragic death, the Japanese government is publishing a guide of helpful phrases for U.S.-bound tourists. The guide will include about thirty phrases that few Japanese learn in their language classes, among them, "Get lost," "Watch out," and "I mean it" (Sanger, 1993: A9). Not only the translations but also the different cultural meanings of the thirty phrases will be imparted as a way of letting the visitors know that the person issuing the warning is serious.

THE AFTERMATH

Victimizations that occur in leisure settings frequently go unreported. The tourist–victim, for instance, may not speak the local language or know how to find the police. If the loss or the injury is not great, the tourist–victim may decide that reporting the incident to the police may not be worth it. Victimizations may also go unreported when the leisure activity is itself regarded as a form of disreputable behavior. Victims who have been drinking or who encounter offenders in a known "deviant context" may be reluctant to bring the incident to the attention of the police. Given the generally negative attitude toward many forms of youthful leisure activities, it is not surprising that crimes that occur in these settings remain undiscovered or unrecorded by police.

Victims may respond to crimes committed against them in leisure settings in other ways. One response may be to avoid the types of encounters or circumstances in which the victimization occurred. Since leisure activity is, by definition, discretionary activity, it is easier to avoid than home- or work-related activities. Thus, the victim of courtship violence may refrain from dating, and the jogger who is mugged may stop jogging and take up "mall walking," which may be perceived as safer than running on city streets or park paths.

In other instances, a participant in a street fight or barroom brawl may prefer to seek revenge rather than report the crime to police. Of course, the status of such individuals as "victims" may itself be questionable, as they themselves may have struck the initial blow or instigated the fight. In addition, many criminal events involving young males may be of little interest to police. In recent times, police have been encouraged to manage their excessive workloads by assigning a higher priority to the victimization of women and children than to young males.

While the long-term consequences of leisure-related victimizations are not yet evident, it may be that, with the exception of the sexual assaults, the effects are short-lived. For example, the punks that Baron (1989) talked with simply shrugged off their own victimization, regarding it as just a routine hazard of life on the streets. The degree to which individuals are deterred from becoming involved in leisure-related crimes may have more to do with the risk of being hurt than with the risk of being arrested. This is not to suggest that the police do not deter; their presence on the street or in bars plays an important role in keeping such potentially dangerous behavior under control. The evidence would seem to indicate that the behavior of young males on the street and in other settings can change from violent to passive fairly easily, particularly given the fact that victims and offenders are often hard to distinguish and that public guardians (police and citizens) are not always available to stop a brewing conflict from becoming serious.

The need for guardianship has long driven the policy whereby police attempt to maintain a high profile on the street. This has been achieved through the use of random patrol (that is, cars cruising neighborhoods looking for problems). As we discussed in Chapter 7, however, patrol tactics appear to have little influence on the amount of neighborhood crime. As a result, police departments are now experimenting with neighborhood ministations and increasing foot patrols and neighborhood consultations—tactics they believe can prevent and deter crime more effectively than can a highly visible police presence in the form of random patrol. Still, the most effective guardians against crime are not the police, but rather other people who frequent leisure settings and who call the police when needed.

Leisure settings are best described as settings in which crimes occur according to opportunity. As we will discuss in Chapter 11, attempts have been made to reduce opportunities for crime by making changes to the environment. Target hardening can include anything from increased and better-situated lighting to surveillance cameras (Newman, 1972). For example, a multimillion-dollar program has been initiated by the New York City Subway Authority to clean all trains of graffiti. After each journey, trains are checked and cleaned of debris. Subway police patrol stations with special night-vision glasses and cameras to catch graffiti artists in the act. Scratch-proof glass on the trains is being developed, and there are plans for paint-resistant exteriors. There is even talk of banning spray cans and wide-tip marker pens in order to limit the resources available to graffiti artists. All of these measures are being taken to increase public confidence in the safety of the subway system.

There have also been attempts to influence the use of leisure as a crime control mechanism. Particularly conspicuous have been efforts to develop **positive leisure** alternatives for young people who are actually or potentially delinquent (Agnew and Peterson, 1989). This approach reflects the maxim, made explicit in social control theory, that "idle hands are the devil's workshop." Youths get themselves into trouble (through various forms of "hanging out") because they lack positive options. The reasoning behind the positive-leisure approach is that summer camps, organized clubs, and other so-called forms of healthy recreation will expose youths to an environment that discourages involvement in crime and delinquency.

A parallel approach focuses on the need to control what are widely viewed in some quarters as negative and corrupting forms of youth leisure. This approach seems to reflect the view that, if they are left to make their own leisure choices, youths will almost always make the wrong ones. The past several decades have witnessed numerous crusades intended to impose legal and social restrictions on the ability of young people to make these choices. These campaigns were directed against feature films in the 1930s; comic books and rock and roll in the 1950s; the presumed drug-influenced protest music of the 1960s; and rap and heavy-metal music, fantasy role-playing games (for example, Dungeons and Dragons), and video games in the 1980s and 1990s. Television violence has been the subject of recurrent crusades every five or ten years since the 1960s (Best, 1990; Gray, 1989).

Graffiti offends and creates unease among those who must confront it on a daily basis.

SUMMARY

■ ■ ■

When people are "at leisure," they are also at risk of involvement in criminal events, as offenders or victims. The relationships that link leisure activity and criminal activity are highly varied. Some forms of leisure might be seen as causes of crime. The content of youth-oriented media, for instance, may seem to provide the motives for crime. Alternatively, engagement in peer activities may suggest freedom from the social controls that might be expected to inhibit offending.

Much leisure activity takes place in public spaces. Street crime involves people who are passing through areas in transit from one place to another or who are simply "hanging out." In these contexts, crime might itself constitute leisure, as appears to be the case with vandalism and graffiti writing. In leisure settings such as streets and bars, it is often difficult to distinguish the offenders from the victims when a conflict escalates into assault or other forms of violence. This form of opportunity crime tends to be based on the risky lifestyles of the individuals involved and is more likely to be deterred by retribution than by reporting the crime to the police.

In date rape, the routine activity of courtship takes on a criminal character when aggressive behavior translates into sexual assault against an unwilling participant. Much of this behavior also goes unreported. Tourism crime targets people who are at leisure in unfamiliar places, where their lack of understanding of what areas are safe or unsafe may put them at risk. It is often difficult for tourists who have been victimized to find someone to whom to report the crime. They may decide that they simply do not want the hassle of getting involved with police in a foreign country. Travel agencies and governments are increasingly briefing tourists on how to travel safely and advising them of areas that should be avoided altogether. A tourist's most effective deterrent against crime is to not travel in unsafe areas at all, thereby removing the opportunity for crime.

Some types of leisure pursuits place people at particular risk of victimization. The risky lifestyles in which people engage may make the search for a "good time" result in a "bad time." It must be emphasized that, in the leisure domain, as in other domains, the processes that we are describing are not deterministic. In other words, exposure to criminogenic influences or to threats of victimization does not guarantee the development of a criminal event, but rather only increases its probability by bringing together opportunities for crime and motivations to offend.

QUESTIONS FOR REVIEW AND DISCUSSION
■ ■ ■

1. Why are bars the site of so much crime? Can you name some bars in your area that are associated with high rates of crime?
2. Is dating violence a serious problem on your campus? What measures (if any) have been taken by school officials to deal with the problem?
3. How do you account for the recurrent tendency on the part of adults to view the cultural trappings of adolescents as troublesome?
4. In what way can vandalism be understood as a juvenile form of leisure activity?
5. How do patterns of leisure activity change over the life cycle, and what implications do these changes have for victimization risk?
6. Why are many of the crimes committed against tourists never reported to the police?

Crime and Work

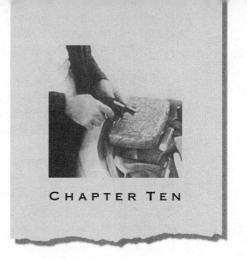

WHAT'S IN CHAPTER TEN

In this chapter, we discuss the work domain from three different perspectives: victimization and work, crime and legitimate work, and crime as work. First, we examine how different types of work can expose individuals to varying forms of crime victimization. Second, we examine how people who are employed in legitimate work activities take advantage of this to commit crimes. Third, we look at crime that takes on the character of work itself, either as a career or in the context of an ongoing illegal enterprise.

KEY TERMS

workplace stress

white-collar crime

occupational crime

corporate crime

criminogenic market structure

enterprise crime

La Cosa Nostra

In this chapter, we consider the social domain of the workplace. As we will see, among the characteristics in which jobs differ is the accessibility to criminal opportunities they afford. Our discussion is organized around two broad topics. The first is the relationship between work in the legitimate labor force and the occurrence of criminal events. Two major issues concern us here. First, in what ways are patterns of victimization associated with patterns of employment? In other words, how do the jobs we have affect the victimization risks we face? Second, in what ways do seemingly honest work make available opportunities for criminal behavior, involving either employers (or employees) or members of the general public?

The second major theme to be explored in this chapter is crime as a type of occupational activity. Here, we examine "enterprise crime," which involves the exploitation of opportunities for the development of criminal business.

CRIME, EMPLOYMENT, AND UNEMPLOYMENT

The U.S. labor force has undergone several important changes in the past few decades. The unemployment rate, which was 4.9 percent in 1970, had risen to 7.1 percent in 1980 and fallen again to 5.5 percent in 1990. By 1993, however, unemployment was again hovering around the 7 percent mark (U.S. Bureau of the Census, 1994). Unemployment is particularly prevalent among young people and minorities—groups that, as we already know, are at high risk for involvement in criminal events as both victims and offenders. The unemployment rate for African-American male teenagers in 1993, for example, was 40.2 percent (U.S. Bureau of the Census, 1994, Table 628).

Female labor force participation has increased greatly in recent years, especially among married women (U.S. Bureau of the Census, 1994, Table 624). The types of jobs available have also changed in the last two decades. While employment in the manufacturing sector fell between 1979 and 1992, the availability of jobs in the service sector increased in the same period (U.S. Bureau of the Census, 1994, Table 642). Compared to goods-producing jobs, however, service jobs tend to be lower paying and to more frequently involve part-time work.

In addition to the size and nature of the work force, the nature of work itself has undergone important changes. Many of these changes are attributable to various types of technological innovations, particularly in computer technology. While these changes are intended to make the workplace more efficient (and, from the employer's viewpoint, more profitable), they affect the pacing and timing of jobs. Employees may have computer hookups in their homes that allow them to reduce the amount of time required at their formal places of work. Fax machines quicken the pace at which information can be transmitted, and cellular telephones have worked to blur, for many, the distinction between private time and work time.

EMPLOYMENT AND VICTIMIZATION

How do patterns of employment or experiences in the labor force relate to patterns of involvement in criminal events? One approach to this question is to ask whether employed and unemployed individuals have different victimization risks. This question is not as straightforward as it may initially appear. Part of the problem concerns how we choose to define the reference group against whom the employed should be compared. If we define this group broadly, including not only those who are unemployed but also those who are retired, institutionalized, or sick or who define their main activity in surveys as "homemakers," then the victimization risks associated with being employed are generally higher for most types of crime (Miethe, Stafford, and Long, 1987). This is because those who constitute this other broad reference group are likely to be people whose social and demographic characteristics are usually associated with lower victimization rates.

When we compare those who are employed with those who are unemployed, the disadvantages associated with employment diminish in many surveys. In other words, unemployment is associated with higher victimization risks (Cohen and Cantor, 1981). The size and significance of this relationship varies. Data from the American National Crime Survey (U.S. Dept. of Justice, 1988) indicate that the unemployed are victimized by violent crime more

The workplace can sometimes be a place where crime occurs.

than twice as often as the employed (76 versus 32 per 1,000 population) and rates of theft victimization are marginally higher for this group (90 versus 81 per 1,000).

UNEMPLOYMENT AND OFFENDING

The relationship between unemployment and offending is studied much more frequently than the relationship between unemployment and victimization. Most of the theories of offending that we reviewed in Chapters 3 and 4 would lead us to expect that risks of offending are greater for unemployed people. Theories that emphasize the role of social inequality in the generation of crime quite naturally suggest that not having a job may encourage the development of criminal motivations. Moreover, this view is perfectly consistent with common sense.

We would expect measures of unemployment to be related, in empirical studies, to measures of criminal offending for many reasons. First, some property crimes may be committed out a sense of need or desire for things that people want but cannot buy. If people lack a stable income, they may experience greater temptations to take what is not theirs. Second, occupational status arguably is an important mechanism for integrating people into conventional society; that is, jobs provide a "stake in conformity" (Toby, 1974). Not having a job may weaken the hold that conformist institutions have over people. Third, being unemployed may result in the adoption of behaviors, such as drug use, that are themselves associated with criminal offending (Hartnagel and Krahn, 1989). Fourth, unemployment may be related to family instability and thus to the ability of parents to monitor the criminal behavior of dependent children (Sampson, 1987). Fifth, since rates of unemployment are high among young people, who seem to be most "crime prone," we might expect the criminogenic effects of unemployment to be particularly strongly related to offending among this segment of the population.

Despite these theoretical and commonsense connections between unemployment and offending, several criminologists question the validity of this relationship (Chiricos, 1987; Freeman, 1983; Gottfredson and Hirschi, 1990). While many criminologists would argue that unemployment is causally related to crime, they are unsure of the size and significance of the effect. Others dispute whether being unemployed has any independent causal influence on the propensity to behave criminally.

Sorting out the relationship between unemployment and offending is no simple task. First, just as efforts to measure crime are fraught with difficulties, it is also quite difficult to measure unemployment in a valid way (Gramling, Forsyth, and Fewell, 1988). Unemployment is usually measured in terms of the number of people who are not employed but who are actively looking for work. Such measures thus exclude those who have "dropped out" of the labor pool. This bias in our measures of unemployment may have the effect of including those who are most highly motivated to gain entry to the "conventional world" and excluding those who are least motivated. The overall effect may be to weaken the measured relationship between crime and unemployment.

Second, some researchers have argued that not only unemployment per se but also the quality of labor force experiences is related to criminal offending (Allan and Steffensmeier, 1989; Currie, 1985; Hartnagel and Krahn, 1989). Precarious, low-paying jobs that offer few of the advantages generally associated with employment are counted as "employment" in labor force surveys, despite the fact that such jobs might not provide a strong cushion against the various criminogenic influences to which the job-holder may be exposed. Third, many researchers attempt to study the relationship between unemployment and crime at the state or national level (for example, by asking if the national unemployment rate is related to the national crime rate) (Chiricos, 1987). However, this may be too broad a level for the investigation of this issue in that it may obscure relationships that exist at the community or neighborhood level.

Despite the popular view of the relationship between unemployment and crime, studies support alternative interpretations. Some researchers have suggested, for instance, that delinquent involvement is greater among employed teenagers than among unemployed ones (Tanner and Krahn, 1991). The former group, it is argued, may be less susceptible to parental controls and more susceptible to delinquent peer influences. Other researchers have suggested that crime causes unemployment (not the other way around) in that people who are criminally inclined are less interested in conforming to the routines demanded by legitimate labor force participation (Wilson, 1983). Still others maintain that the relationship between crime and unemployment is "spurious" in the sense that no real relationship exists between them; the appearance of a relationship is created by the fact that being unemployed and behaving criminally are both related to a "common cause" such as a low degree of self-control (Gottfredson and Hirschi, 1990; Wilson and Herrnstein, 1985).

Ultimately, it may be impossible to generalize about the relationship between unemployment and crime. The nature of the relationship may depend on the type of crime, the social characteristics of the labor force group, and the social policies in place to assist those who are not employed (Allan and Steffensmeier, 1989; Currie, 1985). Cantor and Land (1985) have argued, moreover, that the rate of unemployment may have more than one type of effect on the overall rate of crime. Consistent with arguments made previously in this chapter, they suggest that unemployment may encourage the development of criminal motivation among some people. This implies that unemployment will be positively related to the crime rate such that the crime rate increases as the unemployment rate increases. However, Cantor and Land also argue that the unemployment rate may have a negative effect on the crime rate. This effect is related not to criminal motivation but to criminal opportunity. According to Cantor and Land, the unemployed are much less likely to engage in routine activities that take them away from the home for predictable and extended periods. In other words, unemployment may be related to increases in the level of guardianship exercised over persons and property. In addition, because the unemployment rate can be understood, at least in part, as a general indicator of the overall well-being of the economy, we can assume that when the unemployment rate is high, there will be fewer goods in circulation for thieves to steal. Cantor and Land's analysis of UCR data for the period 1946 to 1982 supports the argument that both types of effects may be possible.

We have reviewed the relationship between the general effects of employment and unemployment on the likelihood of committing crime. Now we can examine how particular forms of labor force participation make crime possible. Two issues concern us here. The first is the relationship between the jobs people have and the victimization risks they face. The second is the ways in which the jobs that people have give them opportunities to behave criminally.

VICTIMIZATION AND WORK

Public awareness of **workplace stress** has been increasing in recent years. Studies have estimated that approximately 15 percent of the U.S work force will experience health problems due to stress (*Business and Health*, 1994). Worker's compensation claims for stress-related problems tripled in the 1980s (Karasek and Theorell, 1990). Stress-related losses are estimated to cost the U.S. economy as much as $150 billion per year (Freudenheim, 1987). Work-related stressors include job demands and hours of work, the threat of layoff, poor interpersonal relations, the risk of accident or injury, harassment, and discrimination—and even fear for one's life.

BOX 10.1 MURDER IN THE WORKPLACE

From the office manager who just fired an employee to the emergency room nurse who fears the stabbing victim's shady companion is fingering a weapon, workers are increasingly worried about being murdered on the job.

By some estimates homicide may now be the third highest work-related cause of death in the United States, according to Joseph Kinney of the Chicago-based National Safe Workplace Institute.

Such crimes are sometimes page one news:

- In Tampa, Fla., a disgruntled former employee killed three men at lunch who were once his supervisors, wounded two others, then took his own life.
- Seven workers at a fried chicken restaurant in suburban Chicago were mowed down during a robbery after the store closed for the evening.
- In 1986 and 1991, two postal workers, one fired and the other threatened with dismissal, took out their rage on postal centers in Oklahoma and Michigan. Nineteen died in all.

But other cases rate only a line or two on the evening news—typically a rejected suitor or ex-spouse stalking his or her mate to a violent death in the office or shop.

"Violence in the workplace is escalating and I think there are two root causes," Kinney says.

"One is a feeling of increased vulnerability that workers and managers now feel. In fact, at least a million managers have lost their jobs because of corporation downsizing or mergers in the last 10 years.

"The other thing is just the increased willingness of people to use violence in our society—to deal with emotions and problems. Stress is rising all over the place."

He says he expects these kinds of violent reactions to escalate.

"Just a generation ago, workers and managers expected to have one employer for life. Now, not only can we expect to have multiple employers, but there is talk about having two or three career changes during a lifetime.

"But, we don't have in place yet the kind of social and educational institutions, public and private, that are responsive to this increased feeling of vulnerability and disloyalty."

Eric Hickey of California State University says mass murders in public places are running at the rate of two or three per month in the United States.

Usually the killer "is making a final statement to the world," he says. "The ultimate motivation is the same—having control over other people when you don't have control over your own life."

Paul Levy of the department of psychology at the University of Akron says he is not 100 percent sure the workplace violence has increased as dramatically as it seems.

"But there probably has been some increase," he says. "When our confidence in our security at work is undermined, that causes a great deal of stress and frustration. In addition, the economic situation is so bad that people feel very insecure in their jobs."

Job loss, Levy says, is nearly as stressful as facing the death of a loved one.

For Discussion

What jobs seem likely to produce the level of stress that might lead individuals to become violent? How might theories that focus on criminal opportunity explain the apparent increase in workplace violence?

SOURCE: "Murder in the Workplace on the Increase in U.S.," *The Toronto Star,* 9 February 1993, p. F10.

INDIVIDUAL AND OCCUPATIONAL CHARACTERISTICS

Although it is not generally recognized as such, the threat of criminal victimization may be an important source of job stress for many people. Victimization surveys tell us that the chances of being a victim of crime are not randomly distributed across occupational groups. While work roles may have much in common, irrespective of the unique characteristics of particular jobs, there are dramatic differences in what types of work people do, where they do it, and with whom it brings them into contact. As we will see, the characteristics of some jobs increase risk while the characteristics of other jobs decrease risk. Such differences may be obscured when the victimization experiences of the employed are compared with those of the unemployed.

Yet, even when we compare the victimization risks associated with different occupations, it may be difficult to determine whether it is the job itself or the characteristics of the people who hold such jobs that affect the risk of victimization. For instance, if we were to discover that part-time employees of fast-food restaurants faced particularly high risks of victimization, we would not necessarily be justified in concluding that there is something about cooking or serving hamburgers that makes one more vulnerable to criminal danger. Fast-food employees tend to be teenagers and, in view of the relationship between age and victimization, the higher risks may involve age-related rather than work-related factors. In fact, we might not even be surprised to discover that, while these employees report higher rates of crime, the experiences that they tell us about typically occur outside of work rather than on the job. Thus, a cursory review of victimization risks and occupation may be misleading.

Information about how victimization risks vary across occupations is hard to come by. This is because the statistical rarity of victimization incidents does not, in many cases, allow survey researchers to compute separate victimization rates for a detailed inventory of occupations. Some research indicates that risks are higher for members of the military (Harlow, 1991), probation officers (Linder and Koehler, 1992), police officers, welfare workers, and those who work in bars (Mayhew, Elliot, and Dowds, 1989) and other occupations that involve regular and frequent contact with high-risk populations.

Perhaps the most comprehensive study of this type was undertaken by Block, Felson, and Block (1984), who calculated the victimization rates for 426 different occupations using data on 108,000 crime incidents reported to National Crime Survey interviewers between 1973 and 1981. For the five of-

Some jobs, such as taxi driver, expose workers to higher risk of crime victimization.

fenses these researchers examined (robbery, assault, burglary, larceny, and automobile theft), victimization risk was inversely related to "occupational status," which they defined as the average income for each occupation. In other words, as the average income of an occupation increased, the risks of being victimized decreased. More specifically, the study revealed marked differences in levels of victimization risk. For instance, amusement and recreation workers and restaurant workers such as busboys, dishwashers, and servers were among the five highest-risk occupations for all offenses. Sheriffs and police officers had the highest assault rates, while taxi drivers and newspaper vendors were among the most frequently robbed. The lowest rates of victimization were found among certain farm workers, as well as telephone and electrical workers, opticians, stenographers, and radio operators.

The authors readily acknowledge that data of this sort are difficult to interpret:

> *On the one hand, better jobs tend to provide more good things in life, presumably including safety and security from crime. More income and credit allow people to purchase security devices, safer locations to live in, better parking spots and the like. Better jobs may also help people avoid public transit and unfavourable hours for trips to work and elsewhere. Better credit allows avoidance of cash. In general, more resources, including money, credit and control over time, should help people to obtain security from crime.*
>
> *On the other hand, better jobs may bring with them more luxury goods to attract offenders. Higher strata individuals may also go out more at night, enjoying sport and cultural events or visiting restaurants or other night spots. Good jobs are often found within a metropolis rather than in rural areas with lower risk. One suspects that modern offenders have little trouble finding the higher occupational strata in order to victimize them, security efforts notwithstanding. (Block, Felson, and Block, 1984: 142)*

Thus, while analyses of the victimization rates of different occupational groups are interesting and informative, they do not necessarily tell us very much about crimes that occur in the workplace. This requires a more focused investigation of the crimes that happen while people are at work.

PRECURSORS

In very general terms, workplace settings have characteristics that both encourage and inhibit victimization. On the one hand, full-time employees spend many hours "at risk" to whatever threats the workplace presents. On the other hand, workplace settings tend to be much more highly structured than, for instance, leisure settings and thus more subject to a variety of social controls that discourage victimization. Some degree of order and control is usually deemed necessary if the organizational goals of the workplace are to be achieved in an efficient fashion.

How much crime occurs in the workplace? Data from the 1992 American National Crime Survey provide a broad answer to this question (U.S. Dept. of

Justice, 1994a). According to this survey, about 11 percent of violent crimes occurred while the respondents were "working or on duty," including 14 percent of assaults, 5 percent of robberies, and 6 percent of rapes. An additional 6.9 percent of violent crimes occurred while respondents were on their way to or from work. With respect to crimes of theft, about 18 percent occurred while the respondents were at work. However, these data underestimate the relative proportion of workplace crime in that they represent proportions of the total number of incidents—that is, incidents involving those who are and who are not members of the paid labor force.

Data from the 1988 British Crime Survey allow us to separate out the proportion of workplace crimes reported by employed respondents (Mayhew, Elliott, and Dowds, 1989). These findings reveal that 71 percent of the thefts, 22 percent of the assaults, 11 percent of the robberies, and 13 percent of the vehicle thefts occurred while respondents were at work. In all cases, the vast majority of the crimes occurred while the victims were inside the workplace rather than in some other work-related location, such as out of doors at work or on the street near the workplace.

One type of worksite for which detailed information regarding the nature of victimization risk is readily available is the school. In recent years, much attention has been focused on schools as settings that pose serious criminal dangers to both students and teachers (Toby, 1983; U.S. Dept. of Justice, 1988). National Crime Survey data (1985–1988) indicate that, with respect to teenage victims aged 12–15, 37 percent of the crimes of violence and 81 percent of the crimes of theft occurred while the victims were at school (Whitaker and Bastian, 1991). A special survey of school crime undertaken by the Department of Justice as a supplement to the 1989 National Crime Survey found that an estimated 9 percent of students aged 12–19 were victims of crime in or around their schools over a six-month period; 2 percent reported experiencing one or more violent crimes; and 7 percent reported at least one property crime (Bastian and Taylor, 1991). Sixteen percent of the respondents claimed that a student had attacked or threatened a teacher at their school in the six months prior to the interview. The violent crimes typically involved "simple assaults" (for example, schoolyard fights) that did not involve weapons and that resulted in relatively minor injuries.

BOX 10.2 VIOLENCE IN SCHOOLS

Because the likelihood of experiencing criminal victimization is dependent at least in part on how (and where) individuals spend their time, not surprisingly, young people have a relatively high risk of being victimized at school. Concern over the rates at which children are victimized while they are in school is reflected in the presence of metal detectors and "hall police" in all too many schools in the United States.

Data from the National Crime Victimization Survey have revealed that teenagers report fairly high rates of victimizations occurring at school or on school property. Table 10.1 provides information regarding the volume and nature of criminal victimization of youths at school between 1985 and 1988.

Table 10.1
Criminal Victimizations of Teenagers, 1985–1988

Type of Crime	Percent Occurring at School		Percent Occurring Elsewhere	
	Age 12–15	Age 16–19	Age 12–15	Age 16–19
Violent crime	37%	17%	63%	83%
Robbery	32	9	68	91
Aggravated assault	23	9	77	91
Simple assault	43	24	57	76
Property crime	81	39	19	61

Crimes that occurred at school or on school property were less likely to be reported to the police than were crimes that occurred on the street. Nine percent of teen crime victimizations that occurred in school and 21 percent of those that took place on school property were reported to the police, as compared with 37 percent of crimes that occurred on the street. Crimes that occurred in school or on school property were also less likely to involve a weapon—weapons were used in 37 percent of street crimes reported, but only 12 percent of crimes that took place in school and 21 percent of those on school property were found to have involved a weapon. Teen victims sustained injuries in 26 percent of school crimes, 31 percent of crimes occurring on school property, and 32 percent of street crimes.

Characteristics of offenders in violent crimes were somewhat different when the crime occurred in school versus on the street. Table 10.2 compares offender characteristics reported by teenaged victims of violent crimes by the location of the event.

Table 10.2
Offender Characteristics in Violent Crimes, by Location, 1985–1988

Offender Characteristics*	In School	On School Property	On Street
Gender			
Male	68%	71%	84%
Female	29	25	10
Race			
White	70	64	55
Black	21	27	31
Other	4	4	5
Age			
Under age 21	95	90	61
Relationship to Victim			
Relative	—	—	1
Well known	22	24	13
Casual acquaintance	38	32	13
Stranger	36	39	66

*Totals may not add up to 100 percent because of the omission of "unknown" or multiple-assailant characteristics.

For Discussion
What do you think would be effective in reducing victimization in schools? How
would you respond to the claim that most of the violence that occurs in schoolyards
is normal adolescent behavior and nothing to be alarmed about?

SOURCE: Based on Catherine Whitaker and Lisa Bastian, *Teenage Victims* (NCJ-128129)
(Washington, D.C.: U.S. Department of Justice, Bureau of Justice Statistics, 1991).

How do workplace characteristics relate to variations in the levels of workplace danger? Do these risks, for instance, have something to do with the nature of the work or with the location of the workplace? Answers to such questions are still fragmentary. Respondents in the 1988 British Crime Survey
blamed the nature of their jobs for nearly one-quarter of the violent and theft
incidents they experienced. The "public" rather than fellow employees were
blamed for nearly three-quarters of the violent incidents and one-half of the
thefts.

Data from victimization surveys have been used to describe the types of
workplace conditions that seem to facilitate employee victimization (Collins,
Cox, and Langan, 1987; Lynch, 1987). These studies suggest that the risks of
becoming a crime victim on the job are greater in the following circumstances:

- When the job involves face-to-face contact with large numbers of people
  on a routine basis (if the workplace restricts access to authorized per-
  sons, the risks of crime are lower)
- When the job involves handling money
- When the job involves overnight travel or travel between worksites
- When the job involves the delivery of passengers and goods.

The importance of these factors becomes apparent when they are assessed in
reference to routine activities theory and associated concepts such as exposure
and guardianship. People who work in settings that leave them unprotected
and at the same time exposed to large numbers of people (some of whom may
be "motivated offenders") are more likely to be victimized in the workplace.

Victimization studies also indicate that it is the nature of the work, rather
than the characteristics of the victims (such as sex and age), that affects an individual's likelihood of becoming a crime victim in the workplace. In the case
of schools, the structure of the school population might lead us to expect more
crime than we observe. Schools, after all, are settings that concentrate on a
daily basis the age groups at greatest risk of offending and victimization. Toby
(1983) argues that the risks associated with school populations are com-
pounded by the requirement of compulsory attendance. Disruptive or troublesome students who do not wish to attend school are required to do so. For this
reason, he suggests, junior high schools have more serious rates of victimization than do senior high schools.

In addition, until recently, schools have been relatively open settings, easily
accessible to potential offenders who do not attend them. These "intruders,"

as they are usually referred to by school officials, might include not only the stereotypical predator but also the angry parent or the student who is disgruntled at having been expelled. Although schools are capable of exercising some degree of guardianship against victimization, a school of above-average size that allows students considerable freedom of movement may provide many settings that facilitate criminal activity. Within school buildings, more victimizations typically take place in less supervised areas, such as hallways and restrooms, than in more controlled places such as classrooms and libraries (Garofalo, Siegel, and Laub, 1987).

TRANSACTIONS

Much of the violent victimization that occurs in the workplace results from conflicts between employees and customers or clients. These situations include the bartender who tells the inebriated customer that he is "cut off," the teacher who tries to enforce classroom discipline, the sales clerk who refuses to accept returned merchandise, and the police officer who tries to intervene in an argument.

BOX 10.3 POLICE OFFICER INJURIES IN DOMESTIC DISTURBANCES

Domestic disturbances are widely believed to be the most dangerous occupational activities in which police officers become involved. Desmond Ellis and two other researchers attempted to discover whether there was empirical support for this claim. To this end, they analyzed the official statistics gathered by three police forces and collected survey information from almost four hundred members of these forces.

Their analysis revealed that, overall, domestic disturbances accounted for 2.5 percent of the reported injuries. However, the researchers reasoned, it is necessary to take into account the relative frequency with which police officers attend domestic disturbances in order to understand the comparative dangerousness of these situations. They discovered that, although domestic disturbances accounted for 2.5 percent of injuries, these disturbances accounted for 0.8 percent of all calls for service. By contrast, robberies accounted for 0.1 percent of all calls but resulted in 2.8 percent of all injuries.

In order to standardize these differences, the researchers calculated a "danger rate" by dividing the number of injuries by the number of calls. This method revealed robberies to be the most dangerous type of encounter in which the police are likely to be involved, followed by the arrest or transportation of suspects or prisoners. Domestic disturbances ranked third (of six occurrence types) in terms of the degree of danger.

What types of factors increase the risks of injury for police who attend domestic disturbances? The survey data revealed several tentative answers. Injury is more likely when the suspect has allegedly assaulted the victim, when the principals in the incident exhibit hostile behavior toward the officer, and when the incident takes

283

Crime and Work

place in a detached house (as opposed to an apartment). The characteristics of the police officer (age, sex, height, weight) had little to do with whether injury occurred.

For Discussion

Why are robberies such a dangerous type of social interaction to police officers? How can we make theoretical sense out of the fact that the characteristics of individual officers appeared in this study to be unrelated to the chance of injury?

SOURCE: Based on D. Ellis, A. Choi, and C. Blaus (1993), "Injuries to Police Officers Attending Domestic Disturbances: An Empirical Study," *Canadian Journal of Criminology* 35(2): 149–168.

This pattern of employee–customer conflict is reflected in British Crime Survey data that describe "verbal abuse" at work. Fourteen percent of respondents in a survey by Mayhew, Elliot, and Dowds (1989) said that they had been verbally abused by someone other than a co-worker during the fourteen-month period preceding the survey. Although not strictly criminal, verbal abuse can contain threatening statements and may precipitate a conflict that escalates to violence. Although male and female workers were about equally likely to be abused in this way, younger women appeared to be particularly susceptible. While incidents involving abuse by an adult were more likely to involve a single offender, incidents involving adolescents were about as likely to involve a group as a single offender. Intoxication was a factor in almost one-tenth of the incidents. In 80 percent of the incidents, workers were sworn at, and insulting comments about job performance were made in 40 percent of the cases.

The nature of the situational context of much workplace victimization is revealed in a study by Salinger and colleagues (1993) of assaults of flight attendants. This study found that flight attendants have rates of assault as much as ten times higher than the average person. Most assaults involved a conflict between the passenger and the attendant over some mandatory aspect of the flight, such as baggage arrangements or food or drink service. The researchers discovered that first-class passengers, who comprise only 10 percent of the traveling public, accounted for 20 percent of the assaults, a finding that may be explained by the higher expectations of service, passengers' perception of their status relative to that of the attendant, and the amount of alcohol that is typically consumed. The study also found that assaults are most likely to occur during takeoff or landing, the most distressing time for passengers who are afraid of flying. In addition, at takeoff, the authority role of the attendant may not yet be clearly understood.

Violent school crimes, except perhaps those involving intruders, are probably more likely than other workplace crimes to include as participants offenders and victims who are known to each other (Whitaker and Bastian, 1991). According to Garofalo, Siegel, and Laub (1987) many of these events result from:

*frictions from peers arising from normal daily activities. School grounds
and trips to and from school provide ample opportunities for interactions
that can escalate into relatively minor victimizations. "Weapons" often
consist of available items grabbed on the spur of the moment. Items stolen
from victims often seem to be the targets of malicious, even mischievous
motivations. (333)*

THE AFTERMATH

Victimizations that occur in the workplace do not seem to differ appreciably from other categories of crime in terms of their levels of property loss and injury (Garofalo, Siegel, and Laub, 1987; Mayhew, Elliot, and Dowds, 1989; Whitaker and Bastian, 1991). One important factor that probably reduces the potential severity of much workplace crime is the presence of other co-workers, who can provide or summon assistance.

As in the case of other social domains, much of the crime that occurs in the workplace is not reported to the police (Mayhew, Elliot, and Dowds, 1989). At least two specific characteristics of the work domain may discourage such reporting. First, many work environments may have alternative means for dealing with crime. The handling of an incident might proceed no further than bringing it to the attention of a supervisor or private security officer. Businesses, restaurants, and even schools may choose to avoid the publicity associated with the visit of a police patrol car by using informal processing or nonprocessing to deal with the majority of less serious incidents.

Second, employees who are victimized as a result of their dealings with the public may be persuaded by their employers that such incidents only occur when they are not doing their job properly. In other words, they may come to believe that among their job responsibilities is "cooling off" belligerent customers or clients. Even in more severe cases, the victim may fear being blamed for having started the incident by behaving rudely toward the customer (Salinger et al., 1993).

Jobs can become hazardous when they expose employees to clients and situations that may provide an opportunity for crime. One step that can be taken to deter these crimes is to provide employees with the resources they need to deal with client-related problems. Employers must further resolve to react strongly to crimes that occur on their premises, thereby ensuring that their employees can do their job with a greater sense of security.

CRIME AND LEGITIMATE WORK

We have seen that the relationship between crime and unemployment is less straightforward than is commonly supposed. Being employed is no guarantee of immunity from crime or victimization. In this section, we explore some of the ways in which work makes offending possible. Put simply, how do particular types of work routines and particular forms of the social organization of work relate to particular styles of offending?

WHAT IS OCCUPATIONAL CRIME?

The scope of work-related crime is potentially as broad as the types of jobs that exist within an economic system (Croall, 1987). Employees who have unsupervised access to the stock of their employers may find that their work role allows them a unique opportunity for theft. Physicians and lawyers may charge for services that are not performed (Arnold and Hagan, 1992). Stores may use illegal sales practices to defraud the public. Large corporations may engage in the sale and manufacture of dangerous products, pollute the environment, and maintain unsafe working conditions. Work-related crime ranges from pilfering by a disgruntled employee to the gargantuan thefts associated with the American savings and loans scandal.

Modern interest in the concept of work-related crime is usually traced back to the writings of the famous American criminologist Edwin Sutherland (see Chapter 3). Sutherland (1940) used the term **white-collar crime** to refer to "a crime committed by a person of respectability and high status in the course of his [sic] occupation." Sutherland saw a need to correct the imbalance in criminological thinking that associated crime almost exclusively with the actions of the poor and the powerless. Through a study of major American corporations, he sought to prove that individuals who were fully and gainfully employed, and whose jobs accorded them considerable power and economic security, were frequently responsible for serious breaches of the law.

Since Sutherland's time, the concept of white-collar crime has undergone adjustments that reflect changes in the meaning of white-collar work. For Sutherland, the term *white-collar crime* denoted the criminal conspiracies of major corporations. Today, many forms of white-collar work (for example, sales or computer programming) do not involve manual labor, but they cannot be considered positions in some sort of economic or corporate elite. Criminologists have attempted to capture important distinctions in the study of crime and legitimate work by introducing such terms as *professional crime, elite deviance, corporate crime, organizational crime, respectable crime,* and *business crime.* Our interest in social domains as the context of criminal events requires us to focus attention not only on the crimes of powerful job-holders but also on the crimes of those whose jobs denote lower-ranked positions. Encompassing both types of crime is the term **occupational crime,** which Akers (1985: 228) defines as the "violation of legal norms governing lawful occupational endeavors."

Occupational crimes may be distinguished in two important ways. First, they differ with respect to the nature of the offender–victim relationship. Some kinds of crimes are intended to provide only the job-holder with direct benefits. The person who pilfers from an employer does so for personal benefit, as does the bank teller who embezzles or the systems analyst who steals computer time. In such cases, the agency or organization is the victim, and the employee is the offender.

In other cases, the organization may be understood not as the victim but as a weapon that is used against those outside of the organization or at the bottom of the organizational hierarchy. In the context of such criminal events, the crime may profit the job-holder indirectly in that direct benefits accrue to the organization itself. Included among the victims might be other business organizations (a corporation hires industrial saboteurs to steal competitors' secrets), clients or customers (a corporation engages in deceptive advertising or sells untested pharmaceutical or food products), or low-level organizational members (employers maintain unsafe working conditions or violate laws relating to labor relations). Finally, we can recognize more general patterns of victimization with respect to offenders who inflict harm on very broad segments of society. Such crimes include political bribery, which undermines the political system; tax frauds, through which people indirectly distribute their losses to members of the tax-paying public; and industrial pollution, which threatens the air, land, and water.

BOX 10.4 FRAUDULENT BUSINESS PRACTICES: LET THE BUYER BEWARE

While a "caveat emptor" (let the buyer beware) attitude may be seen to characterize many business transactions in the United States, the law sets limits on the ways in which Americans can (and cannot) do business. While no one knows exactly how much consumer fraud takes place in the United States, fraudulent business practices clearly are far from uncommon. Christopher Stone describes one blatantly fraudulent practice in his book *Where the Law Ends: The Social Control of Corporate Behavior.* The case involved Holland Furnace Company, an organization clearing about $30 million in sales annually. One of the ways in which Holland boosted sales of its furnaces, however, involved flagrant fraud.

A Holland representative, posing as an inspector from the gas company, would visit private homes, ostensibly to inspect the furnace. The "inspector" would dismantle the furnace and then refuse to reassemble it because of an alleged safety violation. In the ensuing confusion, a second representative of Holland Furnace would appear at the door, conveniently selling furnaces in the neighborhood. The distraught householder quite often proceeded to purchase a new heating unit from Holland.

After twenty-two years of legal wranglings, three company executives were found guilty of criminal contempt. The company's president was subsequently sentenced to six months in jail.

For Discussion
What steps can individuals take to make sure they are not victims of fraudulent business practices? Why might victims of these kinds of household fraud be reluctant to report the incident to the authorities?

SOURCES: Based on William Coleman, *The Criminal Elite,* 3rd ed. (New York: St. Martin's Press, 1994); and Christopher Stone, *Where the Law Ends: The Social Control of Corporate Behavior* (New York: Harper & Row, 1975).

A second way in which occupational crimes differ concerns the nature of the organizational settings in which they occur. Some types of occupational crime involve an offender who acts alone or only a small number of offenders. Medical fraud or dishonest household repair schemes might each involve the actions of a single offender who deals directly with victims and whose activities are not dependent on institutional support from co-workers. At the other extreme, **corporate crime** might involve "large vertical slices" of complex organizations (Snider, 1993). In such cases, it may be difficult to say who did and who did not behave criminally, since each individual's actions contribute in small ways to the criminal event (see Box 10.4).

We now examine the social organization of work routines in order to understand how and why occupational crimes occur.

PRECURSORS

The relationship between work routines and criminal offending may be understood with reference to the concepts of opportunity and motivation (Coleman, 1987, 1991). In other words, the social organization of work may give people the means with which to violate the law, while their feelings about their jobs or employers may supply them with the reasons for doing so.

In terms of opportunity, some work routines give employers or employees access to people and things to victimize. Doctors have access to patients, lawyers have access to clients, corporations have access to markets, and bank tellers have access to "other people's money" (Calavita and Pontell, 1991). While such access does not necessarily result in criminal action, it does make such action possible.

According to Coleman (1987, 1991), at least four factors influence the evaluation of opportunities to commit white-collar crime. The first factor is the perception of how large a gain can be expected from using the opportunity. The second is the perception of potential risks associated with the opportunity. The exploration of criminal opportunities is more likely when effective control is lacking. Many professional groups, for example, claim to be self-regulating and discourage the efforts of government agencies to assume an investigative function, except in the most extreme cases. Many crimes that are associated with large corporations are so complex that they are policed only with great difficulty. Some observers have argued that the power of professional groups and large corporations discourages effective enforcement by state agencies (Hagan, 1992). The third factor is the degree of compatibility between the use of the opportunity and the potential offender's beliefs, attitudes, and ethical view of the situation. Finally, the evaluation of the opportunity is based on the potential offender's perception of the benefits of one opportunity relative to other opportunities to which the person has access.

The motivations for occupational crime are a matter of considerable debate. Some observers claim that these motivations reside in the nature of work itself or in the wider socioeconomic setting of the workplace. Insofar as capitalism promotes a "culture of competition" that encourages the pursuit of economic profit, the profit motive may be said to be the criminal motive (Calavita and Pontell, 1991). However, the ways in which particular businesses and industries are organized may also serve as important motivating factors. Industries that experience severe competition, that are engaged in the sale or distribution of—and therefore highly regulated—potentially dangerous goods, or that operate in an uncertain economic environment may feel pressure to operate unlawfully as a means of achieving organizational goals (Coleman, 1991; Keane, 1991; Snider, 1993).

In very large corporations or businesses, the pressures to behave criminally may be accentuated by the pressure placed on underlings to achieve organiza-

Wall Street, the center of American commerce, has been racked by major stock crime in the last few years.

tional goals. In what Simon and Eitzen (1993) describe as "corporate Franken-steins," senior management may establish goals or quotas that everyone knows cannot be achieved within the limits imposed by current regulations. At the same time, management may be able to insulate itself from any covert criminal action that results from the establishment of such corporate objectives (Hagan, 1992). Those who make decisions about criminal wrongdoing may be actively or passively discouraged from reporting their activities to senior management (Coleman, 1987; Hagan, 1985). If the acts are discovered by enforcement agencies or the public, management can disavow any knowledge of wrong-doing. If the acts are not discovered, management can claim credit for the high profit yields (Snider, 1993).

By way of illustration, Farberman (1975) argues that the North American automobile industry is characterized by a **criminogenic market structure.** He maintains that the economic organization of the automobile industry almost necessitates criminal behavior on the part of car dealers. The large automobile manufacturers require dealership franchises to sell cars in large numbers but at comparatively low prices. A small profit markup per unit on a large number of units benefits the car manufacturer, but not the dealer, who, as a result, feels compelled to compensate for financial losses by resorting to dishonest repair schemes and other forms of fraud.

The role of market forces in shaping criminal events in the automobile in-dustry is even more clearly illustrated in the case of the Ford Pinto. This car was placed on the market in 1970, largely in response to feared competition from Japanese car manufacturers. Lee Iacocca, who was president of Ford at the time, told his engineers that they had to produce a car that weighed less than 2,000 pounds and that cost less than $2,000. While the Pinto met these specifications, it also contained serious design flaws. Most critical was the placement of the gas tank, which increased the likelihood that the car would explode in a rear-end collision. It was subsequently discovered that the corporate officers had known about this design flaw and about the actions that could be taken to correct it. Rather than act on this knowledge, however, they calculated the cost of these modifications and compared them to the costs likely to be incurred in lawsuits resulting from injuries to or deaths of Pinto drivers. Because the costs of the improvements were estimated to be greater than the costs associated with death and injury, Ford decided not to repair the defect.

Despite organizational and market pressures and a culture that seems to ex-tol success at any cost, not everyone uses his or her occupational role to achieve criminal ends. Criminologists have stressed the significant role played by "definitions of the situation" that favor criminal offending (Benson, 1985). Coleman (1987) proposes the following six such definitions:

1. Defining acts of theft as "borrowing"
2. Denying that white-collar crimes result in any real harm
3. Claiming that the laws that prohibit the behavior are unfair or unjust

4. Claiming that certain types of criminal behavior are necessary if organizational goals are to be achieved
5. Claiming that the behavior is normal and "everybody does it"
6. Claiming that employee theft is not really stealing since the money was owed (for example, uncharged overtime)

Thus, acts that may be seen as criminal by others may be seen as excusable behaviors by the embezzler who defines theft as "borrowing" and by the corporate executive who defines the violation of fair labor laws as "just good business."

Much of the debate about the motivations to commit occupational crime has centered on questions about the distinctiveness of occupational offenders. Many criminologists have long argued that white-collar offenders differ from street criminals in important ways that influence the likelihood of law violation. Many white-collar offenders are neither poor nor powerless. Their crimes are not impulsive, irrational, or the product of inadequate planning. Thus, many factors that are usually associated with crime and criminals would seem to have little to do with the behavior of those white-collar offenders, particularly those at the top of corporate hierarchies. Therefore, the causes of these types of crime must lie elsewhere.

By contrast, Gottfredson and Hirschi (1990), argue that the similarities between street criminals and occupational criminals are more important than the differences. For Gottfredson and Hirschi, the key explanatory mechanism for both groups is "self-control." Special theories are no more necessary to explain the criminal in a legitimate business than they are to explain the criminal in the university, the military, or the church. People who have low self-control are likely to engage in a variety of types of crime and deviance, as the opportunities to do so present themselves.

Because occupations that present significant criminal opportunities tend to be occupations that require a considerable degree of self-control, Gottfredson and Hirschi argue that the rates of occupational crime are lower than is popularly believed. Moreover, they suggest that when differences in opportunity are taken into account, demographic correlates of street and occupational crime are similar. They conclude that there is no need to presume special motivational circumstances in the case of the occupational offender, such as "the culture of competition" or other types of factors described here. Instead, they assert that "the distinction between crime in the street and crime in the suite is an *offense* rather than an *offender* distinction [and] that offenders in both cases are likely to share similar characteristics" (Gottfredson and Hirschi, 1990: 200).

In a recent study, Benson and Moore (1992) used data on the sentencing patterns for a large number of white-collar crimes (bank embezzlement, bribery, income tax evasion, false claims, and mail fraud) and common crimes (narcotics offenses, postal forgery, and bank robbery) to test some of the implications of Gottfredson and Hirschi's theory. Specifically, they attempted to determine whether white-collar offenders were as "criminally versatile" as common offenders and whether they were as prone to as wide a range of deviant activities. They found that, while a minority of white-collar offenders behaved as the theory predicted, the majority did not.

According to Benson and Moore, low self-control is not the only path to occupational crime. Offenders with high self-control may employ it to pursue ego gratification in an aggressive and calculating manner. The culture of competition rewards such individuals by giving them positions of trust and opportunities for committing serious but frequently undetected crimes. In between those with high self-control and those with low self-control are individuals who may take advantage of occupational opportunities depending on their personal situations. For these individuals, fear of economic or occupational failure may create a circumstance in which a previously adequate level of self-control may become inadequate; as a result, the individual's ability to resist occupational opportunities for crime may be weakened.

TRANSACTIONS

It is very difficult to determine the amount of crime that is committed in the course of legitimate work, for many reasons. Above all, the nature of much of this crime ensures that it will never be discovered. Corporate crimes that victimize consumers, clients, or members of the general public are very often "in-

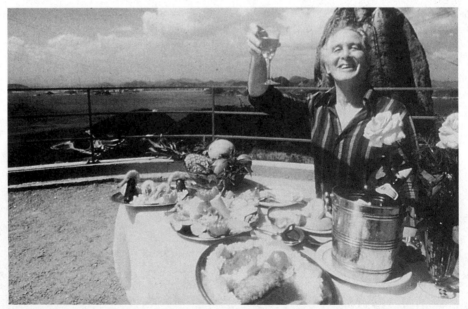

Ronald Biggs, the Great Train Robber, enjoys the spoils of his crime while in hiding in Brazil.

visible" (Coleman, 1987). For example, people do not necessarily know that some of the illnesses they experience are the result of inadequately tested drugs. Workers who are injured by hazardous working conditions may be inclined to blame themselves rather than their employers for their injuries (Croall, 1987). Our terminology encourages this tendency—we routinely call such occurrences "accidents" rather than "assaults."

Unlike more garden variety forms of offending, occupational crimes are largely hidden from public view. The employee who has access to opportunities for offending may escape public scrutiny. The offender who uses the computer to embezzle may do so in such a way that the crime goes undetected by the employer, co-workers, or enforcement agencies. Corporate conspiracies are even less visible. Evidence about corporate decisions regarding offending are not accessible to those outside the corporation. Moreover, because a corporate crime may involve actions by members at all levels of the organization, many of those who participate in the event may not even be aware of the true character of their actions.

As is the case with other categories of crime, occupational crimes do not come to the attention of policing or regulatory agencies as a result of vigorous enforcement practices. At the same time, victims may be poorly positioned to know about—and respond to—the occupational crimes that victimize them. The regulatory agencies that are supposed to police and scrutinize corporate behavior face many obstacles. According to Snider (1992), these obstacles include the following:

- The massive economic and political power of corporations that favor nonenforcement
- Lack of staff and funds
- Frequent lack of support from the governments that appoint them
- The high cost of investigating each complaint
- Support only from weak consumer or labor groups
- Minimal accountability to public or media scrutiny

A consequence of these obstacles is that many kinds of occupational crimes that are discovered are not reported. A business that learns that its employees have been embezzling funds may not wish the matter to be widely known because it would in all likelihood reduce public trust in the company. Thus, the long-range negative consequences of reporting may be seen to outweigh the immediate benefits of doing so.

Police data on occupational offenses are of only limited use. Not only are such offenses underreported, but in many cases (for example, fraud) it is not possible to determine whether the crimes occurred in the context of work roles. This is due in part to the fact that occupational crime is a conceptual rather than a legal category. While victimization surveys may supplement official record-keeping systems, they, too, are limited, given the absence in many cases of a "direct victim" as well as the inability of the victim to recognize occupational and corporate offending.

BOX 10.5 PUBLIC PERCEPTIONS OF COMMERCIAL CRIME

Frank Pearce describes a British victimization survey (the Second Islington Crime Survey) that asked respondents not only about their experiences with "conventional" crime but also about their experiences with several forms of "commercial" crime. Of 889 community residents:

- Nine percent believed that they had been given misleading information about goods or services. As a result, 45 percent complained and 49 percent received some kind of compensation.
- Nineteen percent believed that they had been deliberately overcharged for goods or services. Of these, 68 percent complained and, in 67 percent of cases, received some kind of compensation.
- Twenty-five percent believed that they had paid for goods or work that turned out to be defective. Of these, 74 percent complained and 72 percent received some kind of compensation.

For Discussion

Why do you think that surveys focusing on this type of crime are relatively rare? How might surveys of this type over- or under-report commercial crime?

SOURCE: Frank Pearce, *Second Islington Crime Survey: Commercial and Conventional Crime in Islington* (Kingston: Queen's University, 1991).

THE AFTERMATH

Our best estimates suggest that the crimes committed by people in the course of legitimate occupational activities result in considerable levels of financial and physical harm and loss of life. Snider (1993) argues that "corporate crime is a major killer, causing more deaths in a month than all the mass murderers combined do in a decade." According to one estimate, Americans are twice as likely to die as a result of unsafe or unhealthy workplace conditions as they are to be murdered (Reiman, 1990). The economic costs of corporate crime also exceed the costs of "street" crimes like burglary or larceny. It is estimated that the savings and loan scandal alone will cost American taxpayers as much as $500 billion by the year 2022 (Calavita and Pontell, 1991). In 1993, the FBI estimated the total dollar losses due to index property crimes to be $14.8 billion (U.S. Dept. of Justice, 1994a).

Controlling crimes that occur as in the context of legitimate work roles is no easy task. It is sometimes assumed that members of the public are less concerned about occupational crimes than about more direct forms of predatory crime; however, this does not appear to be the case (Hans and Erman, 1989). Nonetheless, the fact remains that the low level of visibility associated with occupational crimes makes effective deterrence difficult (Coleman, 1987). Some studies suggest that the threat of legal sanction has less impact on corporate crime than does the market environment in which companies operate (Keane, 1991; Simpson and Koper, 1992).

ENTERPRISE VERSUS ORGANIZED CRIME

In some cases, crime can itself be thought of as an occupation or business. We can define **enterprise crimes** as the "sale of illegal goods and services to customers who know that the goods or services are illegal" (Haller, 1990: 207). The nature of such goods or services may be highly varied and ultimately depend on what the law disallows. The sale of illegal drugs or pornography, the operation of illegal gambling houses, loan-sharking, and "contract killing" all represent examples of enterprise crime.

What we call enterprise crime is usually referred to by criminologists and noncriminologists alike as "organized crime." This concept conjures up a number of familiar images gleaned from movies like *The Godfather,* novels, and newspaper coverage of "mob trials" (exemplified by the trial of John Gotti). However, for reasons that will become clear, the concept of organized crime obscures rather than enhances our understanding of the types of events in which we are interested.

WHAT IS ORGANIZED CRIME?

In popular usage, the term *organized crime* refers to long-term, highly organized criminal syndicates that are involved in a number of criminal businesses (U.S. Dept. of Justice, 1988). These syndicates are said to be organized along ethnic lines and to function in much the same way as legitimate business corporations (Cressey, 1969). In this sense, they have well-established patterns of recruitment and authority.

The most widely discussed group of organized criminals in the criminological and popular literature on the subject is the Mafia, also known as **La Cosa Nostra.** This particular form of criminal conspiracy is said to be the major such group operating in North America (Abadinsky, 1987). According to many observers, the Mafia has its origins in the Sicilian Mafia and came to the United States along with the waves of European immigration in the latter days of the nineteenth century (Smith, 1975).

Observers further claim that the modern Mafia has its origins in the so-called "Black Hand" gangs that operated in the ethnic enclaves of major American cities. These gangs were simply groups of extortionists who preyed on their fellow emigres (Pitkin and Cordasco, 1977). Their name derived from the fact that they would send their victims letters signed with a black hand print. The American experiment with national prohibition of liquor in the 1920s allegedly gave organized crime groups an opportunity to consolidate their economic power. Throughout the 1930s, the theory asserts, these gangs developed into a national federation that came to control the operation of illegal business in all regions of the continent.

This view of organized crime has been legitimated in the stories told by former Mafiosi (Maas, 1969), in the reports of undercover law enforcement officers, in federal investigations of organized crime (Moore, 1974; Smith, 1975), and in the writings of academic criminologists (Galliher and Cain, 1974). The major academic architect of this view was the sociologist Donald Cressey (1969), who, as a consultant to the President's Commission on Law Enforcement and the Administration of Justice in the late 1960s, wrote a highly influential report on the nature and influence of organized crime groups in the United States. In a revised version of that report, published in 1969, Cressey argued that any attempt to understand American organized crime required recognition of eight "facts":

1. A nationwide alliance of at least twenty-four tightly knit crime "families" exists in the United States.
2. The members of these "families" are all Italians and Sicilians, or of Italian and Sicilian descent, and those on the eastern seaboard, especially, call the entire system "Cosa Nostra."
3. The names, criminal records, and principal criminal activities of about five thousand of the participants have been assembled.
4. The persons occupying key positions in the skeletal structure of each "family" are well known to law enforcement officials.
5. The "families" are linked to one another and to non–Cosa Nostra syndicates by understandings, agreements, and "treaties," as well as by mutual deference to the "Commission," which is made up of the leaders of the most powerful families.
6. The boss of each family directs the activities (especially the illegal ones) that are undertaken by the members of his "family."
7. The organization as a whole controls all but a tiny part of illegal gambling, loan-sharking, and narcotics importation.
8. Information about the Commission, the "families," and family activities has come from detailed reports made by a wide variety of police observers, informants, wiretaps, and electronic "bugs."

Even though the focus of concern regarding organized crime in America has been largely on the Mafia, or La Cosa Nostra, both researchers and law enforcement officials recognize the fact that participation in organized crime in the United States is, in reality, much more broad-based. Members of other racial/ethnic groups are known to be involved in this type of crime—criminal organizations like the Dixie Mafia, the Mexican Connection, and others are becoming increasingly common in the United States (Kenney and Finchenauer, 1995). Table 10.3 provides an overview of some of the other organized crime units thought to be active in America.

Table 10.3
Recent Ethnic Organized-Crime Groups in the United States

Ethnic Group	Origins	Exemplars	Notable Illicit Activities	North American Locales	Comments (unique or notable characteristics)
Chinese (Tongs, Triads, street gangs)	17th-century China	Wo, 14 K	Gambling, extortion, drug trafficking, robbery, prostitution, murder, arms dealing, racketeering	California, New York	Tongs and street gangs possess many of the characteristics we used to define organized crime groups.
Japanese Yakuza	7th-century Japan	Yamaguchi Gumi	Weapons trafficking (to Japan), methamphetamines trafficking (to Japan), murder, gambling, extortion, bookmaking	California, Hawaii	All Yakuza gangs are highly structured/hierarchical. Legitimate activities include banking and real estate. Annual revenue estimated to be $32 billion.
Colombian drug traffickers	Colombia has a long history of social banditry	Medellin and Cali cartels	Cocaine trafficking	New York area, Miami, Los Angeles, Houston	Complex infrastructures employ about 24,000 according to one estimate. Criminal activities limited to those associated with the drug trade.
Vietnamese gangs	Arrival of immigrants in U.S. in the 1970s	Born to Kill	Extortion, prostitution, auto theft, arson, gambling, armed robbery	Chicago, New Orleans, Houston, Washington, D.C., Los Angeles, Boston	Not a major problem compared to other ethnic organized-crime groups. Closely linked to Chinese organized crime. Considered to be the most ruthless of Asian groups
Jamaican posses	Kingston, Jamaica. Came to U.S. in mid-1970s	Shower Posse, Spangler Posse	Cocaine (crack) distribution, firearms trafficking, money laundering, fraud, robbery, kidnapping, murder, auto theft	New York, Miami, Los Angeles, San Francisco, Detroit, Philadelphia, Dallas, Washington, D.C., Chicago, Houston	One of the most violent organized-crime groups in the country. Forty posses in the U.S. have 22,000 members. Control 30 to 40 percent of U.S. crack trade.
Russian Mafia	Emigres arrived in large numbers in the 1970s	Odessa Malina, Organizatsiya	Marketing illegal goods (drugs, weapons, stolen cars), extortion, forgery, loan-sharking, racketeering, gasoline bootlegging (#1 activity)	New York, New Jersey, Philadelphia, Los Angeles, Chicago, Baltimore, Dallas, Cleveland, Phoenix, Toronto	Perestroika reforms coupled with economic mayhem fueled a tremendous growth in new forms of organized crime.

SOURCE: D. J. Kenney and J. O. Finckenauer, *Organized Crime in America* (Belmont, Calif. Wadsworth, 1995). pp. 272–273.

Despite the popularity of the view of organized crime just outlined, many researchers have called into question both its accuracy and value. Several shortcomings have been noted. First, the view of organized crime as an "organized parasitic conspiracy" deflects our attention from any critical assessment of the ways in which our own society makes such crime possible. Despite the obvious implications of this view, it has been shown that the types of activity associated with La Cosa Nostra have not developed in all societies that have large numbers of Italian immigrants.

Second, researchers over the past two decades have called into question every one of Cressey's eight "facts" as well as the orthodox history of organized crime that is told and retold in the works of popular and academic writers. For example, critics of the orthodox view seriously question the following:

- Whether something called the "Mafia" has ever existed *as a formal organization* in Sicily or anywhere else (Blok, 1975; Hess, 1973; Servadio, 1976)
- Whether a bureaucratically organized group known as La Cosa Nostra exists in North America (Albanese, 1989; Albini, 1971; Smith, 1975)
- Whether contemporary organized crime groups composed of Italian-Americans find their origins in the Black Hand or Prohibition gangs of earlier eras (Hawkins, 1969; Jenkins and Potter, 1987; Smith, 1975)
- Whether police investigations or the investigations by government commissions or task forces have provided any independent evidence that such organizations exist (Albanese, 1989; Hawkins, 1969; Moore, 1974; Smith, 1975)
- Whether the activities of organized crime groups are overseen or coordinated by a national commission (Hawkins, 1969; Ianni and Reuss-Ianni, 1972)

Third, and most basically, the concept of organized crime is itself confusing and misleading (Smith, 1991). Logically, we might suggest that it refers to any type of activity that involves more than one offender acting in coordinated fashion. From this point of view, two juveniles who break into a house could be said to have engaged in organized crime. However, the term is almost never used this way. Instead, it is used to refer to large-scale criminal efforts that are diverse in nature and that seem to have little in common beyond the fact that we associate them with particular stereotypical notions of who organized criminals are. Adding to the confusion, the term *organized crime* is sometimes used to refer to a particular type of activity (as in the statement, "Gambling is a form of organized crime") and other times to particular groups of criminals (as in the statement, "We must prosecute members of organized crime"). Such usage results in circular reasoning (Maltz, 1976). If we say, for example, "Organized crime is involved in the drug trade," we have not really said anything because, by definition, the drug trade is an organized crime and any group involved in this activity must necessarily be involved in organized crime.

One way out of this impasse is to shift our attention away from the focus on alien, parasitic conspiracies and "organized crime" and toward the study of enterprise crime.

As previously defined, enterprise crime involves the sale and distribution of illegal goods and services. What kinds of social conditions make enterprise crime likely? The first such condition, of course, is the existence of laws prohibiting the goods and services in question. In other words, enterprise crime is made possible when the reach of law creates market opportunities. Prohibition, which was in force in the United States between 1920 and 1933, in a very real sense created the opportunity for financial gain that could be exploited by criminal entrepreneurs (Packer, 1969; Schelling, 1967). In a similar way, attempts to use the law to control the availability of illicit drugs—such as marijuana or cocaine—or to use high rates of taxation to control the availability of legal drugs such as tobacco, make enterprise crime possible. The gap between what people want and what the law allows them to legitimately have suggests an important way in which our society provides the sources of enterprise crime. This point is obscured when we think of such crime as merely the product of an alien, parasitic conspiracy.

The second such factor is systematic corruption. To the degree that enterprise criminals have access to police or political officials who are interested in the development of cooperative ventures with these entrepreneurs, the effects of agencies of legal control may be neutralized. Bribery and corruption may afford some enterprise criminals protection from the law, while others may discover that they are the objects of much more aggressive enforcement. Just as occurs in the more legitimate sectors of the economy, the establishment of cozy relationships between those who do the policing and those who are supposed to be policed may facilitate the conditions by which greater market control is assured. In the absence of such mutually advantageous relationships, criminal enterprise markets are more unstable.

BOX 10.6 THE DRUG BUSINESS

The sale and distribution of drugs represents a major form of enterprise crime. In the 1980s, the concern about drugs dominated much of the discussion about crime and violence in North America.

The reporting of drug crimes differs from the reporting of crimes that involve a direct and immediate victim. Given that both sides are willing participants in a drug transaction, no one is likely to notify the police that a crime has been committed. Drug users, like other types of offenders, are interested in ensuring that their behavior has low visibility. This means that official data on drug crimes are likely to reflect the vigor with which policing agencies pursue such crime.

According to the FBI, supply offenses (sale and manufacture of illegal drugs) have increased as a proportion of total drug crimes since 1981. This has been accompanied by a drop in the total proportion of possession offenses during the same time period. Possession offenses still comprise the majority of arrests associated with illegal drugs. Figure 10.1 shows the distribution of arrests for drug law violations; Figure 10.2 shows the distribution of arrests by drug type.

Figure 10.1
Percent Distribution of Arrests for Drug Law Violations, 1981–1992

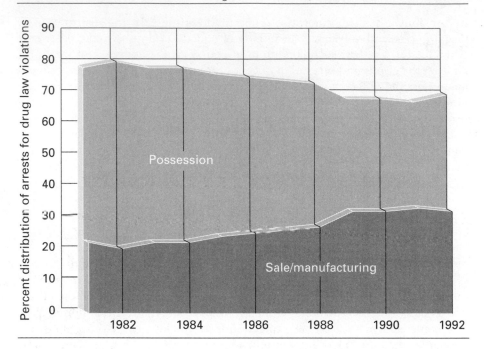

Figure 10.2
Percent Distribution of Arrests for Drug Law Violations, by Type of Drug,
1981–1992

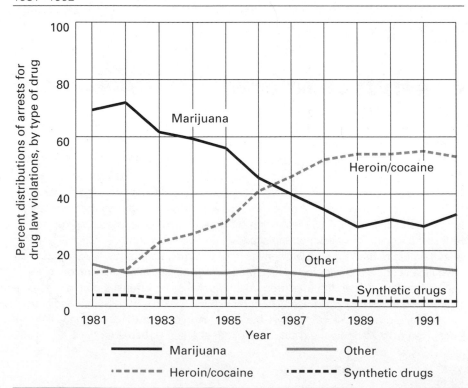

For Discussion

What do you think contributes to the strong growth in arrests for heroin/cocaine versus marijuana in recent years? What effect do police enforcement activities have on rates of drug crime?

SOURCE: Based on Kathleen Maguire and Ann Pastore (eds.), *Sourcebook of Criminal Justice Statistics, 1993,* U.S. Department of Justice, Bureau of Justice Statistics (Washington, D.C.: Government Printing Office, 1994), p. 458.

A third precondition for the establishment of stable enterprise crime is the existence of partnership arrangements. Such arrangements have the same role in illegal businesses that they have in legal business ventures. They allow entrepreneurs to share risks (especially the risk of business failure), and they allow people with different types of resources to pool these resources. This means that individuals who have political influence, capital, or managerial skills can combine their talents in a way that increases the potential for profit.

This emphasis on partnerships suggests that, rather than being hierarchically or bureaucratically organized, enterprise crime is much more likely to involve informal styles of association (Albini, 1971; Ianni and Reuss-Ianni, 1972). Partnerships may arise when they are deemed necessary or desirable for business purposes, and they may be dissolved when they have served their purpose or when they cease to be profitable. Moreover, Haller (1990) notes, not everyone need be thought of as equal in these partnerships. Some entrepreneurs exercise much more power than others because they have the political or economic resources that allow them to participate in several enterprises simultaneously. In the book *Wiseguy,* by Nicholas Pileggi, ex-mobster Henry Hill describes the influence of mob boss Paul Vario in terms that clearly indicate the nature of these partnership arrangements:

> *There were hundreds of guys who depended on Paulie for their living, but he never paid out a dime. The guys who worked for Paulie had to make their own dollar. All they got from Paulie was protection from other guys looking to rip them off. That's what it's all about. That's what the FBI can never understand—that what Paulie and the organization offer is protection of the kinds of guys who can't go to the cops. They're like the police department for wiseguys. (Pileggi, 1985: 56–57)*

More generally, Haller (1990) suggests that, like the Chamber of Commerce or Rotary Club, La Cosa Nostra should be viewed, not as an organization that operates illegal (or legal) businesses, but as an association that businesspeople join partly to further their business careers.

Finally, Haller notes, many types of economic factors shape the structure of illegal enterprises—factors that serve both to enhance and to reduce cooperation (Schelling, 1967). Enterprises that involve the importation of drugs like cocaine or heroin may involve a high degree of cooperation among many groups located in both the exporting and receiving countries. Drug networks also exist at the local level. In addition, substantial drug transactions may require a large initial capital investment. Factors of this type may encourage the development of monopolistic tendencies, since relatively few groups are able to marshall the economic resources or possess the contacts needed to facilitate large-scale arrangements. By contrast, the illegal market for marijuana may be structured quite differently (Rogers, 1973). This illicit commodity does not have to be imported and can be distributed on a small-scale basis by independent entrepreneurs who cater to the needs of a small, local clientele. Markets of this type are much more resistant to monopolization.

TRANSACTIONS

If we think about enterprise crime as a type of business, then the questions to which we seek answers are not unlike the questions we might ask about more legitimate businesses. What is the nature of the market? How are goods and services produced and distributed? What are the sources of capital that underwrite the costs of doing business? How do the various groups involved in these businesses cope with changing markets? What types of people are attracted to this particular line of work, and why?

Criminologists are particularly concerned, however, with the fact that the business is illegal (Haller, 1990). As economist Thomas Schelling (1967) notes, when a business is made illegal, entry into the marketplace is restricted to those who are willing and able to behave criminally. In other words, the illegal nature of the business is perhaps most attractive to those who have no strong reservations about involvement in behaviors that are prohibited by law.

As we pointed out previously, much has been made of the ethnic character of organized crime. Apart from La Cosa Nostra, commonly cited groups include the Chinese Triad, the Jamaican Posse, and associations loosely referred to in the popular press as the Colombian, Irish, and Vietnamese mafias. This emphasis on ethnicity has frequently served to reinforce the popular view that criminal enterprise is an "alien" problem because it is associated with ethnic groups.

In rejecting this view, sociologist Daniel Bell (1953) argued four decades ago that organized crime functions as a "queer ladder of social mobility" in societies that emphasize material success but fail to provide all racial and economic groups with equal opportunities for achieving it. Like Robert Merton (1938), Bell maintained that, as a result of the pressure to achieve social goals, groups that find the legitimate channels of upward mobility blocked may turn to illegal alternatives. A key implication of this argument is that enterprise crime, seen as a form of economic activity, is most attractive to those located at or near the bottom of the social hierarchy.

Ianni (1974), like Bell before him, argued that involvement in enterprise crime is characterized by an ethnic succession rather than by an enduring criminal conspiracy. Particular ethnic groups may dominate organized crime until legitimate channels of upward mobility become generally accessible. At this point, the influence of any particular group may decline as other groups move in to fill the void created by the outward movement. Thus, the Italian presence in organized crime, which peaked in the period immediately before Prohibition, was preceded by an Irish and Jewish presence and succeeded by a Cuban and African-American presence (Ianni, 1974).

This is not to say that the domination of enterprise crime by any particular group is irrelevant to the ways in which markets are structured or exploited (Light, 1977). Members of ethnic groups may be able to draw on their cultural capital in ways that enable them to be especially effective in particular types of enterprise crime. They may also share in particular forms of cultural traditions that facilitate criminal organization. According to Ianni (1971), the significance of the family as a central organizing theme in Italian culture has contributed to the creation of criminal enterprises—structured along kinship lines—that are remarkably durable.

A second important implication that flows from the illegal nature of criminal enterprises relates to the role of regulation. Obviously, when a market is declared illegal, it cannot be controlled by the government agencies responsible for the mediation of disputes or the resolution of conflicts (Reuter, 1984b). As Henry Hill's earlier remarks make clear, criminal entrepreneurs are unable to seek recourse for harm done against them by going to the police or initiating lawsuits. One mobster cannot sue another because a promised shipment of heroin was not delivered or because a promise to influence the vote of a labor union was not kept. It is for such reasons that violence, or the threat of violence, looms so large in the business affairs of criminal entrepreneurs. Violence represents one of the few means by which contracts can be enforced and compliance with agreements can be assured (Black, 1983; Reuter, 1984b).

The types of criminal events that are central to enterprise crime—the acquisition and distribution of illegal goods and services—are complicated affairs, but much popular thinking on the subject glosses over these complexities. We are used to thinking about enterprise crime as nothing more than the acts of vicious gangsters whose ways of thinking and acting are foreign to the societies in which we find them. While this makes for good pulp fiction, it is not very illuminating. Organized-crime events are shaped by the societal context and are in no fundamental way alien to it. The gap between popular demand and efforts to legally control supply makes illegal markets possible in the first place. By declaring these markets off limits to legal regulation, society helps to create circumstances in which the potential for violence is considerable. The stratified nature of society and the restrictions it imposes on upward mobility cause some who are adversely affected to see enterprise crime as a viable means of achieving the goals toward which their societies encourage them to aspire.

THE AFTERMATH

Public reactions to enterprise crime often fail to take account of the wider context, which, we have argued, is necessary if we hope to achieve an appropriate understanding of this type of crime (Morash, 1984). When we read about a gangland killing in an urban ethnic restaurant or a police seizure of drug assets, we rarely consider the social character of these crimes. We are encouraged to think about organized crime as a force at war with "decent society," as it preys on citizens and threatens to corrupt our public officials and undermine our basic social institutions. Rarely are we encouraged to think about criminal enterprise as a logical product of prevalent social conditions. As McIntosh (1975) argues, criminal entrepreneurs are part of a larger configuration that includes not only the criminal but also victims, the police, politicians, customers, and others. The activities of the criminal entrepreneur cannot be understood by focusing on the entrepreneur alone. As these larger configurations change, so do the types of events in which criminal entrepreneurs are likely to be involved. In the absence of this more complex and detailed understanding, enterprise crime will be seen as alien and parasitic.

One important implication of traditional views of enterprise crime relates to the means by which such crime is to be controlled. The image of enterprise crime as an alien, parasitic conspiracy, rather than as a social product, supports the position that this type of crime is a law enforcement problem. From this perspective, enterprise crime is best controlled through the aggressive prosecution of criminal entrepreneurs. And yet, when we conceptualize the problem in terms of criminal enterprise rather than in terms of organized crime, we recognize that this "gangbuster mentality" has serious limitations. If enterprise crime really does function like other economic markets, then the removal of criminal entrepreneurs (through arrest and imprisonment) will not significantly affect market operation, since such actions have no effect on the demand for illegal goods. We recognize this fact quite explicitly in the case of legal markets. When an entrepreneur who sells legal goods—for instance, shoes—is removed from the market as a result of death, illness, or retirement, shoes remain available (Van den Haag, 1975). This is because the demand for shoes will prompt others to enter the market to fill the void. In fact, it might even be argued that, because an aggressive policy of prosecution increases the risks of doing business, the going rate for goods and services will increase and the profits to be gained may increase accordingly.

SUMMARY

■ ■ ■

We have seen in this chapter that the roles we play in the workplace domain structure the kinds of involvement we are likely to have in various types of criminal events. Some jobs increase employees' risks of criminal victimization, while others provide them with opportunities to victimize others, be they subordinates, co-workers, clients, customers, or society at large. Alternatively, illegal though they may be, various types of enterprise crime nevertheless constitute a form of work.

Throughout much of its history, criminology has focused attention on how exclusion from the world of legitimate work motivates criminality. While this remains an important (if unresolved) issue, it is equally important to understand how the organization of the domain of work facilitates or hinders the development of criminal events within this domain. Theories that emphasize the role of social inequality in the generation of crime quite naturally suggest that not having a job may encourage the development of criminal motivations. Victimization risks differ between those who are employed and those who are not. More importantly, particular forms of labor force participation make crime possible. Relevant here are two factors: (1) the relationship between the jobs people have and the victimization risks they face and (2) the ways in which jobs provide people with opportunities to behave criminally.

Victimization risk at work is inversely correlated to occupational status, measured by income, with those in lower-income occupations being more vulnerable. However, occupation alone is not enough to define victimization risk. Workplace settings can be very important in influencing the opportunity for crime. Risk can be heightened by the fact that money is available to be stolen. Sometimes, the nature of the job has a provoking effect on customers, who may vent their anger and frustration at the employee. Crimes that occur in these circumstances are not easy to deter and are underreported. In the aftermath of violent encounters, employees may accept the blame or assume that the employer will blame them for handling the situation poorly. Alternatively, these incidents may be handled informally to avoid the problems associated with police involvement.

Work-related crime may range all the way from pilfering by a disgruntled employee to the gargantuan thefts associated with the American savings and loan scandal. Sutherland (1940) used the term *white-collar crime* to refer to "a crime committed by a person of respectability and high status in the course of his [sic] occupation." He saw a need to correct the imbalance in criminological thinking that associated crime almost exclusively with the actions of the poor and the powerless.

Occupational crimes may be distinguished in two important ways. First, they differ with respect to the nature of the offender–victim relationship. Some kinds of crimes are intended to provide direct benefits only for the job-holder, as in the case of the employee who steals. In such instances, the agency or organization is the victim and the employee is the offender. In other cases, the organization may be used to attack those outside of the business or at the bottom of the organizational hierarchy. With respect to these criminal events, the crime may profit the job-holder indirectly in that more direct benefits accrue to the organization itself. Finally, more general patterns of victimization result from crimes that inflict harm on very broad segments of society. Such crimes include political bribery, tax fraud, and industrial pollution.

Occupational crimes differ according to the nature of the organizational settings in which they occur. Some types of occupational crime involve either a lone offender or a small number of offenders, as is exemplified by medical frauds and dishonest household repair services. At the other extreme, corporate crime might involve "large vertical slices" of complex organizations. In such cases, it may be difficult to say who did and did not behave criminally, since each individual's actions constitute only a small portion of the criminal event.

Gottfredson and Hirschi (1991) argue that the mechanism of self-control is equally applicable to understanding the behavior of the occupational criminal as it is to understanding the behavior of the street criminal. What distinguishes occupational crime from street crime is, in Gottfredson and Hirschi's view, not the offender but rather the offense. People who have low self-control are likely to engage in a variety of types of crime and deviance, as the opportunities to do so present themselves. Despite the significant financial and physical harm caused by occupational crimes, their low visibility makes them difficult to detect and deter.

We can also view crime as operating in a marketplace in which illicit substances and services are sold to customers who know that they are illegal. Rather than viewing such activity in terms of ethnically based organized crime, we instead use the term *enterprise crime* to refer to this type of criminal activity. Enterprise crime occurs as a result of laws that prohibit certain goods and services. In other words, enterprise crime is made possible when the reach of law creates market opportunities. More than requiring a definition of illegality, however, enterprise crime needs the presence of systematic corruption, partnership arrangements between illegal and legal businesses, and favorable market conditions such as a monopoly on the illegal goods.

When we conceptualize the problem of "organized crime" in terms of criminal enterprise rather than in terms of organized crime, it becomes apparent that law enforcement responses to crime have serious limitations. If enterprise crime functions like other economic markets, removing criminal entrepreneurs (through arrest and imprisonment) will not significantly affect market operation or reduce the demand for illegal goods.

QUESTIONS FOR REVIEW AND DISCUSSION
■ ■ ■

1. What criminological factors would help to explain why taxi drivers tend to experience high rates of robbery?
2. What measures could be taken to reduce the problems of crime and victimization in high schools? Do these solutions interfere with the basic mission of schools to provide education?
3. Do you agree with the view that corporate crime is a more serious problem than street crime? How do corporations discourage us from adopting this view?
4. In reference to a job you currently hold (or perhaps a past summer job), what opportunities for crime did your employment make available to you?

5. How do television and movie portrayals of organized crime distort public understanding of the problem of organized crime? Can you think of some specific examples?

6. "Despite their differences, most offender-based theories lead us to expect a higher rate of crime among people who are unemployed than among people who are employed." Discuss this statement.

PART SIX

RESPONSES TO CRIME

A VARIETY OF PUBLIC POLICY RESPONSES TO THE CRIME PROBLEM HAVE BEEN PROPOSED. BY REVIEWING WHAT WE HAVE STUDIED ABOUT THE CRIMINAL EVENT AND THEN EXAMINING POSSIBLE SOLUTIONS, WE CAN BETTER UNDERSTAND CRIME IN GENERAL.

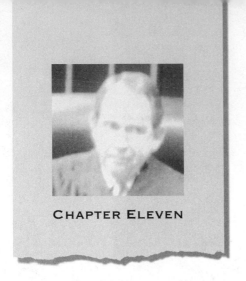

Summary and Review of Public Policy Responses to Crime

KEY TERMS

crime prevention

opportunity reduction

social development

community-based policing

situational crime prevention

resource mobilization

WHAT'S IN CHAPTER ELEVEN

In this chapter, we begin by reviewing the criminal event. We then examine potential public policy responses to the crime problem from an event perspective, focusing on public health and public safety issues and crime prevention through social development. We conclude by discussing recent initiatives in community policing.

311

*Summary and
Review of
Public Policy
Responses
to Crime*

INTRODUCTION

The objectives of this chapter are (1) to summarize what we have learned in previous chapters about the nature, causes, and consequences of criminal events, and (2) to sketch some of the major policy responses available to us. These objectives are interrelated in that what we can do about criminal events should follow logically from a detailed understanding of their causes and content.

SUMMARY OF FINDINGS ON THE CRIMINAL EVENT

We began in Chapter 1 by discussing some important concepts that guide the study of criminal events. Most notably, we emphasized that there are no simple answers to the questions, What is crime? and How is crime to be studied? It is too glib to say that crime is simply behavior that violates the law; such a definition obscures our view of the complex social realities that demand our attention. We emphasized a need to recognize that there is more to crime than the behavior of a lawbreaker. As social events, crimes involve not only offenders but other participants as well, including victims, the police, witnesses, and bystanders, all of whom act and react within particular social and physical circumstances.

Chapter 1 sketched a general picture of crime in the United States. We saw that the amount of crime has increased fourfold over the past thirty years and that the majority of crime is directed against property rather than against people. Public views of crime, as articulated in the mass media and day-to-day conversations, influence our views of crime. Unfortunately, media images of crime tend to exaggerate the frequency of serious violent crime and to emphasize the sensationalist character of both crime and the solutions to crime.

In Chapter 2, we introduced the criminal event framework. Most fundamentally, we observed that criminal events are social events in that they involve interaction between human beings. The dynamics of this interaction shape the content of the event and thus the consequences of the event for those involved. We discussed the roles played by the principal protagonists in criminal events—offenders, victims, bystanders, and the police. In examining the social and demographic characteristics of victims and offenders, we noted that, for many categories of crime, offenders and victims have much in common (a finding contrary to what media reporting sometimes leads us to expect). Both victims and offenders tend to be young, socially disadvantaged, and, for many categories of crime, males. There are, of course, important exceptions to this pattern. For obvious reasons, corporate crimes are not typically perpetrated by disadvantaged young males, and many forms of violence uniquely victimize women. We also pointed out that criminal events do not occur with equal frequency in all types of communities or within communities, or at all types of locations.

Chapters 3–6 described the major theoretical orientations that have dominated criminology in recent decades. We defined criminological theories as generalized explanations of criminal phenomena. We look to theories to make sense out of our observations of the empirical world. Conversely, we look to the empirical world for confirmation or refutation of our theoretical views.

Theoretical interest in crime has generally meant theoretical interest in offenders. For this reason, we devoted two chapters to describing alternative conceptualizations of the offender. Chapter 3 focused on theories that derive from "positivist" views of the offender, while Chapter 4 presented explanations that find their origins in "classical" thought. The distinction between positivist and classical views, which we introduced in Chapter 1, has to do with the degree to which human will is thought to dominate social action. Broadly stated, positivist theories seek to understand the factors that cause offenders to do what they do, while classical theories emphasize the significance of rational choice in influencing the behavior of the criminal offender.

Chapter 3 discussed many of the causal theories that have been offered to explain criminal behavior. While some of these theories emphasize biological, constitutional, or genetic causes of criminal conduct, most emphasize the role of social factors. We examined two major types of social explanations. The first considers the ways in which socially induced frustration can contribute to the development of criminal motivations. Robert Merton discerned in the gap between the things that people are encouraged by their culture to want and what is actually available to them a major source of frustration that manifests itself in criminal conduct.

The second social explanation of criminal motivation stresses the role of culture. Subcultural theories suggest that people learn the motivations to behave criminally in the same way that they learn motivations to do anything else. The emphasis here is on the immediate environment in which offenders operate and on how these environments encourage or facilitate the learning of cultural lessons that support criminal behavior. The foremost architect of this view was Edwin Sutherland, whose theory of differential association stressed an understanding of crime as a learned behavior. While Sutherland and the subcultural theorists who followed him encourage us to think about the relationship between criminal behavior and exposure to criminal cultures, theorists like David Matza and Gresham Sykes have argued for the need to appreciate how lessons that might motivate offending can be learned from mainstream culture.

In Chapter 4, we focused on offenders' decision-making processes rather than their motivations. For theorists who adhere to the classical school, there is little to be gained from attempts to search for unique factors that motivate offending behavior. Instead, they suggest that such behavior is better understood in relation to the formal and informal social controls that might be expected to restrain offending behavior. When these controls are ineffective or when individuals are insensitive to them, potential offenders are primed to become actual offenders. In such circumstances, people are free to act in ways that, criminal though they may be, also reflect rational self-interest. Social controls that discourage individuals from engaging in the criminal pursuit of self-interest include their social bonds to conformist others, their relationships with their communities, and the sanctions promised by the legal system.

The theoretical explanations discussed in Chapter 5 differ in a fundamental way from those presented in previous chapters. Specifically, they do not focus on the behavior of offenders, but rather on the opportunities to which offenders have access and on the situations in which they find themselves. According to these theories, an individual who is ready, willing, and able to break the law will not necessarily do so. Other elements must come into play, and depending on how these elements come together, the offender may end up committing one type of crime rather than another.

Opportunity theories suggest that the ways in which people distribute their time and energies over time and across space either increase or decrease the number of opportunities to violate the law that are presented to them. Lifestyle exposure theory argues that, for individuals who pursue lifestyles that bring them into contact with people who have offender characteristics or that put them in places where crimes frequently occur, the risks of becoming crime victims increase. Similarly, routine activities theory suggests that crimes result when motivated offenders, suitable targets, and an absence of capable guardianship converge in time and space. Other theories reviewed in Chapter 5 focus on the ways in which the interactions between offenders and their victims influence criminal outcomes. Relatively simple theories that speak of "victim precipitation" have been replaced in recent years by theories about crime as a situated transaction that is the product not only of an offender's will or motivation but also of social interaction.

Chapter 6 discussed theories and research relating to the aftermath of the criminal event. We examined the variety of ways—obvious and not so obvious—in which involvement in such events may affect victims and offenders. Labeling theorists maintain, for instance, that the societal reaction to minor or petty acts of nonconformity may result in stigmatization, which frustrates the labeled person and thereby contributes indirectly to more serious violations of the law. We also discussed how the effects of crime extend beyond the immediate victim. The fear of crime, for example, can have important implications for the well-being of individuals and their communities. In extreme cases, the public response in the aftermath of criminal events may approximate a panic situation.

Our theoretical elaboration of criminal events led us to conclude that there is value to be derived from investigating these events in the context of particular social domains. Social domains can be defined as the major spheres of life in which we spend most of our time and energy. Three such domains—the family and the household, recreation and leisure, and the workplace—provided the organizing themes for the substantive analysis of criminal events presented in Chapters 8–10. We argued that a comprehensive examination of criminal events in these domains requires us to focus on three important components: precursors, the transaction, and its aftermath. This approach helps us to understand (1) how social arrangements affect the distribution and timing of criminal events, (2) why some groups in society are more likely than others to be involved in criminal events, whether as offenders or victims, (3) why particular types of criminal events have the content that they have, and (4) how victims and others are affected by these events.

Our analyses of criminal events were grounded in empirical data, the sources of which we investigated in Chapter 7. In that chapter, we saw that the data on crime derive principally from two types of investigative strategies: observations and reports. Some researchers attempt to gather information about crime through their observations of crime in naturalistic settings and/or experimental and quasi-experimental settings. Most contemporary research, however, focuses on reports of crime from police, victims, and offenders. While there is much debate about the innate superiority of one type of report over another, we suggested that each type must be appreciated in terms of its own particular strengths and weaknesses. Each type of report provides us with different perspectives on and data about criminal events. Their variable nature does not make these data unusable; however, we should be critical and judicious in employing them.

Our discussion of criminal events in specific social domains in Chapters 8–10 enabled us to apply the theoretical and research lessons that emerged from earlier chapters. In Chapter 8, we took up the issue of criminal events in the home. Two general categories of events were discussed. The first involved interpersonal violence in the context of familial relationships. As we saw, such violence emerges from and reflects the social organization of family life. The very factors that lead us to idealize family life—intimacy and privacy—increase the risks of danger to more vulnerable family members. The data clearly indicate that women and children suffer most from violence in the home.

The second major type of criminal event in the family and household domain is property crime. Breaking and entering and the theft of household goods are very common crimes, and they result in substantial financial loss. As we suggested, much of this crime is opportunistic in nature, involving as it does rational offenders who encounter opportunities for theft. Our discussion of family life and family organization revealed how routine activities create such opportunities.

In Chapter 9, we took up several issues relating to criminal events in the leisure domain. We saw that (particularly in the case of juveniles) leisure is frequently understood as a "cause" of crime. It has been argued that many leisure pursuits in which youths engage promote criminal conduct directly or indirectly. This argument has been made most passionately with respect to television violence, but it also encompasses most other leisure activities pursued by young people. We also saw how leisure pursuits among youths may free them from social controls while at the same time providing them with opportunities for offending. Finally, we investigated how particular leisure contexts—the street, bars and taverns, dating, and tourism—provide settings for criminal events.

A final social domain, the workplace, was discussed in Chapter 10. Here, we saw that the nature and degree of people's involvement in the work domain

315

Summary and
Review of
Public Policy
Responses
to Crime

has important implications for the kinds of criminal events in which they might find themselves. Two major issues emerged from our discussion of the work domain. The first concerned the relationship between involvement in the legitimate world of work and involvement in criminal events. We saw that particular kinds of work expose employees to particular kinds of victimization and offending risks. In the former case, jobs that involve handling money, travel between remote work sites, or regular exposure to high-risk populations increase the risks people face at work. Highly publicized homicides in the workplace have brought this issue into sharp relief. The jobs people have may also provide them with unique opportunities to break the law. For instance, corporate criminals have access to highly profitable offending opportunities and very frequently remain insulated from controls that are supposed to deter their behavior.

The second major issue discussed in Chapter 10 has to do with crime as a form of work. Like legitimate business enterprises, criminal enterprises are sensitive to market conditions, endeavor to forge stable partnership arrangements, and attempt to manage their relationships with state agencies that try to control their activities.

Over the course of this book, we have developed an appreciation for the variety and the complexity of criminal events. The fact that these events occur in diverse social domains and involve different categories of actors does not mean that they are not amenable to criminological analysis. Throughout our analysis of criminal events, the same fundamental questions have kept recurring: Why do offenders and victims come together when they do, as they do, and where they do? Why does the event evolve as it does? What are the consequences of what transpired in the event for its participants? Instead of seeking highly specific answers to these questions, we have attempted to link specific concerns to theoretical ones. Moreover, we have been attentive to the pictures of criminal events that are revealed to us by the major criminological data sources. We conclude with a brief consideration of how the criminological understanding of these events helps us to make sense of public attempts to deal with the problem of crime.

RESPONDING TO CRIME

Criminal events occur because offenders encounter opportunities to violate the law. Controlling the occurrence of these events might involve attempts to discourage potential offenders. Depending on our theoretical model, we may wish to remove the factors that we believe motivate offending, or we may wish to make crime appear less rewarding to those who regard it as a rational course of action. With respect to the latter strategy, we have commented repeatedly on the role of legal deterrence.

Rather than attempt to prevent criminal events by controlling offenders, we might try instead to empower victims in ways that make them more resistant to victimization. One way of achieving this would be to develop policies that allow potential victims greater access to law or that teach them about measures they can take to make themselves less vulnerable to crime. Similarly, we might try to reduce the numbers of criminal opportunities available to offenders by manipulating the physical environments or social situations in which crimes occur.

THE "GET-TOUGH" APPROACH

These preliminary observations suggest several fronts along which any campaign against crime might be conducted. Too often, however, our thinking about crime is less imaginative than it might be. Fed by sensationalist media reporting and political rhetoric, we tend to think of the appropriate response to crime as what some call the "get-tough" approach: hire more police, hand down longer sentences, build more prisons, and execute more offenders.

BOX 11.1 A PUNITIVE PUBLIC?

Support for the death penalty in the United States is generally perceived to be at an all-time high. Since 1982, public opinion polls have consistently found that 70–75 percent of Americans favor the use of execution as a punishment for at least some crimes. This widespread support among citizens for capital punishment has also been cited as a possible factor in decisions by the Supreme Court upholding the right of states to execute convicted criminals.

Some recent research, however, has begun to challenge the supposition that the American public is so completely enamored with the death penalty. Criminologist William Bowers has proposed that public support for capital punishment may actually be "a reflection of the public's desire for a genuinely harsh but meaningful punishment for convicted murderers" (Bowers, 1993: 162). Thus, people support the use of the death penalty because they do not perceive an adequate or appropriate alternative to this punishment.

In a series of opinion surveys (begun by Amnesty International, a human rights organization, and continued by William Bowers and his associates), citizens were asked some version of the following question: "Suppose convicted first-degree murderers in this state could be sentenced to life in prison without parole and also be required to work in prison for money that would go to the families of their victims. Would you prefer this as an alternative to the death penalty?" Responses to this question suggest a different interpretation of Americans' attitudes toward use of the death penalty. When faced with the possibility of this alternative punishment, surveys have found that expressed support for the death penalty falls between 32 and 62 percentage points. That is, people who responded positively to standard opinion poll questions regarding their support for execution were likely to abandon this support when provided with a choice of a sentence of life without parole and victim restitution requirements.

This research suggests that the findings of opinion polls showing high support for use of the death penalty may be somewhat flawed. Americans do seem to want harsh and meaningful punishment for those who commit serious crimes. However, they may not perceive execution as being the only way in which these individuals can be adequately sanctioned.

317

*Summary and
Review of
Public Policy
Responses
to Crime*

For Discussion

Why do so many people view the criminal justice system as excessively lenient? What does this study tell us about the limitations of survey research?

SOURCES: Based on William Bowers (1993), "Capital Punishment and Contemporary Values: People's Misgivings and the Court's Misperceptions," *Law and Society Review* 27(1): 157–175; and Phoebe Ellsworth and Samuel Gross (1994), "Hardening of the Attitudes: Americans' Views on the Death Penalty," *Journal of Social Issues* 50(2): 19–52.

In a similar vein, police forces respond to the rising dangers in their jobs with requests for greater firepower. For example, the police in Winnetka, Illinois, have recently proposed the purchase of Uzi submachine guns to replace their shotguns. These machine guns, which can shoot through walls and fire up to ten rounds a second, are being demanded by a force that patrols a village of 13,000 residents.

Concerns about police safety have risen in response to changes in the nature of street crimes involving drugs. In the aftermath of a sting operation that went awry, resulting in a police officer being wounded, the special narcotics prosecutor in New York City commented, "The rules of engagement in the drug war have changed. . . . It's getting vicious out there" (*The New York Times*, 1989: B2). He attributed this new attitude to the youthfulness of the members of the drug-dealing organizations. Whereas experienced drug dealers tend to flee when confronted with a police officer, teenage gunmen seem to believe that they can escape prosecution by killing the officer. This attitude leaves the police more inclined to take strong precautions when dealing with gun-toting offenders, including the option of shooting first. "Deadly force" options probably deter, but they may also heighten feelings of desperation in those who see them as just another risk of criminal activity.

The use of deadly force raises concerns about breaches in a criminal justice system that theoretically promises fair treatment for all. Still, there appears to be public support for a get-tough response to crime. Are these responses justified, or are they symptomatic of a traumatized society more afraid of the mythology of crime than its reality? This is a difficult question to answer, particularly for people who feel that they have high chances of victimization.

Mandatory charging and sentencing practices that remove discretion from the police and courts have been implemented in some jurisdictions in the belief that greater certainty of punishment will create greater deterrence. In addition, some states have made a concerted effort to implement the death penalty as the appropriate sanction for capital crimes. The severity of the

Judges are increasingly losing their discretion in sentencing for certain types of crimes.

sentence has not been complemented by swiftness of imposition as the queue on death rows gets longer (in some cases, inmates have waited up to ten years for punishment).

Some observers have argued that get-tough responses to the problem of crime are inherently limited (European and North American Conference on Urban Safety and Crime Prevention, 1989). As they see it, the problem is twofold. First, there seems to be little convincing evidence that we effectively control crime when we simply invest more resources in the criminal justice system (Graham, 1990). Second, when we view the criminal justice system as the principal social mechanism for responding to crime, we approach the problem in a reactive rather than a proactive manner and thus never really address the underlying factors associated with crime and criminality.

As with other social problems, it is perhaps more sensible to think about strategies of prevention. **Crime prevention** has been defined as "the anticipation, recognition and appraisal of a crime risk and the initiation of some action to reduce or remove it" (National Crime Prevention Institute, 1986: 2). Clearly, the criminal justice system is itself part of an overall crime prevention strategy in that (1) the threat of legal penalty is meant to deter potential offenders and (2) prison terms, in their capacity to either punish or rehabilitate, are intended to prevent re-offending.

Get-tough approaches to crime tend to involve options that are specifically associated with the criminal justice system. As used by criminologists, the term *crime prevention* is more broadly based, referring to strategies or tactics that, while they might involve the police (or other criminal justice functionaries), are rooted in the physical and social character of the local community (Lab, 1992; van Dijk and de Waard, 1991). From this perspective, crime prevention involves a range of strategies, including installing lights on city streets, initiating citizen police patrols, developing Neighborhood Watch programs, mounting public information campaigns, locking doors, carrying weapons or alarms, and introducing programs aimed at reducing unemployment or poverty.

BOX 11.2 THE CRIME PREVENTION "ARMCHAIR VARIABLES"

Sociologist Marcus Felson has proposed four "armchair variables" that help us to summarize much of what we do, or could do, in the area of crime prevention. He presents these variables as dichotomies, although he indicates that they are better understood as continuous dimensions:

1. *Strategy vs. tactics.* These are military terms that describe the nature of our organizational efforts. A strategy is an overall plan to deal with a problem, while a tactic is a more detailed procedure for carrying out the strategy. Crime prevention tactics may work at cross-purposes if we lack an overall strategy; and a crime prevention strategy may fail if our tactics are not part of a strategic plan.

2. *Simple vs. complex.* Strategies or tactics may be simple or complex. Felson advises us that "making automobiles more difficult to steal" is a simple strategy but one that may involve many complex tactics, such as the use of antitheft computers or policing strategies.

3. *Small area vs. large area.* Some crime prevention efforts may target a single building or a single neighborhood. Others may address crime on a citywide or national basis.

4. *Narrow vs. broad.* Some types of programs might be directed toward a very narrow range of crimes or a single type of crime (for example, shoplifting), while others (for example, social development approaches) might be intended to prevent a wide variety of crimes.

For Discussion

Can you think of crime prevention programs that operate in your community and suggest how they relate to these "armchair variables"?

SOURCE: Based on M. Felson (1992), "Routine Activities and Crime Prevention," *Studies on Crime and Crime Prevention* 1(1): 30–34.

Public policy in the area of health care suggests interesting parallels to the issue of crime prevention. One way society can deal with medical problems is to wait until people get sick and then make health-care services available to them. Similarly, we can wait until people commit crimes and then take action by using criminal justice resources to catch and then confine or treat them. The use of the word *rehabilitation* in reference to prison programs suggests a quite literal application of the medical model to our thinking about crime and punishment.

In the area of public health, however, most policy planners recognize the value of applying limited resources in a preventive rather than a reactive manner. If we can prevent illness, we won't need to treat it after the fact. For this reason, we are advised to get regular medical checkups, exercise, and watch our diets. We might view the problem of crime in a similar way. It is more sensible to take action *before* crimes occur than after harm has been done.

Borrowing from the language of public health, we can think of crime prevention as having primary, secondary, and tertiary dimensions (Brantingham and Faust, 1976; Lab, 1992; van Dijk and de Waard, 1991). Primary prevention includes programs aimed at either the entire community or the population at risk. Exemplifying primary prevention are crime prevention programs that teach risk-reducing skills to the large audiences (Sacco and Silverman, 1982). Pamphlets, brochures, and posters providing information on family violence are examples of (mass media) primary prevention. Secondary prevention refers to programs aimed at those segments of the population that are at particularly high risk (or, in public health language, that show early symptoms of the problem). Examples of secondary prevention include targeting high-crime areas for special treatment (such as neighborhood redevelopment or Neighborhood Watch programs) and installing security equipment in schools that have experienced problems with intruders. Finally, tertiary prevention refers to strategies that are intended to prevent the recurrence of crime. Examples of tertiary prevention include victim–offender mediation, training courses for drunk drivers, treatment programs for wife assaulters, and various forms of diversion and community service.

There have been efforts in the United States to focus on violent crime as one would certain forms of disease (Meredith, 1984). James Mason, then the head of the Atlanta-based Centers for Disease Control (CDC)—which studies violent crime as a form of life-threatening disease—has stated that public health measures have been successful in treating poverty-related problems (for example, venereal disease, lead poisoning, and tuberculosis) *in the absence of* attempts to alleviate the social ills associated with them. The campaign against smoking has been particularly successful. Warnings about the health hazards, the political activism of nonsmokers, demands for nonsmoking areas, and interest in public fitness are all factors that have forced smokers to reconsider their habits (Meredith, 1984: 48).

321

Summary and
Review of
Public Policy
Responses
to Crime

According to Mason, we can do something about violence without first having to come up with solutions to poverty (Meredith, 1984: 45). Among his recommendations for reducing violence are developing programs that teach people how to handle conflict and restricting the availability of handguns.

The gun control debate is highly contentious. It ranges from the facile observation that "guns don't kill people, people kill people" to evidence that gun control laws appear to have little effect on the amount of homicide by firearms that we see in the United States (Kleck and Patterson, 1989). Nonetheless, controlling guns is viewed by the CDC as a major factor in the successful eradication of violence in the United States

Guns are the most popular means of committing homicide in the United States. In 1993, for example, 70 percent of homicides were perpetrated using some type of firearm (U.S. Dept. of Justice, 1994). Moreover, increasing numbers of young people now possess—and use—guns. The issue of gun control is complicated by those who argue that they have a right to use guns for sporting purposes or that the Second Amendment (guaranteeing the right to bear arms) implies that no restrictions on the ownership of weapons are allowed under the Constitution of the United States. Despite such protests, guns provide a symbolic as well as real threat to the well-being of crime-racked societies.

BOX 11.3 GUNS AND YOUTH

Gun crime involving young people has become a significant concern in recent years. Data from the Rochester Youth Development Study suggest that the concern may be well founded.

Under the direction of criminologist Terence Thornberry, the Rochester Youth Development Study tracked a large cohort of Rochester youths over a fifty-four-month period. In addition, data were collected from a variety of social agencies, including the schools, the police, and the courts. Overall, the study provides a thorough picture of adolescent development during the junior and senior high school years.

With respect to guns, the study found that by the ninth and tenth grades, more boys own illegal guns (7 percent) than own legal guns (3 percent). Of the boys who own illegal guns, about half of the whites and African-Americans and nearly 90 percent of the Hispanics carry them on a regular basis.

As Figure 11.1 shows, a strong relationship exists between owning illegal guns and delinquency. Among illegal gun owners, 74 percent commit street crimes, 24 percent commit gun crimes, and 41 percent use drugs. Boys who own legal guns, however, have much lower rates of delinquency and are even slightly less delinquent than nonowners of guns.

The research also showed that socialization into gun ownership is also vastly different for legal and illegal gun owners. Those who own legal guns have fathers who own guns for sport and hunting. On the other hand, illegal gun owners are more likely to be gang members.

Figure 11.1

Relationship Between Gun Ownership by Young Males and Street, Gun, and Drug Crimes

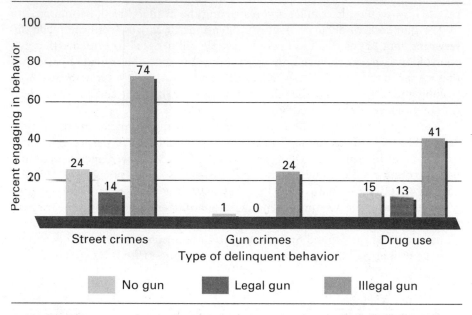

For Discussion

How are the socialization experiences regarding gun use likely to differ between legal and illegal gun owners? Is it sufficient or appropriate to think about illegal gun ownership and street crime in simple cause-and-effect terms?

SOURCE: Based on D. Huizinga, R. Loeber, and T. P. Thornberry, *Urban Delinquency and Substance Abuse: Initial Findings* (Washington, D.C.: U.S. Department of Justice, 1994).

Public opinion surveys in the United States would suggest that many Americans are not opposed to increasing controls on the purchase of handguns. For example, a 1993 poll found that 76 percent of Americans favored stricter firearms control laws, 40 percent favored an outright ban on handguns, and 77 percent favored a ban on assault weapons (Thomas, 1995). Lawmakers have not always acted on these concerns of citizens, although some form of gun control is becoming more politically popular in the United States. For example, the Brady Bill (named for former White House press secretary James Brady, who was wounded in a 1981 assassination attempt on President Reagan), passed by Congress in 1994, provides for a mandatory five-day waiting period in the purchase of handguns. Proposals to ban (and alternatively, to prevent a ban on) a variety of assault, automatic, and semi-automatic weapons are currently being debated in the legislature. Many states have passed laws in

323

*Summary and
Review of
Public Policy
Responses
to Crime*

Fearing that the police can no longer protect them, many people are looking for ways to protect themselves.

recent years as well, limiting the ease with which guns may be purchased. For example, in 1993, the Virginia legislature approved a measure that limited citizens to the purchase of one gun per month (aimed at reducing or eliminating gunrunning in the state). A public health approach to reducing violence would emphasize educating citizens about the dangers associated with the improper use of firearms.

Despite the valuable insights that the public health model provides, its application to crime prevention is problematic (Graham, 1990). First, the model is so wide-ranging that it is unclear where we should draw the boundaries between what is and what is not a crime prevention practice. Second, the distinctions between primary, secondary, and tertiary prevention are frequently less clear in practice than they are in theory. Third, the attempt to classify crime prevention practices in this way assumes that our understanding of what causes crime (and, therefore, of how it can be prevented) is more scientifically precise than it really is. Harries (1990) further cautions that public health as an institution has, at the present time, neither the resources nor the personnel to make a lasting impression on the problem of crime incidence.

In the remainder of this section and in the two sections that follow, we examine three major approaches to crime prevention that extend well beyond traditional get-tough approaches. Each picks up an important theme in the study of criminal events. **Opportunity reduction** focuses on how social and environmental factors might be brought to bear on the reduction of crime opportunities. **Social development** approaches attempt to create social conditions that discourage long-term serious offending and empower potential victims while at the same time contributing to the rebuilding of communities. Finally, **community-based policing** (or problem-oriented policing) considers ways in which the policing role may be expanded beyond the narrow reactive role that brings the police into criminal events only when such events are either already underway or finished.

CRIME PREVENTION THROUGH OPPORTUNITY REDUCTION

As we have seen, the event conceptualization of crime stresses the importance of opportunity in elucidating where and when crimes occur. Only when people who are ready, willing, and able to offend encounter conditions favorable to offending are criminal events likely to develop. From a policy standpoint, therefore, actions that control the appearance or accessibility of opportunities to engage in crime may help to prevent much crime. The important implication of this approach is that we can manage the risks of crime without changing the character of offenders. Because the emphasis in opportunity reduction is on the modification of the situations in which crimes occur, crime prevention through opportunity reduction is sometimes referred to as **situational crime prevention.**

Situational prevention is based on two important assumptions. The first is that crimes are most effectively prevented when we are attentive to their particular characteristics (Brantingham and Brantingham, 1990). Thus, the first step in opportunity reduction is careful crime analysis: Who commits these crimes? When are they committed? Where do they most frequently occur? What do offenders hope to achieve by committing crimes? How might certain characteristics of the physical environment contribute to these events? Are there natural forces of guardianship that might be activated in the situations in which crimes typically occur? The answers to such questions help crime prevention planners tailor specific solutions to specific crime problems.

BOX 11.4 CASE STUDIES IN SITUATIONAL PREVENTION

Patricia L. Brantingham and Paul J. Brantingham are known as international experts in the area of situational crime prevention. Their research provides the following examples, which clearly illustrate the logic and the value of the approach.

Example 1: In a large suburban municipality, a brewer's warehouse had experienced repeated problems with people breaking into delivery vans at night. The vans were empty but were backed up to the loading bay doors and locked up overnight. Offenders, apparently in search of beer, repeatedly cut through a fence on the perimeter of the warehouse lot and broke into the vans. No beer was stolen, since the vans were empty, but the brewer incurred repeated repair costs to fix the damaged fence and delivery vans.

A crime prevention officer convinced the warehouse manager to park the delivery vans away from the loading bay doors (which were themselves very secure) and leave them unlocked overnight. The vans were opened on a few subsequent occasions, but they were not damaged as before.

Example 2: A church experienced a less serious but more common problem. A high school was located opposite the church, and a convenience store was located on the street behind the church. As might be expected, students from the high school walked through the church parking lot to get to and from the convenience store. Unfortunately, the students dumped lots of litter in the church parking lot. Church members were upset by the mess but unable to stop either the trespassing teenagers or their littering.

A crime prevention officer found an effective, low-cost solution. He convinced the church to dig a ditch across the front of its property (except for an entrance way) and to build a direct pathway from the school to the convenience store along one edge of the church property. The new pathway had a tall cedar fence on one side to separate it from adjacent houses and a chain-link fence on the other side. The littering on the church grounds stopped, and, perhaps surprisingly, the student pathway stayed litter- and graffiti-free. General research on littering and graffiti finds that keeping an area "clean" is a deterrent to further problems.

Example 3: To combat shoplifting, video stores are changing how they display the videos they have for rental. Previously, they tended to place the actual cassettes out on the shelves. Customers would select a cassette and carry it to a central desk for rental. This system had the benefit of reducing staff time spent on telling customers whether particular videos were available for rental: If they were on the shelves, they were available; if they were not on the shelves, they were not available.

Most stores now display the small empty boxes that the videos originally came in or else small plastic display cards with advertising material. The customer must exchange the box or card for the actual video at a central station. Although this system requires more staff time, it reduces shoplifting dramatically.

For Discussion

Can you think of examples in your community of situational crime prevention? Why do some critics worry that prevention activities of this type merely displace crime from one locale to another?

SOURCE: Based on P. L. Brantingham and P. J. Brantingham (1990), "Situational Crime Prevention in Practice," *Canadian Journal of Criminology* 32(1): 29–30.

325

*Summary and
Review of
Public Policy
Responses
to Crime*

The second key assumption relates to the nature of the offender. Opportunity reduction approaches reflect the model of the rational offender (Cornish and Clarke, 1986). In other words, offenders' decisions are based on their assessment of the various costs and benefits associated with a particular course of action. How easily can a crime be committed? Is anyone who might take action to prevent the crime standing guard? Are there less risky ways of obtaining the rewards that the commission of the crime promises? Offenders will seek answers to such questions and behave in ways that reflect their best interests. If the opportunities conducive to crime can be made less attractive or less plentiful, many types of crimes (particularly those that are largely opportunistic in nature) may occur much less frequently. According to Clarke (1992), situational prevention involves increasing the risks and decreasing the rewards associated with crime. As offending situations become more difficult, riskier, and less rewarding, rational offenders will be discouraged from offending.

One obvious way in which people increase the difficulties associated with crime is through target hardening, which refers to those measures that decrease the vulnerability of personal or household property. Entry into a house with locked doors and windows is more difficult than entry into a house in which such measures have not been taken. Various forms of access control, such as locked gates and entry phones, also increase the degree of effort needed to commit certain crimes.

The deadbolt lock is one of the most effective deterrents to property crime.

BOX 11.5 VICTIMIZATION PREVENTION ADVICE

Much crime prevention literature encourages people to reduce their vulnerability to crime by adopting behaviors that make them harder targets. Women, in particular, have been given much advice—in booklets, brochures, and pamphlets—about what they can do to make themselves safer.

DeKeseredy, Burshtyn, and Gordon provide examples from a government booklet published in 1990 that advises women:

- Never remain alone in an apartment, laundry room, mailroom, or parking garage.
- Do not put your first name on your mailbox or in the telephone book.
- Do not overburden yourself with packages and a bulky purse.
- Try to avoid isolated bus stops.
- If you babysit, be escorted home after dark.

Such advice has a familiar ring and may even be considered by many to be common sense. But is it good crime prevention policy? DeKeseredy and colleagues, as well as feminist writer Elizabeth Stanko, find this information troubling for several reasons.

327

*Summary and
Review of
Public Policy
Responses
to Crime*

First, it focuses women's attention on "stranger danger," despite the fact that women face greater risks from men who are familiar to them. These tips will do little to protect a wife from an abusive husband or a teenager from an assaultive boyfriend. In fact, their effect may be to encourage women to be even more dependent on male protectors from whom they may have more to fear.

Second, it implicitly adopts a "victim-blaming" position by telling women that their safety is their own problem; if they become victims, it is because they failed to take appropriate precautions.

Third, long lists of safety tips deny women's experiences. Many women already organize their lives around safety issues. When and where they go, and what kinds of activities they do and do not engage in, are decisions that reflect their awareness of their vulnerability to danger. Such lists tell women that no matter how much they do, they are not doing enough.

Fourth, crime prevention tips tend to aggravate women's fear of victimization without doing anything that actually makes them any safer.

Stanko suggests that, rather than communicate to women what they have to do to make themselves safer, it makes more sense to discourage men from engaging in behavior that makes women feel unsafe.

In contrast to the target-hardening advice given to women, a pamphlet issued by the British Home Office tells men the following:

- If you are walking in the same direction as a woman on her own, don't walk behind her. This may worry her. Cross the road and walk on the other side. This may reassure her that you are not following her.
- Don't sit too close to a woman on her own in a railway carriage.
- Remember that a woman on her own may feel threatened by what you think are admiring looks.

For Discussion
How might the advice cited by DeKeseredy and colleagues contribute to women's fear? Why do some critics argue that advice addressed to potential victims is really just a form of victim-blaming?

SOURCES: British Home Office, *Crime: Together We'll Crack It* (London: The Home Office, 1989); W. S. DeKeseredy, H. Burshtyn, and C. Gordon (1992), "Taking Woman Abuse Seriously: A Critical Response to the Solicitor General of Canada's Crime Prevention Advice," *International Review of Victimology* 2: 1–11; and E. Stanko, "When Precaution Is Normal: A Feminist Critique of Crime Prevention." In L. Gelsthorpe and A. Morris (eds.), *Feminist Perspectives in Criminology* (Philadelphia: Open University Press, 1990).

The risks involved in the commission of crime may be increased by measures that make it more likely (or, at least, make it *appear* more likely) that the offender will be discovered and apprehended. A high level of surveillance by security guards, citizen patrols, and security cameras clearly is intended to serve this purpose. Perhaps less obvious is the role played by other types of crime prevention measures, such as locks. As Felson (1992: 32) argues, "The strategic role of a lock is not to prevent entry! Rather, its strategic role is to force the offender to make a lot of noise, in hope that others will hear that noise. Ideally, the potential offender will take a look at the lock, note the noise it will force him to make, fear the consequences of that noise, and decide against committing the crime."

The role of prevention goes beyond the introduction of defensible space. According to Merry (1981), a neighborhood may be architecturally designed to discourage crime but still not be adequately defended, because it has little or no social cohesion. Krupat and Kubzansky (1987: 61) note that "even when buildings are low and the entrances and public spaces focus around a small set of families, people will not react to crime when they believe that they are on someone else's turf, when they do not consider the police effective or when they fear retribution."

Among the most popular measures intended to activate natural surveillance at the local level are Block Watch or Neighborhood Watch programs that are sponsored by the local police. These programs are supposed to encourage neighborhood residents to "share information about local crime problems, exchange crime prevention tips, and make plans for engaging in surveillance ('watching') of the neighborhood and crime-reporting activities" (Rosenbaum, 1987: 104). Surveillance programs increase interaction among neighbors at the same time as they remove opportunities for crime. The Bureau of Justice Statistics reported in 1986 that about one family in five lives in a neighborhood with a surveillance program and that, in those areas, 38 percent of residents participate (Garofalo and McLeod, 1988).

BOX 11.6 WHO IS THE CRIME PREVENTION ACTIVIST?

What kinds of individuals take the initiative to organize crime prevention efforts in their communities? In attempting to answer this question, researcher Stanley Shernock compared a sample of Neighborhood Watch leaders with a sample of nonparticipants from the same nonurban area of the United States.

He found that, compared to nonactivists, crime prevention activists tended to be older, married, and of higher socioeconomic status. No significant differences existed with respect to the gender composition or employment status of the two groups. In addition, crime prevention activists were found to have a larger number of memberships in other voluntary associations.

Activists were no more likely than nonactivists to report having been victimized; nor were they more likely to report having witnessed a crime. Crime prevention activism was also unrelated to feelings of personal safety. Activists were more likely than nonactivists to perceive the crime rate as increasing, but they were also more inclined to view their own neighborhoods as less dangerous than the surrounding ones.

Based on this analysis, Shernock concluded that these crime prevention activists viewed crime as more of a potential threat than as a present reality. As such, they did not see their activities as directed toward the control of crime that actually occurs, but rather toward the deterrence of crimes that could occur and toward the preservation of neighborhood stability.

For Discussion

Why are some people more likely than others to get involved in crime prevention activities?

SOURCE: Based on S. K. Shernock (1986), "A Profile of the Crime Prevention Activist," *Journal of Criminal Justice* 14: 211–228.

While opportunity for crime can be thwarted by the self-help actions of potential victims, individuals who take the law into their own hands may do so in a manner that constitutes vigilantism (Rosenbaum and Sederberg, 1976). Black (1983) describes "self-help crime" as a potent and frequently used form of punishment and deterrence. The equation of guns with independence and security is evident in the sales pitch for LadySmith, a handgun designed to meet the "physical requirements of women." Here, a potential victim is provided the means with which to enact summary justice on her assailant. A National Rifle Association ad that appeared in *USA Today* in 1987 justifies the arming of women by arguing that only 3 percent of rape attempts are completed against victims carrying weapons.

Self-help deterrence can become outright retribution. Bernard Goetz (the "subway vigilante") admitted to having purposely carried a gun when riding on the New York subways in search of trouble. He found trouble when a number of youths carrying screwdrivers approached him and demanded money. Goetz shot at them, hitting one youth in the back as he was running away. Initially proclaimed a hero for standing up to his "assailants," Goetz's image was badly tarnished by his admission that he had been seeking revenge for an earlier mugging. What had first appeared a defensive strategy was in fact an offensive act. Goetz had tried to assume the role of police officer, the difference being that the police are normally constrained by professional codes of conduct and due process of the law.

Finally, crime may be made less attractive by reducing the rewards associated with the offense. For example, requiring bus riders to have exact change decreases the amount of money that must be handled by any particular bus driver and makes the robbery of drivers a less attractive proposition. Similarly, markings that identify individual ownership of property may discourage the conspicuous use of stolen merchandise and seriously hurt the chances for resale. As we saw in Chapter 5, the amount of money available in 7-Elevens at any given time is another way in which the rewards for criminality can be curtailed.

Unquestionably, opportunity reduction has proven effective in a variety of specific settings. However, this approach is not without its critics. Some have suggested that removing opportunity is more likely to displace crime than to prevent it (Gabor, 1990b). In other words, if we make it difficult for a motivated offender to offend in one situation, he or she might simply find another situation more conducive to offending. If one store takes precautions to prevent theft, can we really be sure that the would-be thief will not simply seek out targets where such precautions are not taken? The evidence suggests that displacement may be a problem with particular types of crime and particular types of offenders. However, many forms of opportunity reduction do in fact prevent crimes rather than just displace them (Brantingham and Brantingham, 1990).

More specific forms of opportunity reduction invite more specific criticisms. Various target-hardening methods, such as installing locks on doors and bars on windows, may be faulted for encouraging a "fortress mentality" that enhances the fear of crime in society (Graham, 1990). Some critics see the use of electronic surveillance as part of a gradual shift toward a "surveillance society" (Clarke, 1992). Critics of Neighborhood Watch programs claim that, despite the highly favorable publicity they receive and the high regard in which they are held by police and politicians, little evidence suggests that they accomplish what they are supposed to accomplish. According to Rosenbaum (1987),

> There is some evidence to suggest (a) if given the opportunity to participate, residents in the majority of high-crime neighborhoods would not participate, and (b) when citizens do participate, the social interaction that occurs at meetings may lead to increases (rather than decreases) in fear of crime, racial prejudice and other crime-related perceptions or feelings. More important, there is little evidence that these block/neighborhood meetings cause local residents to engage in neighborhood surveillance, social interaction, and bystander intervention—behaviors that are posited as the central mechanism for strengthening informal social controls and reducing opportunities for crime. (127)

Perhaps the most frequent and general criticism of opportunity reduction approaches is that, by placing so much emphasis on reducing opportunities for crime, they ignore the underlying causes of crime. It has been argued that, because these strategies do not address the root causes of crime, the best they can hope to achieve is short-term benefits. If we wish to consider these root causes, we must turn to another major approach—crime prevention through social development.

CRIME PREVENTION THROUGH SOCIAL DEVELOPMENT

Crime prevention through social development focuses not on the criminal act, but on the serious, repeat offender. As we saw in previous chapters, research suggests that a relatively small number of offenders are responsible for a disproportionately large number of crimes. These offenders begin their criminal careers early in life and end them (if at all) late in life. Over the course of their offending careers, they commit a wide variety of predatory offenses. The research also indicates that these individuals tend to come from disadvantaged backgrounds, that they abuse alcohol and other drugs, and that they have experienced serious family problems as well as school- and employment-related problems.

A range of social problems, from family victimization to poverty and racism, can provide a fertile breeding ground for crime. The building of communities is seen by advocates of the social development approach to provide a comprehensive strategy that reduces crime by discouraging potential offenders while at the same time strengthening potential victims. The aim of crime prevention through social development is to correct the criminogenic social conditions that are assumed to be the root causes of crime. Oriented toward the achievement of long-range prevention, this approach seeks to eliminate the underclass from which serious, repeat offenders typically emerge.

BOX 11.7 CRIME PREVENTION THROUGH SOCIAL DEVELOPMENT

Elements of a social development agenda toward crime prevention can be seen in recent legislation that has been both proposed and enacted by the Congress of the United States. Even as citizens and lawmakers are increasingly moving toward a "get tough on crime" attitude, we also see attention being paid to the importance of crime prevention, especially among young people. The following excerpt from Attorney General Janet Reno's remarks to the Senate subcommittee on Children, Family, Drugs and Alcoholism illustrates this legislative concern with crime prevention:

It is a pleasure to be with you today to speak about one of the key elements of the President's anti-crime effort—workable and effective prevention programs.

. . . The key components of the President's anti-crime program are police, punishment, and prevention. . . . The crime bills that will soon be reconciled in Congress will put more police on our streets and provide swift and severe punishment for violent offenders. But, it will also steer young people away from crime and drugs, giving them instead, as the President has said, "something to say yes to."

We have the opportunity to develop and nurture crime prevention programs for young Americans through employment, recreational and educational opportunities.

We have the opportunity to break the cycle of violence—a cycle that so often begins with children seeing violence against their mothers by family members— by doing something serious about domestic violence and other forms of violence against women.

The crime bills passed by the Senate and House contain numerous programs which take advantage of the opportunity presented by the growing consensus that we must seek to prevent crime.

I would like to highlight briefly some of the prevention programs in the crime bill:

- *The President's Youth Employment Skills program . . . will give young people something other than crime to say yes to by providing employment and skills to young people in hard-hit, high crime areas. The young people of America want to be involved. They want to contribute, and to work to build a better future for themselves and their families. . . .*
- *The Ounce of Prevention programs . . . can provide . . . a terrific mechanism for coordinating and effectively integrating the delivery of the federal government's new youth development and youth oriented crime prevention initiatives. . . .*

The activities to be supported by the Ounce of Prevention are simple and workable. Let me give you one example: the Community Schools Initiative contained in the Ounce of Prevention. Children face the greatest risks after school, on weekends, and during school vacations—when they are idle and their parents are at work or not around. It is during these hours that kids fall prey to drugs and crime. A recent study found that eighth graders who were unsupervised for 11 or more hours a week were twice as likely to abuse drugs or alcohol as those who had adult supervision. Boredom and isolation may also be the best recruitment devices that violent gangs have.

Through recreation and organized sports and other activities, young people can develop self esteem, learn to play by the rules and experience the thrill of playing fair. We have resources available in every neighborhood, now, to use for this purpose: $250 billion worth of public school buildings and facilities. The problem is that these schools are generally open only seven hours a day, and often for only 180 days a year. . . .

If we keep these schools open, they can bring the community together and provide the space for activities, learning and a safe place to be a kid. . . . The Community Schools Initiative is just one example of what we can do. . . . It demonstrates that crime prevention ideas are there waiting for us to act.

For Discussion

What type of success do you believe we will witness from each of the components of the crime bills—that is, police, punishment, and prevention? In your view, how workable are the proposals presented here?

SOURCE: Prepared statement of Attorney General Janet Reno before the Senate subcommittee on Children, Family, Drugs and Alcoholism, 17 May 1994, pp. 27–30.

The notion that crime can be prevented by eliminating the social ills that breed crime (particularly teenage crime) is not new. There is a long history of social reformism that argues that we can best fight crime by fighting poverty, racism, unemployment, and other forms of social disadvantage (Graham, 1990; Rosenbaum, 1988). The social development approach differs from these older approaches in its more systematic efforts to identify and attack the root causes of crime.

Because predatory crime is part of a "tangle of pathologies" (Wilson, 1987) that characterizes the lives of the socially disadvantaged, our policy approaches to crime prevention must extend beyond the criminal justice system into the areas of family, educational, housing, and health policy (Graham, 1990). One important theme emphasizes **resource mobilization,** which addresses crime issues in terms of whether the law helps people—especially the poor and powerless—protect themselves against victimization. Browne and Williams (1989) note that the enactment of domestic violence legislation (which makes arrest of offenders more likely), coupled with high levels of resource mobilization (including the provision of shelters for battered women), tended to reduce the rate of female-perpetrated homicide. That is, the more women feel empowered to deal with violence directed against them, the less likely they are to react with fatal violence.

Browne and Williams admit that some issues remain unclear. They cannot establish the degree of awareness that individuals have of available resources. In addition, they have no way of measuring the accessibility that individual women have to the mandated resources. Further, it is not clear how many people actually use the resources that are available or how effective these resources are in meeting individual needs (Browne and Williams, 1989: 91–92). What *is* clear from this research, however, is that, where these resources are available, criminal victimization from fatal assaults is lower. This finding provides a strong argument for the need to assess the extent to which society can provide alternatives to women that will enable them to avoid becoming victims.

Advocates of the social development approach see crime prevention not as the exclusive domain of any one social or governmental agency. Instead, they place considerable emphasis on the need to establish crime prevention councils at both the federal and municipal levels. These councils would bring together those responsible for health, family, employment, and housing policy, as well as the police and voluntary agencies that are concerned with a broad range of social welfare issues. The idea behind such an arrangement is that, by sharing the ownership of the crime problem, more comprehensive solutions will be developed.

While the social development approach has proven more popular in some European countries than in North America, it is clearly gaining momentum. However, some advocates of opportunity reduction maintain that the social development strategy fails to recognize that crime is not a homogeneous event and that different crimes require different intervention strategies (Brantingham, 1989).

Other critics question whether we have the political will or, in times of fiscal restraint, we are truly prepared to make the financial commitments that a comprehensive social development approach might entail. We might also ask if the linkages that social development advocates draw between factors such as family upbringing, employment, and school experience are as obvious and as straightforward as they are sometimes made out to be. The list of causative factors to which the social development approach draws our attention is long and unwieldy, and as we have seen, there is honest debate among criminologists about the relative importance of these factors (Graham, 1990).

How will changes in the nature of our communities condition our ability to implement crime prevention strategies in the future? Some general trends are apparent. For example, the development of new information technologies clearly is transforming the nature of social life, and in so doing is suggesting the possibility of new prevention opportunities. Cellular telephones allow people to intervene anonymously in a variety of situations that would not have been possible before. Computer terminals in patrol cars allow police to tap databases that provide instant information about known offenders and unsafe locations.

Other trends that bring with them increases in the levels of guardianship and decreases in levels of victimization risk include the growth of remote work sites, which can reduce commuting time (Felson, 1987); the spread of computer technologies, which allow many people to spend part of the working day at home; the expansion of part-time work in the service economy; and the increasing popularity of video and other home entertainment technologies. All of these changes suggest that the shift in routine activities away from the home may be undergoing a reversal. While the long-term impact of such changes on the community remains to be seen, they may eventually permit some forms of community prevention that were not viable in the past.

Modern technology has made policing more efficient.

335

*Summary and
Review of
Public Policy
Responses
to Crime*

Felson (1987) provides an interesting example of how our prevention planning must be informed by careful social forecasting. He argues that metropolitan areas in North America are undergoing profound changes that involve the emergence of the "metroquilt" as the new dominant urban form. Within the context of the metroquilt, the city becomes "a patchwork of coterminous facilities intervening between homes, business and the larger society. The metroquilt would divide urban space among a large set of corporations, whose facilities managers would be responsible for organizing everyday movements, including security" (Felson, 1987: 920). This patchwork is apparent in the landscape of any major city. Stores are replaced by malls, single-family dwellings by condominiums and apartment complexes, and businesses and factories by industrial parks. In the metroquilt, Felson maintains, we have decreasing need to walk from one place to another and increasing need to drive from the parking lot of one facility to the parking lot of another facility.

In Felson's view, the growth of the metroquilt has far-reaching implications for crime prevention. As facilities develop, the distinction between public urban space and private space becomes increasingly blurred. As people spend increasing amounts of their time shopping in malls, working in office complexes, and visiting friends and relatives in apartment complexes, private businesses rather than the government assume greater responsibility for their safety. As a result, the facility could become the major organizational tool for crime prevention. Felson is optimistic about these developments because they seem to suggest the possibility that prevention can be rationalized and that security can be planned. He maintains that safety will become part of the marketing strategy because, as facilities compete for customers and tenants, private developers will have a strong incentive to make environments more crime-free (see also Shearing and Stenning, 1983; Walsh and Donovan, 1989).

However, there is a more disturbing side to all of this. If the production of safety is increasingly the domain of the private developer, then safety becomes a commodity accessible only to those who can afford it. The patron of the upscale shopping center, the resident of the luxurious condo, and the employee in a gleaming office tower may find safety more accessible than those who spend most of their time in facilities where profit motives or government cost-cutting militate against extensive crime prevention planning. The risk that safety may become a commodity to be bought and sold, rather than a public good, suggests that issues other than technical effectiveness must inform prevention efforts. The prevention of crime must involve not only logistical matters but also matters of justice and equality. This concern is one that police are now facing as they attempt to adopt crime prevention as a primary focus of their activities.

COMMUNITY-BASED POLICING

Gottfredson and Hirschi (1990) argue that the natural limits of law enforcement are set by the spontaneous nature of crime: The offender sees that he or she can get something for nothing and seizes the opportunity. No increases in law enforcement, they suggest, can truly deter this type of behavior. Research has provided strong evidence that there is no relationship between the level of crime in a society and the number of police available to control this crime (Bayley, 1985; Jackson, 1989). Gottfredson and Hirschi (1990: 270), maintain that, in the overwhelming majority of robberies, burglaries, assaults, homicides, thefts, and drug deals, "the offender does not know or care about the probability of being observed by the police." The primary role of the police, they suggest, is to respond to criminal activity and to maintain social control; there is no evidence that increasing police tactical resources has the effect of reducing crime rates.

BOX 11.8 COMMUNITY-BASED POLICING AND THE FEAR OF CRIME

A broad definition of crime prevention extends well beyond efforts to control crime levels. It may also include attempts to alleviate public worries or anxieties about the problem of crime. This is an important function since many observers have come to recognize the fear of crime—separate and distinct from crime itself—as a social problem that requires attention.

It has been argued that traditional methods of policing, which emphasize motorized patrols, rapid response, and crime investigation, have done little to assuage public fears. Some criminologists suggest that new styles of community-based policing may more effectively combat the problem of public fear. In particular, some research studies have shown that, in areas where police use foot patrols, residents exhibit lower levels of concern and worry.

Why should foot patrols and other forms of community-based policing have this effect? In general, such measures increase the level of contacts between police and residents. These contacts increase communication, which, in turn, increases trust and the two-way flow of information. As communication between the police and members of the local community improves, confidence in the police may be enhanced. The police may then be better able to deal with problems in a proactive rather than a reactive manner. Police and citizens may inform each other about community problems and solutions. Many of the conditions that give rise to fear may thus be eradicated.

For Discussion

Do you think community-based policing has the effect of lowering public fear? Should controlling the fear of crime be a policy priority?

SOURCE: Based on M. H. Moore and R. C. Trojanowicz, *Perspectives on Policing: Policing and the Fear of Crime* (Washington, D.C.: U.S. Department of Justice, 1988).

Unfortunately, police resources have become scarcer, and what the police do primarily is respond to complaints (not crime), maintain visibility in neighborhoods, and control traffic. In a study of police activity, Lawson (1982) discov-

337

*Summary and
Review of
Public Policy
Responses
to Crime*

ered that the police spend only 10–15 percent of their time engaged in actual law enforcement; the rest of their time is taken up with order maintenance.

The pressures of order maintenance and restricted resources have forced police agencies to begin to rethink their strategy of law enforcement. The police role has expanded partly as a result of the fact that the police belong to the only twenty-four-hour social agency that is easy to reach and that will make house calls. The police emergency line (911) leaves police overwhelmed with calls that require them to serve not a law enforcement function, but rather a regulatory or order maintenance function. In addition, the police are being called upon to become more actively involved in crime prevention, partly as a response to the increased levels of unease that people feel in urban areas.

Given the assumption of routine activities theory that crime is made possible not only by the availability of offenders and victims but also by the absence of visible guardians (such as the police), it is hard to believe that the police have *no* effect on deterring crime. However, as the research consistently indicates, a direct correlation between policing levels and crime does not exist. Hiring more police does not necessarily lower crime, for many reasons. In previous chapters, we examined the police role in defining criminal events. The criteria that the police use in determining whether to arrest a person are shaped by a number of factors, including the nature of the police organization and its strategies of policing, differing interpretations of criminal events and differing assessments of the characteristics and motivations of participants in these events, and variations in the interpretations of the law and the cooperation of the public. We will examine how each of these factors can influence the new problem-oriented strategies (also referred to as community-based policing and compliance-based policing) that are intended to assist the police in dealing with crime. But first, we will consider the changes that have taken place in the ways in which the police have functioned over the years.

The original mandate of the police in the nineteenth century was order maintenance (Wilson, 1983). The order maintenance or compliance role of the police was coterminous with "community relations." The police were to protect the community from disorderly behavior and to control conflict where they found it (Monkkonen, 1983). This role required them to act as "watchmen," keeping track of the comings and goings in the community and looking out for behavior that might constitute a threat to public order. The compliance role is associated with the "proactive" policing we discussed in Chapters 1 and 5. As Klockars (1985: 106–107) has stated, the police are not law enforcement agencies, but rather regulatory institutions—their job is not to enforce the laws but to regulate relationships between people.

The principal objective of compliance law enforcement is to secure conformity with the law by resorting to means that induce that conformity (Reiss, 1984). Compliance systems return to the original mandate of the police whereby one seeks to create law-abidingness through preventive or remedial actions. Under these systems, the primary focus of policing shifts from detecting and penalizing violators to providing incentives to individuals to comply

The cop on the street has proven to be the most effective form of policing.

with the law. Compliance-based policing also recognizes the need to include the public in controlling social disorder, beyond merely reporting crime to the police. The public is encouraged to include the police as intermediaries in situations of community conflict (Lawson, 1982).

The public has demanded more social order since at least the 1850s (Monkkonen, 1983). In fact, in comparison to crime control, order control as practiced by the police has had a long and successful record. As Monkkonen states, Victorian morality has triumphed in most of America's city streets. We expect, and get, quiet and predictable behavior from almost everyone. Vice is no longer highly visible. Yet the dramatic rise in crime rates, and the apparent ineffectiveness of the police in dealing with crime and its consequences, has again raised concerns about social order. Monkkonen attributes the increases in crime rates to a number of factors, including urbanization and changes in the demographic composition of the population. The effect of these increases early in this century was to narrow the focus of police agencies to crime control alone, leaving the problems of general order maintenance to other agencies.

The principal objective of crime control or deterrence law enforcement is to detect violations of the law, identify offenders responsible for violations, and penalize perpetrators. This is done to diminish the chance of future offenses both by the offender (specific deterrence) and by others who may contemplate the same criminal act (general deterrence) (Reiss, 1984: 91). Until recently, contemporary policing has had as a stated objective the apprehension of offenders through arrest, which has led to the form of "reactive" policing that dominates the way that police agencies operate (Reiss, 1984: 84).

339

*Summary and
Review of
Public Policy
Responses
to Crime*

Police have now begun to realize that crime control, by necessity, requires broadening their mandate once again to include order maintenance or compliance law enforcement. However, this notion is being resisted by police agencies that still regard law enforcement as their principal mandate.

The internal workings of police organizations are such that peacekeeping and order maintenance functions are seen as residual matters. Real policing, some argue, involves arrest. The philosophy of community-based policing challenges this view, but the problem remains that many compliance-based actions are without legitimation in police organizations. In addition, little training is provided for compliance-based operations. As Mastrofski (1983: 34) notes, the crime-fighting and the noncrime public service functions coexist uneasily in the police profession. The former dominates training curricula, career incentives, and organization evaluations, while the latter dominates the workload.

Notwithstanding this trend, community-based policing has replaced professional crime control policing as the dominant ideological and organizational model of progressive policing. Bayley (1988: 226) identifies four major features of community-based policing: (1) community-based crime prevention, (2) proactive servicing, as opposed to emergency response, (3) public participation in the planning and supervision of police operations, and (4) the shifting of command responsibility to lower-level ranks. Accompanying these organizational and procedural changes is an emphasis on identifying and solving problems, which are defined in terms of breaches of both law and social order. Further, the solutions to these problems do not merely reside in the rules and regulations of the police service; they must also acknowledge the concerns and desires of the community in which the problems occur.

According to Goldstein (1990), community-based policing requires at least five major adjustments in current thinking. First, to do their job

> ## WHAT DOES IT MEAN?
>
> ### *Community-Based Policing*
>
> Community-based policing includes (1) community based crime prevention, (2) proactive servicing, as opposed to emergency response, (3) public participation in the planning and supervision of police operations, and (4) the shifting of command responsibility to lower-level ranks.

well, police officers must be encouraged to search for alternatives to law enforcement. This encouragement must be reflected in a consistent, agencywide commitment to improving the quality of police service. Second, the police must not restrict their attention to those actions that have a potential for reducing crime. In some cases, crime is only the final consequence of unresolved noncrime-related problems. Third, consistent with the view that policing encompasses all of a community's problems, those that do not fit strict law enforcement criteria must also be addressed. Fourth, some effort must be made to understand the nature of the problems that are encountered in any given area prior to setting out alternatives. Too often, alternatives are prescribed that simply do not work because they are not suited to the area being policed. Like any other large organization, police have difficulty resisting internal pressures to follow established but rigid objectives and procedures. Fifth, police must be open to the idea of allowing other agencies to fulfill the job in conjunction with (or in place of) the police. According to Goldstein (1990: 104), this strategy "is intended to dissuade the police from applying a generic response to a generic problem, or to applying a single response haphazardly to a wide range of different types of problems."

Bayley (1988: 226) suggests that, if implemented correctly, community-based policing will constitute the most fundamental change in policing since the rise in police professionalism early in this century. However, while community-based policing appears to be gaining acceptance in police circles, few attempts have been made to understand how it actually works or to evaluate its overall performance (Kennedy, 1991). This means that the police may simply be doing the same thing as before but labeling it as something different, or doing something differently but not as well as before.

In fact, community-based policing has had differing levels of success (Rosenbaum, 1994). At the heart of the concept is neighborhood team policing, which involves the long-term assignment of officers to a particular area. This strategy allows officers to make a commitment to an area and to assume a broader level of authority in providing policing that is more sensitive to community needs. Neighborhood team programs have not been embraced by many police managers, however, who see the decentralization that is associated with them as limiting their control over their officers (Scheingold, 1984: 134). In addition, aggressive patrol tactics used in crime control may diminish police rapport with the public, thereby undermining the effectiveness of community-based policing (Scheingold, 1984: 135). Finally, their fear of being seen as indecisive may cause many officers to play the role of order restorer rather than that of peacemaker (Palenski, 1984: 35).

Police must look to community members to support them in their efforts to bring about order in the community. This support can take the form of self-help, as discussed earlier, or it can involve a kind of coproduction, whereby the police use community members as supporters of police activity (Krahn and Kennedy, 1985). Coproduction can range from passive responses, such as locking doors, to more active responses, such as participating in crime prevention programs or acting as informants (Skolnick, 1966). As Black (1980) points out, since the typical criminal act occurs at an unpredictable time and place, the police must rely on citizens (most often the victims of a crime) to involve them.

Providing resources for community-based policing (outside of community support) has proven to be problematic. Police budgets still depend on caseloads of calls for service and on crime rates. Community-based policing activity, directed as it is at problem solving and referral to outside programs, may create an impression of reduced activity, which, in turn, would suggest a need for lower budgets. The use of alternative programs also brings the police into conflict with other agencies, which makes it more difficult for them to define their role in the community and obtain the resources they need to realize their objectives.

341

*Summary and
Review of
Public Policy
Responses
to Crime*

Further, it is very difficult for some police agencies to remain apolitical when fighting for budget allocations and arguing for certain policing strategies. The lobbying by communities and by volunteers in community-based policing programs may make the police appear more politically active than local politicians would want them to be, thereby making their requests for more funds even more tenuous. Police chiefs are thus confronted with a plethora of community constraints. These constraints need to be overcome before the chiefs can show that they are fulfilling the objectives of compliance-based policing. In her discussion of policing programs in Britain, Shaffer (1980: 38) argues that improving police–community relations is a crucial first step. The members of a community must get to know the police as concerned and sympathetic individuals as well as controlling and disciplining law officers. Without communication and cooperation between the police and the public, she concludes, "policing in a democratic society is impossible."

SUMMARY
■ ■ ■

One response to crime is to see it as a public health problem that is best addressed by removing some of the major instruments that bring about injury (for example, guns). A second view advocates the mobilization of social institutions and resources as a means of empowering victims to defend themselves against criminal attack. Given the already formidable challenges that public health institutions face in dealing with diseases and injuries that originate from noncrime sources, our heavy reliance on the police to confront the crime problem is unlikely to change (at least in the near future).

We can look at prevention from the viewpoint of opportunity reduction or social development. Prevention can include a number of factors, ranging from target hardening to increased surveillance. It can also set as a priority the targeting of violence and offer ways in which violence can be averted. Situational prevention is based on two important assumptions. The first is that crime is most effectively prevented when we attend to the particular characteristics of the type of crime in question. The second is that, in most cases, we are dealing with a rational offender, who calculates such things as risks, benefits, and ease of accomplishment before committing a crime. It follows from this that raising the costs associated with crimes (which are largely opportunistic in nature) may reduce the frequency with which they occur. Neighborhood Watch and Block Watch programs assume that crime can be prevented by increasing surveillance and, by extension, the risk of detection and apprehension, as it is perceived by the potential offender.

In contrast to the other prevention strategies, crime prevention through social development focuses on the serious, repeat offender. A relatively small number of offenders may be responsible for a disproportionately large number of crimes. These individuals tend to have in common many social and demographic characteristics. The aim of crime prevention through social development is to correct the criminogenic social conditions that are assumed to be important causes of crime. The focus of the social development approach is on long-range outcomes that enhance social security and reduce crime incidence.

Combining opportunity reduction and social development is a new approach known as community-based policing. The police are shifting their attention from crime fighting (that is, deterrence-based policing) to compliance policing, which is more directly integrated into the community. The principal objective of compliance law enforcement is to secure conformity with law through systems that encourage community participation in defining and solving problems. The former emphasis on the detection and punishment of violators has given way to an emphasis on the need to provide incentives to individuals as a means of encouraging them to comply with the law.

Compliance-based policing recognizes the need to include the public in controlling social disorder, beyond merely reporting crime to the police. Bringing together a number of services within the community, as well as community members, can help to form a multipronged attack on crime involving re-education, mediation, opportunity removal, resource mobilization, the targeting of the roots of crime, and problem solving. Our success in controlling crime and diminishing the incidence of criminal events depends on our ability to understand where crime comes from and on our commitment to expend resources in broadening our responses to it.

QUESTIONS FOR REVIEW AND DISCUSSION
■ ■ ■

1. Why is there a popular tendency to think about "more police and more prisons" as the *obvious* solution to the crime problem?
2. What similarities are there in the ways in which American society approaches the problem of crime and the problem of disease?
3. With reference to the community in which you reside, what are some of the implications for crime prevention of Felson's analysis of changing urban forms?
4. How do policies of situational prevention emerge quite logically from theoretical ideas that emphasize "rational offenders" and "social control"?
5. What does it mean to say that "there is much more to community-based policing than law enforcement"?
6. According to critics, what are some of the more important limitations of traditional responses that assign the central responsibility for crime control to the criminal justice system?

References

Abadinsky, H. 1987. *Organized Crime,* 2nd ed. Chicago: Nelson-Hall.

Adler, F. 1975. *Sisters in Crime.* New York: McGraw-Hill.

Agnew, R. S. 1992. "Foundation for a General Strain Theory of Crime and Delinquency." *Criminology* 30: 47–87.

———. 1990. "The Origins of Delinquent Events: An Examination of Offender Accounts." *Journal of Research in Crime and Delinquency* 27(3): 267–294.

———. 1985. "A Revised Strain Theory of Delinquency." *Social Forces* 64(1): 151–167.

Agnew, R. S., and S. Huguley. 1989. "Adolescent Violence Toward Parents." *Journal of Marriage and the Family* 51: 699–711.

Agnew, R. S., and A. R. Peters. 1986. "The Techniques of Neutralization: An Analysis of Predisposing and Situational Factors." *Criminal Justice and Behavior* 13: 81–97.

Agnew, R. S., and D. M. Peterson. 1989. "Leisure and Delinquency." *Social Problems* 36(4): 332–350.

Agnew, R. S., and H. R. White. 1992. "An Empirical Test of General Strain Theory." *Criminology* 30: 475–499.

Akers, R. L. 1985. *Deviant Behavior: A Social Learning Approach.* Belmont, Calif.: Wadsworth.

Albanese, J. 1989. *Organized Crime in America,* 2nd ed. Cincinnati, Ohio: Anderson.

Albini, J. L. 1971. *The American Mafia: Genesis of a Legend.* New York: Irvington.

Allan, E. A., and D. J. Steffensmeier. 1989. "Youth, Underemployment and Property Crime: Differential Effects of Job Availability and Job Quality on Juvenile and Young Adult Arrest Rates." *American Sociological Review* 54: 107–123.

Amir, M. 1971. *Patterns of Forcible Rape.* Chicago: University of Chicago Press.

Anderson, J., and L. Whitten. 1976. "Auto Maker Shuns Safer Gas Tank." *The Washington Post* (December 30), p. B7.

Arneklev, B. J., H. G. Grasmick, C. R. Tittle, and R. J. Bursik. 1993. "Low Self-Control and Imprudent Behavior." *Journal of Quantitative Criminology* 9(3): 225–247.

Arnold, B. L., and J. Hagan. 1992. "Careers of Misconduct: Prosecuted Professional Deviance Among Lawyers." *American Sociological Review* 57(6): 771–780.

Bachman, R. 1994. *Violence Against Women.* Washington, D.C.: U.S. Department of Justice, Bureau of Justice Statistics (NCJ-145325).

———. 1992. *Elderly Victims.* Washington, D.C.: Bureau of Justice Statistics.

Baldassare, M. 1986. "The Elderly and Fear of Crime." *Sociology and Social Research* 70: 218–221.

Balkin, S. 1979. "Victimization Rates, Safety and Fear of Crime." *Social Problems* 26(3): 343–358.

Bandura, A. A., D. Ross, and S. A. Ross. 1963. "Imitation of Film-Mediated Aggressive Models." *Journal of Abnormal and Social Psychology* 66: 3–11.

Barnhorst, R., S. Barnhorst, and K. L. Clarke. 1992. *Criminal Law and the Canadian Criminal Code,* 2nd ed. Toronto: McGraw-Hill/Ryerson.

Baron, S. 1989. "The Canadian West Coast Punk Subculture: A Field Study." *Canadian Journal of Sociology* 14(3): 289–316.

Bartol, C. R. 1980. *Criminal Behavior: A Psychological Approach.* Englewood Cliffs, N.J.: Prentice-Hall.

Bastian, L. D., and B. M. Taylor. 1991 (September). *School Crime: A National Crime Victimization Survey Report.* Washington, D.C.: U.S. Department of Justice.

Baumer, T. L. 1978. "Research on Fear of Crime in the United States." *Victimology* 3: 254–264.

Baunach, P. J. 1990. "State Prisons and Inmates: The Census and Survey." In D. L. Mackenzie, P. J. Baunach, and R. R. Roberg (eds.), *Measuring Crime: Large-Scale, Long-Range Efforts.* Albany: State University of New York.

Bayley, D. H. 1988. "Community Policing: A Report from the Devil's Advocate." In J. R. Greene and D. Mastrofski (eds.), *Community Policing: Rhetoric or Reality.* New York: Praeger.

———. 1986. "The Tactical Choices of Police Patrol Officers." *Journal of Criminal Justice* 14: 329–348.

———. 1985. *Patterns of Policing: A Comparative International Analysis.* New Brunswick, N.J.: Rutgers University Press.

Bechhofer, L., and A. Parrot. 1991. "What Is Acquaintance Rape?" In A. Parrot and L. Bechhofer (eds.), *Acquaintance Rape: The Hidden Crime.* New York: John Wiley.

Becker, H. S. 1963. *Outsiders: Studies in the Sociology of Deviance.* New York: Free Press.

Bell, D. 1953. "Crime as an American Way of Life." *The Antioch Review* 13 (June): 131–154.

Bell, D. J. 1987. "The Victim–Offender Relationship: A Determinant Factor in Police Domestic Dispute Dispositions." *Marriage and Family Review* 12(1/2): 87–102.

Bennett, T. 1989. "Burglars' Choice of Targets." In D. J. Evans and D. T. Herbert (eds.), *The Geography of Crime.* London: Routledge.

Bennett, T., and R. Wright. 1984. *Burglars on Burglary.* Brookfield, Vt.: Gower.

Benson, D., C. Charlton, and F. Goodhart. 1992. "Acquaintance Rape on Campus: A Literature Review." *College Health* 40 (January): 157–165.

Benson, M. L. 1985. "Denying the Guilty Mind: Accounting for Involvement in a White-Collar Crime." *Criminology* 23(4): 583–607.

Benson, M. L., and E. Moore. 1992. "Are White Collar and Common Offenders the Same? An Empirical and Theoretical Critique of a Recently Proposed General Theory of Crime." *Journal of Research in Crime and Delinquency* 29(3): 251–272.

Bequai, A. 1987. *Technocrimes.* Lexington, Mass.: D. C. Heath.

Bernard, T. J. 1981. "The Distinction Between Conflict and Radical Criminology." *Journal of Criminal Law and Criminology* 72(1): 362–379.

Best, J. 1990. *Threatened Children.* Chicago: University of Chicago Press.

————. 1988. "Missing Children: Misleading Statistics." *The Public Interest* 92 (Summer): 84–92.

Birkbeck, C., and G. LaFree. 1993. "The Situational Analysis of Crime and Deviance." *Annual Review of Sociology* 19: 113–137.

Black, D. J. 1983. "Crime as Social Control." *American Sociological Review* 48 (February): 34–45.

————. 1980. *The Manners and Customs of the Police.* New York: Academic Press.

————. 1976. *The Behavior of Law.* New York: Academic Press.

————. 1971. "The Social Organization of Arrest." *Stanford Law Review* 23: 1087–1111.

————. 1970. "Production of Crime Rates." *American Sociological Review* 35: 733–747.

Black, D. J., and A. J. Reiss. 1967. "Patterns of Behavior in Police and Citizen Transactions." In *U.S. President's Commission on Law Enforcement and the Administration of Justice, Studies in Crime and Law Enforcement in Major Metropolitan Areas, Field Surveys III,* Vol. 2. Washington, D.C.: U.S. Government Printing Office.

Blau, J. R., and P. M. Blau. 1982. "The Cost of Inequality: Metropolitan Structure and Violent Crime." *American Sociological Review* 4 (February): 114–129.

Block, C. R., and R. L. Block. 1993. *Street Gang Crime in Chicago.* Washington, D.C.: U.S. Department of Justice.

Block, C. R., and R. L. Block. 1984. "Crime Definition, Crime Measurement, and Victim Surveys." *Journal of Social Issues* 40(1): 137–160.

Block, R. 1974. "Why Notify the Police?: The Victim's Decision to Notify the Police of an Assault." *Criminology* 11(4): 555–569.

Block, R., M. Felson, and C. R. Block. 1984. "Crime Victimization Rates for Incumbents of 246 Occupations." *Sociology and Social Research* 69(3): 442–451.

Blok, A. 1975. *The Mafia of a Sicilian Village, 1860–1960.* New York: Harper & Row.

Blumstein, A., J. Cohen, and D. P. Farrington. 1988a. "Criminal Career Research: Its Value for Criminology." *Criminology* 26(1): 1–36.

————. 1988b. "Longitudinal and Criminal Career Research: Further Clarifications." *Criminology* 26(1): 57–74.

Blumstein, A., J. Cohen, and R. Rosenfeld. 1992. "The UCR-NCS Relationship Revisited: A Reply to Menard." *Criminology* 30(1): 115–124.

Bockman, L. S. 1991. "Interest, Ideology and Claims-Making Activity." *Sociological Inquiry* 61(4): 452–470.

Bograd, M. 1988. "How Battered Women and Abusive Men Account for Domestic Violence: Excuses, Justifications or Explanations." In G. T. Hotaling, D. Finkelhor, J. T. Kirkpatrick, and M. A. Straus (eds.), *Coping with Family Violence.* Newbury Park, Calif.: Sage.

Booth, A., D. R. Johnson, and H. M. Choldin. 1977. "Correlates of City Crime Rates: Victimization Surveys Versus Official Statistics." *Social Problems* 25(2): 187–197.

Boritch, H. 1992. "Gender and Criminal Court Outcomes: An Historical Analysis." *Criminology* 30(3): 293–325.

Borofsky, G. L., G. E. Stollak, and L. A. Messe. 1971. "Sex Differences in Bystander Reactions to Physical Assault." *Journal of Experimental Social Psychology* 7: 313–318.

Bottomley, A. K., and K. Coleman. 1981. *Understanding Crime Rates: Police and Public Roles in the Production of Official Statistics.* Farnborough, U.K.: Gower.

Bottomley, A. K., and K. Pease. 1986. *Crime and Punishment—Interpreting the Data.* Philadelphia: Open University Press.

Bowers, W. 1993. "Capital Punishment and Contemporary Values: People's Misgivings and the Court's Misperceptions." *Law and Society Review* 27(1): 157–175.

Box, S. 1981. *Deviance, Reality, and Society.* London: Holt, Rinehart & Winston.

Braithwaite, J. 1989. *Crime, Shame and Reintegration.* Cambridge: Cambridge University Press.

———. 1981. "The Myth of Social Class and Criminality Reconsidered." *American Sociological Review* 46 (February): 36–57.

Brantingham, P. J., and P. L Brantingham. 1984. *Patterns in Crime.* New York: Macmillan.

Brantingham, P. J., and F. L. Faust. 1976. "A Conceptual Model of Crime Prevention." *Crime and Delinquency* 22: 284–296.

Brantingham, P. L. 1989. "Crime Prevention: The North American Experience." In D. J. Evans and D. T. Herbert (eds.), *The Geography of Crime.* London: Routledge.

Brantingham, P. L., and P. J. Brantingham. 1990. "Situational Crime Prevention in Practice." *Canadian Journal of Criminology* 32(1): 17–40.

Brillon, Y. 1985. "Public Opinion About the Penal System: A Cynical View of Criminal Justice." In D. Gibson and J. K. Baldwin (eds.), *Law in a Cynical Society? Opinion and Law in the 1980s.* Calgary: Carswell.

Bromley, D. G. 1991. "Satanism: The New Cult Scare." In J. T. Richardson, J. Best, and D. G. Bromley (eds.), *The Satanism Scare.* New York: Aldine de Gruyter.

Browne, A. 1987. *When Battered Women Kill.* New York: Free Press.

Browne, A., and K. Williams. 1989. "Exploring the Effect of Resource Availability and the Likelihood of Female-Perpetrated Homicides." *Law and Society Review* 23(1): 75–94.

Brunvand, J. H. 1993. *The Baby Train.* New York: Norton.

———. 1989. *Curses! Broiled Again!* New York: Norton.

———. 1986. *The Mexican Pet.* New York: Norton.

———. 1984. *The Choking Doberman and Other "New" Urban Legends.* New York: Norton.

———. 1981. *The Vanishing Hitchhiker: American Urban Legends and Their Meaning.* New York: Norton.

Burgess, A. W., L. L. Holmstrom, and M. P. McCausland. 1977. "Child Sexual Assault by a Family Member: Decisions Following Disclosure." *Victimology: An International Journal* 2(2): 236–250.

Burke, P., J. E. Stets, and M. A. Pirog-Good. 1989. "Gender Identity, Self-Esteem, and Physical and Sexual Abuse in Dating Relationships." In J. Stets and M. Pirog-Good (eds.), *Violence in Dating Relationships,* pp. 72–93. New York: Praeger.

Bursik, R. J., Jr., and H. G. Grasmick. 1993. *Neighborhoods and Crime: The Dimensions of Effective Community Control.* New York: Lexington Books.

Burt, M. R., and B. L. Katz. 1985. "Rape, Robbery and Burglary: Responses to Actual and Feared Criminal Victimization with Special Focus on Women and the Elderly." *Victimology* 10: 325–358.

Business and Health. 1994. "Helping to Eliminate Stress in the Workplace." Vol. 12(4) (Depression Supplement): 28–31.

Cain, M., and K. Kulscar. 1981–82. "Thinking Disputes: An Essay on the Origins of the Dispute Industry." *Law and Society Review* 16(3): 375–402.

Calavita, K., and H. N. Pontell. 1991. "'Other People's Money' Revisited: Collective Embezzlement in the Savings and Loan Insurance Industries." *Social Problems* 38(1): 94–112.

Cantor, D., and K. C. Land. 1985. "Unemployment and Crime Rates in the Post–World War II United States: A Theoretical and Empirical Analysis." *American Sociological Review* 50 (June): 317–332.

Carter, D. L. 1985. "Hispanic Perceptions of Police Performance: An Empirical Assessment." *Journal of Criminal Justice* 13: 487–500.

Castro, M. T., and L. Bumpass. 1989. "Trends in Marital Disruption." *Demography* 26: 37–52.

Cater, J., and T. Jones. 1989. "Crime and Disorder." In J. Cater and T. Jones (eds.), *Social Geography—An Introduction to Contemporary Issues*. New York: Routledge, Chapman & Hall.

Chaiken, J., and M. Chaiken. 1982. *Varieties of Criminal Behavior*. Rand Report r-2814-NIJ. Santa Monica, Calif.: Rand Corporation.

Chambliss, W. 1975. "On the Paucity of Original Research on Organized Crime: A Footnote to Galliher and Cain." *The American Sociologist* 10: 36–39.

Chibnall, S. 1977. *Law-and-Order News*. London: Tavistock.

Chicago Tribune. 1993. "Driveby Shooting at Park Pool Leaves 1 Dead, 4 Hurt in Cicero." (July 21), Section 2, p. 1.

Chilton, R. 1991. "Images of Crime: Crime Statistics and Their Impact." In J. F. Sheley (ed.), *Criminology: A Contemporary Handbook*, pp. 45–65. Belmont, Calif.: Wadsworth.

Chiricos, T. G. 1987. "Rates of Crime and Unemployment: An Analysis of Aggregate Research Evidence." *Social Problems* 34(2): 187–242.

Clark, R. D. 1988. "Celerity and Specific Deterrence: A Look at the Evidence." *Canadian Journal of Criminology* 30(2): 109–120.

Clarke, R. V. 1992. "Introduction." In R. V. Clarke (ed.), *Situational Crime Prevention*. Albany, N.Y.: Harrow & Heston.

Clarke, R. V., P. Ekblom, M. Hough, and P. Mayhew. 1985. "Elderly Victims of Crime and Exposure to Risk." *Journal of Criminal Justice* 23: 1–9.

Clarke, R. V., and M. Felson. 1993. "Introduction: Criminology, Routine Activity, and Rational Choice." In R. V. Clarke and M. Felson (eds.), *Routine Activity and Rational Choice*. New Brunswick, N.J.: Transaction.

Cloward, R. A. 1959. "Illegitimate Means, Anomie, and Deviant Behavior." The Bobbs-Merrill Reprint Series in the Social Science. Reprinted by permission of *American Sociological Review* 24 (April): 164–176.

Cloward, R. A., and L. E. Ohlin. 1960. *Delinquency and Opportunity*. New York: Free Press.

Cohen, A. K. 1955. *Delinquent Boys: The Culture of the Gang*. New York: Free Press.

Cohen, L. E., and D. Cantor. 1981. "Residential Burglary in the United States: Lifestyle and Demographic Factors Associated with the Probability of Victimization." *Journal of Research in Crime and Delinquency* 18(1): 113–127.

Cohen, L. E., D. Cantor, and J. R. Kleugel. 1981. "Robbery Victimization in the U.S.: An Analysis of a Non-Random Event." *Social Science Quarterly* 62(4): 644–657.

Cohen, L. E., and M. Felson. 1979. "Social Change and Crime Rate Trends: A Routine Activity Approach." *American Sociological Review* 44 (August): 588–608.

Cohen, L. E., J. R. Kluegel, and K. C. Land. 1981. "Social Inequality and Predatory Criminal Victimization: An Exposition and Test of a Formal Theory." *American Sociological Review* 46 (October): 505–524.

Cohen, S. 1972. *Folk Devils and Moral Panics*. London: MacGibbon & Kee.

Coleman, J. W. 1991. "Respectable Crime." In J. F. Sheley (ed.), *Criminology: A Contemporary Handbook,* pp. 219–239. Belmont, Calif.: Wadsworth.

———. 1987. "Toward an Integrated Theory of White-Collar Crime." *American Journal of Sociology* 93(2): 406–439.

Coleman, W. 1994. *The Criminal Elite,* 3rd ed. New York: St. Martin's Press.

Collins, J. J., B. G. Cox, and P. A. Langan. 1987. "Job Activities and Personal Crime Victimization: Implications for Theory." *Social Science Research* 16: 345–360.

Conklin, J. E. 1975. *The Impact of Crime.* New York: Macmillan.

Cook, F. L., and W. G. Skogan. 1990. "Agenda Setting and the Rise and Fall of Policy Issues: The Case of Criminal Victimization of the Elderly." *Environment and Planning C: Government and Policy* 8: 395–415.

Cook, P. J. 1977. "Punishment and Crime: A Critique of Current Findings Concerning the Preventive Effects of Punishment." *Law and Contemporary Problems* 41(1): 164–204.

Corcoran, T. 1993. "Media an Accomplice in Pepsi Hoax." *Globe and Mail* (June 18), p. B2.

Cornish, D. B., and R. V. Clarke. 1986. *The Reasoning Criminal.* New York: Springer-Verlag.

———. 1986. "Introduction." In D. B. Cornish and R.V. Clarke (eds.), *The Reasoning Criminal: Rational Choice Perspectives on Offending.* New York: Springer-Verlag.

Cornwall, A., and H. N. Bawden. 1992. "Reading Disabilities and Aggression: A Critical Review." *Journal of Learning Disabilities* 25(5): 281–288.

Cressey, D. R. 1969. *Theft of the Nation.* New York: Harper & Row.

Crimebeat. 1992. "Crime Tours." (January): 29–31.

Croall, H. 1987. "Who Is the White-Collar Criminal?" *British Journal of Criminology* 29(2): 157–174.

Cromwell, P. F., J. N. Olson, and D. W. Avary. 1991. *Breaking and Entering: An Ethnographic Analysis of Burglary.* Newbury Park, Calif.: Sage.

Crystal, S. 1988. "Elder Abuse: The Latest Crisis." *The Public Interest* 88: 56–66.

Cullen, F. T., B. G. Link, and C. W. Polanzi. 1982. "The Seriousness of Crime Revisited: Have Attitudes Towards White-Collar Crime Changed?" *Criminology* 20(1): 83–102.

Culliver, C., and R. Sigler. 1991. "The Relationship Between Learning Disabilities and Juvenile Delinquency." *International Journal of Adolescence and Youth* 3(1–2): 117–128.

Cumberbatch, G., and A. Beardsworth. 1976. "Criminals, Victims and Mass Communications." In E. C. Viano (ed.), *Victims and Society.* Washington, D.C.: Visage Press.

Currie, E. 1985. *Confronting Crime: An American Challenge.* New York: Pantheon Books.

Cusson, M. 1993. "Situational Deterrence: Fear During the Criminal Event." In R. V. Clarke (ed.), *Crime Prevention Studies, Volume 1.* Monsey, N.Y.: Criminal Justice Press.

Daly, M., and M. Wilson. 1988. *Homicide.* Chicago: Aldine de Gruyter.

Davis, N. J. 1988. "Battered Women: Implications for Social Control." *Contemporary Crises* 12: 345–372.

Davis, P. W. 1991. "Stranger Intervention into Child Punishment in Public Places." *Social Problems* 38(2): 227–246.

Dechenes, E. P. 1990. "Longitudinal Research Designs." In K. L. Kempf (ed.), *Measurement Issues in Criminology,* pp. 152–166. New York: Springer-Verlag.

DeKeseredy, W. S. 1988. *Woman Abuse in Dating Relationships: A Critical Evaluation of Research and Theory*. Toronto: Canadian Scholar's Press.

DeKeseredy, W. S., and R. Hinch. 1991. *Woman Abuse: Sociological Perspectives*. Ottawa: Thompson Educational Publishing.

Desrocher, F. 1991. "Tearoom Trade: A Law Enforcement Problem." *Canadian Journal of Criminology* 33(1): 1–21.

DiIulio, J. J. 1989. "The Impact of Inner-City Crime." *Public Interest* 96: 28–46.

Dominick, J. R. 1978. "Crime and Law Enforcement in the Mass Media." In C. Winick (ed.), *Deviance and Mass Media*. Beverly Hills, Calif.: Sage.

Doob, A. N. 1982. "The Role of Mass Media in Creating Exaggerated Levels of Fear of Being the Victim of a Violent Crime." In P. Stringer (ed.), *Confronting Social Issues: Applications of Social Psychology*. Toronto: Academic Press.

Doob, A. N., and G. E. MacDonald. 1976. "Television Viewing and Fear of Victimization: Is the Relationship Causal?" *Journal of Personality and Social Psychology* 37: 170–179.

Dorfman, A. 1984. "The Criminal Mind." *Science Digest* 92(10): 44–47, 98.

Douglas, J. D., and F. C. Waskler. 1982. *The Sociology of Deviance*. Boston: Little, Brown.

Dowie, M. 1977. "Pinto Madness." *Mother Jones* 2 (September): 18–32. Reprinted in J. Skolnick and E. Currie (eds.), *Crisis in American Institutions*. 1982. Boston: Little Brown.

DuBow, F., E. McCabe, and G. Kaplan. 1979. *Reactions to Crime: A Critical Review of the Literature*. Washington, D.C.: U.S. Department of Justice.

Durkheim, E. 1964. *The Rules of Sociological Method*. New York: Free Press. (Orig. pub. in 1938.)

———. 1933. *The Division of Labor in Society*. Trans. G. Simpson. Glencoe, Ill.: Free Press.

Dutton, D. G. 1987. "The Criminal Justice Response to Wife Assault." *Law and Human Behavior* 11(3): 189–206.

Dutton, D., S. Hart, L. W. Kennedy, and K. Williams. 1992. "Arrest and the Reduction of Repeat Wife Assault." In E. Buzawa and C. Buzawa (eds.), *Domestic Violence: The Changing Criminal Justice Response*. Westport, Conn.: Greenwood Press.

Elliott, D. S., and S. S. Ageton. 1980. "Reconciling Race and Class Differences in Self-Reported and Official Estimates of Delinquency." *American Sociological Review* 45 (February): 95–110.

Ellis, D. 1984. "Video Arcades, Youth and Trouble." *Youth and Society* 16(1): 47–65.

Ellis, D., A. Choi, and C. Blaus. 1993. "Injuries to Police Officers Attending Domestic Disturbances: An Empirical Study." *Canadian Journal of Criminology* 35(2): 149–168.

Ellis, L. 1982. "Genetics and Criminal Behavior." *Criminology* 20(1): 43–66.

Ellsworth, P., and S. Gross. 1994. "Hardening of the Attitudes: Americans' Views on the Death Penalty." *Journal of Social Issues* 50(2): 19–52.

Ericson, R. V. 1991. "Mass Media, Crime, Law, and Justice: An Institutional Approach." *The British Journal of Criminology* 31(3): 219–249.

———. 1982. *Reproducing Order: A Study of Police Patrol Work*. Toronto: University of Toronto Press.

———. 1981. *Making Crime: A Study of Detective Work*. Toronto: Butterworths.

Ericson, R. V., P. M. Baranek, and J. B. L. Chan. 1991. *Representing Order: Crime, Law, and Justice in the News Media*. Toronto: University of Toronto Press.

―――. 1989. *Negotiating Control: A Study of News Sources*. Toronto: University of Toronto Press.

―――. 1987. *Visualizing Deviance*. Toronto: University of Toronto Press.

European and North American Conference on Urban Safety and Crime Prevention. 1989. *Final Declaration*. Montreal.

Evans, D. J. 1989. "Geographical Analyses of Residential Burglary." In D. J. Evans and D. T. Herbert (eds.), *The Geography of Crime*. London: Routledge.

Fagan, J., and S. Wexler. 1987. "Family Origins of Violent Delinquents." *Criminology* 25: 643–669.

Farberman, H. A. 1975. "A Criminogenic Market Structure: The Automobile Industry." *Sociological Quarterly* 16: 438–457.

Farrington, D. P. 1989. "Implications of Longitudinal Studies for Social Prevention." *Canadian Journal of Criminology* 31(4): 453–463.

Farrington, D. P., S. Bowen, A. Buckle, T. Burns-Howell, and J. Burrows. 1993. "An Experiment on the Prevention of Shoplifting." In R. V. Clarke (ed.), *Crime Prevention Studies*, pp. 93–119. Monsey N.Y.: Criminal Justice Press.

Fattah, E. A. 1993. "The Rational Choice/Opportunity Perspectives as a Vehicle for Integrating Criminological and Victimological Theories." In R. V. Clarke and M. Felson (eds.), *Routine Activity and Rational Choice*, pp. 225–228. New Brunswick, N.J.: Transaction.

―――. 1991. *Understanding Criminal Victimization*. Scarborough, Ont.: Prentice-Hall.

Fattah, E. A., and V. F. Sacco. 1989. *Crime and Victimization of the Elderly*. New York: Springer-Verlag.

Feld, S. L., and M. A. Straus. 1990. "Escalation and Desistance from Wife Assault in Marriage." In M. A. Straus and R. J. Gelles (eds.), *Physical Violence in American Families: Risk Factors and Adaptations to Violence in 8,145 Families*. New Brunswick, N.J.: Transaction.

Felson, M. 1994. *Crime and Everyday Life*. Newbury Park, Calif.: Pine Forge Press.

―――. 1992. "Routine Activities and Crime Prevention." *Studies in Crime and Crime Prevention Annual Review* 1(1): 30–34.

―――. 1987. "Routine Activities and Crime Prevention in the Developing Metropolis." *Criminology* 25(4): 911–931.

―――. 1986. "Linking Criminal Choices, Routine Activities, Informal Control, and Criminal Outcomes." In D. B. Cornish and R. V. Clarke (eds.), *The Reasoning Criminal*. New York: Springer-Verlag.

Felson R. B., W. F. Baccaglini, and S. A. Ribner. 1985. "Accounting for Criminal Violence: A Comparison of Official and Offender Versions of the Crime." *Sociology and Social Research* 70(1): 93–101.

Ferraro, K. J. 1989. "Policing Woman Battering." *Social Problems* 36(1): 61–74.

Ferraro, K. J., and J. M. Johnson. 1983. "How Women Experience Battering: The Process of Victimization." *Social Problems* 30: 325–335.

Figlio, R. M. 1990. "Measurement in Criminology and Criminal Justice: A Brief 20-Year Retrospective." In D. L. MacKenzie, D. J. Baunach, and R. R. Roberg (eds.), *Measuring Crime: Large-Scale, Long-Range Efforts*. Albany: State University of New York Press.

Finkelhor, D., and J. Dzuiba-Leatherman. 1993. "The Victimization of Children." Paper presented at the meetings of the American Society of Criminology, Phoenix, October 1993.

Finkelhor, D., G. T. Hotaling, and A. Sedlak. 1990. *Missing, Abducted, Runaway, and Thrownaway Children in America: First Report.* Washington, D.C.: Juvenile Justice Clearinghouse.

Fischer, C. S. 1981. "The Public and Private Worlds of City Life." *American Sociological Review* 46 (June): 306–316.

———. 1976. *The Urban Experience.* New York: Harcourt Brace Jovanovich.

———. 1975. "The Effect of Urban Life on Traditional Values." *Social Forces* 53: 420–432.

Fishman, M. 1981. "Police News: Constructing an Image of Crime." *Urban Life* 9(4): 371–394.

———. 1978. "Crime Waves as Ideology." *Social Problems* 25(5): 531–543.

Flowers, R. B. 1989. *Demographics and Criminality: The Characteristics of Crime in America.* New York: Greenwood Press.

Freeman, R. B. 1983. "Crime and Unemployment." In J. Q. Wilson (ed.), *Crime and Public Policy.* San Francisco: ICS Press.

Freudenheim, M. 1987. "Business and Health." *New York Times* (May 26).

Frieze, I. H., and A. Browne. 1989. "Violence in Marriage." In L. Ohlin and M. Tonry (eds.), *Family Violence.* Chicago: University of Chicago Press.

Frinell, D. E., E. Dahlstrom III, and D. A. Johnson. 1980. "A Public Education Program Designed to Increase the Accuracy and Incidence of Citizens' Reports of Suspicious and Criminal Activities." *Journal of Police Science and Administration* 8(2): 160–165.

Furstenberg, F. 1971. "Public Reactions to Crime in the Streets." *The American Scholar* 40: 601–610.

Gabor, T. 1990a. "Crime Prevention: The Agenda." *Canadian Journal of Criminology* 32(1): 1–7.

———. 1990b. "Crime Displacement and Situational Prevention: Toward the Development of Some Principles." *Canadian Journal of Criminology* 32(1): 41–73.

Gabor, T., and A. Normandeau. 1989. "Armed Robbery: Highlights of a Canadian Study." *Canadian Police College Journal* 13(4).

Galliher, J. F., and J. A. Cain. 1974. "Citation Support for the Mafia Myth in Criminology Textbooks." *The American Sociologist* 9 (May): 68–74.

Gans, H. 1962. *The Urban Villagers.* New York: Free Press.

Garofalo, J. 1981a. "Crime and the Mass Media: A Selective Review of Research." *Journal of Research in Crime and Delinquency* (July): 319–350.

———. 1981b. "The Fear of Crime: Causes and Consequences." *The Journal of Criminal Law and Criminology* 72: 839–857.

Garofalo, J., and M. McLeod. 1988. *Improving the Use and Effectiveness of Neighborhood Watch Programs.* Washington, D.C.: U.S. Department of Justice.

Garofalo, J., L. Siegel, and J. Laub. 1987. "School-Related Victimizations Among Adolescents: An Analysis of National Crime Survey (NCS) Narratives." *Journal of Quantitative Criminology* 3(4): 321–338.

Garofalo, R. 1914. *Criminology.* Boston: Little, Brown.

Gartner, R., and B. McCarthy. 1991. "The Social Distribution of Femicide in Urban Canada, 1921–1988." *Law and Society Review* 25(2): 287–311.

Gastil, R. D. 1971. "Homicide and a Regional Culture of Violence." *American Sociological Review* 36 (June): 412–427.

Gates, L. B., and W. M. Rohe. 1987. "Fear and Reactions to Crime: A Revised Model." *Urban Affairs Quarterly* 22: 425–453.

Gelles, R. J., and M. A. Straus. 1990. "The Medical and Psychological Costs of Family Violence." In M. A. Straus and R. J. Gelles (eds.), *Physical Violence in American Families: Risk Factors and Adaptations to Violence in 8,145 Families*. New Brunswick, N.J.: Transaction.

———. 1988. *Intimate Violence*. New York: Simon & Schuster.

Geran, L. 1992. "Occupational Stress." *Canadian Social Trends* 26 (Autumn): 14–17.

Gibbons, D. C. 1988. "Some Critical Observations on Criminal Types and Criminal Careers." *Criminal Justice and Behavior* 15: 8–23.

Gibbs, J. P. 1981. *Norms, Deviance, and Social Control: Conceptual Matters*. New York: Elsevier.

———. 1966. "Conceptions of Deviant Behavior: The Old and the New." *Pacific Sociological Review* 9: 9–14.

Gibbs, J. P., and M. L. Erikson. 1976. "Crime Rates of American Cities in an Ecological Context." *American Journal of Sociology* 82(3): 605–620.

Gilbert, N. 1991. "The Phantom Epidemic of Sexual Assault." *The Public Interest* 103 (Spring): 54–65.

Gillespie, C. 1989. *Justifiable Homicide: Battered Women, Self Defense, and the Law*. Columbus: Ohio State University Press.

Gillespie, D. L., and A. Leffler. 1987. "The Politics of Research Methodology in Claims-Making Activities: Social Science and Sexual Harassment." *Social Problems* 34(5): 490–501.

Gilsinan, J. F. 1990. *Criminology and Public Policy: An Introduction*. Englewood Cliffs, N.J.: Prentice-Hall.

———. 1989. "They Is Clowning Tough: 911 and the Social Construction of Reality." *Criminology* 27(2): 329–344.

Giordano, P. C., S. A. Cernkovich, and M. D. Pugh. 1986. "Friendships and Delinquency." *American Journal of Sociology* 91(5): 1170–1202.

Glick, P. C. 1990. "American Families: As They Are and Were." *Sociology and Social Research* 74(3): 139–145.

The Globe and Mail. 1993. "Westray Charges Thrown Out." (July 21), p. A1.

Goff, C., and N. Nason-Clark. 1989. "The Seriousness of Crime in Fredericton, New Brunswick: Perceptions Toward White-Collar Crime." *Canadian Journal of Criminology* 31(1): 19–34.

Goffman, E. 1963. *Stigma: Notes on the Management of Spoiled Identity*. Englewood Cliffs, N.J.: Prentice-Hall.

———. 1959. *The Presentation of Self in Everyday Life*. Garden City, N.J.: Doubleday.

Golant, S. M. 1984. "Factors Influencing the Nighttime Activity of Old Persons in Their Community." *Journal of Gerontology* 39: 485–491.

Gold, M. 1970. *Delinquent Behavior in an American City*. Belmont, Calif.: Brooks/Cole.

Goldstein, H. 1990. *Problem-Oriented Policing*. Philadelphia: Temple University Press.

Gondolf, E. W., and J. R. McFerron. 1989. "Handling Battering Men and Police Action in Wife Abuse Cases." *Criminal Justice and Behavior* 16: 429–439.

Goode, E., and N. Ben-Yehuda. 1994. *Moral Panics: The Social Construction of Deviance*. Oxford: Blackwell.

Goodstein, L., and R. L. Shotland. 1982. "The Crime Causes Crime Model: A Critical Review of the Relationship Between Fear of Crime, Bystander Surveillance, and Changes in the Crime Rate." *Victimology* 5(2–4): 133–151.

Gordon, M. T., and L. Heath. 1981. "The News Business, Crime and Fear." In D. A. Lewis (ed.), *Reactions to Crime*. Beverly Hills, Calif.: Sage.

Gordon, M. T., and S. Riger. 1989. *The Female Fear.* New York: Free Press.

Gorelick, S. M. 1989. "'Join Our War': The Construction of Ideology in a Newspaper Crimefighting Campaign." *Crime and Delinquency* 35(3): 421–436.

Gottfredson, M. R. 1984. "Victims of Crime: The Dimensions of Risk." A Home Office Research and Planning Unit Report. London: HMSO Books.

Gottfredson, M. R., and D. Gottfredson. 1988. *Decisionmaking in Criminal Justice,* 2nd ed. New York: Plenum.

Gottfredson, M. R., and T. Hirschi. 1990. *A General Theory of Crime.* Stanford, Calif.: Stanford University Press.

———. 1988. "Science, Public Policy and the Career Paradigm." *Criminology* 26: 37–55.

———. 1986. "The True Value of Lambda Would Appear to Be Zero: An Essay on Career Criminals, Criminal Careers, Selective Incapacitation, Cohort Studies, and Related Topics." *Criminology* 24 (2): 213–234.

Gould, L. C. 1989. "Crime, Criminality, and Criminal Events." Paper presented at the Annual Meetings of the American Society of Criminology, Reno, Nevada.

Gove, W. R. 1975. *The Labelling of Deviance: Evaluating a Perspective.* New York: Sage.

Gove, W. R., M. Hughes, and M. Geerken. 1985. "Are Uniform Crime Reports a Valid Indicator of the Index Crimes? An Affirmative Answer with Minor Modifications." *Criminology* 23(3): 451–501.

Graber, D. A. 1980. *Crime News and the Public.* New York: Praeger.

Graham, J. 1990. *Crime Prevention Strategies in Europe and North America.* Helsinki: Helsinki Institute for Crime Prevention and Control.

Gramling, R., C. Forsyth, and J. Fewell. 1988. "Crime and Economic Activity: A Research Note." *Sociological Spectrum* 8: 187–195.

Gray, H. 1989. "Popular Music as a Social Problem: A Social History of the Claims Against Popular Music." In J. Best (ed.), *Images of Issues.* New York: Aldine de Gruyter.

Greenberg, D. F. 1992. "Comparing Criminal Career Models." *Criminology* 30(1): 141–147.

Greenberg, M. S., R. B. Ruback, and D. R. Westcott. 1982. "Decision Making by Crime Victims: A Multimethod Approach." *Law and Society Review* 17: 47–84.

Gurr, T. R. 1980. "Development and Decay: Their Impact on Public Order in Western History." In J. Inciardi and C. E. Faupel (eds.), *History and Crime.* Beverly Hills, Calif.: Sage.

Gusfield, J. 1989. "Constructing the Ownership of Social Problems: Fun and Profit in the Welfare State." *Social Problems* 36(5): 431–441.

———. 1963. *Symbolic Crusade: Status Politics and the American Temperance Movement.* Urbana: University of Illinois Press.

Hagan, J. 1992. "White Collar and Corporate Crime." In R. Linden (ed.), *Criminology: A Canadian Perspective.* Toronto: Harcourt Brace Jovanovich.

———. 1989. *Structural Criminology.* New Brunswick, N.J.: Rutgers University Press.

———. 1985. *Modern Criminology.* New York: McGraw-Hill.

———. 1980. "The Legislation of Crime and Delinquency: A Review of Theory, Method and Research." *Law and Society Review* 14(3): 603–628.

Hagan, J., A. R. Gillis, and J. H. Simpson. 1985. "The Class Structure of Gender and Delinquency: Toward a Power-Control Theory of Common Delinquent Behavior." *American Journal of Sociology* 90(6): 1151–1178.

————. 1979. "The Sexual Stratification of Social Control: A Gender-Based Perspective on Crime and Delinquency." *British Journal of Sociology* 30(1): 25–38.

Hagan, J., J. Simpson, and A. R. Gillis. 1988. "Feminist Scholarship, Relational and Instrumental Control, and a Power-Control Theory of Gender and Delinquency." *The British Journal of Sociology* 39(3): 301–336.

————. 1987. "Class in the Household: Deprivation, Liberation and a Power-Control Theory of Gender and Delinquency." *American Journal of Sociology* 92(4): 788–816.

Haller, M. H. 1990. "Illegal Enterprise: A Theoretical and Historical Interpretation." *Criminology* 28(2): 207–235.

Hamlin, J. E. 1988. "The Misplaced Role of Rational Choice in Neutralization Theory." *Criminology* 26: 425–438.

Hanmer, J., and S. Saunders. 1984. *Well-Founded Fear: A Community Study of Violence to Women*. London: Hutchinson, in association with The Explorations in Feminism Collective, an affiliation of the Women's Research and Resources Centre.

Hans, V. P. 1990. "Law and the Media: An Overview and Introduction." *Law and Human Behavior* 14(5): 399–407.

Hans, V. P., and D. Ermann. 1989. "Responses to Corporate Versus Individual Wrongdoing." *Law and Human Behavior* 13(2): 151–166.

Hansel, M. K. 1987. "Citizen Crime Stereotypes—Normative Consensus Revisited." *Criminology* 25: 455–485.

Harlow, C. W. 1994. *Comparing Federal and State Prison Inmates, 1991*. Washington, D.C.: Bureau of Justice Statistics.

————. 1991. *Female Victims of Violent Crime*. Washington, D.C.: U.S. Department of Justice.

————. 1989. *Injuries from Crime*. Washington, D.C.: Bureau of Justice Statistics.

Harney, P. A., and C. L. Muehlenhard. 1991. "Factors That Increase the Likelihood of Victimization." In A. Parrot and L. Bechhofer (eds.), *Acquaintance Rape: The Hidden Crime*. New York: John Wiley.

Harries, K. D. 1990. *Serious Violence*. Springfield, Ill.: Charles C. Thomas.

Harris, M. K. 1991. "Moving into the New Millennium: Toward a Feminist Vision of Peace." In H. E. Pepinsky and R. Quinney (eds.), *Criminology as Peacemaking*. Bloomington: Indiana University Press.

Hartman, D. P., D. M. Gelfand, B. Page, and P. Walder. 1972. "Rates of Bystander Observation and Reporting of Contrived Shoplifting Incidents." *Criminology* (November): 247–267.

Hartnagel, T. 1992. "Correlates of Criminal Behavior." In R. Linden (ed.), *Criminology: A Canadian Perspective*. Toronto: Harcourt Brace Jovanovich.

Hartnagel, T. F., and H. Krahn. 1989. "High School Dropouts, Labor Market Success, and Criminal Behavior." *Youth and Society* 20(4): 416–444.

Harwood, R. 1993. "Is TV to Blame for Violence?" *Washington Post* (April 17), p. A23.

Hasell, M. J., and F. D. Peatross. 1990. "Exploring Connections Between Women's Changing Roles and House Forms." *Environment and Behavior* 22(1): 3–26.

Hawkins, G. 1969. "God and the Mafia." *The Public Interest* 14 (Winter): 24–51.

Heath, L. 1984. "Impact of Newspaper Crime Reports on Fear of Crime: Multimethodological Investigation." *Journal of Personality and Social Psychology* 47: 263–276.

Hennigen, K. M., L. Heath, J. D. Wharton, M. L. Del Resario, T. D. Cook, and B. J. Calder. 1982. "Impact of the Introduction of Television on Crime in the United States: Empirical Findings and Theoretical Implications." *Journal of Personality and Social Psychology* 42(3): 461–477.

Henshel, R. L., and R. A. Silverman. 1975. *Perception in Criminology.* Toronto: Methuen.

Hepburn, J. 1977. "Social Control and the Legal Order: Legitimated Repression in a Capitalist State." *Contemporary Crises* 1(1): 77–90.

Hess, H. 1973. *Mafia and Mafiosi: The Structure of Power.* Farnborough, U.K.: Saxon House.

Hickey, E. 1991. *Serial Murderers and Their Victims.* Belmont, Calif.: Wadsworth.

Hicks, R. D. 1991. *In Pursuit of Satan.* Buffalo: Prometheus Books.

Hindelang, M. J., M. R. Gottfredson, and J. Garofalo. 1978. *Victims of Personal Crime: An Empirical Foundation for a Theory of Personal Victimization.* Cambridge, Mass.: Ballinger.

Hindelang, M. J., T. Hirschi, and J. Weis. 1981. *Measuring Delinquency.* Beverly Hills, Calif.: Sage.

Hirschi, T. 1969. *Causes of Delinquency.* Berkeley: University of California Press.

Hocker, J. L., and W. W. Wilmot. 1985. *Interpersonal Conflict,* 2nd ed. Dubuque, Iowa: William C. Brown.

Hollinger, R. C., and L. Lanza-Kaduce. 1988. "The Process of Criminalization: The Case of Computer Crime Laws." *Criminology* 26(1): 101–113.

Horowitz, A. V. 1990. *The Logic of Social Control.* New York: Plenum.

Hotaling, G. T., and D. Finkelhor. 1990. "Estimating the Number of Stranger-Abduction Homicides of Children: A Review of Available Evidence." *Journal of Criminal Justice* 18: 385–399.

Hotaling, G. T., and M. A. Straus (with A. J. Lincoln). 1990. "Intrafamily Violence and Crime and Violence Outside the Family." In M. A. Straus and R. J. Gelles (eds.), *Physical Violence in American Families: Risk Factors and Adaptations to Violence in 8,145 Families.* New Brunswick, N.J.: Transaction.

Hough, M. 1987. "Offenders' Choice of Target: Findings from Victim Surveys." *Journal of Quantitative Criminology* 3(4): 355–370.

———. 1985. "The Impact of Victimisation: Findings from the British Crime Survey." *Victimology* 10: 488–497.

Humphries, D. 1981. "Serious Crime, News Coverage, and Ideology: A Content Analysis of Crime Coverage in a Metropolitan Paper." *Crime and Delinquency* 27(2): 191–205.

Hunt, J. 1985. "Police Accounts of Normal Force." *Urban Life* 13(4): 315–341.

Ianni, F. A. J. 1974. *Black Mafia.* New York: Simon & Schuster.

———. 1971. "The Mafia and the Web of Kinship." *The Public Interest* 16: 78–100.

Ianni, F. A. J., and E. Reuss-Ianni. 1972. *A Family Business: Kinship and Social Control in Organized Crime.* New York: Russell Sage Foundation.

Innes, C. A., and L. A. Greenfeld. 1990. "Violent State Prisoners and Their Victims." *Bureau of Justice Statistics Special Report.* Washington, D.C.: U.S. Department of Justice.

Iso-Ahola, S. 1980. *The Social Psychology of Leisure and Recreation.* Dubuque, Iowa: William C. Brown.

Jackson, M. 1989. "The Clinical Assessment and Prediction of Violent Behavior: Toward a Scientific Analysis." *Criminal Justice and Behavior* 16(1): 114–131.

Jackson, P. G. 1990. "Sources of Data." In K. L. Kempf (ed.), *Measurement Issues in Criminology*. New York: Springer-Verlag.

Jackson, P. I. 1989. *Minority Group Threat, Crime, and Policing*. New York: Praeger.

Jacobs, N. 1965. "The Phantom Slasher of Taipei: Mass Hysteria in a Non-Western Society." *Social Problems* 12: 318–328.

Janoff-Bulman, R., and I. H. Frieze. 1983. "A Theoretical Perspective for Understanding Reactions to Victimization." *Journal of Social Issues* 39(2): 1–17.

Jason, J. 1983. "Child Homicide Spectrum." *American Journal of Diseases of Children* 137: 578–581.

Jeffery, C. R. 1990. *Criminology: An Interdisciplinary Approach*. Englewood Cliffs, N.J.: Prentice-Hall.

Jenkins, P. 1994. *Using Murder: The Social Construction of Serial Homicide*. New York: Walter de Gruyter.

———. 1992. *Intimate Enemies: Moral Panic in Great Britain*. New York: Aldine de Gruyter.

Jenkins, P., and D. Meier-Katkin. 1992. "Satanism: Myth and Reality in a Contemporary Moral Panic." *Crime, Law and Social Change* 17: 53–75.

Jenkins, P., and G. Potter. 1987. "The Politics and Mythology of Organized Crime: A Philadelphia Case-Study." *Journal of Criminal Justice* 15: 473–484.

Jensen, G. F., and D. Brownfield. 1986. "Gender, Lifestyles, and Victimization: Beyond Routine Activity." *Violence and Victims* 1(2): 85–99.

Johnson, D. M. 1945. "The 'Phantom Anesthetist' of Mattoon: A Field Study of Mass Hysteria." *Journal of Abnormal and Social Psychology* 40: 175–186.

Johnson, G. D., G. J. Palileo, and N. B. Gray. 1992. "Date Rape on a Southern Campus." *Sociology and Social Research* 76(2): 37–41.

Johnson, I. M. 1990. "A Loglinear Analysis of Abused Wives' Decisions to Call the Police in Domestic Violence Disputes." *Journal of Criminal Justice* 18: 147–159.

Junger, M. 1987. "Women's Experiences of Sexual Harassment: Some Implications for Their Fear of Crime." *British Journal of Criminology* 27(4): 358–383.

Jupp, V. 1989. *Methods of Criminological Research*. London: Unwin Hyman.

Kalmuss, D. S., and M. A. Straus. 1990. "Wife's Marital Dependency and Wife Abuse." In M. A. Straus and R. J. Gelles (eds.), *Physical Violence in American Families: Risk Factors and Adaptations to Violence in 8,145 Families*. New Brunswick, N.J.: Transaction.

Kantor, G. K., and M. A. Straus. 1987. "The Drunken Bum Theory of Wife Beating." *Social Problems* 34(2): 213–230.

Kapferer, J. N. 1989. "A Mass Poisoning Rumor in Europe." *Public Opinion Quarterly* 53: 467–481.

Kappeler, V. E., M. Blumberg, and G. W. Potter. 1993. *The Mythology of Crime and Criminal Justice*. Prospect Heights, Ill.: Waveland Press.

Karasek, R., and T. Theorell. 1990. *Healthy Work*. New York: Basic Books.

Karmen, A. 1990. *Crime Victims: An Introduction to Victimology*, 2nd ed. Pacific Grove, Calif.: Brooks/Cole.

Katz, J. 1993. "Guns, Guns, Guns: The War in the United States." *Globe and Mail* (July 2), p. A15.

———. 1988. *Seductions of Crime: Moral and Sensual Attractions in Doing Evil*. New York: Basic Books.

———. 1987. "What Makes Crime 'News'." *Media, Culture and Society* 9: 47–75.

Keane, C. 1991. "Corporate Crime." In R. A. Silverman, J. J. Teevan, and V. F. Sacco (eds.), *Crime in Canadian Society*, 4th ed. Toronto: Butterworths.

Kelling, G., T. Pate, D. Dieckman, and C. E. Brown. 1974. *The Kansas City Preventive Patrol Experiment: A Summary Report.* Washington, D.C.: The Police Foundation.

Kempf, K. L. 1987. "Specialization and the Criminal Career." *Criminology* 25: 399–420.

Kennedy, L. W. 1991. "Evaluating Community Policing." *Canadian Police College Journal* 15(4): 275–290.

———. 1990. *On the Borders of Crime: Conflict Management and Criminology.* New York: Longman.

———. 1988. "Going It Alone: Unreported Crime and Individual Self-Help." *Journal of Criminal Justice* 16(5): 403–412.

Kennedy, L. W., and S. Baron. 1993. "Routine Activities and a Subculture of Violence: A Study of Violence on the Street." *Journal of Research in Crime and Delinquency* 30(1): 88–112.

Kennedy, L. W., and D. R. Forde. 1990. "Routine Activities and Crime: An Analysis of Victimization in Canada." *Criminology* 28(1): 101–115.

Kennedy, L. W., and R. A. Silverman. 1985. "Significant Others and Fear of Crime Among the Elderly." *International Journal of Aging and Human Development* 20(4): 241–256.

———. 1985. "The Elderly Victim of Homicide: An Application of the Routine Activities Approach." *Sociological Quarterly* 31(2): 307–319.

Kenney, D., and J. Finckenauer. 1995. *Organized Crime in America.* Belmont, Calif.: Wadsworth.

Kinderlehrer, J. 1983. "Delinquent Diets: Partners in Crime." *Prevention* (October): 141–144.

Kirby, C., and T. C. Renner. 1986. *Mafia Assassin: The Inside Story of a Canadian Biker, Hitman and Police Informer.* Toronto: Methuen.

Kitsuse, K. I. 1962. "Societal Reaction to Deviant Behavior: Problems of Theory and Method." *Social Problems* 9: 247–256.

Klaus, P. A. 1994. *Crime Data Brief: The Costs of Crime to Victims.* Washington, D.C.: U.S. Department of Justice.

Klaus, P. A., and M. R. Rand. 1984. *Family Violence.* Washington, D.C.: Bureau of Justice Statistics.

Kleck, G., and B. Patterson. 1989. "The Impact of Gun Control and Gun Ownership Levels on City Violence Rates." Paper presented at the annual meetings of the American Society of Criminology, Reno, Nevada, November.

Kleck, G., and S. Sayles. 1990. "Rape and Resistance." *Social Problems* 37(2): 149–162.

Klockars, C. B. 1985. *The Idea of Police.* Beverly Hills, Calif.: Sage.

Koenig, D. J. 1991. *Do Police Cause Crime?: Police Activity, Police Strength, and Crime Rates.* Ottawa: Canadian Police College.

Kornhauser, R. 1978. *Social Sources of Delinquency.* Chicago: University of Chicago Press.

Krahn, H., and Kennedy, L. W. 1985. "Producing Personal Safety: The Effects of Crime Rates, Police Force Size, and Fear of Crime." *Criminology* 23(4): 697–710.

Krohn, M. D., L. Lanza-Kaduce, and R. Akers. 1984. "Community Context and Theories of Deviant Behavior: An Examination of Social Learning and Social Bonding Theories." *The Sociological Quarterly* 25: 353–371.

Krupat, E., and P. Kubzansky. 1987. "Designing to Deter Crime." *Psychology Today* (October): 58–61.

Kurz, D. 1987. "Emergency Department Responses to Battered Women: Resistance to Medicalization." *Social Problems* 34(1): 69–81.

Lab, S. P. 1992. *Crime Prevention: Approaches, Practices and Evaluations,* 2nd ed. Cincinnati: Anderson.

LaGrange, R. L., and K. F. Ferraro. 1989. "Assessing Age and Gender Differences in Perceived Risk and Fear of Crime." *Criminology* 27: 697–719.

———. 1987. "The Elderly's Fear of Crime: A Critical Examination of the Research." *Research on Aging* 9: 372–391.

LaGrange, R. L., K. F. Ferraro, and M. Supancic. 1992. "Perceived Risk and Fear of Crime: Role of Social and Physical Incivilities." *Journal of Research in Crime and Delinquency* 29: 311–334.

Langan, P. A. 1983. "Career Patterns in Crime." *Bureau of Justice Statistics: Special Report.* Washington, D.C.: U.S. Department of Justice.

Lasley, J. R., and J. L. Rosenbaum. 1988. "Routine Activities and Multiple Personal Victimization." *Sociology and Social Research* 73(1): 47–50.

Laub, J. H. 1990. "Patterns of Criminal Victimization in the United States." In A. J. Lurigio, W. G. Skogan, and R. C. Davis (eds.), *Victims of Crime: Problems, Policies and Programs.* Newbury Park, Calif.: Sage.

———. 1987. "Data for Positive Criminology." In M. R. Gottfredson and T. Hirschi (eds.), *Positive Criminology.* Newbury Park, Calif.: Sage.

Lauritsen, J. L., R. J. Sampson, and J. H. Laub. 1991. "The Link Between Offending and Victimization Among Adolescents." *Criminology* 29(2): 265–292.

Lawson, P. E. 1982. *Solving Somebody Else's Blues.* Latham, Md.: University Press of America.

Lejeune, R., and N. Alex. 1973. "On Being Mugged." *Urban Life and Culture* 2(3): 259–283.

Lemert, E. M. 1951. *Social Pathology.* New York: McGraw-Hill.

Letkemann, P. 1973. *Crime as Work.* Englewood Cliffs, N.J.: Prentice-Hall.

Levi, K. 1981. "Becoming a Hit Man: Neutralization in a Very Deviant Career." *Urban Life* 10: 47–63.

Light, I. 1977. "The Ethnic Vice Industry, 1880–1944." *American Sociological Review* 42 (June): 464–479.

Lindner, C., and R. J. Koehler. 1992. "Probation Officer Victimization: An Emerging Concern." *Journal of Criminal Justice* 20(1): 52–62.

Lindquist, J. H., and J. M. Duke. 1982. "The Elderly Victim at Risk." *Criminology* 20(1): 115–126.

Liska, A. E., and W. Baccaglini. 1990. "Feeling Safe by Comparison: Crime in the Newspapers." *Social Problems* 37(3): 360–374.

Liska, A. E., and B. D. Warner. 1991. "Functions of Crime: A Paradoxical Process." *American Journal of Sociology* 6: 1441–1463.

Lizotte, A. J. 1985. "The Uniqueness of Rape: Reporting Assaultive Violence to the Police." *Crime and Delinquency* 31(2): 169–190.

Lloyd, S. A., J. E. Koval, and R. M. Cale. 1989. "Courtship and Violence in Dating Relationships." In M. A. Pirog-Good and J. E. Stets (eds.), *Violence in Dating Relationships.* New York: Praeger.

Loftus, E. F. 1979. *Eyewitness Testimony.* Cambridge, Mass.: Harvard University Press.

Loree, D. J., and R. W. Walker. 1991. *Community Crime Prevention: Shaping the Future.* Ottawa: The Royal Canadian Mounted Police Public Affairs Directorate.

Los Angeles Times. 1993. "Ex-Bank Manager Gets 24 Years in Drug Money Case." (July 21), p. B2.

Loseke, D. R. 1989. "'Violence' Is 'Violence' . . . or Is It?: The Social Construction of 'Wife Abuse' and Public Policy." In J. Best (ed.), *Images of Issues: Typifying Contemporary Social Problems.* New York: Aldine de Gruyter.

Lotz, R., E. D. Poole, and R. M. Regoli. 1985. *Juvenile Delinquency and Juvenile Justice.* New York: Random House.

Luckenbill, D. F. 1984. "Murder and Assault." In R. F. Meier (ed.), *Major Forms of Crime.* Beverly Hills, Calif.: Sage.

———. 1977. "Criminal Homicide as a Situated Transaction." *Social Problems* 25(2): 176–186.

Luckenbill, D. F., and J. Best. 1981. "Careers in Deviance and Respectability: The Analogy's Limitation." *Social Problems* 29: 197–206.

Lurigio, A. J. 1987. "Are All Victims Alike? The Adverse, Generalized and Differential Impact of Crime." *Crime and Delinquency* 33: 452–467.

Lurigio, A. J., and P. A. Resick. 1990. "Healing the Psychological Wounds of Criminal Victimization: Predicting Postcrime Distress and Recovery." In A. J. Lurigio, W. G. Skogan, and R. C. David (eds.), *Victims of Crime: Problems, Policies and Programs.* Newbury Park, Calif.: Sage.

Luxton, M. 1988. "Thinking About the Future." *Family Matters: Sociology and Contemporary Canadian Families.* Toronto: Methuen.

Lynch, C. 1994. "Pocketsful of Fear." *Globe and Mail* (February 6), p. D5.

Lynch, J. P. 1987. "Routine Activity and Victimization at Work." *Journal of Quantitative Criminology* 3(4): 283–300.

Lynch, J. P., and D. Cantor. 1992. "Ecological and Behavioral Influences on Property Victimization at Home: Implications for Opportunity Theory." *Journal of Research in Crime and Delinquency* 29(3): 335–362.

Maas, P. 1968. *The Valachi Papers.* New York: Putnam.

McCarthy, B., and J. Hagan. 1991. "Homelessness: A Criminogenic Situation?" *British Journal of Criminology* 31(4): 393–410.

McClearly, R. M., B. C. Nienstedt, and J. M. Erven. 1982. "Uniform Crime Reports as Organizational Outcomes: Three Time Series Experiments." *Social Problems* 29(4): 361–372.

McCord, J. 1991. "Family Relationships, Juvenile Delinquency, and Adult Criminality." *Criminology* 29(3): 397–417.

McCorkle, R. C. 1992. "Personal Precautions to Violence in Prisons." *Criminal Justice and Behavior* 19: 160–173.

McIntosh, M. 1975. *The Organization of Crime.* London: Macmillan.

Maguire, K., and A. Pastore (eds.). 1994. *Sourcebook of Criminal Justice Statistics, 1993.* Washington, D.C.: U.S. Department of Justice, Bureau of Justice Statistics.

Maguire, M., with T. Bennett. 1982. *Burglary in a Dwelling: The Offence, the Offender and the Victim.* London: Heinemann.

Malamuth, N. M. 1983. "Factors Associated with Rape as Predictors of Laboratory Aggression Against Women." *Journal of Personality and Social Psychology* 45: 432–442.

Malamuth, N. M., and E. Donnerstein. 1984. *Pornography and Sexual Aggression.* Orlando: Academic Press.

Maltz, M. D. 1976. "On Defining 'Organized Crime': The Development of a Definition and a Typology." *Crime and Delinquency* 22: 338–346.

Martin, R., R. J. Mutchnick, and W. T. Austin. 1990. *Criminological Thought: Pioneers Past and Present.* New York: Macmillan.

Massey, J. L., M. D. Krohn, and L. M. Bonati. 1989. "Property Crime and the Routine Activities of Individuals." *Journal of Research in Crime and Delinquency* 26(4): 378–400.

Mastrofski, S. 1983. "The Police and Noncrime Services." In G. Whitaker and C. D. Phillips (eds.), *Evaluating Performance of Criminal Justice Agencies.* Beverly Hills, Calif.: Sage.

Matza, D., and G. M. Sykes. 1961. "Juvenile Delinquency and Subterranean Values." *American Sociological Review* 26: 712–719.

Maxfield, M. G. 1990. "Homicide Circumstances, 1976–1985: A Taxonomy Based on Supplementary Homicide Reports." *Criminology* 28: 671–695.

———. 1987. "Household Composition, Routine Activity, and Victimization: A Comparative Analysis." *Journal of Quantitative Criminology* 3(4): 301–320.

Mayhew, P., D. Elliott, and L. Dowds. 1989. *The 1988 British Crime Survey: A Home Office Research and Planning Unit Report.* London: HMSO Books.

Mayhew, P., N. Maung, and C. Mirrlees-Black. 1993. *The 1992 British Crime Survey.* London: HMSO Books.

Mednick, S., T. Moffitt, and S. Stack. 1987. *The Causes of Crime: New Biological Approaches.* New York: Cambridge University Press.

Menard, S., and H. C. Covey. 1988. "UCR and NCS: Comparisons over Space and Time." *Journal of Criminal Justice* 16: 371–384.

Meredith, N. 1984. "The Murder Epidemic." *Science* (December): 41–48.

Merry, S. E. 1981. *Urban Danger.* Philadelphia: Temple University Press.

Merton, R. K. 1938. "Social Structure and Anomie." *American Sociological Review* 3: 672–682.

Messner, S. 1989. "Economic Discrimination and Societal Homicide Rates: Further Evidence on the Cost of Inequality." *American Sociological Review* 54: 597–611.

Messner, S. F., and J. R. Blau. 1987. "Routine Leisure Activities and Rates of Crime: A Macro-Level Analysis." *Social Forces* 65: 1035–1051.

Messner, S. F., and R. Rosenfeld. 1994. *Crime and the American Dream.* Belmont, Calif.: Wadsworth.

Michalowski, R. J., and E. W. Bohlander. 1976. "Repression and Criminal Justice in Capitalist America." *Sociological Inquiry* 46(2): 95–106.

Miethe, T. D. 1982. "Public Consensus on Crime Seriousness: Normative Structure or Methodological Artifact?" *Criminology* 20: 515–526.

Miethe, T. D., and G. R. Lee. 1984. "Fear of Crime Among Older People: A Reassessment of the Predictive Power of Crime-Related Factors." *The Sociological Quarterly* 25: 397–415.

Miethe, T. D., and R. F. Meier. 1994. *Crime and Its Social Context.* Albany: State University of New York Press.

———. 1990. "Opportunity, Choice and Criminal Victimization: A Test of a Theoretical Model." *Journal of Research in Crime and Delinquency* 27(3): 243–266.

Miethe, T. D., M. C. Stafford, and J. S. Long. 1987. "Social Differentiation in Criminal Victimization: A Test of Routine Activities/Lifestyle Theories." *American Sociological Review* 52 (April): 184–194.

Miller, D. T., and C. A. Porter. 1983. "Self-Blame in Victims of Violence." *Journal of Social Issues* 39: 139–152.

Miller, G. 1978. *Odd Jobs.* Englewood Cliffs, N.J.: Prentice-Hall.

Miller, J. L., and A. B. Anderson. 1986. "Updating the Deterrence Doctrine." *Journal of Criminal Law and Criminology* 77(2): 418–438.

Miller, L. J. 1990. "Violent Families and the Rhetoric of Harmony." *British Journal of Sociology* 41(2): 263–288.

Miller, W. 1958. "Lower Class Culture as a Generating Milieu of Gang Delinquency." *Journal of Social Issues* 14: 5–19.

Minor, W. W. 1981. "Techniques of Neutralization: A Reconceptualization and Empirical Examination." *Journal of Research in Crime and Delinquency* 18: 295–318.

Moeller, G. L. 1989. "Fear of Criminal Victimization: The Effects of Neighborhood Racial Composition." *Sociological Inquiry* 59: 208–221.

Moffitt, T. E., D. R. Lynam, and P. A. Silva. 1994. "Neuropsychological Tests Predicting Persistent Male Delinquency." *Criminology* 32(2): 277–300.

Monkkonen, E. H. 1983. "The Organized Response to Crime in Nineteenth- and Twentieth-Century America." *Journal of Interdisciplinary History* 14(1): 113–128.

Moore, W. H. 1974. *The Kefauver Commission and the Politics of Crime, 1950–1952.* Columbia: University of Missouri Press.

Morash, M. 1984. "Organized Crime." In R. F. Meier (ed.), *Major Forms of Crime.* Beverly Hills, Calif.: Sage.

Morin, E. 1971. *Rumor in Orleans.* New York: Pantheon.

Morris, N. 1988. "Insanity Defense." *Crime File Study Guide.* Washington, D.C.: National Institute of Justice.

Morris, N., and G. Hawkins. 1970. *The Honest Politician's Guide to Crime Control.* Chicago: University of Chicago Press.

Moysa, M. 1992. "Crown Backs Off Murder Charge." *Edmonton Journal* (February 12), p. A1.

Muehlenhard, C. L., and M. A. Linton. 1987. "Date Rape and Sexual Aggression in Dating Situations: Incidence and Risk Factors." *Journal of Counseling Psychology* 34(2): 186–196.

Mundt, R. J. 1990. "Gun Control and Rates of Firearm Violence in Canada and the United States." *Canadian Journal of Criminology* 32(1): 137–154.

Murphy, C. 1988. "Community Problems, Problem Communities and Community Policing in Toronto." *Journal of Research in Crime and Delinquency* 25(4): 392–410.

Murray, C., and R. Herrnstein. 1994. *The Bell Curve.* New York: Free Press.

Naffine, N. 1987. *Female Crime: The Construction of Women in Criminology.* Sydney: Allen & Unwin.

National Crime Prevention Institute. 1986. *Understanding Crime Prevention.* Boston: Butterworths.

Nelson, B. 1984. *Making an Issue of Child Abuse.* Chicago: University of Chicago Press.

Nettler, G. 1984. *Explaining Crime.* New York: McGraw-Hill.

Newman, G. R. 1990. "Popular Culture and Criminal Justice: A Preliminary Analysis." *Journal of Criminal Justice* 18: 261–274.

Newman, O. 1972. *Defensible Space: Crime Prevention Through Urban Design.* New York: Macmillan.

New York Times. 1989. "Two Men Arrested in Shooting of Officer." (May 7), p. B2.

New York Times Magazine. 1989. "China Erupts: The Reasons Why." (June 4), pp. 26–29.

Normandeau, A. 1987. "Crime on the Montreal Metro." *Sociology and Social Research* 71(4): 289–292.

O'Brien, R. M. 1986. "Rare Events, Sample Sizes and Statistical Problems in the Analysis of the NCS City Surveys." *Journal of Criminal Justice* 14: 441–448.

———. 1985. *Crime and Victimization Data*, Vol. 4. Law and Criminal Justice Series. Beverly Hills, Calif.: Sage.

O'Hare, W. P., K. Pallard, T. Mann, and M. Kent. 1991. "African Americans in the 1900s." *Population Bulletin* 46 (1). Washington, D.C.: Population Reference Bureau.

O'Keefe, G. J. 1984. "Public Views on Crime: Television Exposure and Media Credibility." In R. N. Bostrom (ed.), *Communication Yearbook 8*. Beverly Hills, Calif.: Sage.

Packer, H. L. 1969. *The Limits of the Criminal Sanction*. Stanford, Calif.: Stanford University Press.

Pagelow, M. D. 1989. "The Incidence and Prevalence of Criminal Abuse of Other Family Members." In L. Ohlin and M. Tonry (eds.), *Family Violence*. Chicago: University of Chicago Press.

Palenski, J. E. 1984. "The Use of Mediation by Police." *Mediation Quarterly* 5: 31–38.

Pandiani, J. A. 1978. "Crime Time TV: If All We Know Is What We Saw . . ." *Contemporary Crises* 2: 437–458.

Parker, G. 1991. "The Structure of Criminal Law." In R. A. Silverman, J. J. Teevan, and V. F. Sacco (eds.), *Crime in Canadian Society*, 4th ed. Toronto: Butterworths.

Parsons, T. 1951. *The Social System*. Glencoe, Ill.: Free Press.

Patterson, G. R., and T. J. Dishion. 1985. "Contributions of Families and Peers to Delinquency." *Criminology* 23: 63–79.

Peek, C. W., J. L. Fischer, and J. S. Kidwell. 1985. "Teenage Violence Toward Parents: A Neglected Dimension of Family Violence." *Journal of Marriage and the Family* 47: 1051–1058.

Pepinsky, H., and P. Jesilow. 1984. *Myths That Cause Crime*. Cabin John, Md.: Seven Locks Press.

Pfohl, S. 1977. "The Discovery of Child Abuse." *Social Problems* 24(3): 315–321.

Pfuhl, E. H. 1986. *The Deviance Process*, 2nd ed. Belmont, Calif.: Wadsworth.

Phelps, T. G. 1983. "The Criminal as Hero in American Fiction." *Wisconsin Law Review* 6: 1427–1454.

Phillips, D. P. 1983. "The Impact of Mass Media Violence on U.S. Homicides." *American Sociological Review* 48 (August): 560–568.

Pileggi, N. 1985. *Wiseguy: Life in a Mafia Family*. New York: Simon & Schuster.

Pillemer, K. A. 1985. "The Dangers of Dependency: New Findings on Domestic Violence against the Elderly." *Social Problems* 33: 146–158.

Pillemer, K. A., and D. Finkelhor. 1988. "The Prevalence of Elder Abuse: A Random Sample Survey." *The Gerontologist* 28(1): 51–57.

Pitkin, T. M., and F. Cordasco. 1977. *The Black Hand: A Chapter in Ethnic Crime*. Totowa, N.J.: Littlefield, Adams.

Population Reference Bureau. 1992. "1992 World Population Data Sheet of the Population Reference Bureau, Inc." Washington, D.C.: Population Reference Bureau.

Pound, R. 1943. "A Survey of Social Interests." *Harvard Law Review* 53: 1–39.

Provenzo, E. F. 1991. *Video Kids: Making Sense of Nintendo*. Cambridge, Mass.: Harvard University Press.

Quinn, M. J., and S. K. Tomita. 1986. *Elder Abuse and Neglect: Causes, Diagnosis and Intervention Strategies*. New York: Springer-Verlag.

Quinney, R., and J. Wildeman. 1991. *The Problem of Crime: A Peace and Social Justice Perspective*. Mountain View, Calif.: Mayfield.

Randall, D. M., L. Lee-Sammons, and P. H. Hagner. 1988. "Common Versus Elite Crime Coverage in Network News." *Social Science Quarterly* 69(4): 910–929.

Rankin, J. H., and L. E. Wells. 1990. "The Effect of Parental Attachments and Direct Controls on Delinquency." *Journal of Research on Crime and Delinquency* 27(2): 140–165.

Reasons, C. E. 1976. "Images of the Crime and the Criminal: The Dope Fiend Mythology." *Journal of Research in Crime and Delinquency* 13: 133–144.

Reasons, C. E., and D. Chappell. 1985. "Continental Capitalism and Crooked Lawyering." *Crime and Social Justice* 26: 38–59.

Reckless, W. 1967. *The Crime Problem*, 4th ed. New York: Meredith.

Reiman, J. H. 1990. *The Rich Get Richer and the Poor Get Prison*, 3rd ed. New York: Macmillan.

Reinarman, C., and H. G. Levine. 1989. "The Crack Attack: Politics and Media in America's Latest Drug Scare." In J. Best (ed.), *Images of Issues*. New York: Aldine de Gruyter.

Reiss, A. J., Jr. 1986a. "Official and Survey Crime Statistics." In E. A. Fattah (ed.), *From Crime Policy to Victim Policy—Reorienting the Justice System*. London: Macmillan.

———. 1986b. "Policy Implications of Crime Victim Surveys." In E. A. Fattah (ed.), *From Crime Policy to Victim Policy—Reorienting the Justice System*. London: MacMillan.

———. 1984. "Consequences of Compliance and Deterrence Models of Law Enforcement for the Exercise of Police Discretion." *Law and Contemporary Problems* 47(4): 83–122.

Reiss, A., and J. A. Roth. 1994. *Understanding and Preventing Violence*. Washington, D.C.: U.S. Department of Justice.

Rengert, G., and J. Wasilchick. 1985. *Suburban Burglary: A Time and a Place for Everything*. Springfield, Ill: Charles C. Thomas.

Reppetto, T. 1974. *A Residential Crime*. Cambridge, Mass.: Ballinger.

Resick, P. A. 1987. "Psychological Effects of Victimization: Implications for the Criminal Justice System." *Crime and Delinquency* 33: 468–478.

Reuter, P. 1984a. "The (Continued) Vitality of Mythical Numbers." *Public Interest* 75: 135–147.

———. 1984b. "Social Control in Illegal Markets." In D. Black (ed.), *Toward a General Theory of Social Control, Volume 2: Selected Problems*. Orlando: Academic Press.

Riger, S. 1981. "On Women." In D. A. Lewis (ed.), *Reactions to Crime*. Beverly Hills, Calif.: Sage.

Riley, D. 1987. "Time and Crime: The Link Between Teenager Lifestyle and Delinquency." *Journal of Quantitative Criminology* 3(4): 339–354.

Roberts, K. 1983. *Youth and Leisure*. London: George Allen & Unwin.

Rogers, A. J. 1973. *The Economics of Crime*. Hinsdale, Ill.: Dryden Press.

Roncek, D. W. 1981. "Dangerous Places." *Social Forces* 60: 74–96.

Roncek, D. W., and P. A. Maier. 1991. "Bars, Blocks and Crimes Revisited: Linking the Theory of Routine Activities to the Empiricism of 'Hot Spots'." *Criminology* 29(4): 725–753.

Roncek, D. W., and M. A. Pravatiner. 1989. "Additional Evidence That Taverns Enhance Nearby Crime." *Sociology and Social Research* 73(4): 185–188.

———. 1988. "Community Crime Prevention: A Review and Synthesis of the Literature." *Justice Quarterly* 5(3): 323–395.

———. 1987. "Coping with Victimization: The Effects of Police Intervention on Victims' Psychological Readjustment." *Crime and Delinquency* 33: 502–519.

Rosenbaum, D. P. 1994. *The Challenge of Community Policing: Testing the Promise.* Newbury Park, Calif.: Sage.

———. 1988. "Community Crime Prevention: A Review and Synthesis of the Literature." *Justice Quarterly* 5(3): 323–395.

———. 1987. "The Theory and Research Behind Neighborhood Watch: Is It a Sound Fear and Crime Reduction Strategy?" *Crime and Delinquency* 33(1): 103–134.

Rosenbaum, H. J., and P. C. Sederberg. 1976. "Vigilantism: An Analysis of Establishment Violence." In H. J. Rosenbaum and P. C. Sederberg (eds.), *Vigilante Politics.* Philadelphia: University of Pennsylvania Press.

Rosnow, R. L. 1988. "Rumour as Communication: A Contextual Approach." *Journal of Communication* 38(1): 12–28.

Rosnow, R. L., and G. A. Fine. 1976. *Rumor and Gossip.* New York: Elsevier.

Ross, R., and G. L. Staines. 1972. "The Politics of Analyzing Social Problems." *Social Problems* 20(1): 18–40.

Rossi, P. H., E. Waite, C. E. Bose, and R. E. Berk. 1974. "The Seriousness of Crimes: Normative Structure and Individual Differences." *American Sociological Review* 39: 224–237.

Ruback, R. B., M. S. Greenberg, and D. R. Wescott. 1984. "Social Influence and Crime-Victim Decision Making." *Journal of Social Issues* 40(1): 51–76.

Rubington, C., and M. S. Weinberg. 1987. *Deviance: The Interactionist Perspective.* New York: Macmillan.

Rush, G. 1994. *The Dictionary of Criminal Justice,* 4th ed. Guilford, Conn.: Dushkin.

Sacco, V. F. 1995. "Media Constructions of Crime." *The Annals of the American Academy of Political and Social Science* 539: 141–154.

———. 1990. "Gender, Fear and Victimization: A Preliminary Application of Power-Control Theory." *Sociological Spectrum* 10: 485–506.

Sacco, V. F., and B. J. Fair. 1988. "Images of Legal Control: Crime News and the Process of Organizational Legitimation." *Canadian Journal of Communication* 13: 113–122.

Sacco, V. F., and H. Johnson. 1990. *Patterns of Criminal Victimization in Canada.* Ottawa: Minister of Supply and Services.

Sacco, V. F., and R. A. Silverman. 1982. "Crime Prevention Through Mass Media: Prospects and Problems." *Journal of Criminal Justice* 10: 257–269.

Sacco, V. F., and E. Zureik. 1990. "Correlates of Computer Misuses: Data from a Self-Reporting Sample." *Behaviour and Information Technology* 9(5): 353–369.

Sagarin, E. 1975. *Deviants and Deviance.* New York: Praeger.

Sales, E., M. Baum, and B. Shore. 1984. "Victim Readjustment Following Assault." *Journal of Social Issues* 40(1): 117–136.

Salinger, L. R., P. Jesilow, H. N. Pontell, and G. Geis. 1993. "Assaults Against Airline Flight Attendants: A Victimization Study." In H. N. Pontell (ed.), *Social Deviance.* Englewood Cliffs, N.J.: Prentice-Hall.

Sampson, R. J. 1987. "Urban Black Violence: The Effect of Male Joblessness and Family Disruption." *American Journal of Sociology* 93(2): 348–382.

———. 1985. "Race and Criminal Violence: A Demographically Disaggregated Analysis of Urban Homicide." *Crime and Delinquency* 31(1): 47–82.

Sampson, R. J., and W. B. Groves. 1989. "Community Structure and Crime: Testing Social Disorganization Theory." *American Journal of Sociology* 94: 774–802.

Sampson, R. J., and J. H. Laub. 1990. "Crime and Deviance over the Life Course: The Salience of Adult Social Bonds." *American Sociological Review* 55: 609–627.

Sampson, R. J., and J. L. Lauritsen. 1990. "Deviant Lifestyles, Proximity Crime, and the Offender–Victim Link in Personal Violence." *Journal of Research in Crime and Delinquency* 27(2): 110–139.

Sanger, D. E. 1993. "How to Visit America and Get Out Alive." *Globe and Mail* (June 18), p. A9.

Saunders, D. G. 1989. "Who Hits First and Who Hurts Most?: Evidence for the Greater Victimization of Women in Intimate Relationships." Paper presented at the Annual Meeting of the American Society of Criminology, Reno, Nevada.

Savitz, L. D. 1982. "Official Statistics." In L. D. Savitz and N. Johnston (eds.), *Contemporary Criminology,* pp. 3–15. New York: John Wiley.

———. 1978. "Official Police Statistics and Their Limitations." In L. D. Savitz and N. Johnston (eds.), *Crime in Society.* New York: John Wiley.

Scheingold, S. A. 1984. *The Politics of Law and Order: Street Crime and Public Policy.* New York: Longman.

Schelling, T. C. 1967. "Economic Analysis of Organized Crime." In *President's Commission on Law Enforcement and Administration of Justice Task Force Report: Organized Crime, Annotations and Consultant's Papers,* pp. 114–126. Washington, D.C.: U.S. Government Printing Office.

Scheppele, K. L., and P. B. Bart. 1983. "Through Women's Eyes: Defining Danger in the Wake of Sexual Assault." *Journal of Social Issues* 39: 63–81.

Schissel, B. 1992. "The Influence of Economic Factors and Social Control Policy on Crime Rate Changes in Canada, 1962–1988." *Canadian Journal of Sociology* 17(1): 405–428.

Schlesinger, P., et al. 1992. *Women Viewing Violence.* London: BFI.

Schneider, V. W., and B. Wieresma. 1990. "Limits and Use of the Uniform Crime Reports." In D. L. MacKenzie, P. J. Baunach, and R. R. Roberg (eds.), *Measuring Crime: Large-Scale, Long-Range Efforts.* Albany: State University of New York Press.

Schur, E. M. 1979. *Interpreting Deviance.* New York: Harper & Row.

———. 1965. *Crimes Without Victims.* Englewood Cliffs, N.J.: Prentice Hall.

Schwartz, M. D. 1988. "Ain't Got No Class: Universal Risk Theories of Battering." *Contemporary Crises* 12: 375–392.

Scott, M., and S. Lyman. 1968. "Accounts." *American Sociological Review* 33: 42–62.

Scully, D., and J. Marolla. 1984. "Convicted Rapists' Vocabulary of Motive: Excuses and Justifications." *Social Problems* 31(5): 530–544.

Sedlak, A. J. 1988. "The Effects of Personal Experiences with Couple Violence on Calling It 'Battering' and Allocating Blame." In G. T. Hotaling, D. Finkelhor, J. T. Kirpatrick, and M. A. Straus (eds.), *Coping with Family Violence.* Newbury Park, Calif.: Sage.

Sellin, T. 1938. "Culture Conflict and Crime." A Report of the Subcommittee on Delinquency of the Committee on Personality and Culture. *Social Science Research Council Bulletin* 41.

Selzer, J. A., and D. Kalmus. 1988. "Socialization and Stress Explanations for Spouse Abuse." *Social Forces* 67(2): 473–491.

Servadio, G. 1976. *Mafioso: A History of the Mafia from Its Origins to the Present Day.* New York: Stein & Day.

Shaffer, E. B. 1980. *Community Policing.* London: Croom Helm.

Shaw, C. R., and H. D. McKay. 1942. *Juvenile Delinquency in Urban Areas.* Chicago: University of Chicago Press.

Shearing, C. D., and P. C. Stenning. 1983. "Private Security: Implications for Social Control." *Social Problems* 30: 493–506.

Sheldon, W. H. 1940. *Varieties of Delinquent Youth: An Introduction to Constitutional Psychiatry.* New York: Harper & Brothers.

Sheley, J. F. 1991. "Conflict in Criminal Law." In J. F. Sheley (ed.), *Criminology: A Contemporary Handbook,* pp. 21–39. Belmont, Calif.: Wadsworth.

Sherman, L. 1992. *Policing Domestic Violence: Experiments and Dilemmas.* New York: Free Press.

Sherman, L., and R. Berk. 1984. "The Specific Deterrent Effects of Arrest for Domestic Assault." *American Sociological Review* 49: 261–272.

Sherman, L., P. R. Gartin, and M. E. Buerger. 1989. "Routine Activities and the Criminology of Place." *Criminology* 27(1): 27–55.

Sherman, L., J. Schmidt, D. Rogan, and C. DeRiso. 1991. "Predicting Domestic Homicide: Prior Police Contact and Gun Threats." In Michael Steinman (ed.), *Woman Battering: Policy Responses.* Cincinnati: Anderson.

Shibutani, T. 1966. *Improvised News: A Sociological Study of Rumor.* Indianapolis, Ind.: Bobbs-Merrill.

Shotland, R. L. 1976. "Spontaneous Vigilantism: A Bystander Response to Criminal Behavior." In H. J. Rosenbaum and P. C. Sederberg (eds.), *Vigilante Politics.* Philadelphia: University of Pennsylvania Press.

Shotland, R. L., and L. I. Goodstein. 1984. "The Role of Bystanders in Crime Control." *Journal of Social Issues* 40(1): 9–26.

Shotland, R. L., and M. K. Straw. 1976. "Bystander Response to an Assault: When a Man Attacks a Woman." *Journal of Personality and Social Psychology* 34: 990–999.

Shover, N. 1983. "The Later Stages of Ordinary Property Offender Careers." *Social Problems* 30: 208–218.

———. 1973. "The Social Organization of Burglary." *Social Problems* 201 (Spring): 499–513.

Sigler, R. T., and M. Johnson. 1986. "Public Perceptions of the Need for Criminalization of Sexual Harassment." *Journal of Criminal Justice* 14: 229–237.

Silverman, I., and S. Dinitz. 1974. "Compulsive Masculinity and Delinquency: An Empirical Investigation." *Criminology* 11: 498.

Silverman, R. A., and L. Kennedy. 1993. *Deadly Deeds: Murder in Canada.* Scarborough, Ont.: Nelson Canada.

———. 1992. "Interpersonal Relations and Means of Lethal Violence in Canada." In A. Kuhl (ed.), *Homicide: The Victim–Offender Connection.* Cincinnati: Anderson.

Silverman, R. A., and M. O. Nielsen. 1992. *Aboriginal Peoples and Canadian Criminal Justice.* Toronto: Butterworths.

Silverman, R. A., J. J. Teevan, and V. F. Sacco. 1991. *Crime in Canadian Society,* 4th ed. Toronto: Butterworths.

Simon, D. R., and D. S. Eitzen. 1993. *Elite Deviance,* 4th ed. Boston: Allyn & Bacon.

Simon, R. 1990. *Women and Crime Revisited.* Washington, D.C.: Bureau of Justice Statistics.

Simpson, S. C., and C. S. Koper. 1992. "Deterring Corporate Crime." *Criminology* 30(3): 347–375.

Simpson, S. S. 1989. "Feminist Theory, Crime and Justice." *Criminology* 27(4): 605–631.

Singer, S. I., and M. Levine. 1988. "Power-Control Theory, Gender and Delinquency: A Partial Replication with Additional Evidence on the Effect of Peers." *Criminology* 26: 627–647.

Skaret, D., and C. Wilgosh. 1989. "Learning Disabilities and Juvenile Delinquency: A Causal Relationship." *International Journal for the Advancement of Counselling* 12: 113–123.

Skinner, B. F. 1948. *Walden Two*. New York: Macmillan.

Skipper, J. K. 1985. "Nicknames of Notorious American Twentieth Century Deviants: The Decline of the Folk Hero Syndrome." *Deviant Behavior* 6: 99–114.

Skogan, W. G. 1993. "The Various Meanings of Fear." in W. Bilsky, C. Pfeiffer, and P. Wetzels (eds.), *Fear of Crime and Criminal Victimization*. Stuttgart, Germany: Ferdinand Enke Verlag.

———. 1990a. "The National Crime Survey Redesign." *Public Opinion Quarterly* 54: 256–272.

———. 1990b. *Disorder and Decline*. New York: Free Press.

———. 1987. "The Impact of Victimization on Fear." *Crime and Delinquency* 33: 135–154.

———. 1986. "Methodological Issues in the Study of Victimization." In E. A. Fattah (ed.), *From Crime Policy to Victim Policy—Reorienting the Justice System*. London: Macmillan.

———. 1984. "Reporting Crimes to the Police: The Status of World Research." *Journal of Research in Crime and Delinquency* 21: 113–137.

———. 1981. "On Attitudes and Behavior." In D. A. Lewis (ed.), *Reactions to Crime*. Beverly Hills, Calif.: Sage.

———. 1977. "Dimensions of the Dark Figure of Unreported Crime." *Crime and Delinquency* 23: 41–50.

———. 1976. "Citizen Reporting of Crime: Some National Panel Data." *Criminology* 13(4): 535–549.

Skogan, W. G., and M. G. Maxfield. 1981. *Coping with Crime: Individual and Neighborhood Reactions*. Beverly Hills, Calif.: Sage.

Skogan, W. G., and M. A. Wycoff. 1987. "Some Unexpected Effects of a Police Service for Victims." *Crime and Delinquency* 33: 490–501.

Skolnick, J. 1966. *Justice Without Trial*. New York: John Wiley.

Smith, D. 1975. *The Mafia Mystique*. New York: Basic Books.

Smith, D. A. 1987. "Police Response to Interpersonal Violence: Defining the Parameters of Legal Control." *Social Forces* 65(3): 767–782.

Smith, D. A., and G. R. Jarjoura. 1989. "Household Characteristics, Neighborhood Composition and Victimization Risk." *Social Forces* 68(2): 621–640.

———. 1988. "Social Structure and Criminal Victimization." *Journal of Research in Crime and Delinquency* 25: 27–52.

Smith, D. C. 1991. "Wickersham to Sutherland to Katzenbach: Evolving an 'Official' Definition for Organized Crime." *Crime, Law and Social Change* 16: 135–154.

Smith, L. N., and G. D. Hill. 1991. "Victimization and Fear of Crime." *Criminal Justice and Behavior* 18: 217–239.

Smith, S. J. 1982. "Victimization in the Inner City." *British Journal of Criminology* 22: 386–401.

Snider, L. 1993. *Bad Business: Corporate Crime in Canada*. Scarborough, Ont.: Nelson Canada.

———. 1992. "Commercial Crime." In V. F. Sacco (ed.), *Deviance: Conformity and Control in Canadian Society,* 2nd ed. Scarborough, Ont.: Prentice-Hall.

Spector, M., and J. I. Kitsuse. 1977. *Constructing Social Problems*. Menlo Park, Calif.: Cummings.

Stafford, M. C., and O. R. Galle. 1984. "Victimization Rates, Exposure to Risk, and Fear of Crime." *Criminology* 22(2): 173–185.

Stafford, M. C., and J. P. Gibbs. 1980. "Crime Rates in an Ecological Context: Extension of a Proposition." *Social Science Quarterly* 61(3–4): 653–665.

Stanko, E. 1990. *Everyday Violence: How Women and Men Experience Sexual and Physical Danger.* London: Pandora.

———. 1985. *Intimate Intrusions: Women's Experience of Male Violence.* London: Routledge & Kegan Paul.

Stark, R. 1987. "Deviant Places: A Theory of the Ecology of Crime." *Criminology* 25(4): 893–909.

Steffensmeier, D. J., and E. Allen. 1991. "Gender, Age, and Crime." In J. F. Sheley (ed.), *Criminology: A Contemporary Handbook,* pp. 67–93. Belmont, Calif.: Wadsworth.

Steffensmeier, D. J., and R. H. Steffensmeier. 1977. "Who Reports Shoplifters?: Research Continuities and Further Developments." *International Journal of Criminology and Penology* 3: 79–95.

Steffensmeier, D. J., and R. M. Terry. 1973. "Deviance and Respectability: An Observational Study of Reactions to Shoplifting." *Social Forces* 51: 417–426.

Steinman, M. 1992. "Going Beyond Arrest: Police Responses to Domestic Violence." Paper presented at the Annual Meeting of the American Society of Criminology, New Orleans.

Steinmetz, S. 1986. "The Violent Family." In M. Lystad (ed.), *Violence in the Home: Interdisciplinary Perspectives.* New York: Brunner/Mazel.

———. 1978. "Battered Parents." *Society* 15(5): 54–55.

———. 1977–78. "The Battered Husband Syndrome." *Victimology: An International Journal* 2: 499–509.

Stoddart, K. 1991. "It's Easier for the Bulls Now: Official Statistics and Social Change in a Canadian Heroin-Using Community." In R. A. Silverman, J. J. Teevan, and V. F. Sacco (eds.), *Crime in Canadian Society,* 4th ed. Toronto: Butterworths.

———. 1981. "As Long As I Can't See You Do It: A Case Study of Drug-Related Activities in Public Places." *Canadian Journal of Criminology* 23(4): 391–405.

Stoker, B. 1975. *The Annotated Dracula.* Annotated by L. Wolf. New York: Clarkson N. Potter.

Stone, C. 1975. *Where the Law Ends: The Social Control of Corporate Behavior.* New York: Harper & Row.

Stout, C. 1991. "Common Law: A Growing Alternative." *Canadian Social Trends* 23: 18–20.

Straus, M. A. 1991. "Discipline and Deviance: Physical Punishment of Children and Violence and Other Forms of Crime in Adulthood." *Social Problems* 38(2): 133–152.

———. 1990a. "The National Family Violence Surveys." In M. A. Straus and R. J. Gelles (eds.), *Physical Violence in American Families: Risk Factors and Adaptations to Violence in 8,145 Families.* New Brunswick, N.J.: Transaction.

———. 1990b. "Social Stress and Marital Violence in a National Sample of American Families." In M. A. Straus and R. J. Gelles (eds.), *Physical Violence in American Families: Risk Factors and Adaptations to Violence in 8,145 Families.* New Brunswick, N.J.: Transaction.

Straus, M. A., and R. J. Gelles. 1990a. "How Violent Are American Families?: Estimates from the National Family Violence Resurvey and Other Studies." In M. A. Straus and R. J. Gelles (eds.), *Physical Violence in American Families: Risk Factors and Adaptations to Violence in 8,145 Families.* New Brunswick, N.J.: Transaction.

―――. 1990b. *Physical Violence in American Families: Risk Factors and Adaptations to Violence in 8,145 Families.* New Brunswick, NJ: Transaction.

Straus, M. A., and C. Smith. 1990. "Family Patterns and Child Abuse." In M. A. Straus and R. J. Gelles (eds.), *Physical Violence in American Families: Risk Factors and Adaptations to Violence in 8,145 Families.* New Brunswick, N.J.: Transaction.

Straus, M. A., and K. R. Williams. 1988. "Homicide Victimization and Offense Rates by Age, Gender, Race, Relation of Victim to Offender, Weapon Used, and Circumstances, for the United States, 1976–1979 and 1980–1984." Unpublished manuscript, Family Research Lab, University of New Hampshire, Durham.

Sugarman, D. B., and G. T. Hotaling. 1989. "Dating Violence: Prevalence, Context and Risk Markers." In M. A. Pirog-Good and J. E. Stets (eds.), *Violence in Dating Relationships.* New York: Praeger.

Surette, R. 1992. *Media, Crime, and Criminal Justice: Images and Realities.* Pacific Grove, Calif.: Brooks/Cole.

Sutherland, E. H. 1961. *White Collar Crime.* New York: Holt, Rinehart & Winston.

―――. 1947. *Principles of Criminology,* 4th ed. Chicago: Lippincott.

―――. 1940. "White-Collar Criminality." *American Sociological Review* 5: 1–12.

Suttles, G. 1972. *The Social Construction of Communities.* Chicago: University of Chicago Press.

Sykes, G., and D. Matza. 1957. "Techniques of Neutralization: A Theory of Delinquency." *American Sociological Review* 22: 664–670.

Taber, J. K. 1980. "A Survey of Computer Crime Studies." *Computer Law Journal* 2: 275–328.

Tanioka, I. 1986. "Evidence Links Smoking to Violent Crime Victimization." *Sociology and Social Research* 71(1): 58ff.

Tanner, J. 1992. "Youthful Deviance." In V. F. Sacco (ed.), *Deviance: Control and Conformity in Canadian Society,* 2nd ed. Scarborough, Ont.: Prentice-Hall.

Tanner, J., and H. Krahn. 1991. "Part-Time Work and Deviance Among High School Seniors." *Canadian Journal of Sociology* 16(3): 281–302.

Taylor, R. B., and S. Gottfredson. 1986. "Environmental Design and Prevention: An Examination of Community Dynamics." In A. J. Reiss, Jr., and M. Tonry (eds.), *Communities and Crime.* Chicago: University of Chicago Press.

Taylor, S. E., J. V. Wood, and R. R. Lichtman. 1983. "It Could Be Worse: Selective Evaluation as a Response to Victimization." *Journal of Social Issues* 39: 19–40.

Thomas, P. 1995. "Gun Control Will Decrease Crime." In P. A. Winters (ed.), *Crime and Criminals,* pp. 153–160. San Diego: Greenhaven Press.

Thompson, W. E. 1986. "Courtship Violence: Toward a Conceptual Understanding." *Youth and Society* 18(2): 162–176.

Thornberry, T. P. 1987. "Toward an Interactional Theory of Delinquency." *Criminology* 25(4): 863–892.

Thornberry, T. P., A. J. Lizotte, M. D. Krohn, M. Farnworth, and S. J. Jang. 1991. "Testing Interactional Theory: An Examination of Reciprocal Causal Relationships Among Family, School, and Delinquency." *Journal of Criminal Law and Criminology* 82(1): 3–33.

Tierney, K. 1982. "The Battered Women Movement and the Creation of the Wife Beating Problem." *Social Problems* 29: 207–220.

Timmer, D. A., and W. H. Norman. 1984. "The Ideology of Victim Precipitation." *Criminal Justice Review* 9: 63–68.

Timrots, A. D., and M. R. Rand. 1987. *Violent Crime by Strangers and Non-Strangers.* Washington, D.C.: Bureau of Justice Statistics.

Toby, J. 1983 (December). "Violence in Schools." *National Institute of Justice: Research in Brief*. Washington, D.C.: U.S. Department of Justice.

———. 1974. "The Socialization and Control of Deviant Motivation." In Daniel Glaser (ed.), *Handbook of Criminology*. Chicago: Rand McNally.

Tracy, P. E., and J. A. Fox. 1989. "A Field Experiment on Insurance Fraud in Auto Body Repair." *Criminology* 27: 509–603.

Trevethan, S., and S. Tajeshwer. 1992. "Gender Differences Among Violent Crime Victims." *Juristat Service Bulletin* 12(21). Ottawa: Canadian Centre for Justice Statistics.

Tunnell, K. D. 1992. *Choosing Crime: The Criminal Calculus of Property Offenders*. Chicago: Nelson-Hall.

Turk, A. 1976. "Law as a Weapon in Social Conflict." *Social Problems* 23: 276–292.

Tyler, T. 1990. *Why People Obey the Law*. Chicago: University of Chicago Press.

Unger, D. G., and A. Wandersman. 1985. "The Importance of Neighbors: The Social, Cognitive, and Affective Components of Neighboring." *American Journal of Community Psychology* 13(2): 139–169.

U.S. Bureau of the Census. 1994. *Statistical Abstract of the United States, 1994*. Washington, D.C.: U.S. Government Printing Office.

———. 1992. *Census and You*. Washington, D.C.: U.S. Government Printing Office.

———. 1991a. "Advance Report of Final Divorce Statistics, 1988." *Monthly Vital Statistics Report* 40(4), Supplement, August 26.

———. 1991b. "Population Profile of the United States 1991." *Current Population Reports*, Special Studies, Series P-23, No. 173. Washington, D.C.: U.S. Government Printing Office.

———. 1991c. *Statistical Abstract of the United States, 1991*. Washington, D.C.: U.S. Government Printing Office.

———. 1989. "Fertility of American Women: June 1988." *Current Population Reports*, Series P-20, No. 432. Washington, D.C.: U.S. Government Printing Office.

———. 1983. *Statistical Abstract of the United States, 1982-83*. Washington, D.C.: U.S. Government Printing Office.

U.S. Department of Justice. 1994a. *Criminal Victimization in the United States, 1992*. Washington, D.C.: U.S. Government Printing Office.

———. 1994b. *Sourcebook of Criminal Justice Statistics, 1993*. (NCJ-148211). Washington, D.C.: Bureau of Justice Statistics.

———. 1994c. *Violence Between Intimates*. (NCJ-149259). Washington, D.C.: U.S. Department of Justice, Bureau of Justice Statistics.

———. 1994d. *Crime in the United States, 1993*. Washington D.C.: U.S. Department of Justice.

———. 1993. *Felony Defendants in Large Urban Counties, 1990*. (NCJ-141872). Washington, D.C.: Bureau of Justice Statistics.

———. 1992. *Criminal Victimization in the United States, 1990*. Washington, D.C.: Bureau of Justice Statistics.

———. 1990. *Violence Against Women*. Washington, D.C.: Bureau of Justice Statistics.

———. 1988. *Report to the Nation on Crime and Justice*, 2nd ed. Washington, D.C.: Bureau of Justice Statistics.

———. 1985a. *Special Report: Reporting Crimes to the Police*. Washington, D.C.: Bureau of Justice Statistics.

———. 1985b. *Electronic Fund Transfer Fraud*. Washington, D.C.: Bureau of Justice Statistics.

Van den Haag, E. 1975. *Punishing Criminals: Concerning a Very Old and Painful Question*. New York: Basic Books.

van Dijk, J. J. M., and J. de Waard. 1991. "A Two-Dimensional Typology of Crime Prevention Projects with a Bibliography." *Criminal Justice Abstracts* (September).

Victor, J. S. 1993. *Satanic Panic.* Chicago: Open Court.

Visher, C. A. 1991. "Career Offenders and Selective Incapacitation." In J. F. Sheley (ed.), *Criminology: A Contemporary Handbook,* pp. 459–477. Belmont, Calif.: Wadsworth.

Vold, G., and T. J. Bernard. 1986. *Theoretical Criminology,* 3rd ed. New York: Oxford University Press.

Voumvakis, S. E., and R. V. Ericson. 1984. *News Accounts of Attacks on Women: A Comparison of Three Toronto Newspapers.* Toronto: Centre of Criminology, University of Toronto.

Wachs, E. 1988. *Crime-Victim Stories: New York City's Urban Folklore.* Bloomington and Indianapolis: Indiana University Press.

Walker, S. 1994. *Sense and Nonsense About Crime: A Policy Guide,* 2nd ed. Pacific Grove, Calif.: Brooks/Cole.

Walklate, S. 1989. *Victimology: The Victim and the Criminal Justice System.* London: Unwin Hyman.

Waller, I. 1989. *Current Trends in European Crime Prevention: Implications for Canada.* Ottawa: Department of Justice Canada.

———. 1982. "Victimization Studies as Guides to Action: Some Cautions and Suggestions." In H. J. Schneider (ed.), *The Victim in International Perspective.* New York: Aldine de Gruyter.

Waller, I., and N. Okihiro. 1978. *Burglary: The Victim and the Public.* Toronto: University of Toronto Press.

Waller, I., and R. Weiler. 1984. *Crime Prevention Through Social Development.* Ottawa: Canadian Council on Social Development.

Walsh, W. F., and E. J. Donovan. 1989. "Private Security and Community Policing: Evaluation and Comment." *Journal of Criminal Justice* 17: 187–197.

Walters, G. D., and T. W. White. 1989. "Heredity and Crime: Bad Genes or Bad Research." *Criminology* 27(3): 455–458.

Warr, M. 1991. "America's Perceptions of Crime and Punishment." In J. F. Sheley (ed.), *Criminology: A Contemporary Handbook,* pp. 5–19. Belmont, Calif.: Wadsworth.

———. 1989. "What Is the Perceived Seriousness of Crime?" *Criminology* 27: 795–821.

———. 1988. "Rape, Burglary, and Opportunity." *Journal of Quantitative Criminology* 4(3): 275–288.

———. 1985. "Fear of Rape Among Urban Women." *Social Problems* 32: 238–250.

Webb, V. J., and I. H. Marshall. 1989. "Response to Criminal Victimization by Older Americans." *Criminal Justice and Behavior* 16(2): 239–258.

Weeks, E. L., J. M. Boles, A. P. Garbin, and J. Blount. 1986. "The Transformation of Sexual Harassment from a Private Trouble to a Public Issue." *Sociological Inquiry* 56: 432–455.

Weis, J. G. 1989. "Family Violence Research Methodology and Design." In L. Ohlin and M. Tonry (eds.), *Family Violence, Crime and Justice—A Review of Research.* Vol. 11. Chicago: University of Chicago Press.

Wellford, C. 1975. "Labelling Theory and Criminology: An Assessment." *Social Problems* 22: 332–345.

Wellman, B., and B. Leighton. 1979. "Networks, Neighborhoods, and Communities: Approaches to the Study of the Community Question." *Urban Affairs Quarterly* 14: 363–390.

Wells, L. E., and J. H. Rankin. 1991. "Families and Delinquency: A Meta-Analysis of the Impact of Broken Homes." *Social Problems* 38(1): 71–93.

———. 1988. "Direct Parental Controls and Delinquency." *Criminology* 26: 263–285.

———. 1986. "The Broken Homes Model of Delinquency: Analytical Issues." *Journal of Research in Crime and Delinquency* 23(1): 68–93.

West, D. J., and D. P. Farrington. 1977. *The Delinquent Way of Life.* London: Heinemann.

Whitaker, C. J., and L. D. Bastian. 1991. *Teenage Victims.* A National Crime Survey Report. Washington, D.C.: U.S. Department of Justice.

Williams, K. R., and R. L. Flewelling. 1988. "The Social Production of Criminal Homicide: A Comparative Study of Disaggregated Rates in American Cities." *American Sociological Review* 53: 421–431.

Williams, K. R., and R. Hawkins. 1986. "Perceptual Research on General Deterrence: A Critical Review." *Law and Society Review* 20: 545–572.

Wilson, J. 1980. "Sociology of Leisure." *Annual Review of Sociology* 6: 21–40.

Wilson, J. Q. 1983. *Thinking About Crime.* New York: Vintage.

Wilson, J. Q., and R. J. Herrnstein. 1985. *Crime and Human Nature.* New York: Simon & Schuster.

Wilson, J. Q., and G. L. Kelling. 1982. "Broken Windows." *Atlantic Monthly* (March): 29–38.

Wilson, N. K. 1985. "Venerable Bedfellows: Women's Liberation and Women's Victimization." *Victimology* 10: 206–220.

Wilson, P. R., R. Lincoln, and D. Chappell. 1986. "Physician Fraud and Abuse in Canada: A Preliminary Examination." *Canadian Journal of Criminology* 28(2): 129–146.

Wilson, W. J. 1987. *The Truly Disadvantaged: The Inner City, the Underclass, and Public Policy.* Chicago: University of Chicago Press.

Wirth, L. 1938. "Urbanism as a Way of Life." *American Journal of Sociology* 44: 3–24.

Wirtz, P. W., and A. V. Harrell. 1987. "Police and Victims of Physical Assault." *Criminal Justice and Behavior* 14: 81–92.

Wolf, D. 1991. *The Rebels: A Brotherhood of Outlaw Bikers.* Toronto: University of Toronto Press.

Wolfgang, M. 1958. *Patterns in Criminal Homicide.* Philadelphia: University of Pennsylvania Press.

Wolfgang, M., and F. Ferracuti. 1967. *The Subculture of Violence: Towards an Integrated Theory in Criminology.* Beverly Hills, Calif.: Sage.

Wolfgang, M., R. M. Figlio, and T. Sellin. 1972. *Delinquency in a Birth Cohort.* Chicago: University of Chicago Press.

Wright, C., and J-P. Leroux. 1991. "Children as Victims of Violent Crime." *Juristat Service Bulletin* 11(8). Ottawa: Canadian Centre for Justice Statistics.

Wright, J. D., and P. Rossi. 1986. *Armed and Considered Dangerous: A Survey of Felons and Their Firearms.* Hawthorne, N.Y.: Aldine de Gruyter.

Wright, R., and T. Bennett. 1990. "Exploring the Offender's Perspective: Observing and Interviewing Criminals." In K. L. Kempf (ed.), *Measurement Issues in Criminology.* New York: Springer-Verlag.

Yin, P. 1982. "Fear of Crime as a Problem for the Elderly." *Social Problems* 30: 240–245.

———. 1980. "Fear of Crime Among the Elderly: Some Issues and Suggestions." *Social Problems* 27: 492–504.

Zatz, M. S. 1987. "Chicago Youth Gangs and Crime: The Creation of a Moral Panic." *Contemporary Crises* 11: 129–158.

Zawitz, M. W., P. A. Klaus, R. Bachman, L. D. Bastian, M. M. DeBerry, Jr., M. R. Rand, and B. M. Tayler. 1993. *Highlights from 20 Years of Surveying Crime Victims*. Washington: Bureau of Justice Statistics.

Ziegenhagen, E. A., and D. Brosnan. 1985. "Victims' Responses to Robbery and Crime Control Policy." *Criminology* 23: 675–695.

Acknowledgments

PHOTO CREDITS

Chapter 1:2, The Bettmann Archives.

Chapter 1:6 (t), Lionel Delevinge / Stock, Boston Inc.

Chapter 1:6 (b), David Wells / The Image Works.

Chapter 1:7, Spencer Grant / Photo Researchers Inc.

Chapter 1:10 (l), The Bettmann Archives.

Chapter 1:10 (c,r), Brandon Carson.

Chapter 1:21, Wide World Photos.

Chapter 1:25, Joe Rodriguez / Black Star.

Chapter 1:30, Phyllis Jenson / Stock, Boston Inc.

Chapter 1:34, Bill Aron / PhotoEdit.

Chapter 1:36, Patsy Davidson / The Image Works.

Chapter 2:47, Jim Mahoney / The Image Works.

Chapter 2:50, Elena Dorfman / Off-Shoot Stock.

Chapter 2:64, Akos Szilvasi / Stock, Boston Inc.

Chapter 2:68, Michael Siluk / The Image Works.

Chapter 3:78, Ulrike Welsch / Photo Researchers Inc.

Chapter 3:89, Gale Zucker / Stock, Boston Inc.

Chapter 3:91, Michael Weisbrot / The Image Works.

Chapter 3:106, Ilene Perlman / Stock, Boston Inc.

Chapter 3:107, The Bettmann Archives.

Chapter 3:109, Wide World Photos.

Chapter 4:115, Spencer Grant / Monkmeyer Press Photo.

Chapter 4:121 (t), George Malave / Stock, Boston Inc.

Chapter 4:121 (b), Amy Etra / PhotoEdit.

Chapter 4:128, The Bettmann Archives.

Chapter 5:139, Mimi Forsyth / Monkmeyer Press Photo.

Chapter 5:142, Zigy Kaluzny / Tony Stone Worldwide.

Chapter 5:145, David Strickler / Monkmeyer Press Photo.

Chapter 6:155, Jim Mahoney / The Image Works.

Chapter 6:157, Gale Zucker / Stock, Boston Inc.

Chapter 6:160, Peter Southwick / Stock, Boston Inc.

Chapter 6:167, Elena Dorfman / Off-Shoot Stock.

Chapter 6:172, Paul Conklin / Monkmeyer Press Photo.

Chapter 7:181, Liama Druskas / Stock, Boston Inc.

Chapter 7:184, Bob Daemmrich / The Image Works.

Chapter 7:201, Richard Levine.

Chapter 7:211, Wide World Photos.

Chapter 8:214, Michael Newman / PhotoEdit.

Chapter 8:221, M. Antman / The Image Works.

Chapter 8:235, Michael Dwyer / Stock, Boston Inc.

Chapter 8:240, Elena Dorfman / Off-Shoot Stock.

Chapter 9:248, Elizabeth Crews / The Image Works.

Chapter 9:257, Spencer Grant / Monkmeyer Press Photo.

Chapter 9:260, Harry Wilks / Stock, Boston Inc.

Chapter 9:266, L. L. T. Rhodes / Tony Stone Worldwide.

Chapter 9:269, Barbara Alper / Stock, Boston Inc.

Chapter 10:273, Peter Menzel / Stock, Boston Inc.

Chapter 10:278, Olive Pierce / Stock, Boston Inc.

Chapter 10:289, Courtesy of the NYSE.

Chapter 10:292, Ronald Biggs / Black Star.

Chapter 11:308, Jim Pickerell / Stock, Boston Inc.

Chapter 11:318, K. D. Lawson / Black Star.

Chapter 11:323, The Bettmann Archives.

Chapter 11:326, Freda Leinwand / Monkmeyer Press Photo.

Chapter 11:334, Glen Korengold / Stock, Boston Inc.

Chapter 11:338, Richard Hutchings / Photo Researchers Inc.

TEXT CREDITS

Chapter 1: 38–39, from Colum Lynch, "Pocketfuls of Fear," *The Globe and Mail,* February 6, 1994, p. D5. Reprinted by permission of the author.

Chapter 3: 87, from Curt R. Bartol, *Criminal Behavior: A Psychological Approach,* 4/e, © 1995, p. 30. Reprinted by permission of Prentice Hall, Upper Saddle River, New Jersey.

Chapter 7: 205–206, from Murray A. Straus and Richard J. Gelles, *Physical Violence in American Families: Risk Factors and Adaptations to Violence in 8,145 Families,* Transaction Publishers, 1990. Reprinted by permission of the publisher.

Chapter 8: 224, from Murray A. Straus and Richard J. Gelles, *Physical Violence in American Families: Risk Factors and Adaptations to*

Violence in 8,145 Families, Transaction Publishers, 1990. Reprinted by permission of the publisher.

Chapter 9: 249–251, from Richard Harwood, "Is TV to Blame for Violence?" *The Washington Post,* April 17, 1993, p. A23. © 1993 *The Washington Post.* Reprinted with permission.

Chapter 9: 265–266, from Elizabeth Wissner-Gross, "Emphasize Safety in the Caribbean as Anywhere Else," *Newsday,* January 30, 1993. Reprinted by permission of Los Angeles Times Syndicate International.

Chapter 10: 276–277, from "Murder in the Workplace on the Increase in U.S.," *The Toronto Star,* February 9, 1993, p. F10. © 1993 Reuters. Reprinted with permission of Reuters.

Author Index

Glossary/Subject Index

Sexual aggression and male control, 264
Sexual assault 58, 61, 71, 77, 107, 141,
    146, 147, 166, 203, 204, 255
  Acquaintance rape, 149
  Reporting rape, 27
  See also Dating violence; Leisure domain
Situational factors, 11, 145
Situated transactions process of interaction
    involving two or more individuals that
    lasts as long as they find themselves in
    one another's presence. 135, 147–149,
    150, 151
Small durable product design, 142
Smoking, 320
Social bonds, 117, 119, 134, 313. See also
    Bond, theory of
Social conditions, 83
Social constraints, 136
Social control the regulatory institutions
    of society, particularly the law enforce-
    ment and judicial systems and how they
    operate, encompassing rule-enforce-
    ment at all levels. 11, 12, 17, 27, 57,
    67, 116, 117, 133, 163, 169, 172, 312,
    314
  Courts and, 17
  Formal social control conventional meth-
    ods of technology and physical coer-
    cion, such as the police force, used to
    maintain social order. 23, 112, 118,
    120, 122, 124, 126, 133
  Informal social control casual methods
    of coercion employed by community
    members to maintain conformity.
    17, 23, 112, 113, 116, 118, 119,
    120–122, 124–126, 133, 171
  Legal controls, 17, 18
  Police and, 17
  Private control, 122
  Public control, 122
  See also Crime prevention; Police
Social disadvantaged, 54, 55, 60. See also
    Inner city; Lower classes; Poverty; Un-
    derclass; Workplace domain
Social disorganization long-term and wide-
    spread deterioration of social order and
    control in a population. 66, 67, 97,
    100, 119, 120, 122, 134, 260. See also
    Incivility; Social organization
Social distance, 120
Social domains major spheres of life in
    which we spend most of our time and
    energy. 69, 313, 315. See also Enter-
    prise crime; Family domain; Household
    domain; Occupational crime; Work-
    place domain
Social exchange, 150, 151
Social inequality results when a social group
    is underprivileged compared with an-
    other. 25, 26, 274. See also Relative in-
    equality
Social interaction, 19
Socialization, 84, 87, 92, 95, 99, 114, 134
Social learning theories, 100
Social organization coherence and continu-
    ity in the social environment, and ratio-
    nal cooperation among individuals and

social institutions. 93. See also Social
    disorganization
Social roles, 136
Sociobiology the study of the biological ba-
    sis of social behavior. 83
  Adoption studies the behavioral compari-
    son of near-birth adoptees to their
    genetic and their adoptive parents. 85
  Body type in order to determine the rela-
    tionship between physique and crimi-
    nality, Sheldon categorized, or "so-
    matotyped," three basic types of
    body build—endomorphic, ectomor-
    phic, and mesomorphic—which are
    associated with a particular type of
    temperament. 86, 87
  Constitutional structure predispositions
    toward criminality are claimed to be ex-
    pressed by biological factors, such as
    phenotypes or body types, and psy-
    chological propensities. 83, 86–89,
    110, 312
    Criticisms of, 86
  Crime gene the sociobiological perspec-
    tive that certain genes may be linked
    to criminality. 85, 90
  Diet the concept that the behavior of cer-
    tain individuals can be affected by
    their diet. 88, 89, 110
  General pedigree studies a nonexperimen-
    tal approach to the study of intergen-
    erational transmission of genetically
    predisposed behavior between related
    individuals. 84
  Genetics and, 83, 89, 110, 312
    Criticisms of, 85
    Genotypes and, 85
    Intergenerational genetic defects and, 83
  Karyotype studies claim that the size, the
    shape and the number of chromo-
    somes, or karyotypes, in individuals
    are causal factors to criminality. 85
  Physiology and, 83
  Predisposition and, 83
  Trace elements mineral content in the
    subject's body determines episodic
    violence or antisocial behavior.
    88, 89
  Twin studies a nonexperimental study de-
    signed to research and compare crim-
    inal predispositions between dizy-
    gotic and monozygotic twins. 84
  See also Atavism; Evolution; Heredity;
    Predetermined behavior
Sociology, 8
Sociopath antisocial personality disorder
    involving a marked lack of ethical or
    moral development. 92. See also Anti-
    social personality; Gacy, John Wayne;
    Psychopath
Strain theory the theory that the constant
    emphasis on success in society and its
    possible attainment consistently contra-
    dicts the actual opportunity facing
    people, especially at the bottom of soci-
    ety where the greatest amount of crime,

or illegitimate adaptive means, occurs.
    96, 128. See also General strain theory
Subcultures a group or groups within a host
    culture with different values evident
    from their expression of deviant behav-
    ior. 60, 103–109
Subculture of violence a subculture in which
    disproportionate rates of criminal vio-
    lence are a product of a group's com-
    mitment to subcultural values and
    norms that condone violence as accept-
    able means of resolving interpersonal
    conflict. 105, 106, 261, 312. See also
    Legitimate violence; Self-help crime
Substance abuse
  Drugs and, 8, 65, 89, 110, 176, 259, 274,
    299–302, 331
  Alcohol and, 11, 89, 227, 257, 259, 261,
    331
Subterranean values values that are held by
    many in society, although they may be
    in conflict with other cherished values.
    107. See also Morals
Symbolic interactionism the role of linguistic
    interaction in developing a social iden-
    tity and functioning according to
    shared norms and values. 148. See also
    Labelling theory

Target hardening, increasing protection of
    premises to deter a criminal through
    fear of detection or because the target
    has been made inaccessible. 143, 151,
    160, 234, 239, 243, 244, 268, 319,
    326–328. See also Crime prevention;
    Defensible space; Deterrence
Tearooms, 65
Territorial marking, 120. See also Gangs
Third parties, 151, 259, 260. See also By-
    standers; Witnesses
Tiananmen Square, 127
Tolerance, 19, 120. See also Domestic vio-
    lence, tolerance of
Trajectories in life course perspective, de-
    scribes the directions in which lives
    seem to be moving. 118. See also Life
    course perspective; Transitions
Transitions in life course perspective, spe-
    cific events that might or might not al-
    ter trajectories. 118. See also Life
    course perspective; Trajectories

Underclass a class of society that almost
    exclusively inhabits segregated, dis-
    advantaged neighborhoods where so-
    cial epidemics are highly concentrated,
    resulting in mutually reinforcing con-
    tagion effects. 25, 68. See also Demo-
    graphic characteristics; Incivility;
    Inner city; Lower classes; Poverty;
    Segregation
Underground economy, 60
Universal form of crime, 100
Urban crime, 67, 68, 82, 168
Urbanization, 100, 118, 119, 197
Utopian world (B.F. Skinner), 100